Clinical Geropsychology

Edited by

Inger Hilde Nordhus
Gary R. VandenBos
Stig Berg
Pia Fromholt

American Psychological Association
Washington, DC

Published by
American Psychological Association
750 First Street, NE
Washington, DC 20002

Copies may be ordered from
APA Order Department
P.O. Box 92984
Washington, DC 20090-2984

In the UK, Europe, Africa, and the Middle East, copies may be ordered from
American Psychological Association
3 Henrietta Street
Covent Garden, London
WC2E 8LU England

In the five Scandinavian countries this book is distributed by
Cappelen Akademisk Forlag a.s
Postboks 9047 Gronland
0133 Oslo, Norway

Typeset in Century Schoolbook by EPS Group Inc., Easton, MD

Printer: United Book Press, Inc., Baltimore, MD
Cover designer: Minker Design, Bethesda, MD
Technical/Production Editor: Catherine R. W. Hudson

Library of Congress Cataloging-in-Publication Data

Clinical geropsychology / edited by Inger Hilde Nordhus ... [et al.].—1st ed.
    p.   cm.
   Includes bibliographical references and index.
   ISBN 1-55798-519-7 (hardcover, acid-free paper)
   1. Aged—Mental health. 2. Psychotherapy for the aged.
 I. Nordhus, Inger Hilde.
  RC451.4.A5C528   1998
  618.97′689—dc21

                                                          98-14132
                                                           CIP

British Library Cataloguing-in-Publication Data
A CIP record is available from the British Library.

Printed in the United States of America
First Edition

Contents

Contributors

Vern L. Bengtson, PhD, *Andrus Gerontology Center, School of Gerontology, University of Southern California, Los Angeles*

Stig Berg, PhD, *Institute of Gerontology, University College of Health Sciences, Jönköping, Sweden*

Raymond Bossé, PhD, *Department of Veterans Affairs, Edith Nourse Rogers Memorial Hospital, Bedford, MA*

Peter Bruhn, PhD, *Center for Gerontopsykologi, Aarhus University, Risskov, Denmark*

Elisabeth O. Burgess, PhD, *Department of Sociology, Georgia State University, Atlanta*

John C. Cavanaugh, PhD, *University of Delaware, Newark*

Bertram J. Cohler, PhD, *Committee on Human Development, The University of Chicago, Illinois*

Frederick L. Coolidge, PhD, *Department of Psychology, University of Colorado, Colorado Springs*

Paul T. Costa, Jr., PhD, *Laboratory of Personality and Cognition, Gerontology Research Center, National Institute on Aging, National Institutes of Health, Baltimore, MD*

Melissa M. Dolan, MA, *Department of Human Development and Family Studies, Pennsylvania State University, University Park*

Bjørn Ellertsen, PhD, *Department of Medical and Biological Psychology, Section of Clinical Neuropsychology, University of Bergen, Norway*

Amy Fiske, PhD, *Department of Psychology, University of Southern California, Los Angeles*

Pia Fromholt, MA, *Center for Gerontopsykologi, Aarhus University, Risskov, Denmark*

Margaret Gatz, PhD, *Department of Psychology, University of Southern California, Los Angeles*

Edith S. Lisansky Gomberg, PhD, *Alcohol Research Center, Department of Psychiatry, and School of Social Work, University of Michigan, Ann Arbor*

Jennifer H. Gray, MA, *Institute for Life-Span Development and Gerontology, The University of Akron, OH*

Michel Hersen, PhD, *School of Professional Psychology, Pacific University, Forest Grove, OR*

Knut Hestad, PhD, *Department of Medical and Biological Psychology, Section of Clinical Neuropsychology, University of Bergen, Norway*

Reidun Ingebretsen, PhD, *NOVA-Norwegian Social Research, Oslo, Norway*

Shannon E. Jarrott, MA, *Department of Human Development and Family Studies, Pennsylvania State University, University Park*

Lennarth Johansson, *The National Board of Health and Welfare, Stockholm, Sweden*

Bertram P. Karon, PhD, *Department of Psychology, Michigan State University, East Lansing*

Julia E. Kasl-Godley, PhD, *Department of Psychology, University of Southern California, Los Angeles*

Hallgrim Kløve, PhD, *Department of Medical and Biological Psychology, Section of Clinical Neuropsychology, University of Bergen, Norway*

Bob G. Knight, PhD, *Andrus Gerontology Center, School of Gerontology, University of Southern California, Los Angeles*

Gerd Kvale, PhD, *Department of Clinical Psychology, Outpatient Clinic for Adults and the Elderly, University of Bergen, Norway*

Richard S. Lazarus, PhD, *Professor Emeritus, University of California, Berkeley*

Sara A. Leitsch, MA, *Department of Human Development and Family Studies, Pennsylvania State University, University Park*

T. J. McCallum, PhD, *Andrus Gerontology Center, School of Gerontology, University of Southern California, Los Angeles*

Robert R. McCrae, PhD, *Gerontology Research Center, National Institute on Aging, National Institutes of Health, Baltimore, MD*

Geir Høstmark Nielsen, PhD, *Department of Clinical Psychology, Outpatient Clinic for Adults and the Elderly, University of Bergen, Norway*

Inger Hilde Nordhus, PhD, *Department of Clinical Psychology, Outpatient Clinic for Adults and the Elderly, University of Bergen, Norway*

Jørgen Bruun Pedersen, *Institute of Psychology, Roskilde University Center, Denmark*

Timothy A. Salthouse, PhD, *School of Psychology, Georgia Institute of Technology, Atlanta*

Maria Schmeeckle, PhD, *Andrus Gerontology Center, University of Southern California, Los Angeles*

Forrest R. Scogin, PhD, *Department of Psychology, The University of Alabama, Tuscaloosa*

Daniel L. Segal, PhD, *Department of Psychology, University of Colorado, Colorado Springs*

Per Erik Solem, PhD, *NOVA–Norwegian Social Research, Oslo, Norway*

Harvey L. Sterns, PhD, *Institute for Life-Span Development and Gerontology, The University of Akron, OH*

Gary R. VandenBos, PhD, *Office of Publications and Communications, American Psychological Association, Washington, DC*

Susan Krauss Whitbourne, PhD, *Department of Psychology, University of Massachusetts, Amherst*

Rosalie S. Wolf, PhD, *Institute on Aging, Memorial Hospital, Worcester, MA*

Jian Yang, PhD, *Gerontology Research Center, National Institute on Aging, National Institutes of Health, Baltimore, MD*

Steven H. Zarit, PhD, *Department of Human Development and Family Studies, Pennsylvania State University, University Park*

Robert A. Zucker, PhD, *Alcohol Research Center, Department of Psychiatry, The University of Michigan, Ann Arbor*

Foreword

The United States and many other countries have had to rethink many national policies and priorities in the last 25 years, as human beings are living longer. These concerns relate to retirement income, health care, housing, psychological services, and much more. It is critical that psychology provide research and service to older people around a full array of issues and topics.

A major policy question in the United States at the moment is whether the social security system will remain solvent in the next century and whether or not Medicare will be sufficient to pay for the health-care needs of our older citizens. Indeed, the Alliance for Aging Research (1997) recently commissioned a report on uncovering facts concerning the high cost of the last year of life. The report labels the following statement as a myth: "As the population ages, health care costs for the elderly will necessarily overwhelm and bankrupt the nation" (p. 14). The authors, using cross national data, point out that there is no necessary relationship between high health-care costs and the proportion of older individuals in that society. Whereas Sweden, for example, has around 18% of its people over the age of 65, the percentage of its gross domestic product spent on health care is similar to the amount spent by countries with considerably smaller numbers of older people. In addition, when one looks at spending for people aged 80 or over, no discernable pattern of spending seems to emerge for industrialized countries. Furthermore, in countries that have experienced a sharp rise in the older population, like Japan, for example, health-care spending has not increased proportionally, the report contends. The overall conclusion on the question of rising health-care costs was that if necessary research on health care toward the end of life begins now, it should be possible to cope with an aging population without experiencing rampaging increases in costs.

Interestingly enough, William Safire (1997) recently commented on a proposal to extend government health insurance to the so called "near-elderly," that is, people as young as 55. He points out that except for the oldest old individuals (those over 85) there is less than total agreement on when old age begins. True, one official definition of elderly given by the U.S. government is 65 years, as that is the year one is currently eligible for Social Security retirement income. However, one can postpone regular Social Security payments until the age of 70 in this country, just as one can receive reduced benefits at age 62. The "official" definition of the beginning of old age is a flexible one, reflecting the fact that striking individual differences exist in the process of aging.

For a number of years now, my graduate students and I at Michigan State University have worked on researching memory complaints in the able older person. We are attempting to popularize the notion of mood and memory checkups for older adults, just as one would encourage individuals to seek checkups for one's physical health. Geropsychologists are well equipped to assess mood and memory functions in older adults and there is evidence that memory workshops are effective in improving memory functions and in reducing memory complaints. Although memory training is not a panacea for all older adults and does not result in long lasting effects, most other life style interventions do not do so either. However, the argument is often made that there is no need for mood and memory interventions for older adults. The usual reasons given are that memory problems in the able older person are not severe enough and that they are so common as to obviate the necessity for interventions. Crook (1993) points out some fallacies in that argument. If one were to follow that argument, then one could reasonably wait until the changes that occur in vision and hearing have reached such proportions that they seriously impair functioning. Just think how much money one could save by postponing the attainment of glasses or hearing aids until serious impairment threatened.

One of the opportunities provided to the President of the American Psychological Association is to choose an agenda during that term of office. Now that our Association was 105 years old, I thought it was high time to focus on the topic of aging. One of the initiatives of my presidency was to appoint a task force to develop guidelines for the evaluation of dementia and age-related cognitive decline. The task force proposed 10 guidelines about such professional practice, which I summarize here:

1. Psychologists who perform evaluations of dementia and age-related cognitive decline are familiar with the prevailing diagnostic nomenclature and specific diagnostic criteria.
2. Psychologists attempt to obtain informed consent.
3. Psychologists gain specialized competence.
4. Psychologists seek and provide appropriate consultation.
5. Psychologists are aware of personal and societal biases and engage in nondiscriminatory practice.
6. Psychologists conduct a clinical interview as part of the evaluation.
7. Psychologists are aware that standardized psychological and neuropsychological tests are important tools in the assessment of dementia and age-related cognitive decline.
8. When measuring cognitive changes in individuals, psychologists attempt to estimate premorbid abilities.
9. Psychologists are sensitive to the limitations and sources of variability and error in psychometric performance.
10. Psychologists recognize that provision of constructive feedback, support, and education, as well as maintenance of a therapeutic alliance, can be important parts of the evaluation process.

My other presidential initiative was designed to give psychologists and other health-care providers information to assist them in working with older adults. This free brochure is titled "What the Practitioner Should Know About Working With Older Adults" and is available from the American Psychological Association. Some of the relevant sections concern the realities of aging for older Americans, psychological problems experienced by older adults, as well as assessment and interventions and broad professional issues of concern to psychologists who work with older adults. These recent initiatives in support of geropsychology occurred during my year as President of the American Psychological Association. That is why I am pleased to write this foreword for *Clinical Geropsychology*.

This volume covers theoretical views, challenges, and practical issues as well as assessment and intervention. It is a broadly based book, and I personally know many of the authors. Clinical geropsychology is coming of age: There is now a proficiency in geropsychology recognized by the Council for the Recognition of Specialties and Proficiencies in Psychology. Interest in geropsychology is spreading, and research efforts are expanding. There are a number of doctoral level programs in this country and abroad that are teaching and fostering research in geropsychology. Postdoctoral opportunities are increasing. One of the sections of the Division of Clinical Psychology is devoted to geropsychology. Division 20 (Adult Development and Aging) of the American Psychological Association is also very supportive of clinical geropsychology. In addition, there are many other national and state level groups that focus on this area. The Aging Revolution is well on its way.

Norman Abeles

References

Alliance for Aging Research. (1997). *Seven deadly myths: Uncovering the facts about the high cost of the last year of life*. Washington, DC: Author.

Crook, T. H. (1993). Diagnosis and treatment of memory loss in older patients who are not demented. In R. Levy, R. Howard, & A. Burns (Eds.), *Treatment and care in old age psychiatry*. London: Wrightson Biomedical Publishing.

Safire, W. (1998, February 8). Don't call me near-elderly. *New York Times Magazine, 147*, 22–24.

Preface

The age distribution of the world's population has changed drastically since 1900. In 1900 only 1 in 25 Americans was age 65 or over, and the average life span was 47 years. Across the Nordic countries, the corresponding figures were 1 in 14 individuals was age 65 or over, and the average life span was 55.5 years.

In 1996, the number of individuals over the age of 65 varied between 1 in 6 and 1 in 10 of the total population in developed countries. The demographic change is dramatic on a historical scale, and it has required every country around the world to alter policies to adjust. It has also required medicine, psychology, and all other disciplines providing treatment and care to individuals to change the nature and content of their training to better furnish relevant materials for their providers regarding older populations. This book is intended to contribute to that process.

Our goal as we began this book was to address "the latter half of life." By that, we were roughly thinking that the starting point of coverage for this book would be 40 years of age and would continue on to cover the rest of life, including old-old age (perhaps meaning 80 to 100 years). However, our interests and concerns were not really anchored in the concrete number of years alive.

One of the basic issues in geropsychology research is whether or not chronological age per se is a significant variable for study. For those involved in teaching geropsychology, this is a question often raised by students. How important is chronological age when doing research or applied work involving aging and older people? A clear and definite answer to this question is not easy to give. At the same time it is a vital question that needs to be made explicit whenever relevant. In this volume, some chapters focus on this as a central topic. In chapter 7, for example, this variable is explicitly amplified by Lazarus, who argues that individuality is the key to understanding coping behavior in old age. As geropsychologists, we should focus on aging adults as individuals with individual histories and problems, rather than as a statistical cohort whose behavior is analyzed by means and averages. Similarly, in describing psychotherapy with older adults (chapter 23), Nordhus and her colleagues note that questions regarding the effectiveness of psychotherapy for older adults are often related to the issue of the extent to which chronological age is an informative variable for therapeutic work. For clinical geropsychology, current psychotherapy does work in clinical practice with older adults, but it is important that the clinician is cognizant of specific types of knowledge (e.g., the diversity of normal as well as pathological aging) and of specific assessment issues (e.g., specific diagnosis and initial case formulation for each elderly patient).

It is our conviction that presenting clinical geropsychology in terms of the special needs of older adults and their persistent low representation in mental health services is not helpful in developing a clinical psychology that is responsive to all persons at all points in life. What we need is a positively framed focus on professional challenges (and research challenges) involved in working with adult individuals, including those typically referred to as in "old age."

Because the average psychologist (perhaps even most psychologists) has little direct contact and experience with a wide range and representative sample of older individuals, it is easy for myths about older people and inappropriate stereotypes to exist. For example, although the availability of nursing home care is an important potential resource for older populations, it is also the case that less than 5% of the elderly population is confined to a nursing home at any one time, and the majority of older people never spend a portion of their old age in a nursing home. In fact, the most typical life-course pattern in old age is one of independent living, successfully coping with whatever chronic conditions face a given elderly individual.

It is essential that psychologists and other health care providers approach older people from a positive perspective rather than from one of pathology, loss, and decline. It is a more optimistic way of approaching older people, and it is a more realistic one. Seligman and Csikszentmihalyi (personal communication, January 25, 1998) have referred to this as taking a "positive social science" approach to human functioning and basic research. Such an approach emphasizes strength, responsibility, resilience, and coping. In addition, such an approach views individuals as active participants in living and in determining the course of their lives. McAdams and de St. Aubin, in their 1998 book, *Generativity and Adult Development: How and Why We Care for the Next Generation*, have provided a rich collection of investigations into adults' concerns for and commitment to promoting the next generation through parenting, teaching, mentoring, and other activities that benefit and foster the development and well-being of those individuals in social systems that outlive the self.

Because, by definition, new professional psychologists are "young" (or younger), there are events in life that they have yet to experience but that their older clients will have experienced. We do not believe that one has to be an older person to work with older patients, and we do not believe that a therapist has to have experienced the exact same life event of a given patient to help that patient explore their reactions to their experience and how they might cope with it. However, we do believe it is critical for newly trained professionals to have factual and experiential information about certain life events that typically occur in middle age or older, so that they do not merely rely on the idiosyncratic experience of their parents or grandparents or on a smaller number of older individuals they might have known. Thus, as we talked about the development of this book, it was vital to us to present the reader with concrete descriptions of challenges as well as problems that older adults experience or may experience. We attempt to achieve this with the short chapters presented in Part II, each of which represents a specialized topic within geropsychology that can be examined in greater depth as it is relevant to a given patient.

This volume is intended for practicing clinical psychologists, psychology graduate students in training, and other scientifically informed mental health professionals working with aging populations. This book, with 26 chapters divided into three parts, provides in-depth coverage of clinical geropsychology. Part I presents a theoretical anchoring across perspectives on psychological, cognitive, and biological aspects of aging. Part II, as noted above, provides brief introductions to an array of practical issues and life challenges in the lives of aging individuals. Part III provides practical advice on clinical assessment and intervention approaches to assisting older individuals and their families. This last section provides the reader with a solid introduction to various psychological interventions, clinical issues that typically arise and how best to address them, and topics that the therapist should consider in the clinical treatment of older adults.

Many individuals have contributed to the final published volume. Above all, we thank the chapter authors who have generously shared their knowledge for use by others in understanding and aiding older populations. We are especially grateful to Elizabeth Bulatao in the Office of Communications, American Psychological Association (APA), for ably serving as the project coordinator for this particular volume. We thank Inger Nordhagen, administrative secretary at the Department of Clinical Psychology, University of Bergen, Norway, for her assistance, persistence, and support. And, we thank the APA editorial staff, particularly Catherine Hudson of APA Books, for her quick and efficient handling of the production aspects of this book.

Part I

Theoretical Views on Older Individuals

1

Life-Span Developmental Perspectives on Aging: An Introductory Overview

Gary R. VandenBos

Life-span developmental psychology became generally accepted in the 1980s, after systematic articulation during the 1970s. The *life-span developmental approach* has been defined as being "concerned with the description, explanation, and modification (optimization) of developmental processes in the human life course from conception to death" (Baltes, Reese, & Lipsitt, 1980, p. 66).

Individual contributions by Hall, Jung, and Hollingsworth provided the seeds for such a life-span perspective in the 1920s and 1930s. However, according to Baltes et al. (1980), it was the convergence of three trends in the 25 years after World War II that led to the eventual description and acceptance of a life-span developmental approach. The three trends were the publication of several longitudinal studies of adults who had originally participated in a child development project begun before World War II, the emergence of the overall interdisciplinary field of gerontology in the 1950s and 1960s, and a commitment to a life-span approach at several major universities in the United States and Europe. These trends, in their opinion, provided a context in which the study of aging, as well as the aged as a distinct population, could be placed in a larger perspective, involving biological as well as psychosocial factors, for the examination of developmental processes across the entire life course.

Although it is common to read statements that life-span developmental psychology is an orientation rather than a theory, Schroots (1996) has nicely summarized seven propositions about the nature of human aging inherent in the theoretical framework of life-span developmental psychology, as articulated by Baltes and his associates (e.g., Baltes, 1987; Baltes et al., 1980; Baltes, Smith, & Staudinger, 1992). These propositions are that

(1) there are major differences between normal, pathological, and optimal aging, the latter defined as aging under development-enhancing and age-friendly environmental conditions; (2) the course of aging shows much interindividual variability (heterogeneity); (3) there is much latent reserve capacity in old age; (4) there is aging loss in the range of reserve capacity or adaptability; (5) individual and social knowledge (crystallized intelligence) enriches the mind and can compensate for age-related decline in fluid intelligence (aging losses); (6) with age, the balance between gains and losses becomes

increasingly negative; and finally, (7) the self in old age remains a resilient system of coping and maintaining integrity. (Schroots, 1996, p. 745)

The above points actually address several levels of detail, but all of these reflect interesting ways of thinking about older people. For example, the first point articulates the view that there are basic normative normal (or common) developmental sequences, as well as commonly observed pathological developmental deviations, which has implications for practice—suggesting that any given person should be evaluated and understood against these normative patterns, but also considered in an individual (or idiosyncratic) manner. The second point reflects the life-span developmental view that there are individual differences across all dimensions of functioning during all periods of development. Interindividual variation becomes greater in old age as compared with the middle portion of adulthood. In general, the magnitude of individual differences, and the array of patterns of functioning, are greatest in infancy and early childhood and then again in old age and old, old age. The third point is the first that directly addresses "old age" per se, and it simply asserts that considerable adaptability or resources to support coping and change exists in older individuals. The fourth and sixth points acknowledge that there is a progressive decline in adaptive ability with age, which becomes increasingly negative. The fifth point emphasizes that previous learning and experience can, to some degree, help to offset or compensate for decline in memory, learning, speed of information processing, and so forth. The seventh point is a simple assertion that the older individual remains a functioning psychological entity with adaptive capacities for self-maintenance.

A life-span developmental approach to aging is seen by some as an effective counter-balance to an "abnormal" psychology approach to aging, which might overemphasize pathological processes, decline, and malfunction. In a parallel fashion, life-span developmental psychology of aging is also particularly focused on the creative adaptation that individuals simultaneously make to changing external demands and personal physical and mental decline. Developmental change is seen as a life-long process, and change is viewed as sequential (i.e., change in later periods of life is influenced by and builds on earlier change and events). The life-span approach uses a biopsychosocial model, as change is viewed as occurring in interrelated biological, psychological, and social domains. In addition, cohort effects, that is, the impact of shared experiences that occurred earlier in time at a given developmental point for a large group of similarly aged individuals, are important to understanding older people as a group and as individuals.

The theme that development occurs throughout the life span and that any given individual is always in some type of developmental or behavioral change is one with which most clinicians are quite familiar—and it typically brings Erikson's (1950) model of eight stages of personality development to mind. Erikson's stages were not tied to specific age periods but rather to broad psychological challenges that needed to be sequentially resolved. Within Erikson's model, it will be recalled, *adulthood* (Stage 7) was concerned with generativity versus stagnation, and *maturity* (Stage 8) was concerned with ego integrity versus despair. Whereas Erikson primarily addressed overarching psychological issues, the life-span development approach incorporates all developmental processes, large and small.

Taxonomy of Life Events in Old Age

The life-span developmental approach focuses on the tasks and activities that each person must face during the course of his or her life and the order (or "time") when they should occur. Thus, a general sense of the "normal life course" is assumed, although rarely described in extensive concrete detail. The chapters in section 2 of the present volume each describe some of the more common life events that most people face.

Life events can occur, for a given individual, either *on time* or *off time*. If an event occurs for a given person at the time or age that most other people experience it, it is said to be on time. An example of an off-time event would be a 45-year-old woman who is just beginning college, something that would occur between 18 and 22 years old for most people. There is nothing right or wrong, or good or bad, about being on or off the expected time schedule. Rather, the most significant factor about a person being off time for a given life event is that his or her experience of that life event is likely to be somewhat different from another person's experience of the same event when it occurred at a more typical period in their life.

Reese and Smyer (1983) reviewed the literature on stressful life events and developed a taxonomy of four types of life stressors: biological factors (e.g., changes in physical capacity with age), psychological factors (e.g., changes in cognitive ability or personality with age), physical and environmental factors (e.g., changes in one's housing or general living conditions with age), and social and cultural factors (e.g., changes in role and expected behavior with age). Table 1 gives a small sampling of some of the life events that can occur during later adulthood and old age. Even within the sampling of listed examples in the table, there may be vast differences in how the events occur and how the events are experienced by any given person. These differences suggest an even more complex array of patterns of impact, psychological change, and behavioral accommodation.

Biological Functioning

Many aspects of biological functioning change as one ages and eventually moves into old age, including the functioning of every major organ system of the body. Such changes in biological functioning influence general health, physical mobility, sleep patterns, sexual functioning, cognition, psychological mood, and so forth. The typical pattern of biological decline is initially gradual and begins in middle adulthood. Different organ systems show different rates and patterns of decline, and there are vast differences among individuals.

The life-span developmental perspective appreciates and explores the interrelationship between physical functioning and psychological functioning in individuals at all ages. The extensive and highly significant interrelationships

Table 1. Some Major Life Events in Old Age

Context	Personal/Psychological Event	Social/Cultural Event	Physical/ Environmental Event	Biological Event
Family	Succeeding father in family business Guilt about a family member	Changing support from or contact with family members Aging parents	Major change in family living Sale of childhood home	Serious illness, injury or death of close family member Worsening health of aging parents
Love & Marriage	Adjusting to death of spouse Changing relationship with spouse	Divorce Remarriage	Changing houses to accommodate spouse	Wife's menopause (male) Husband's testosterone decline (female) Spouse's or ex-spouse's death
Parenting	Redefining parenting role in mid-life Grown children returning home to live	Last child leaving home (empty nest) Assuming grandparenting roles	Moving in with children Major change in living conditions	Leaving childrearing stage Child's severe illness, accident, or death
Health	Changing activity level Accepting and adjusting to physiological changes of middle age Adjusting to decreasing physical strength and health Becoming aware of own mortality	Change in physical dependence Changing medical care for older adults	Living conditions enhancing or impairing health	Changing physical health Declining testosterone production (males) Menopause (females) Injury, disability

Friendships & Social Relations	Adjusting friendship patterns after widowhood Learning age-appropriate friendship patterns	Making new friends Change in social network Marked change in church or synagogue activities (e.g., increase or decrease in attendance)	Change in friendship pattern after forced relocation Change in activities after change in physical housing arrangements	Close friend injured or dying Inability to get treatment for illness or injury
Finances	Adjusting to changing economic standard of living Going on welfare	Marked improvement or decline in financial status Financial loss or property loss unrelated to work	Winning a lottery Receiving a large inheritance or windfall profit on sale of home	Serious illness requiring unexpected and extensive health care cost
Work	Stopping work for an extended period without retiring Being unemployed Returning to work after long period Adjusting to retirement and reduced income	Business readjustment Leaving the paid labor force Retirement	Redesign of workplace Relocation of workplace Transportation to work changes	Physical injury or illness causing partial or total work disability

Note. Adapted from H. W. Reese & M. A. Smyer, The dimensionalization of life events. In E. J. Callahan & K. A. McCluskey (Eds.), *Life-span developmental psychology: Nonnormative life events* (pp. 1–33). Copyright 1983 by Academic Press.

between these aspects of development are clearest and most dramatic during infancy and early childhood. They continue to play a large developmental role in late childhood and adolescence, but, for most people, adulthood becomes a period of relative stability in biological and physical changes. For most healthy adults the interplay between physical functioning and psychological functioning is subtle and not of striking relevance (in the absence of physical injury or serious disease) during adulthood. However, in late life, the interrelationship between physical functioning and psychological functioning again takes on a more central role as physical changes (primary declines) begin to be a more common occurrence for all aging individuals. Hence, the direct effects of changes in biological functioning, as well as the psychological reactions to such changes, become more significant with older populations.

Psychological Functioning

A vast array of psychological phenomena can be included in the term *psychological functioning*—for example, emotional reactivity, perceptual processes, personality, memory, interpersonal styles, and so forth. However, the study of changes in cognitive functioning during adulthood and old age has probably been one of the most active research topics regarding psychological functioning over the latter half of the life span. Different patterns of cognitive decline have been noted, across an array of cognitive tasks using standardized tests, for successive cohorts of older individuals.

The general pattern of cognitive functioning over the entire course of a life span is, in general, the rapid acquisition of a broad range of cognitive abilities during childhood and adolescence, followed by a long period of stability (or extremely slow decline) during one's extended adulthood, followed again by a variety of patterns of decline in later life (with the pattern being influenced by many biological, psychological, and social factors). Much research has gone into charting the relationship between chronological age and cognitive performance on specific tasks, as well as into statistically determining the age of peak performance and points of significant decline (as measured against some population-based criteria on these specific tasks).

Both theoretically and empirically, significant attention has been given to the differences between acquiring new knowledge as compared with using previously acquired knowledge. Hebb (1942) described these as *Type A intelligence* (the capacity to develop new patterns of response) and *Type B intelligence* (the functioning of already acquired patterns of response). He argued that these two types of intelligence were highly correlated during childhood and adolescence, but that vast individual differences existed after maturity—with Type B processes being more stable and more lasting throughout adulthood and into old age, whereas Type A processes were more susceptible to decline in varying patterns within the same individual.

In a parallel manner, Cattell (1972) labeled this distinction as one between fluidity and crystallization, whereby a fluid ability reflected a general ability to discriminate and perceive relationships, and crystallized ability referred to habits and knowledge acquired through the prior use of fluid abilities. Cattell's observations of the relationship between fluid and crystallized abilities in childhood and adolescence, as well as across the bulk of adulthood, were quite similar to those of Hebb. These distinctions are supported by a considerable body of research about their basic existence (e.g., Kline & Cooper, 1984; Undheim & Gustafsson, 1987), although no simple, specific widely accepted explanations of how or why they occur have been established.

Some proportion of age-related decline in cognitive functioning is related to biological factors, including the slowing of peripheral and central sensory and motor processes. However, in most cases, this probably explains only a small part of the change in cognitive functioning. Likewise, the degree to which a given individual varies in his or her disuse versus continued and increasingly specialized use of a specific cognitive ability also seems to affect the rate and pattern of decline. In most cases, external environment and sociocultural factors do not appear to be strikingly related to cognitive performance on standardized tests.

Person–Environment Interaction

Throughout the life span, there is a continual interaction between any given individual and the various environments in which he or she lives. An *environment* can refer to one's family, a neighborhood, a school classroom (during childhood and adolescence), a workplace (during adulthood), or any other setting in which the individual has regular ongoing contact and involvement. This environment, obviously, includes other people, as well as the tasks and activities conducted in the environment and the demands, constraints, and facilitating social and environmental aspects related to those activities.

Lawton and Nahemow (1973) provided a conceptual model for considering the person–environmental interface. They suggested that an individual's "internal representation" of the external world mediates the actual person–environment interaction, with *internal representation* meaning how the given individual conceives, views, and experiences the environment (this definition implies that two different people may have two quite different internal representations of the same external environment). The five components described by Lawton and Nahemow are

1. degree of individual competence (which includes an array of abilities and processes, with considerable differences both within and between individuals);
2. environmental press (which includes all of the environmental demands impacting and affecting the individual, such as the need to prepare a report for work or the expectation of preparing a family meal at home);
3. adaptive behavior (which means the outward behavioral manifestation of an individual's competency in responding to a specific environmental press, such as completing a report at work or successfully providing a meal for one's family);
4. affective responses (which means the internal and unobservable response to the environmental demand and one's adaptive behavior in

response to it, such as feeling proud or ashamed about the completed report at work or the meal provided to one's family); and

5. adaptation level (which refers to a range within which the individual is functional in relation to the external demands at an adaptively comfortable level—where the environmental press seems reasonable and the affective response and adaptive behavior also seems reasonable and appropriate).

This way of conceptualizing the person–environment interaction has been used to look at the "match" (or fit) between the knowledge, skills, and abilities of an individual in relation to the environmental demands for task performance, interpersonal relating, and so forth. This conceptualization also has been successfully applied by life-span development psychologists to job or workplace design for working adults. In a somewhat parallel manner, life-span developmental psychologists have used this model when analyzing and designing living environments, transportation needs, and informational material for elderly individuals to best meet the needs of the older person within the skills and abilities of that individual.

The physical living environment (or housing arrangements) of the elderly adult is probably one of the more extensively considered aspects of living during the later years. Retirement often leads to changes in where one lives. Change in economic conditions can have a similar effect. The death of a spouse may, likewise, result in a change in living environment, as may a significant decline in mental and physical capacities. Elderly people face a high probability of needing to relocate, change living arrangements, or change physical housing at some point during their older years. This could mean going to a nursing home, living alone, moving from a house to an apartment, gaining a relative stranger as a roommate, or moving in with one's children. Such environmental changes in housing often represent highly significant events for the older person.

Social and Cultural Factors

Any number of social and cultural factors can be looked at from a life-span developmental perspective, with particular emphasis on their impact and influence on older individuals. Such sociocultural factors can either be looked at as external variables (societal perceptions and valuing or devaluing of older individuals), or as internal phenomena (such as one's own assessment of self-worth in light of changing contributions to society or one's family on retirement). It is also the case that such sociocultural factors can be viewed through an interactive lens, such as the changing parent–child relationship over the course of one's life.

One way of looking at how sociocultural factors influence older individuals is to look at the social institutions or mechanisms that affect them in positive or negative ways. Burgess, Schmeeckle, and Bengtson (chapter 2, this volume) detail the pervasive influence wielded by four major social structures: the family, the workplace, the state, and religious institutions. Changes in the family structure can lead to ambiguity in roles and responsibilities of older family members toward younger family members. Changes in the work context affect older adults, especially women, and may alter their financial situation. Changes in the programs and policies of national governments privilege some groups over others, shape the lives of all individuals, and regulate activities at all stages of the life course. Likewise, changes in religious beliefs and programs offered by religious institutions influence interpersonal relations, support interactions by and activities of older individuals, and impact their definition and evaluation of their life and their functioning in old age.

Two of the social roles or social interactions that have been examined most extensively from a life-span developmental perspective are parent–child role relations (often a caregiving versus care-receiving phenomenon) and the education–work–retirement continuum (often a definition of role or life purpose phenomenon).

When one mentions "parent–child relationships" the image that most people have is a parent, who is most typically in his or her 20s, and a young child. Everyone has experienced the half of the relationship that involves being a young child, and the majority of adults have experienced the other half of that relationship, namely, being a parent. However, those two roles in this form exist during only a small portion of an individual's life span. Most people are surprised to realize that the amount of time in the parent–child relationship during which both parties are adults far exceeds the amount of time when the child is really a child and the parent is an adult.

The grandparent–parent–child relationship, in the most typical pattern, would occur when the original parent (now grandparent) is about 50 years old and the adult child (now parent) is about 25 years old. This three generational relationship has been common for many decades, and empirical data, as well as common myths, exist regarding it.

However, given the increased longevity of elderly individuals today, additional new relationships have emerged. Within the life-span developmental approach, considerable attention has been devoted to the middle-aged adult who has multiple caregiving responsibilities, that is, responsibility for seeing after the needs of a frail elderly parent as well as continuing caregiving responsibilities toward their adolescent or young-adult child. Such responsibilities have typically fallen to the female in most cultures. The general topic of caregiving is considered in greater detail elsewhere in this volume.

The role of work over the life span of the individual has also been studied from a life-span developmental perspective. To a young child, "work" is something that his or her parent does. By adolescence, however, issues regarding the need for future employment begin to take on meaning and relevance to the teenager. Schooling now begins to take on a new meaning, and the continuing education of the teenager is now more likely to be viewed as preparation for a job or career. At some age, typically between 16 and 24 years old, most individuals begin working. For most people, work is initially seen as "just a job"; but at some point, their job becomes a career. For many individuals the work they do as a "productive worker" over the majority of their adult life becomes a central aspect of their life and an important defining characteristic of who they are. Thus, when an individual retires, becoming a retiree can take on considerable and varied significance for the person—including a redefinition of who they are and what about them is worthwhile and valuable.

Successful Aging

As noted earlier, one of the definitions of the life-span developmental approach (Baltes, Reese, & Lipsitt, 1980) used the word *optimization*. A psychological model of "successful aging" has been conceptualized, particularly by Baltes, within the life-span developmental approach. This model is based on "selective optimization with compensation," which uses the concept of adaptation, the gains and losses in skills and abilities over the course of the life span, and the interaction among the elements within the model. Schroots (1996) summarizes these three elements as follows:

> First, there is the element of selection, which refers to an increasing restriction of one's life to fewer domains of functioning because of an age-related loss in the range of adaptive potential. The second element, optimization, reflects the view that people engage in behaviors to enrich and augment their general reserves and to maximize their chosen life courses (and associated forms of behavior) with regard to quantity and quality. The third element, compensation, results also (like selection) from restrictions in the range of adaptive potential. It becomes operative when specific behavioral capacities are lost or are reduced below a standard required for adequate functioning. (p. 745)

Successful aging is said to occur, therefore, through the process of "selective optimization with compensation" over the course of the lifetime, whereby a given individual continues to perform life tasks that are important to him or her despite decreases in skills, ability, memory, and performance. Schroots (1996) presented an example of such functional change in a highly gifted (and, hence, atypical) individual, but this process can be illustrated in more typical individuals as well. For example, an aging used car salesman who was earlier highly conversant about a broad array of car and truck makes and models, each over a 10-year range, might, in his later years of semi-retirement, change over to new car sales from used car sales to reduce the range of needed knowledge (selection), while simultaneously developing and reviewing charts summarizing the features and options for each of the models (optimization). In addition, he might develop preprogrammed computer forms for generating purchase agreements with different configurations of options so that he does not need to slowly write them by hand as he did earlier (compensation).

Clinical Relevance of the Life-Span Perspective

Psychotherapists working with older patients need to be mindful of the myriad life events, some more stressful and others less so, that a given patient has faced over the course of his or her lifetime—particularly in his or her old age

(VandenBos, 1993). A life-span approach provides a nonclinical, nonpathological perspective for considering the entirety of a person's life, both from an individual psychological perspective and in comparison with a normative set of commonly experienced life events. Psychotherapists should feel comfortable with a life-span developmental approach, because it places the target behavior (or symptom) within a pattern of antecedent, current, and subsequent functioning; it addresses strengths, not just weaknesses; and it is concerned with change and adaptation.

In assessing patients' concerns about changing biological functioning, the psychotherapist explores at least three questions: (a) What is the nature and extent of the change on the patient's daily routine and everyday functioning? (b) Is the pattern of change sudden, gradual, or alternating back and forth, and how does the patient's current functioning relate to their recent baseline functioning as well as to their highest level of such functioning at earlier times? and (c) What is the meaning and psychological experience of the biological change for the individual within his or her life experience and knowledge of the life experiences of others, such as family members and peers? Specifics regarding changes in biological functioning are addressed in detail in several other chapters in this volume. It is important that the psychotherapist working with older patients give equal consideration to the functional and psychological consequences of these physical changes and the actual physical changes themselves.

In considering patients' complaints about cognitive functioning, the same basic questions apply (effect on daily functioning, nature of decline, and meaning to the patient). However, the clinician should also analyze the components involved in the specific cognitive abilities about which the patient is concerned. Likewise, it is frequently important to consider the best or highest level of such cognition ever achieved by the patient as well as their recent baseline level of functioning (Zarit & VandenBos, 1990). Moreover, the relationship between the patients' health status and the cognitive decline about which they are expressing concern also needs to be examined. Useful resources in conducting such cognitive assessments of the elderly are provided in Storandt and VandenBos (1994).

The psychologist often needs to help the patient assess environmental demands and personal competencies in relation to those external demands, to help identify what about the environment can or cannot be modified to accommodate the elderly person's capacities, and to explore with the patient (and possibly with his or her family) the alternatives that the patient may have. However, central to all of this is the exploration of the personal meaning and significance of all of these factors to the patient within his or her personal life and interpretation of events.

These types of analysis of behavior and functioning should be comfortable to the clinician. A life-span approach provides a clinician with additional ways of thinking about the specific behavioral strengths and weaknesses of a given elderly patient. Conceptualizing the patient within the totality of the life experiences, assessing current functioning and comparing it to earlier functioning, and planning interventions based on the strengths and abilities of the patient and those around them represent common clinical assessments and interventions with older patients. Life-span developmental psychology is about change, just as psychotherapy is.

References

Baltes, P. B. (1987). Theoretical propositions of life-span developmental psychology: On the dynamics between growth and decline. *Developmental Psychology, 23,* 611–626.

Baltes, P. B., Reese, H. W., & Lipsitt, L. P. (1980). Life-span developmental psychology. *Annual Review of Psychology, 31,* 65–110.

Baltes, P. B., Smith, J., & Staudinger, U. M. (1992). Wisdom and successful aging. In T. Sonderegger (Ed.), *Nebraska symposium on motivation* (Vol. 39, pp. 123–167). Lincoln: University of Nebraska Press.

Cattell, R. B. (1972). *Abilities: Their structure, growth, and action.* Boston: Houghton Mifflin.

Erikson, E. H. (1950). *Childhood and society.* New York: Norton.

Hebb, D. O. (1942). The effect of early and late brain injury upon test scores, and the nature of normal adult intelligence. *Proceedings of the American Philosophical Society, 85,* 275–292.

Kline, P., & Cooper, C. (1984). The factor structure of the Comprehensive Adult Battery. *British Journal of Educational Psychology, 54,* 106–110.

Lawton, M. P., & Nahemow, L. (1973). Ecology and the aging process. In C. Eisdorfer & M. P. Lawton (Eds.), *The psychology of adult development and aging* (pp. 619–674). Washington, DC: American Psychological Association.

Reese, H. W., & Smyer, M. A. (1983). The dimensionalization of life events. In E. J. Callahan & K. A. McCluskey (Eds.), *Life-span developmental psychology: Non-normative life events* (pp. 1–33). New York: Academic Press.

Schroots, J. J. F. (1996). Theoretical developments in the psychology of aging. *The Gerontologist, 36,* 742–748.

Storandt, M., & VandenBos, G. R. (Eds.). (1994). *Neuropsychological assessment of dementia and depression in older adults: A clinician's guide.* Washington, DC: American Psychological Association.

Undheim, J. O., & Gustafsson, J. E. (1987). The hierarchical organization of cognitive abilities: Restoring general intelligence through the use of linear structural relations (LISREL). *Multivariate Behavioral Research, 22,* 149–171.

VandenBos, G. R. (1993). Psychology and the mental health needs of the elderly. In F. Lieberman & M. F. Collen (Eds.), *Good health: A quality lifestyle for later years* (pp. 189–202). New York: Plenum Press.

Zarit, S. H., & VandenBos, G. R. (1990). Effective evaluation of memory in older persons. *Hospital and Community Psychiatry, 41,* 9–16.

2

Aging Individuals and Societal Contexts

Elisabeth O. Burgess, Maria Schmeeckle,
and Vern L. Bengtson

Sociological perspectives on aging emphasize the importance of group member-ship and the effects of historical events on the experiences of later life. Consider a 70-year-old woman who is being admitted for psychological evaluation. What if anything can we know about her based solely on her age and personal ex-periences? Is turning 70 a significant milestone or a common occurrence? Is she likely to be in good health? What avenues are available to her for financial support? Is she embedded in a social network? What opportunities were avail-able to her over the life course? What historical events on a societal level shaped her life? What more do we know about her if we have information on her eth-nicity, social class, and education level?

Situating individuals in social contexts is essential if we want to under-stand the lives and psychological disabilities of older people. Many clinicians acknowledge this but may not recognize how it applies at a broad societal and historical level. It is all too easy to stereotype older patients from the perspec-tive of our own class background and the current historical period. When we recognize the importance of broad-level social contexts, we can better under-stand the diversity of experiences of aging across time and location.

In this chapter, we explore how social structures shape the lives and prob-lems of older individuals. We focus on family, work, the state, and religion—four significant contexts that have changed greatly over the past century. By understanding these changing contexts, geropractitioners can better work to address the needs, concerns, and psychopathologies of older individuals.

Social Structures

Individuals live and interact in social contexts that affect their everyday lives. These contexts can be understood as *social structures*, large-scale patterns of behavior that are ordered across time and location and reflect accepted patterns of values and beliefs. Social structures can operate at two levels: those of whole societies and those representing integral components of society (Connell, 1987). At the latter level, commonly recognized social structures include family, work, the state, religion, the legal system, and education.

Social structures shape individual practices in marked ways through the establishment of social rules (norms) and the distribution of resources (power). These rules and resources govern practices such as entry into school, the timing of marriage, exit from the paid labor force, and receipt of government-sponsored health care. Through rituals, individuals celebrate these accepted life transitions and use them to give meaning to their lives.

At the same time, people shape change in social structures in direct and indirect ways. Individuals and groups can challenge social structures directly through organized resistance to dominant ideology and indirectly through nonadherence to social norms. The interplay between individuals and social structures provides the vital force that brings about social change.

The pace of change between individual lives and social structures is often uneven. Because of the routinized nature of social structures, structural norms are slow to change. In contrast, people can change their lives very rapidly to meet their individual needs. Thus, social structures lag behind individual lives (Riley, Kahn, & Foner, 1994). When individuals are faced with an increasingly out-of-date social structure, they develop creative adaptations for their personal lives and may challenge the social structure itself. For example, in the past few decades, middle-aged women from the middle and upper classes have returned to school when caregiving responsibilities have lessened in the home. These women directly challenged notions of *student* and *experienced* worker by adapting their unpaid homemaking skills for use in the paid labor force.

The goal of this chapter is to highlight selected social structures that influence the lives of aging individuals and to describe these changing contexts as we approach the twenty-first century. We have chosen to focus on the social structures of family, work, state, and religion because of their widespread significance in older people's lives.

Family

The boundaries of family are hotly contested by politicians, academics, and the public (Stacey, 1996). Family can be thought of in several ways; its meaning has changed over time and across cultures and differs by context within cultures. How *family* is defined legally has implications far beyond the home: for insurance coverage eligibility, tax bracket status, pension levels and distribution, child custody decisions, probate outcomes, medical intervention decisions, and immigration options (Weston, 1991). In this section, we focus on family as a social structure. Next, we examine (a) historical change in family structures and definitions, and (b) increased diversity in the experiences of family and how these shape the lives of older people.

Family as a social structure. As a social structure, families represent a symbolic context in which individuals' needs for love and support are met and reciprocated. Family members exchange significant levels of help and support throughout the life course (Cicerelli, 1990; Silverstein, Parrott, & Bengtson, 1995). They help each other in many ways, providing assistance with regular tasks, financial support, and advice. They share companionship, love, and leisure time. They experience shared history that comes from long-term relationships with kin who recognize their multiple facets. Many experience pride in seeing the continuation of their family lines in younger generations.

Here we mainly emphasize the positive potentials of family life, but note that family conflict can play a real and serious role in the lives of older people. Although conflict, disagreement, and competition can coexist with affection and support in families (Bengtson, Rosenthal, & Burton, 1996), they also can lead to negative memories and decreased willingness to help in times of need (Whitbeck, Hoyt, & Huck, 1994). Thus, although we acknowledge that families' interactions reflect the imperfections of their members, we emphasize that despite this, the social structure of family remains powerfully important.

Historical changes in family structures and definitions. One of the most profound changes that has influenced our understanding of family over the last century is the lengthening of average life expectancy. Improved sanitary conditions, better nutrition, and medical advances have lowered levels of infant and child mortality and increased average life expectancy at birth. In 1900, the average life expectancy of a child born in the United States was 47 years. Ninety years later, it was 75.4 years (Treas, 1995). For older people, having longer lives means having increased time in family roles. For example, the average duration of relationships between parents and children has increased dramatically. On average, adult children today experience twice as much shared time with a living parent as their counterparts in 1800 and triple the amount of time with both parents living (Watkins, Menken, & Bongaarts, 1987). This means that adult children have more potential for contact and support from parents but they may also have more responsibility for aging parents throughout the life course.

Beyond parent–child relationships, higher average life spans have increased the potential for extended intergenerational relationships. Grandparenting and great-grandparenting, which were less common in 1900, have become enduring life roles for many as we approach the year 2000. Many grandparents have a lot to offer to younger generations, and this interaction can also provide older people with an increased sense of purpose (Robertson, 1995).

In addition to intergenerational ties, the potential for long-term relationships between siblings and cousins of the same generation has grown. For example, the longevity and indissolubility of many biological and adoptive sibling relationships make them vital to a sense of security in old age. Siblings are more likely to be companions than other types of relatives and are better at maintaining active long-distance relationships than are friends (Bedford, 1995).

Recent decades have shown a decrease in marriages that result in lifelong relationships. Since 1800, the average number of years spent in marriage has increased, but at a far lower rate than its potential (Watkins et al., 1987). People are more likely to marry later, have fewer children, have children outside of marriage, cohabit outside of marriage, divorce, belong to step- and blended families, and live in nonfamily households, and are less likely to remarry after divorce, than they were a few decades ago (Stacey, 1996; Tucker & Mitchell-Kernan, 1995). These trends are generally evident throughout the

Western world, despite some variations across different racial, social class, and age groups (Stacey, 1996; Tucker & Mitchell-Kernan, 1995). One in two marriages in the United States is now expected to end in divorce. Although a significant proportion of divorced people remarry, many do not (Cherlin, 1992).

New forms of chosen partnerships are becoming increasingly socially acceptable. These most commonly take the form of cohabitation without legal marriage or gay male or lesbian partnerships, which may or may not be legally sanctioned. Although these forms of partnerships have been found among most cultures for centuries, in the past few decades, societies have begun to recognize these partnerships as legitimate alternatives to marriage. Cohabitation has become extremely common in the United States. Among the formerly married, declining rates of remarriage are more than offset when those who have substituted cohabitation for remarriage are incorporated (Cherlin & Furstenberg, 1994). In addition, some people cohabit as a precursor to marriage. Recent U.S. data indicate that about 90% of cohabiting relationships at any age result in marriage or break up within 5 years (Cherlin, 1992). For the remaining 10%, long-term cohabitation may be due to ideological beliefs or financial necessity. For example, two romantically involved elderly people may chose not to marry, to maintain higher pension levels.

The increased acceptance of lesbian and gay male partnerships is evident in the increased political dialogue around their rights to legally marry. In some countries, gay men and lesbians have gained ground in their rights to claim a legally sanctioned form of marriage. Denmark, Norway, and Sweden have legalized a form of lesbian or gay male marriage called *registered partnerships* (Stacey, 1996). A limited legal recognition has been achieved in Canada as well for same-gender relationships (Bala, 1994). Until quite recently, gay male and lesbian partners were uniformly denied familial rights commonly given to heterosexual spouses. These include the rights to coparent children, to co-own property, and to receive benefits from a partner's employment. These rights continue to be challenged in many countries.

The tenuousness of marriage and the increased visibility of alternative partnerships lead to several implications for older people. One is that although older people today may not experience the same high levels of divorce, cohabitation, and publicly open homosexuality as their younger counterparts, they are affected by these practices in their children and other younger relatives. They will need to make decisions about how to negotiate their changing kinship networks. A second implication for older people is that more in the future are likely to enter old age while divorced or in short-term remarriages or cohabitations. Ex- and short-term spouses may not be as likely to provide the depth of personal care that long-term spouses typically gave in the past. As a result, it may fall more to children, siblings, and other long-term family members to supplement relatively weak spousal support systems. Older men who are divorced may also lose contact or closeness with intergenerational kin, because they are less likely to enact strong "kinkeeping" roles than women (Hagestad, 1986). Older women who are divorced may face compounded economic problems with aging, because many have been in the paid labor force only sporadically and their retirement incomes are only a fraction of men's. As new forms of chosen partnerships are becoming socially acceptable, the meanings of family life have become increasingly diverse. It is this phenomenon that we explore next.

Diversity in experiences of family. Many researchers are now recognizing what much of the public already knows: Family and kinship are often not bounded by marriage, adoption, or biology. This has been stated in the past about specific subgroups such as African Americans (Stack, 1970) but is increasingly acknowledged for the majority of society. Regardless of family form, adult intergenerational relationships are structurally diverse (Bengtson, Rosenthal, & Burton, 1990; Silverstein & Bengtson, 1997). Widespread changes in structural family forms and lived family lives have many important implications for aging individuals. Riley and Riley (1993) describe an emerging kinship structure they call a "latent matrix" of kin connections. This matrix consists of a large and complex network of kin relationships, which are flexible, voluntary, not constrained by age or generation in closeness and support, and latent in quality until they are called on. The Rileys conceptualize the latent matrix as a network of kin that is continually shifting, allowing for the activation and intensification of close kin relationships. Boundaries are wide, to encompass several degrees of stepkin and in-laws, single-parent families, and cohabitation-related, adopted, and other "relatives" chosen from outside the family.

This type of socially constructed family, or *opportune* family (C. L. Johnson, 1995), includes individuals who are selectively accumulated through marriage, divorce, and remarriage. These relationships are variable and negotiable for those of all ages, adding complexity to many family relationships. This complexity has influenced the role of grandparents (Giarrusso, Silverstein, & Bengtson, 1996). For example, C. L. Johnson and Barer (1987) examined four different ways divorce or remarriage among family members altered kinship networks for grandparents: (a) when relationships with relatives of a child's divorce were retained while new relatives were added with a child's remarriage, (b) when the divorces and remarriages of multiple children created several subsets of relatives, (c) when the divorces and remarriages of the grandparents added another set of step- and in-law relations, and (d) when they retained relationships with former children-in-law after these children remarried.

Nearly half of the grandparents in C. L. Johnson and Barer's (1987) study experienced kinship expansion fitting these criteria, during the 3 years after a child's marital separation. Those grandmothers who severed relations with former in-laws after their children divorced experienced a temporary contraction in the kinship system, which expanded again if the children remarried. C. L. Johnson and Barer's research highlights the voluntary aspect of relationships formed after divorce and remarriage. Like the grandparents in their study, a great number of individuals of all ages do and will face choices about kinship expansion and reduction throughout their lives. We can no longer assume that help and support are exchanged across only certain family structures.

The structural changes described above and the diversity of decisions people might make about them can bring a great deal of ambiguity into the lives of older individuals. Boss and Greenberg (1984) described a state of *boundary ambiguity*, in which individuals can feel a lack of clarity about who is in or out of a family system at any given time. Step-relatives, cohabiting partners of relatives, and even biological relatives may be seen as physically present but psychologically absent or as psychologically present but physically absent. In these cases, the family boundaries are ambiguous, contributing to confusion over the roles and tasks individuals perform. Should stepgrandchildren living with biological grandchildren be invited for the holidays and given comparable gifts? Should a child's cohabiting partner be included in a family portrait? Should former stepchildren be called on for assistance in times of need?

These and many other everyday decisions shape whether ambiguously related family members are treated as integral, peripheral, or negligible to a larger family system. Family members may disagree about who should be included and the level of inclusion or exclusion. This kind of conflict may be bewildering for older individuals, many of whom grew up during a time when family boundaries were perceived as more clear. While negotiable kinship provides more potential for emotional and financial support, it can also leave aging individuals in a precarious situation, because obligations among family members may also become more ambiguous.

Work

The relationship among work, careers, and aging is changing. The nineteenth-century notion of work did not include retirement. People worked until they died or were physically disabled. By the end of the twentieth century, retirement has become something that most workers expect to experience; yet changes in the structure of labor markets, economies, and societal attitudes have led to differential experiences of work. In this section, we begin by discussing work as a social structure. We then explore how trajectories and transitions in work careers vary due to two main factors: (a) changes over historical time in labor markets and economies and (b) diversity in the experience of work.

Work as a social structure. The social structure of work provides an opportunity structure of available occupations, norms about appropriate people for these occupations, and a reward structure related to these occupations. Like family, work can be thought of in a multitude of ways. It can incorporate many types and situations of labor. This labor can be physical or mental. It can be paid or unpaid. It may take place in the public sphere or inside a private home. Work can take the form of a recognized position in an established labor market or it can be a marginal position in the underground economy. Workers can work full-time or part-time, and they can be paid in salaries, hourly wages, by the job, or in exchange for other goods and services.

Here we focus on the context of the paid labor force and older people's relationships with it. Our understanding of work is based on patterns established in the paid labor force. Even with this caveat, the meaning and experience of work is extremely complex. Transitions in and out of work are not clearly delineated at any stage of life. For instance, many contemporary entry-level jobs require high levels of education. As a result, many young people are spending more years in education, and delaying entry into the paid workforce. Similarly, the process of exiting the paid labor force is not simple. It involves not only individual choices, but overall opportunity structures. Although retirement can be viewed as a separate social structure (Atchley, 1993), the boundaries between retirement and work are becoming increasingly permeable. The transition between work and retirement is blurred (Mutchler, Burr, Pienta, & Massagli, 1997), and decisions to retire may not be final (Hayward, Grady, & McLaughlin, 1988). Although the decision to exit or remain in the labor force is a very personal one, larger societal factors play a role by either pushing older workers out of work or pulling them into the labor force (Kohli, 1994).

Historical changes in labor markets and economies. As labor markets change, work opportunities for older adults also change. A major indication of this is the changes to the overall availability of certain types of jobs. Service and high-tech positions have replaced the large number of agricultural and manufacturing jobs available in the early 1900s. As the labor market has shifted to a postindustrial, service-based economy, the types of jobs available are less likely to be the career jobs that contemporary elderly (middle-class men) entered into as young adults. In the United States, corporate downsizing and restructuring in the past decade also have reduced the demand for senior workers. Instead, the jobs available to many older workers are "contingent jobs," with no promise of lifetime employment or company loyalty (Henretta, 1994). Many of the skills of contemporary older workers are obsolete in today's marketplace, which emphasizes advanced technological skills. Another component of the changing workplace is that certain types of people are funneled into certain jobs. For instance, only when the demand for labor is high, such as during World War II, have concerted efforts been made to retrain older workers (Kohli, 1994).

Partly because of these factors, there has been a downward trend in labor force participation among men over 55 (Easterlin, Crimmins, & Ohanian, 1984; Treas, 1995). This reflects a pattern of early retirement among a significant proportion of the male workforce. This pattern has stabilized during the last quarter century, especially since the 1980s. Retirement trends for older women are more varied than for men: whereas some women fit the male pattern, others are entering the paid labor force in later life for the first time (Quinn & Burkhauser, 1994).

In addition, the size and skills of the available pool of younger workers influence the job opportunities open to aging people. When the size of younger cohorts is smaller, there may be more demand for older workers. Nevertheless, many employers will hire supplemental workers from the pool of women and immigrants before they will approach older workers (Kohli, 1994). In contrast, a rise in unemployment among younger workers can increase the push toward early exit for older workers.

Changes in economies can result in changes in the value of income. The more people depended on work for their preretirement income, instead of assets or savings, the more likely they are to return to work if their pensions and savings decrease in value (Hayward et al., 1988). Part-time and self-employment are increasingly common among older workers, the majority of whom are working part-time by choice. "Bridge jobs," the part-time jobs that workers obtain between careers and retirement, are becoming more prevalent among older workers (Quinn & Kozy, 1996).

Diversity in experiences of work. The work history of individuals influences their subsequent opportunities as they age. Diversity in careers by gender, race, and class can lead to differences in opportunities and marketability in later life. The establishment of seniority both within and between occupations is also diverse (Henretta, 1994). The type or prestige of an occupation influences individual decisions to remain in the labor force. For instance, high-prestige jobs that focus on mental work may retain older workers who continue to find their work gratifying and whose expertise continues to be highly valued. For menial laborers, the situation is reversed. Remaining in a job may be less desirable for older workers whose skills are devalued. Ironically, these workers are more likely to be in need of additional income in old age.

Opportunity structures during primary working years affect opportunities and access to resources during retirement (Calasanti, 1993). For workers with a career of manual and low-paying jobs, exit from the workforce is often more about health issues and disability than gaining leisure time. Hayward, Friedman, and Chin (1996) found that in the United States, African Americans' unequal footing in the labor force persisted into retirement years with significantly higher rates of disability.

Women's work trajectories reflect the opportunities available to them in society and deeply held beliefs about gender roles. Most occupations in the United States remain gender segregated, and most women continue to hold low-status, female-typed, dead-end jobs, earning much lower wages than men (Blum, 1991). Because women are more likely to spend time outside the paid labor force, they are even less marketable in later life.

Industrialization and workplace patterns encourage lives that are structured around age norms. Many Western notions of appropriate life activities have come to be organized around work (Kohli, 1986). Work has become more individualized historically, as it has been pulled away from community and family life.

The State

The state, or government, shapes older people's lives in profound ways. First, we provide a sociological perspective on the state as a social structure and how it influences the lives of aging individuals. Next, we highlight how states or governments act as both (a) providers for the well-being of older individuals and (b) regulators of life course activities.

The state as a social structure. The state is the largest social structure and wields incredible power over individual lives. As a social structure, the state manages collective resources and maintains social order. Toward these ends, the state privileges some groups over others, and its programs and policies reflect the ideologies of those in control.

The *state* can be defined as a combination of "executive, legislative, and judicial branches of government, the military, the criminal justice system, educational institutions, and public health and welfare institutions" (Estes, Linkins, & Binney, 1996, p. 347). Our perspective draws from the work of political economists who emphasize the social construction and value-laden nature of state activities (Estes et al., 1996; Minkler & Estes, 1991).

As societies have become more industrialized, states have become increasingly complex, to meet the needs of individuals. Through legislation, states establish rules about citizenship, employment, health care, and many other things. Through funding, states facilitate research and development in the fields of science and technology.

State activities have played a major role in constructing what people think of as "old age." Since the 1930s in the United States, "older people" were designated as all people over age 65. This was the age limit required for receipt of full Social Security benefits. Sixty-five as an age marker originated in Germany in the 1880s (Myles, 1984) with the introduction of the first social insurance program. Today, certain segments of society provide benefits for "seniors" at a range of ages. The U.S. government has pushed the old age eligibility marker of 65 upward, with the planned increase in the retirement age from 65 to 67 (Torres-Gil, 1992).

In its functions as manager of resources and maintainer of social order, the state shapes the lives of older individuals in two key ways: It provides for later life social welfare through programs such as Social Security and Medicare, and it regulates activities at all stages of the life course.

The state as provider. The term *welfare state* refers to government entitlement programs that distribute income, health care, and social services (Myles, 1984; Schulz, 1996). It is this aspect of the state that most concerns us here, because states have taken on significant responsibilities for the economic maintenance of older people (Myles, 1984). As a result, older people depend on state policies more than people of other age groups (Estes, 1991a).

In recent decades across the industrialized world, government programs benefiting older people have expanded (Jacobs, 1990; Mayer & Schoepflin, 1989; Myles, 1984). Some describe the years 1930–1990 as the era of Modern Aging, in which governments took on a major role in the provision of services and benefits for older people (Torres-Gil, 1992). This expansion has made the practice of retirement more accessible (Quadagno & Myles, 1991) and has led to an increase in independent living for those over 65 (Jacobs, 1990).

Nations differ from each other and across time in their provision of social welfare programs for older people. Cross-national variations can be linked to levels of industrialization, economic development, and political culture and values (Binstock & Day, 1996). For example, the United States is set apart from other nations in its focus on individualism and its resistance to government action (Binstock & Day, 1996; Parrott, Reynolds, & Bengtson, 1997). As a result, only in the United States is health care a part of the politics of old age (Estes, 1991b). Other capitalistic Western nations have health care for people of all ages.

Although welfare state expansion has contributed to the economic well-being of older people in general, certain groups remain at risk under current systems. Disadvantaged groups include women, minorities, the poor, the frail, and those in rural areas (Torres-Gil, 1992). This can be explained in part by policies that benefit certain groups over others. For example, the application of Social Security in the United States is not gender neutral. Benefits based on spousal wages reinforce women's dependence on men. Women's prior economic dependence (resulting from societal norms of women providing the bulk of unpaid home care) has led to gender inequality in retirement income for men and women. Single women are particularly impoverished (Estes et al., 1996).

Another issue is that the needs of older people exceed the programs available to fill those needs. Governments expect that much of the care that older people need will be provided by family members and other loved ones. When older people are financially able to hire private in-home companions, family members still must take the responsibility for monitoring and managing these services. Informal and private care is compromised when primary caregivers, often women, are unable to "do it all" and dependent older people are placed into impersonal, institutionalized forms of care, such as day care and nursing homes (Hochschild, 1995). Even if paid workers strive to give high-quality care, it is doubtful that state-provided care offers the same level of mental, emotional, and physical attention to well-being that someone with a long-term emotional bond would give (Hochschild, 1995).

The size and scope of welfare state activities, including entitlement programs for older people, continue to be a matter of public debate. The state is now being framed as a social structure unable to handle the increasing needs of older people. Social policy discussions have shifted from a focus on improvement to one of crisis and budget cutting (Estes, 1991b). Three long-term developments challenge whether older people's income security can be maintained at current levels: (a) the accelerated rate of population aging, (b) anticipated rises in public expenditures, and (c) the trend toward early retirement (Quadagno & Myles, 1991). A basic question comes up again and again: "What should be the role of the public sector in caring for citizens in later life?" (Jacobs, 1990, p. 358). Although this question will continue to be a major one facing policymakers in upcoming decades, it is unlikely that there will be dramatic changes in governmental policies toward the aged in the near future (Parrott et al., 1997).

The state as regulator of the life course. State policies regulate many aspects of life, including the structure of schooling, the legal marriage age, and the age of pension eligibility (Mayer & Schoepflin, 1989). In these and other ways, the state provides a structure for people to fit into as they live their lives.

One aspect of this regulation occurs as a by-product of welfare state provision. By providing age-based transfer incomes, states decrease older people's dependency on others and allow for decision making that might otherwise be impossible (Mayer & Schoepflin, 1989). For instance, in the past when people reached retirement age in the United States, they forfeited income if they delayed retirement, because public pensions did not increase if receipt was delayed. This provided a strong incentive to stop working at age 65 for financial reasons. Age-based eligibility contributes to sharp life transitions that are arbitrarily and universally applied rather than based on need (Neugarten & Neugarten, 1986) or individual preferences (Mayer & Schoepflin, 1989). "Whenever the state establishes rules, provides services, or offers monetary incentives, it is functionally rational for individuals to make use of such opportunities" (Mayer & Schoepflin, 1989, p. 202).

Other regulation of older people occurs through general legislation that shapes decision making. Certain laws have a particularly strong impact on older people. One example is "right to die" regulation. This has become an issue in many industrialized countries and encompasses various forms of euthanasia and assisted suicide (Glick & Smith, 1993).

Another example of regulation that is extremely relevant to older people is legislation surrounding "autonomy" and "competency." When an individual becomes unable to make his or her own decisions about medical treatment or health care, others must be brought in to help make these decisions. A variety of options exist in this realm, depending on the specifics of the situation (Wilber & Reynolds, 1995). States are involved in regulating the practices of surrogacy and guardianship, which in turn affect health care and financial outcomes in the lives of older people who have become incapacitated.

Due to state involvement, aging individuals experience a context that promotes transitions that are ordered yet are not individually motivated (Mayer & Schoepflin, 1989). This is a powerful force that geropractitioners may want to consider—that externally and universally applied rules are shaping the lives of older individuals. Further, these rules do not evolve in a vacuum but in specific historical and political contexts.

Some groups, including gerontologists, have challenged the necessity of a life course segmented by age, arguing instead for an "age-integrated" society, in which individuals of all ages can move between educational, occupational, unpaid work, and leisure activities (Riley et al., 1994). They argue that there is a lack of productive and meaningful role opportunities for the rising numbers of strong, healthy, and capable older people (Riley et al., 1994). States may encourage continued productive roles in the future by raising the eligibility age of public pensions (Burkhauser & Quinn, 1994).

In summary, states, with their entitlement programs, age-based rules, and general legislation, act as major providers and regulators in the lives of older people. Their policies do not have an equal impact on all individuals: Some are privileged and others disadvantaged under current systems. It is important to guard against seeing this as "natural"—states have developed over time and location within specific historical contexts. They enable and constrict the lives of older people. They make some preferred decisions possible and others unattainable.

Religion

Organized religion plays a major role in the lives of billions of people worldwide. Taken collectively, the major world religions—Christianity, Judaism, Islam, Buddhism, Hinduism, Confucianism, and Taoism—condition the lives and belief structures of people of all ages. These religions have varying influences at multiple levels: Some shape government policy and societal norms, whereas others have an influence primarily at a personal and small-group level. This section focuses on (a) the role of religion in articulating a system of beliefs and values and (b) religious institutions as locations of social interaction and support for older people.

Religion as a social structure. Religious organizations transmit values and beliefs to members of society. As mentioned above, they have varying influences on people's lives. Nevertheless, viewing religion as a social structure allows us to see how at a broad societal level, religion offers a context in which individual and collective needs for meanings are met through established beliefs and rituals.

The role of religion in articulating a system of beliefs and values. Religion seeks to define the spiritual world and give meaning to events that are difficult to explain or understand. Religious values, beliefs, and rituals can integrate members of a community and provide a source of strength in difficult times. Religion facilitates the process of older people making sense of their lives by providing hope, emotional strength, and coping strategies for dealing with death and suffering (Ellison, 1994; T. R. Johnson, 1995; Koenig, 1994). These can serve as resources for older individuals, even in the absence of tangible social support (Payne & McFadden, 1994). Religion acts as a source of continuity for many older people, but it can also be a source of conflict. Religious beliefs and meanings may clash with other aspects of people's lives, such as conventional medical practices, legal rights, and expectations at the workplace (O'Connell, 1994). Other times, people's beliefs clash with the beliefs of others, leading to social conflict. This can result in generational conflict as younger members of a religious community seek to adapt rituals and values to contemporary society. On a more personal level, individuals might feel that they have not lived up to the expectations of their religion, leading to a sense of guilt or a fear of damnation, which may have an effect on psychological well-being (Moberg, 1983). Others may feel let down by a religion that could not prevent sorrow and loss of loved ones.

Religion as a facilitator of social interaction and support for older people. Religion provides a meeting ground for its members. These meeting grounds can be physical spaces, such as temples and shrines, or social spaces, such as prayer groups and religious festivals. Older individuals who are lonely or depressed may be particularly comforted by the social opportunity provided by religious participation. Religious communities enable the creation of social networks and the exchange of support in times of need (Ellison, 1994). Because people of older ages are currently more likely to be involved in religion than those of younger ages (Payne & McFadden, 1994), religious activities may be an important site for peer interaction among older individuals and comfort in the face of losses of family and friends. The interaction and support provided by religion also afford additional benefits. Increased social support and stronger social networks provided by religious involvement are correlated with better health. Religion promotes a sense of intimacy and a feeling of belonging among older individuals (T. R. Johnson, 1995). The mental health benefits of religious involvement are consistent over the life course (Levin, Chatters, & Taylor, 1995). Recently, researchers have been careful to point out that health benefits are not simply due to religious participation, but a result of related factors, such as social support (Atchley, 1997). In the United States, African American churches have been shown to provide the kind of social and psychological support that links older people with health communities (Levin et al., 1995). However, although the interaction that comes with religion can be a major support for older individuals, it can have some negative effects also. Noncompliance with religious norms may lead to social stigma within a religious community, or meddling on the part of "well-meaning" religious members.

Implications for Practitioners

Understanding aging individuals in the context of social structures is important for practitioners because social contexts define and shape the lives of older people. As Mills (1959) stated in *The Sociological Imagination*, "neither the life of an individual nor the history of a society can be understood without understanding both" (p. 3). Older people seeking the services of geropractitioners are living in an increasingly complex world. Social contexts condition the opportunities and social support available to them. The rapid changes to social institutions that have occurred across the twentieth century can be hard to continually adapt to, and older people may find themselves increasingly alienated, confused, and even estranged from the society in which they live. By recognizing the historically changing structural diversity of their clients' lives, geropractitioners can adapt their treatments to best fit clients' particular life situations.

Older people have many needs, and geropractitioners play a critical role in helping them adjust to the changes of later life. Many of these changes can be linked to broader trends in society that vary across time and location. Recognition of these broad trends enables geropractitioners to anticipate issues and to develop programs to better meet the needs of the older people they serve. In addition, geropractitioners can influence the social context in which their clients live by sharing their expertise with the larger community. For instance, by serving on civic, educational, or religious organizations, practitioners can help their community adapt to the needs of older individuals. By recognizing and incorporating the structural contexts discussed in this chapter, practitioners can develop services that help older individuals cope with their changing world.

Each social structure discussed in this chapter has been linked to the lives of aging individuals. The changing family context can lead to ambiguity in terms of older family members' responsibility toward younger family members. By providing them with information on (grand)child custody and visitation, estate planning, and strategies to manage family conflict, practitioners empower the lives of aging people negotiating family relationships. The changing work context can place older people, especially women, in precarious financial circumstances. Practitioners can address these needs by creating programs that focus on job retraining, strategies for reentering the workforce, and retirement planning. The changing context of the state structures the lives of aging individuals. By developing services for them that emphasize political action, interpret new laws and regulations, and negotiate the health care system, practitioners can help older individuals recognize their own agency in dealing with the monolithic structure of the state. The changing context of religion can leave older individuals isolated from like-minded peers. Practitioners can address these needs by encouraging religious organizations to reach out to the older population and by providing information to older clients about diverse religious communities that service elders.

Conclusion

There has been a tendency for geropractitioners to think of older people in individualistic terms. Although this is important, it is incomplete because it ignores structural constraints and the power of social norms. The main thrust of this chapter has been to show the importance of four societal contexts to the lives of aging individuals. These four contexts—family, work, the state, and religion—are in constant flux, and a change in one area can precipitate changes in each of the others, which all affect the individual. A recognition of these broad-level contexts enhances the understanding of behavior, and it will assist geropractitioners in the practice of service to older individuals.

References

Atchley, R. C. (1993). Critical perspectives on retirement. In T. R. Cole, W. A. Achenbaum, P. L. Jakobi, & R. Kastenbaum (Eds.), *Voices and visions of aging: Toward a critical gerontology* (pp. 3–19). New York: Springer.

Atchley, R. C. (1997). The subjective importance of being religious and its effects on health and morale 14 years later. *Journal of Aging Studies, 11,* 131–141.

Bala, N. (1994). The evolving Canadian definition of the family: Towards a pluralistic and functional approach. *International Journal of Law and the Family, 8,* 293–318.

Bedford, V. H. (1995). Sibling relationships in middle and old age. In R. Blieszner & V. H. Bedford (Eds.), *Handbook of aging and the family* (pp. 201–222). Westport, CT: Greenwood Press.

Bengtson, V. L., Rosenthal, C. J., & Burton, L. M. (1990). Families and aging: Diversity and heterogeneity. In R. Binstock & L. George (Eds.), *Handbook of aging and the social sciences* (3rd ed., pp. 263–287). New York: Academic Press.

Bengtson, V. L., Rosenthal, C. J., & Burton, L. M. (1996). Paradoxes of familes and aging. In R. Binstock & L. George (Eds.), *Handbook of aging and the social sciences* (4th ed., pp. 253–282). New York: Academic Press.

Binstock, R. H., & Day, C. L. (1996). Aging and politics. In R. H. Binstock & L. K. George (Eds.), *Handbook of aging and the social sciences,* (4th ed., pp. 362–387). New York: Academic Press.

Blum, L. M. (1991). *Between feminism and labor: The significance of the Comparable Worth Movement.* Berkeley: University of California Press.

Boss, P., & Greenberg, J. (1984). Family boundary ambiguity: A new variable in family stress theory. *Family Process, 23,* 535–546.

Burkhauser, R. V., & Quinn, J. F. (1994). Changing policy signals. In M. W. Riley, R. L. Kahn, & A. Foner (Eds.), *Age and structural lag: Society's failure to provide meaningful opportunities in work, family, and leisure* (pp. 237–262). New York: Wiley.

Calasanti, T. M. (1993). Bringing in diversity: Toward an inclusive theory of retirement. *Journal of Aging Studies, 7*, 133–150.

Cherlin, A. J. (1992). *Marriage, divorce, remarriage* (Rev. and enl. ed.). Cambridge, MA: Harvard University Press.

Cherlin, A. J., & Furstenberg, F. F. (1994). Stepfamilies in the United States: A reconsideration. *Annual Review of Sociology, 20*, 359–381.

Cicerelli, V. G. (1990). Family support in relation to health problems of the elderly. In T. H. Brubaker (Ed.), *Family relationships in later life* (2nd ed., pp. 212–228). Newbury Park, CA: Sage.

Connell, R. W. (1987). *Gender and power: Society, the person and sexual politics.* Stanford, CA: Stanford University Press.

Easterlin, R. A., Crimmins, E. M., & Ohanian, L. (1984). Changes in labor force participation of persons 55 and over since World War II: Their nature and causes. In J. Livingston & J. E. Birren (Eds.), *Aging and technological advances* (pp. 89–97). New York: Plenum.

Ellison, C. G. (1994). Religion, the life stress paradigm, and the study of depression. In J. S. Levin (Ed.), *Religion in aging and health: Theoretical foundations and methodological frontiers* (pp. 78–121). Newbury Park, CA: Sage.

Estes, C. L. (1991a). The new political economy of aging: Introduction and critique. In M. Minkler & C. L. Estes (Eds.), *Critical perspectives on aging: The political and moral economy of growing old* (pp. 3–18). Amityville, NY: Baywood.

Estes, C. L. (1991b). The Reagan legacy: Privatization, the welfare state, and aging in the 1990s. In J. Myles & J. Quadagno (Eds.), *States, labor markets, and the future of old age policy* (pp. 59–83). Philadelphia: Temple University Press.

Estes, C. L., Linkins, K. W., & Binney, E. A. (1996). The political economy of aging. In R. H. Binstock & L. K. George (Eds.), *Handbook of aging and the social sciences* (4th ed., pp. 346–361). New York: Academic Press.

Giarrusso, R., Silverstein, M., & Bengtson, V. L. (1996). Family complexity and the grandparent role. *Generations, 20*, 17–23.

Glick, H. R., & Smith, J. D. (1993). *The right to die: A comparative perspective.* Tallahassee: Florida State University, Pepper Institute on Aging and Public Policy, Working Paper Series (No. PI-93-13).

Hagestad, G. (1986). The family: Women and grandparents as kinkeepers. In A. Pifer & L. Bronte (Eds.), *Our aging society* (pp. 141–160). New York: Norton.

Hayward, M. D., Friedman, S., & Chin, H. M. (1996). Race inequities in men's retirement. *Journal of Gerontology: Social Sciences, 55*, S1–S10.

Hayward, M. D., Grady, W. R., & McLaughlin, S. D. (1988). Changes in retirement process among older men in the United States: 1972–1980. *Demography, 24*, 371–386.

Henretta, J. (1994). Social structures and age-based careers. In M. W. Riley, R. L. Kahn, & A. Foner (Eds.), *Age and structural lag: Society's failure to provide meaningful opportunities in work, family, and leisure* (pp. 57–79). New York: Wiley.

Hochschild, A. R. (1995, Fall). The culture of politics: Traditional, postmodern, cold-modern, and warm-modern ideals of care. *Social Politics, 2*, 331–346.

Jacobs, B. (1990). Aging and politics. In R. H. Binstock & L. K. George (Eds.), *Handbook of aging and the social sciences* (3rd ed., pp. 350–361). New York: Academic Press.

Johnson, C. L. (1995). Cultural diversity in the late-life family. In R. Blieszner & V. H. Bedford (Eds.), *Handbook of aging and the family* (pp. 307–331). Westport, CT: Greenwood Press.

Johnson, C. L., & Barer, B. M. (1987). Marital instability and the changing kinship networks of grandparents. *Gerontologist, 27*, 330–335.

Johnson, T. R. (1995). The significance of aging well. *American Behavioral Scientist, 39*, 186–208.

Koenig, H. G. (1994). Religion and hope for the disabled elder. In J. S. Levin (Ed.), *Religion in aging and health: Theoretical foundations and methodological frontiers* (pp. 18–51). Newbury Park, CA: Sage.

Kohli, M. (1986). The world we forgot: A historical review of the life course. In V. W. Marshall (Ed.), *Later life: The social psychology of aging* (pp. 271–303). Beverly Hills, CA: Sage.

Kohli, M. (1994). Work and retirement: A comparative perspective. In M. W. Riley, R. L. Kahn, & A. Foner (Eds.), *Age and structural lag: Society's failure to provide meaningful opportunities in work, family, and leisure* (pp. 80–106). New York: Wiley.

Levin, J. S., Chatters, L. M., & Taylor, R. J. (1995). Religious effects on health status and life satisfaction among Black Americans. *Journal of Gerontology: Social Sciences, 50B*, S154–S163.

Mayer, K. U., & Schoepflin, U. (1989). The state and the life course. *Annual Review of Sociology, 15*, 187–209.

Mills, C. W. (1959). *The sociological imagination*. New York: Oxford University Press.

Minkler, M., & Estes, C. L. (Eds.). (1991). *Critical perspectives on aging: The political and moral economy of growing old*. Amityville, NY: Baywood.

Moberg, D. O. (1983). Religion in the later years. In W. W. Morris, I. M. Bader, & A. M. Hoffman (Eds.), *Daily needs and interests of old people* (pp. 119–133). Springfield, IL: Charles C Thomas.

Mutchler, J. E., Burr, J. A., Pienta, A. M., & Massagli, M. P. (1997). Pathways to labor-force exit: Work transitions and work instability. *Journal of Gerontology: Social Sciences, 52*, S4–S12.

Myles, J. (1984). *Old age in the welfare state: The political economy of public pensions*. Boston: Little, Brown.

Neugarten, B. L., & Neugarten, D. A. (1986). The changing meanings of age in the aging society. In A. Pifer & L. Bronte (Eds.), *Our aging society: Paradox and promise* (pp. 33–51). New York: Norton.

O'Connell, L. J. (1994). The role of religion in health-related decision making for elderly patients. *Generations, 18*, 27–30.

Parrott, T. M., Reynolds, S. L., & Bengtson, V. L. (1997). Aging and social welfare in transition: The case of the United States. *Scandinavian Journal of Social Welfare, 6*, 168–179.

Payne, B. P., & McFadden, S. H. (1994). From loneliness to solitude: Religious and spiritual journeys in later life. In L. E. Thomas & S. A. Eisenhandler (Eds.), *Aging and the religious dimension* (pp. 13–27). Westport, CT: Auburn House.

Quadagno, J., & Myles, J. (1991). Introduction: States, labor markets, and the future of old-age policy. In J. Myles & J. Quadagno (Eds.), *States, labor markets, and the future of old age policy* (pp. 3–18). Philadelphia: Temple University Press.

Quinn, J. F., & Burkhauser, R. (1994). Retirement and labor force behavior of the elderly. In L. Martin & S. Preston (Eds.), *Demography of aging* (pp. 50–101). Washington, DC: National Research Council.

Quinn, J. F., & Kozy, M. (1996). The role of bridge jobs in the retirement transition: Gender, race and ethnicity. *Gerontologist, 36*, 363–372.

Riley, M. W., Kahn, R. L., & Foner, A. (1994). Introduction: The mismatch between people and structures. In M. W. Riley, R. L. Kahn, & A. Foner (Eds.), *Age and structural lag: Society's failure to provide meaningful opportunities in work, family, and leisure* (pp. 1–12). New York: Wiley.

Riley, M. W., & Riley, J. W. (1993). Connections: Kin and cohort. In V. L. Bengtson & W. A. Achenbaum (Eds.), *The changing contract across generations* (pp. 169–189). New York: Aldine de Gruyter.

Robertson, J. F. (1995). Grandparenting in an era of rapid change. In R. Blieszner & V. H. Bedford (Eds.), *Handbook of aging and the family* (pp. 243–260). Westport, CT: Greenwood Press.

Schulz, J. H. (1996). Economic security policies. In R. H. Binstock & L. K. George (Eds.), *Handbook of aging and the social sciences* (4th ed., pp. 410–426). New York: Academic Press.

Silverstein, M., & Bengtson, V. L. (1997). Intergenerational solidarity and the structure of adult child–parent relationships in American families. *American Journal of Sociology, 103*, 429–460.

Silverstein, M., Parrott, T. M., & Bengtson, V. L. (1995). Factors that predispose middle-aged sons and daughters to provide social support to older parents. *Journal of Marriage and the Family, 57*, 465–476.

Stacey, J. (1996). *In the name of the family: Rethinking values in the postmodern age*. Boston: Beacon Press.

Stack, C. B. (1970). *All our kin: Strategies for survival in a Black community*. New York: Harper & Row.

Torres-Gil, F. (1992). *The new aging: Politics and change in America*. New York: Auburn House.

Treas, J. (1995). Older Americans in the 1990s and beyond. *Population Bulletin, 50*(2).

Tucker, M., & Mitchell-Kernan, B. C. (1995). *The decline in marriage among African Americans: Causes, consequences and policy implications*. New York: Russell Sage Foundation.

Watkins, S., Menken, A., & Bongaarts, J. (1987). Demographic foundations of family change. *American Sociological Review, 52,* 346–358.

Weston, K. (1991). *Families we choose: Lesbians, gays, kinship.* New York: Columbia University Press.

Whitbeck, L., Hoyt, D. R., & Huck, S. M. (1994). Early family relationships, intergenerational solidarity, and support provided to parents by their adult children. *Journal of Gerontology: Social Sciences, 49,* S85–S94.

Wilber, K., & Reynolds, S. L. (1995). Rethinking alternatives to guardianship. *Gerontologist, 35*(2), 248–257.

3

Aging and Personality Traits: Generalizations and Clinical Implications

Paul T. Costa, Jr., Jian Yang, and Robert R. McCrae

In the very first textbook on personality psychology, Allport (1937) listed some 50 different definitions of *personality*, and the list has only grown since then. Perhaps the most common definition, however, refers in some way to personality *traits*, a person's attributes or qualities measured by personality inventories. Traits such as timidity, cheerfulness, unconventionality, generosity, and dependability are familiar to laypersons as well as psychologists; one way to characterize a person's personality is by listing all of his or her traits.

To dynamically oriented psychologists, traits sometimes seem too superficial a level at which to analyze personality. But that view probably stems from a confusion of traits with habits or other overt behaviors. Traits are related to behaviors—although only probabilistically—but they are also related to motives and drives, to feelings and fantasies, to cognitive styles and intellectual interests. They affect interpersonal interactions (Shaver & Brennan, 1992), sexuality (Costa, Fagan, Piedmont, Ponticas, & Wise, 1992), coping and defense (Costa, Zonderman, & McCrae, 1991), religious orientations (Piedmont, 1996), health practices (Marshall, Wortman, Vickers, Kusulas, & Hervig, 1994), and psychological well-being (Emmons & Diener, 1985). Personality traits are truly pervasive influences on the psychological functioning of the person.

Although personality traits can be inferred from observed behavior, they are usually best assessed through questionnaires that ask respondents to summarize long-term patterns of behavior. A substantial body of research has now demonstrated the validity of self-reports, most notably through their correlation with observer ratings (McCrae, 1994). Agreement between self-reports and ratings from knowledgeable informants, and between independent informants, is typically in the range of .30 to .60, suggesting substantial overlap but also some differences. As a result, these methods should be considered complementary, and both self-reports and observer ratings have been used in longitudinal studies of adult personality.

We thank Gian Vittorio Caprara, Claudio Barbarnelli, Alois Angleitner, Willem K. B. Hofstee, Jolijn Hendriks, and Boele De Raad, for making their inventories available to us, and Alois Angleitner, for sharing German data on these instruments.

For decades, progress in research on trait psychology was hindered by the lack of a generally accepted model of trait structure. Different researchers examined different traits, or the same traits under different labels; a few major figures (including Raymond B. Cattell and Hans J. Eysenck) dominated the long-standing debates surrounding the issue of the most adequate model of traits. It was not until the 1980s that several different groups of researchers independently concluded that almost all traits could be understood in terms of five broad trait domains or factors, commonly labeled Neuroticism, Extraversion, Openness to Experience, Agreeableness, and Conscientiousness (McCrae & John, 1992). In turn, each of these factors is defined by many more specific and narrow traits, which provide a more detailed description of personality.

Much of the research on this hierarchical five-factor model (FFM) of personality has used the Revised NEO Personality Inventory (NEO–PI–R; Costa & McCrae, 1992b), a 240-item questionnaire developed specifically to operationalize the FFM. The NEO–PI–R has 30 scales, which measure six different facets of each of the five factors. For example, the Agreeableness factor is represented by facet scales measuring Trust, Straightforwardness, Altruism, Compliance, Modesty, and Tendermindedness.

In a series of studies (Costa & McCrae, 1992b), the NEO–PI–R has been related to most other major personality inventories, yielding a guide to the classification of many widely used scales in terms of the FFM. For example, the Thoughtfulness scale of the Guilford–Zimmerman Temperament Survey (GZTS; Guilford, Zimmerman, & Guilford, 1976) is a measure of Openness; the GZTS Ascendance scale is a measure of Extraversion. This mapping allows researchers to integrate findings from studies using many different instruments and to plan systematic research that efficiently covers the full range of personality traits.

The generalizability of the FFM is now well established across male and female, White and non-White, and older and younger adult samples (Costa, McCrae, & Dye, 1991). And although the FFM was originally identified through studies of English-language trait terms (John, Angleitner, & Ostendorf, 1988), it appears to be a universal structure. Studies in languages and cultures as distinct as Filipino, Estonian, Hebrew, and Japanese have all shown nearly identical factor structures (McCrae, Costa, del Pilar, Rolland, & Parker, 1988). In every culture so far examined, people who are sociable also tend to be energetic, assertive, and cheerful: Extraversion—like the other major factors—is a universal dimension of individual differences.

The fast of universality suggests that personality structure may be a specieswide part of human nature, and that hypothesis is consistent with a large body of data on the heritability of the five factors. Findings from twin, family, and adoption studies consistently show that most traits are, to a substantial degree, determined by genetic influences (Jang, McCrae, Angleitner, Riemann, & Livesley, in press) and are largely unaffected by childhood experiences (Rowe, 1994). The whole range of personality traits—including characteristics not ordinarily seen as aspects of temperament, such as trust, dutifulness, and aesthetic sensitivity—appear to be constitutional predispositions that find some form of expression in every culture.

Personality Traits in Adulthood

Those findings stand in stark contrast to the view of personality that has dominated psychological thinking in this century. From Freud on, personality psychologists generally presumed that the major determinants of personality were life experiences: infant attachment, enculturation, learned self-efficacy, traumatic life events, role requirements, and losses. Although psychoanalysts argued that in the absence of analysis, little of importance changed after the first few years, most other psychologists saw personality as a relatively fluid system that would adapt to changing life circumstances. We know that children raised in the Great Depression differ from those raised in the affluent 1950s in their sense of economic security and their political views, that retirement can lead to role loss and new challenges to marital adjustment, and that life-threatening illnesses such as cancer or heart disease sometimes transform one's outlook on life. Few psychologists would have been surprised if longitudinal studies of personality traits had shown that these, too, were readily shaped and reshaped by historical circumstances and life events.

The real surprise was that longitudinal studies in fact showed nothing of the sort. The predominant pattern is instead one of stability, and where there are changes, they appear to be due to intrinsic maturational processes largely independent of environmental influences. Results from studies of adult personality development are entirely consistent with results from behavior genetics studies in depicting personality traits not as learned adaptations but as endogenous and enduring dispositions that are more likely to be contributing causes than simple effects of life experiences. These are surely findings for clinical psychologists to ponder.

Stability of Individual Differences

The evidence for these assertions comes first from longitudinal studies of the stability of individual differences in personality traits. Cross-sectional studies, in which individuals of different ages are compared at the same time, are useful for looking at mean-level changes with age, but they do not speak to the issue of rank-order stability. To determine how well individual differences are preserved over time, it is necessary to measure the same people on at least two different occasions. When the retest interval is short—a week or a month—the retest correlation is interpreted as a measure of the reliability of the instrument: Researchers presume that the underlying trait has not changed, so correlations less than 1.0 must be due to transient fluctuations. When the retest interval is long—a year or a decade—the same retest correlation is usually construed as evidence of the stability of the trait itself, although it is clear that the observed correlation will be affected by retest unreliability as well as by real changes in the underlying trait.

In one of the first longitudinal studies of adults, Costa, McCrae, and Arenberg (1980) examined 6- and 12-year retest correlations for the 10 scales of the GZTS. In a subsample of 114 men with complete data at three times, they reported 6-year retest correlations ranging from .70 to .84 and 12-year retest correlations ranging from .68 to .85. In addition, the availability of 3-point data made it possible to separate reliability from stability and to estimate the stability of the true score for each of the 10 GZTS scales. These values ranged from .80 to 1.00, with a median of .91, suggesting almost no change in real personality over a 12-year interval.

Since that time, many other studies have been reported, using different samples, instruments, and retest intervals (see Costa & McCrae, 1997, for a review). Results from studies of women closely parallel those from studies of men. Three general conclusions seem warranted: (a) Personality traits from all five factors are stable, and equally stable, in adults; (b) stability coefficients are higher for adults over age 30 than for younger adults (e.g., Finn, 1986); and (c) stability gradually decreases over long time intervals. Projecting from 24-year data, Costa and McCrae (1992c) estimated that about three fifths of the variance in personality traits is stable over a typical 50-year adult life span.

Most longitudinal studies are based on self-reports, and conclusions based on a single methodology are always suspect. In particular, it might be hypothesized that individuals have a stable self-concept that accounts for their unchanging responses to personality questionnaire items. Perhaps their true personality is in fact changing, as unbiased observers could attest. That hypothesis is testable by conducting longitudinal studies of observer ratings of personality. In 1988, Costa and McCrae reported 6-year retest correlations of spouse ratings of Neuroticism, Extraversion, and Openness in samples of 89 men and 78 women. Correlations ranged from .77 to .86, values almost identical to those seen in self-reports over the same interval.

In a subsequent study, peer ratings of all five factors were collected over a 7-year interval. Retest correlations for single peer raters ranged from .74 to .78 for men and from .63 to .84 for women. Note again that these coefficients are uncorrected for retest unreliability. Because multiple peer ratings were collected, the design of this study allowed an estimate of the stability of true scores. These estimates all exceeded .84, with a median of .90 (Costa & McCrae, 1992c). Self, spouse, and peers concur in showing that individual differences are highly stable in adults.

When such findings were first reported, they were so unexpected that many psychologists believed some artifact was responsible. Perhaps on retest, respondents recalled their original responses and, in the interest of appearing consistent, simply repeated them. But Woodruff (1983) showed that respondents could not accurately recall earlier responses even when instructed to. Perhaps what was stable was not personality itself but merely response styles like acquiescence and extreme responding. But analyses controlling for such influences did not reduce the stability of trait scores (Costa, McCrae, & Arenberg, 1983).

Even if personality traits were stable for most people, surely (it was claimed) there must be subsets of people who showed important changes (Spiro, Levenson, & Aldwin, 1992). But most attempts to demonstrate meaningful change (as opposed to random and unreliable fluctuation, which can be found in any distribution of change scores) were unsuccessful. Major changes in physical health status, such as the development of cancer and coronary disease, did not affect personality scores (Costa, Metter, & McCrae, 1994). Despite theoretical predictions, individuals high in self-monitoring or low in personal agency did not show lower retest stability than others (McCrae, 1993). Even a small group of respondents who claimed that their personality had changed "a good deal" over the previous 6 years showed 6-year retest correlations ranging from .66 to .90 in self-reports and spouse ratings (Costa & McCrae, 1989b).

Fluidity of Individual Differences in the 20s

Adolescents as a group do consistently show somewhat lower retest stabilities than older adults (Finn, 1986; Siegler et al., 1990). Developmentally, this suggests that significant change occurs in the decade of the 20s and that this might be an important life period in which to intervene to change undesirable aspects of personality. Methodologically, it implies that life-span developmental research should not use the personality traits of college students as the endpoint of child development (Kagan & Moss, 1962) or the baseline for adult life outcomes (Siegler et al., 1990). The relative fluidity of individual differences in this decade also suggests that group-level changes may also occur at this age.

Stability of Mean Levels

The stability of individual differences is understandable in terms of the genetic basis of traits—after all, one's genetic blueprint is essentially fixed for life. But many processes under genetic control (e.g., hair color) change across the life span, and mean-level changes are entirely consistent with stability in individual differences. If everyone uniformly declined in Extraversion or Openness by 1 standard deviation per decade, rank order would be maintained despite major changes in the mean level of the trait.

Stereotypes of aging in the United States suggest these types of mean-level changes. Older people are often depicted as being socially withdrawn and emotionally disengaged, conservative in beliefs and rigid in behavior, depressed and apathetic. Although efforts to combat ageism have probably made some progress, these stereotypes are still widespread: Krueger and Heckhausen (1993) found that German adults of all ages anticipated declines in desirable personality traits in the latest decades of life.

These stereotypes are not supported by objective personality data, however (Costa & McCrae, 1997). For example, Krueger and Heckhausen's (1993) participants showed no age differences when asked to describe their own personalities (rather than their expectations of change in general). One of the largest cross-sectional studies of age trends in personality was conducted as part of the National Health and Nutrition Examination Survey I Epidemiologic Follow-Up Study. About 10,000 respondents to that national probability survey were assessed with brief measures of Neuroticism, Extraversion, and Openness (Costa et al., 1986). Separate analyses of Black and White men and women across the age range from 35 to 85 showed no marked declines or increases. Correlations with age ranged only from −.12 to −.19 and, although statistically significant, suggested that age accounts for less than 4% of the variance in these personality traits. Note also that the correlation with Neuroticism was negative; older persons are not more prone to depression and anxiety but slightly less.

The peer-rating study reported by Costa and McCrae (1992c) offers an entirely different method of measurement on which to base age–personality correlations. The results are strikingly similar, however: Correlations of age with peer-rated Neuroticism, Extraversion, and Openness were −.15, −.16, and −.16, respectively. In that study, both Agreeableness and Conscientiousness showed positive correlations with age (.18 and .05), although the latter was not statistically significant.

Intrinsic Maturational Changes in Personality

The very small age correlations seen among adults over age 30 could be easily dismissed as cohort differences or age differences in some response bias if they did not show a familiar pattern. But in fact the same age-related declines in Neuroticism, Extraversion, and Openness and increases in Agreeableness and Conscientiousness were seen also when adolescents were compared with midlife adults (Costa & McCrae, 1994). That initially became clear when the NEO–PI (Costa & McCrae, 1985) was first published. Most research with that instrument had used adult samples, and when investigators began to use it on college samples, divergences from adult norms quickly became apparent. Patterns of age differences were similar for men and women and were found in several different college samples. Revisions of the NEO–PI (Costa & McCrae, 1989a, 1992b) included separate norms for college-age respondents.

The pattern of age differences between 18-year-olds and 30-year-olds, especially at the level of specific facets, is not surprising. The data show that adolescents are higher in Neuroticism, especially in *impulsiveness*, an inability to control cravings and urges; in Extraversion, especially excitement seeking; and in Openness to a variety of forms of experience. They also show that adolescents score low in Agreeableness and Conscientiousness, especially in compliance, dutifulness, and self-discipline facets. These cross-sectional findings are supported by the results of a number of longitudinal studies (Jessor, 1983; Mortimer, Finch, & Kumka, 1982) and are consistent with the commonsense view that age leads to increased self-control, stability, and maturity.

Are these age changes an intrinsic part of human maturation, or are they the result of American patterns of child rearing and American educational and economic structures in the second half of the twentieth century? There is reason to think that they may be universal. The developmental progression toward stability, tranquillity, and compliance is the theme of a famous dictum by Confucius (cited in Levinson, Darrow, Klein, Levinson, & McKee, 1978, p. 326):

> At 15 I set my heart upon learning.
> At 30, I had planted my feet firm upon the ground.
> At 40, I no longer suffered from perplexities.
> At 50, I knew what were the biddings of heaven.
> At 60, I heard them with docile ear.
> At 70, I could follow the dictates of my own heart; for what I desired no longer overstepped the boundaries of right.

Those 2,500-year-old hypotheses have received recent support in two studies of age differences in personality traits among contemporary Chinese (Tarnowski, Shen, Diehl, & Labouvie-Vief, 1996; Yang, McCrae, & Costa, 1997). Both studies used Chinese translations of the California Psychological Inventory (CPI; Gough, 1987), and both found that younger Chinese adults scored higher on scales measuring preference for variety and change (Flexibility) and understanding of others (Empathy), whereas older Chinese scored higher on scales measuring even-temperedness and self-discipline (Self-Control), taking duties seriously (Responsibility), and adhering to conventional rules (Norm-Favoring). These are not uniquely Chinese effects; instead, the same effects were also seen in two American samples (Tarnowski et al., 1996; Yang et al., 1997).

The Confucian view of adult development seems to imply that change continues across the life span well after age 30. There is some empirical evidence in favor of that view: Yang et al. (1997) found linear increases or decreases in their sample across the range from 18 to 67. At this time, it is not clear whether there are real cultural differences in the rate of change of personality traits in adults over age 30.

Studies using the full NEO−PI−R in translation have found similar patterns of age differences in German, Italian, Portuguese, Croatian, and Korean samples (McCrae et al., 1997). These cross-sectional comparisons carry considerable weight because they are also cross-cultural. Any single cross-sectional study confounds age effects with generational differences that reflect the effects of the historical experience of a birth cohort. But the United States, Germany, Croatia, and Korea have had vastly different histories in the twentieth century; when similar patterns of age differences are found, it is unlikely that they are attributable to cohort effects. Declines in Neuroticism, Extraversion, and Openness to Experience and increases in Agreeableness and Conscientiousness appear to be universal maturational effects, only modestly influenced by historical experience. Just as behavior genetics studies suggest a very limited role for child rearing practices in the formation of adult personality, so these cross-national age difference studies suggest a limited role for culturally shared life experiences in shaping basic personality dispositions.

This does not mean, of course, that culture is irrelevant to personality development, or vice versa. Adaptation to life will be facilitated to the extent that socially assigned life tasks and privileges are congruent with intrinsic developmental processes. The prohibition of alcohol to minors is based on the social perception that on average, their levels of excitement seeking are too high and their levels of self-control too low to make alcohol consumption safe.

Between age 21 and age 65, contemporary American culture makes few age-graded requirements. Teenage athletes and musicians earn millions; middle managers in their 50s face corporate downsizing. By contrast, Chinese society, guided for centuries by Confucian ideals of filial piety, reserves increasing authority and respect for older individuals. Young Chinese, like young Americans, aspire to set up their own lives and begin careers and families, but they are perhaps more ready to acknowledge their own inexperience and immaturity and to benefit from advice from their elders. As they gain life experience, they also gain ascribed authority, and respect follows them into old age. American culture minimizes the importance of maturation in personality; Chinese culture emphasizes it.

American Personality From a European Perspective

Psychology as a discipline is dominated by Americans, and much of the world's personality research uses English or American models and measures. Evidence on the cross-cultural generalizability of the FFM shows that questionnaires like the NEO–PI–R can be successfully translated and adapted for use in other cultures. However, if personality is indeed universal, then it should also be possible to use in the United States instruments developed elsewhere. Importing instruments from abroad may offer new insights into the relations between age and personality.

In parallel with the development of the FFM in the United States, investigators from several other countries have attempted to create personality measures based on their own natural language lexicons of personality trait terms. The Five-Factor Personality Inventory (FFPI; Hendriks, 1997; Hendriks, Hofstee, De Raad, & Angleitner, 1995) was based primarily on analyses of the Dutch lexicon, although parallel German and English versions were also developed. The Big Five Questionnaire (BFQ; Caprara, Barbaranelli, Borgogni, & Perugini, 1993) grew out of lexical studies in Italian and was subsequently translated into English. Both of these instruments were interpreted as personality models that were particularly appropriate for their indigenous culture; it is possible that the features that differentiate the Dutch and Italian measures from the American FFM are particularly responsive to adult age changes.

Volunteer participants in the Baltimore Longitudinal Study of Aging completed either the FFPI or the BFQ by computer administration at their regular visit to the Gerontology Research Center in 1996 or 1997. Most of these participants had completed the NEO–PI–R on a previous visit, from 2 to 8 years earlier; 52 of the 252 participants completed the NEO–PI–R on the same occasion as the FFPI or BFQ. The mean interval between administrations of the NEO–PI–R and the other instrument was 3.1 years.

Table 1 summarizes results of this study. All 10 scales showed adequate-to-good internal consistency, and convergent correlations with factors from the NEO–PI–R were generally quite high, despite the passage of as much as 8 years between administrations of the two instruments—indirect evidence of the stability of traits themselves. The two exceptions are FFPI Intellect/Autonomy and BFQ Friendliness, which are not strongly related to any single NEO–PI–R factor. These divergences are not unexpected, as reflected in the fact that the test authors chose labels for these constructs from outside the standard FFM.

Of primary interest, however, are the correlations in the last column, which are easily summarized: With the exception of FFPI Conscientiousness, which shows a moderate positive correlation with age, none of these scales appears to be age related. Conclusions about the stability of personality based on American scales in the United States and abroad are supported by data on European scales administered in the United States.

Table 1. Internal Consistency, Cross-Instrument Validity, and Age Correlations of Dutch and Italian Personality Inventories in an American Sample

| Scale | α | Correlation with NEO–PI–R factor | | | | | r_{age} |
		N	E	O	A	C	
FFPI[a]							
Neuroticism	.90	**.57*****	−.01	.09	.03	−.18	−.14
Extraversion	.91	−.01	**.71*****	.03	.10	−.18	−.01
Intellect/Autonomy	.84	−.28**	.13	**.32*****	−.24*	.40***	.04
Agreeableness	.73	−.05	.06	.09	**.52*****	−.07	−.02
Conscientiousness	.83	−.02	−.01	−.31**	.01	**.65*****	.26**
BFQ							
Neuroticism	.86	**.69*****	−.11	−.35***	−.20*	.02	−.07
Energy	.82	−.38***	**.59*****	.38***	−.24**	.33***	.00
Openness	.80	−.30***	.33***	**.65*****	−.02	.19*	−.06
Friendliness	.75	−.27**	.41***	.29***	**.37*****	.02	−.07
Conscientiousness	.78	.11	.07	.19*	.07	**.66*****	−.10

Note. NEO–PI–R = Revised NEO Personality Inventory; N = Neuroticism; E = Extraversion; O = Openness to Experience; A = Agreeableness; C = Conscientiousness; FFPI = Five-Factor Personality Inventory; BFQ = Big Five Questionnaire. For FFPI, *n*s = 39 men age 27 to 58, 77 women age 21 to 67. For BFQ, *n*s = 50 men age 19 to 59, 86 women age 27 to 58. Hypothesized convergent correlations are presented in boldface.

[a]Coefficient alpha is calculated for the FFPI scales; correlations are based on FFPI estimated factor scores.

*p < .05. **p <.01. ***p <. 001.

Of course, this study is limited both in the modest size of the samples and in the age range studied—primarily 30 to 60. It is therefore fortunate that replications are available from two studies using German versions of the same instruments (personal communication, A. Angleitner, August 7, 1997; Rosendahl, 1997). The significant correlation between age and FFPI Conscientiousness in the American sample was replicated in both German samples; in addition, FFPI Neuroticism, BFQ Openness, and BFQ Friendliness all showed significant negative correlations with age. However, none of the correlations exceeded .26 in absolute magnitude. If we assume that BFQ Friendliness is more akin to Extraversion than Agreeableness, as both Table 1 and the German data suggest, then these small age changes are all consistent with the generalization that Neuroticism, Extraversion, and Openness decline slightly, whereas Agreeableness and Conscientiousness increase slightly, with age. Variations across instruments, models, languages, and cultures do not obscure these universal developmental trends.

Effects of Mental Disorders on Personality

Although changes in physical health have no more than a transient effect on personality, it is certainly possible that mental disorders would have direct and lasting effects. Indeed, some clinicians are reluctant to administer personality questionnaires to clients because they believe results would be seriously distorted by concurrent psychiatric disorders.

That hypothesis has been tested in the case of major depression. Bagby, Joffe, Parker, Kalemba, and Harkness (1995) assessed 57 depressed patients before and after treatment. They found that Neuroticism scores decreased and Extraversion scores increased with remission but that the other three factors were unaffected. And although Neuroticism scores declined after the depressive episode, they remained a full standard deviation higher than adult norms even in remission. Similar results were reported by Trull, Useda, Costa, and McCrae (1995) for an outpatient psychiatric clinic with a 6-month follow-up. They found a decrease in Neuroticism *t* scores from 64 to 59 and an increase in Agreeableness *t* scores from 43 to 47 but no significant change in Extraversion, Openness, or Conscientiousness.

High postdepression Neuroticism scores led Bagby et al. (1995) to conclude that lifelong Neuroticism probably predisposed these patients to develop clinical depression. An alternative explanation could be that depressive episodes leave psychological scars and permanently alter personality. But a prospective test of that hypothesis examining the effects of first depressive episode in a large sample of relatives of psychiatric patients found no lasting effects of the episode on self-reported personality traits (Shea et al., 1996). Acute mental disorders such as depression and anxiety do not appear to alter adult personality.

In contrast, there is clear evidence that progressive neurological disorders and other forms of brain damage can affect personality. Clinical observation has suggested for years that personality change is an early feature of Alzheimer's disease, but empirical support for that hypothesis has only recently been provided. After all, most personality instruments use self-reports, and it is unlikely that Alzheimer's patients could meaningfully complete such questionnaires. The first clear demonstration of personality changes came in 1991 when Siegler et al. asked caregivers of mildly-to-moderately demented patients to provide personality ratings. Caregivers completed the observer rating form of the NEO–PI twice, once to describe the patients as they had been before the onset of the disorder and once to describe them as they currently were. On average, most premorbid ratings were within the normal range, although patients were described as having been somewhat lower than norms in Openness to Experience. Concurrent descriptions, however, showed high levels of Anxiety, Depression, and especially Vulnerability and low levels of Extraversion, Openness, and especially Conscientiousness. On average, patients appeared to have declined over 2 standard deviations in Conscientiousness as a result of the disorder.

This striking pattern of results has subsequently been replicated in several other studies of patients with Alzheimer's disease (e.g., Chatterjee, Strauss, Smyth, & Whitehouse, 1992), but it does not appear to be specific to that disorder. Glosser et al. (1995) used a similar design to show that patients with Parkinson's disease also increased in Neuroticism and decreased (although not as markedly) in Extraversion and Conscientiousness. Similar results were reported by Mendelsohn, Dakof, and Skaff (1995), using both spouse ratings and self-reports on an adjective checklist. These two studies also included control groups that demonstrated that the changes were not due to aging itself or to the presence of a medical disorder. Finally, two unpublished studies of individuals who had experienced traumatic brain injuries also showed a similar, if less extreme, pattern (Costa, 1996). Together, these studies suggest that diffuse brain damage increases Neuroticism (negative affect and vulnerability to stress), reduces Extraversion (activity and assertiveness), and disrupts Conscientiousness (organization and planning).

In retrospect, these findings are not surprising, although very little in the literature anticipated the marked loss of Conscientiousness. Most important, these kinds of changes are not aspects of normal aging; instead, they are probably an indication of underlying pathology.

Implications for Geropsychology

Research over the past 20 years has made it increasingly clear that personality traits are endogenous and enduring dispositions. They are substantially inherited, show little permanent effect of child rearing or enculturation in a particular historical era, change modestly in patterns that suggest intrinsic maturation, and change dramatically, not in response to life experience, but as a result of underlying brain disease. Although traits influence moods, habits, and attitudes, they themselves are more basic psychological forces to be reckoned with by every clinician. In this concluding section, we list some of the implications of trait research for geropsychology.

Life-Span Continuity

The discipline of geropsychology is based on the premise that older individuals have unique psychological needs and capacities. In many respects, that is undoubtedly true: Older adults differ from younger adults in the life stressors they typically face, in the social support available, in their physical health, and in their susceptibility to cognitive impairment. But with respect to personality, the predominant pattern is continuity: Older men and women as a group do not differ much from younger men and women, and individuals preserve their own configuration of traits for decades. In many respects, it is less important for a clinician to know that a client is 80 years old than to know that he or she is low in Agreeableness or high in Openness.

Personality and Psychopathology

Personality trait dimensions are important to clinicians because they are associated with diagnosable mental disorders and, more broadly, with problems in living. Despite the traditional distinction between normal and abnormal psychology, it is now well established that many forms of psychopathology are associated with personality traits within the FFM. People high in Neuroticism are prone to depression (Bagby et al., 1995) and a variety of other disorders. Low Agreeableness and low Conscientiousness are associated with drug addiction (Brooner, Herbst, Schmidt, Bigelow, & Costa, 1993). Not surprisingly, a wide range of normal personality traits are systematically related to the personality disorders and to subclinical problems in living (Costa & Widiger, 1994). Assessing traits in the FFM gives clinicians a basis for anticipating characteristic forms of psychopathology.

Client Strengths

Personality involves more than predispositions to pathologies. Assessing personality allows the clinician to explore systematically possible strengths. High levels of Agreeableness, for example, are associated with higher levels of marital satisfaction (McCrae, Stone, Fagan, & Costa, in press) and social support (Costa & McCrae, 1992a) and are thought to contribute to the formation of a therapeutic alliance (Miller, 1991). Openness to Experience contributes flexibility and a willingness to attempt change. Introversion may facilitate self-sufficiency, and high Conscientiousness promotes hard work on assigned therapeutic tasks.

Realistic Expectations

At one time, clinicians working with older clients were advised to raise their expectations: Older people can indeed respond to psychotherapy (Speer, 1994) when the goal of therapy is adjustment to bereavement or resolution of a family crisis or amelioration of depression. But clinicians sometimes suppose that the goal of therapy is a complete restructuring of personality, and at least in our present state of knowledge, that goal is probably unrealistic for patients of any age. The stability of personality across the vicissitudes of life suggests that deliberate interventions to change it will have modest effects at best. As Harkness and Lilienfeld (in press) argued, "the single greatest misconception that patients (and perhaps some therapists) hold about therapy is that a high [Neuroticism] person can be turned into a low [Neuroticism] person." Instead, they argue, psychotherapy offers constructive ways to manage the recurring negative affect that such people experience. Psychotherapy is more about learning to live with one's personality than about changing it.

Designing Treatment

If personality cannot be changed, why bother to assess it at all? One answer is that personality traits may influence a client's response to various forms of therapy. On the basis of his clinical experience, Miller (1991) argued that Extraversion and Openness are particularly relevant to the selection of an appropriate form of therapy. Therapies that rely on talk, on sharing experiences in a group, or on freely expressing feelings may appeal more to extraverts than introverts; reading and writing assignments or pharmacological interventions may be preferred by introverts (cf. Shea, 1988). Variations in Openness are likely to affect the client's receptiveness to novel experiences in therapy: Open people may appreciate role playing and dream analysis; closed people may prefer directive therapy or biofeedback. Matching treatments to traits is an underresearched topic that could profit immensely by systematic application of the FFM framework.

Unity in Diversity

Clinical psychologists have become increasingly aware of the need for sensitivity to issues of diversity (Yutrzenka, 1995). Gender, ethnicity, and age are all conditions that can affect the client's problems, possible solutions, and relations to the clinician. Surely no one would dispute that by attending to these features the clinician can develop a broader and more empathic understanding of the client. But it is also worth recalling that in some respects human nature is universal, providing common ground for understanding people from every class, culture, and age group. Personality structure is one of these universals of human nature (McCrae et al., 1998): Young Americans, middle-aged Germans, and older Chinese men and women can all be characterized in terms of their enduring levels of Neuroticism, Extraversion, Openness, Agreeableness, and Conscientiousness. These are central features of their psychological makeup to which geropsychologists must attend.

References

Allport, G. W. (1937). *Personality: A psychological interpretation*. New York: Holt.

Bagby, R. M., Joffe, R. T., Parker, J. D. A., Kalemba, V., & Harkness, K. L. (1995). Major depression and the five-factor model of personality. *Journal of Personality Disorders, 9,* 224–234.

Brooner, R. K., Herbst, J. H., Schmidt, C. W., Bigelow, G. E., & Costa, P. T., Jr. (1993). Antisocial personality disorder among drug abusers: Relations to other personality diagnoses and the five-factor model of personality. *Journal of Nervous and Mental Disease, 181,* 313–319.

Caprara, G. V., Barbaranelli, C., Borgogni, L., & Perugini, M. (1993). The "Big Five Questionnaire": A new questionnaire to assess the five factor model. *Personality and Individual Differences, 15,* 281–288.

Chatterjee, A., Strauss, M. E., Smyth, K. A., & Whitehouse, P. J. (1992). Personality changes in Alzheimer's disease. *Archives of Neurology, 49,* 486–491.

Costa, P. T., Jr. (1996, March). *Personality assessment of neurologically impaired patients using Form R of the Revised NEO Personality Inventory (NEO–PI–R)*. Paper presented at the Midwinter Meeting of the Society for Personality Assessment, Denver, CO.

Costa, P. T., Jr., Fagan, P. J., Piedmont, R. L., Ponticas, Y., & Wise, T. (1992). The five-factor model of personality and sexual functioning in outpatient men and women. *Psychiatric Medicine, 10,* 199–215.

Costa, P. T., Jr., & McCrae, R. R. (1985). *The NEO Personality Inventory manual*. Odessa, FL: Psychological Assessment Resources.

Costa, P. T., Jr., & McCrae, R. R. (1988). Personality in adulthood: A six-year longitudinal study of self-reports and spouse ratings on the NEO Personality Inventory. *Journal of Personality and Social Psychology, 54,* 853–863.

Costa, P. T., Jr., & McCrae, R. R. (1989a). *The NEO–PI/NEO–FFI manual supplement*. Odessa, FL: Psychological Assessment Resources.

Costa, P. T., Jr., & McCrae, R. R. (1989b). Personality continuity and the changes of adult life. In M. Storandt & G. R. VandenBos (Eds.), *The adult years: Continuity and change* (pp. 45–77). Washington, DC: American Psychological Association.

Costa, P. T., Jr., & McCrae, R. R. (1992a). Normal personality assessment in clinical practice: The NEO Personality Inventory. *Pyschological Assessment, 4,* 5–13, 20–22.

Costa, P. T., Jr., & McCrae, R. R. (1992b). *Revised NEO Personality Inventory (NEO–PI–R) and NEO Five-Factor Inventory (NEO–FFI) professional manual.* Odessa, FL: Psychological Assessment Resources.

Costa, P. T., Jr., & McCrae, R. R. (1992c). Trait psychology comes of age. In T. B. Sonderegger (Ed.), *Nebraska Symposium on Motivation: Vol. 39. Psychology and aging* (pp. 169–204). Lincoln: University of Nebraska Press.

Costa, P. T., Jr., & McCrae, R. R. (1994). Stability and change in personality from adolescence through adulthood. In C. F. Halverson, G. A. Kohnstamm, & R. P. Martin (Eds.), *The developing structure of temperament and personality from infancy to adulthood* (pp. 139–150). Hillsdale, NJ: Erlbaum.

Costa, P. T., Jr., & McCrae, R. R. (1997). Longitudinal stability of adult personality. In R. Hogan, J. A. Johnson, & S. R. Briggs (Eds.), *Handbook of personality psychology* (pp. 269–290). Orlando, FL: Academic Press.

Costa, P. T., Jr., McCrae, R. R., & Arenberg, D. (1980). Enduring dispositions in adult males. *Journal of Personality and Social Psychology, 38,* 793–800.

Costa, P. T., Jr., McCrae, R. R., & Arenberg, D. (1983). Recent longitudinal research on personality and aging. In K. W. Schaie (Ed.), *Longitudinal studies of adult psychological development* (pp. 222–265). New York: Guilford Press.

Costa, P. T., Jr., McCrae, R. R., & Dye, D. A. (1991). Facet scales for Agreeableness and Conscientiousness: A revision of the NEO Personality Inventory. *Personality and Individual Differences, 12,* 887–898.

Costa, P. T., Jr., McCrae, R. R., Zonderman, A. B., Barbano, H. E., Lebowitz, B., & Larson, D. M. (1986). Cross-sectional studies of personality in a national sample: 2. Stability in neuroticism, extraversion, and openness. *Psychology and Aging, 1,* 144–149.

Costa, P. T., Jr., Metter, E. J., & McCrae, R. R. (1994). Personality stability and its contribution to successful aging. *Journal of Geriatric Psychiatry, 27,* 41–59.

Costa, P. T., Jr., & Widiger, T. A. (Eds.). (1994). *Personality disorders and the five-factor model of personality.* Washington, DC: American Psychological Association.

Costa, P. T., Jr., Zonderman, A. B., & McCrae, R. R. (1991). Personality, defense, coping, and adaptation in older adulthood. In E. M. Cummings, A. L. Greene, & K. H. Karraker (Eds.), *Life-span developmental psychology: Perspectives on stress and coping* (pp. 277–293). Hillsdale, NJ: Erlbaum.

Emmons, R. A., & Diener, E. (1985). Personality correlates of subjective well-being. *Personality and Social Psychology Bulletin, 11,* 89–97.

Finn, S. E. (1986). Stability of personality self-ratings over 30 years: Evidence for an age/cohort interaction. *Journal of Personality and Social Psychology, 50,* 813–818.

Glosser, G., Clark, C., Freundlich, B., Kliner-Krenzel, L., Flaherty, P., & Stern, M. (1995). A controlled investigation of current and premorbid personality: Characteristics of Parkinson's disease patients. *Movement Disorders, 10,* 201–206.

Gough, H. G. (1987). *California Psychological Inventory administrator's guide.* Palo Alto, CA: Consulting Psychologists Press.

Guilford, J. S., Zimmerman, W. S., & Guilford, J. P. (1976). *The Guilford–Zimmerman Temperament Survey handbook: Twenty-five years of research and application.* San Diego, CA: EDITS.

Harkness, A. R., & Lilienfeld, S. O. (in press). Individual-differences science for treatment planning: Personality traits. *Psychological Assessment.*

Hendriks, A. A. J. (1997). *The construction of the Five-Factor Personality Inventory.* Unpublished doctoral dissertation, University of Groningen, Groningen, The Netherlands.

Hendriks, A. A. J., Hofstee, W. K. B., De Raad, B., & Angleitner, A. (1995). *The Five-Factor Personality Inventory (FFPI).* Unpublished manuscript, University of Groningen, Groningen, The Netherlands.

Jang, K. L., McCrae, R. R., Angleitner, A., Riemann, R., & Livesley, W. J. (in press). Heritability of facet-level traits in a cross-cultural twin study: Support for a hierarchical model of personality. *Journal of Personality and Social Psychology.*

Jessor, R. (1983). The stability of change: Psychosocial development from adolescence to young adulthood. In D. Magnusson & V. L. Allen (Eds.), *Human development: An interactional perspective* (pp. 321–341). New York: Academic Press.

John, O. P., Angleitner, A., & Ostendorf, F. (1988). The lexical approach to personality: A historical review of trait taxonomic research. *European Journal of Personality, 2,* 171–203.

Kagan, J., & Moss, H. A. (1962). *From birth to maturity*. New York: Wiley.

Krueger, J., & Heckhausen, J. (1993). Personality development across the adult life span: Subjective conceptions vs. cross-sectional contrasts. *Journal of Gerontology, 48*, P100–P108.

Levinson, D. J., Darrow, C. N., Klein, E. B., Levinson, M. L., & McKee, B. (1978). *The seasons of a man's life*. New York: Knopf.

Marshall, G. N., Wortman, C. B., Vickers, R. R., Jr., Kusulas, J. W., & Hervig, L. K. (1994). The five-factor model of personality as a framework for personality–health research. *Journal of Personality and Social Psychology, 67*, 278–286.

McCrae, R. R. (1993). Moderated analyses of longitudinal personality stability. *Journal of Personality and Social Psychology, 65*, 577–585.

McCrae, R. R. (1994). The counterpoint of personality assessment: Self-reports and observer ratings. *Assessment, 1*, 159–172.

McCrae, R. R., Costa, P. T., Jr., del Pilar, G. H., Rolland, J. P., & Parker, W. D. (1998). Cross-cultural assessment of the five-factor model: The Revised NEO Personality Inventory. *Journal of Cross-Cultural Psychology, 29*, 171–188.

McCrae, R. R., Costa, P. T., Jr., Lima, M. P., Simoes, A., Ostendorf, F., Angleitner, A., Marusic, I., Bratko, D., Caprara, G. V., Barbaranelli, C., Chae, J. H., & Piedmont, R. L. (1997). *Age differences in personality across the adult lifespan: Parallels in five cultures*. Unpublished manuscript, Gerontology Research Center, Baltimore.

McCrae, R. R., & John, O. P. (1992). An introduction to the five-factor model and its applications. *Journal of Personality, 60*, 175–215.

McCrae, R. R., Stone, S. V., Fagan, P. J., & Costa, P. T., Jr. (in press). Identifying causes of disagreement between self-reports and spouse ratings of personality. *Journal of Personality*.

Mendelsohn, G. A., Dakof, G. A., & Skaff, M. (1995). Personality change in Parkinson's disease patients: Chronic disease and aging. *Journal of Personality, 63*, 233–257.

Miller, T. (1991). The psychotherapeutic utility of the five-factor model of personality: A clinician's experience. *Journal of Personality Assessment, 57*, 415–433.

Mortimer, J. T., Finch, M. D., & Kumka, D. (1982). Persistence and change in development: The multidimensional self-concept. In P. B. Baltes & O. G. Brim, Jr. (Eds.), *Life-span development and behavior* (Vol. 4, pp. 264–315). New York: Academic Press.

Piedmont, R. L. (1996, August). *The five-factor model and its value for religious research*. Symposium presented at the 104th Annual Convention of the American Psychological Association, Toronto, Ontario, Canada.

Rosendahl, M. (1997). *Ein Vergleich verschiedener Instrumente zur Erfassung fünf zentraler Persönlichkeitsdimensionen* [A comparison of different instruments assessing five central dimensions of personality]. Unpublished diploma thesis, University of Bielefeld, Bielefeld, Germany.

Rowe, D. C. (1994). *The limits of family influence: Genes, experience, and behavior*. New York: Guilford Press.

Shaver, P. R., & Brennan, K. A. (1992). Attachment styles and the "Big Five" personality traits: Their connection with each other and with romantic relationship outcomes. *Personality and Social Psychology Bulletin, 18*, 536–545.

Shea, M. T. (1988, August). *Interpersonal styles and short-term psychotherapy for depression*. Paper presented at the 96th Annual Convention of the American Psychological Association, Atlanta, GA.

Shea, M. T., Leon, A. C., Mueller, T. I., Solomon, D. A., Warshaw, M. G., & Keller, M. B. (1996). Does major depression result in lasting personality change? *American Journal of Psychiatry, 153*, 1404–1410.

Siegler, I. C., Welsh, K. A., Dawson, D. V., Fillenbaum, G. G., Earl, N. L., Kaplan, E. B., & Clark, C. M. (1991). Ratings of personality change in patients being evaluated for memory disorders. *Alzheimer Disease and Associated Disorders, 5*, 240–250.

Siegler, I. C., Zonderman, A. B., Barefoot, J. C., Williams, R. B., Jr., Costa, P. T., Jr., & McCrae, R. R. (1990). Predicting personality in adulthood from college MMPI scores: Implications for follow-up studies in psychosomatic medicine. *Psychosomatic Medicine, 52*, 644–652.

Speer, D. C. (1994). Can treatment research inform decision makers? Nonexperimental method issues and examples among older outpatients. *Journal of Consulting and Clinical Psychology, 62*, 560–568.

Spiro, A., III, Levenson, M. R., & Aldwin, C. M. (1992, August). *How stable is personality?* Paper presented at the 100th Annual Convention of the American Psychological Association, Washington, DC.

Tarnowski, A., Shen, J., Diehl, M., & Labouvie-Vief, G. (1996, November). *Adult age differences in personality: Similarity of US and Chinese patterns.* Paper presented at the 49th Annual Scientific Meeting of the Gerontological Society of America, Washington, DC.

Trull, T. J., Useda, J. D., Costa, P. T., Jr., & McCrae, R. R. (1995). Comparison of the MMPI–2 Personality Psychopathology Five (PSY–5), the NEO–PI, and the NEO–PI–R. *Psychological Assessment, 7,* 508–516.

Woodruff, D. (1983). The role of memory in personality continuity: A 25 year follow-up. *Experimental Aging Research, 9,* 31–34.

Yang, J., McCrae, R. R., & Costa, P. T., Jr. (1997, October). *Adult age differences in Chinese personality.* Paper presented at the Conference on Temperament and Personality Development Across the Life Span, Carbondale, IL.

Yutrzenka, B. A. (1995). Making a case for training in ethnic and cultural diversity in increasing treatment efficacy. *Journal of Consulting and Clinical Psychology, 63,* 197–206.

4

Cognitive and Information-Processing Perspectives on Aging

Timothy A. Salthouse

As is the case with other areas of adult development, both continuity and change are dominant themes in the area of aging and cognition. However, because the type of change that is most often found is decline, the age relations in this area are frequently referred to as *stability* and *decline.*

A distinction between two types of cognition, one that remains stable with advancing age and another that declines, has been recognized for decades among researchers interested in aging (e.g., see Salthouse, 1991, for a review). Measures of knowledge presumed to be acquired through experience tend to remain stable, or sometimes even increase, across the adult years. In contrast, measures of flexibility of thinking, or the ability to solve novel problems, tend to decline with increasing age. The two types of cognition have been labeled *crystallized* and *fluid* intelligence, respectively, but a more descriptive characterization is in terms of the accumulated *products* of processing carried out in the past versus the efficiency or effectiveness of *processing* at the time of assessment.

The different age trends in the two aspects of cognition are readily apparent in many standardized test batteries. For example, in the Wechsler Adult Intelligence Scale (Wechsler, 1981), the verbal scale scores (including Vocabulary and Information) often tend to be stable from the early 20s through the 70s, whereas the performance scale scores (including Block Design and Object Assembly) tend to decrease almost linearly from the late 20s or early 30s onward. The two types of cognition are also evident in individual tests of vocabulary and of abstract reasoning, such as Raven's Progressive Matrices (Raven & Court, 1989). Figure 1 illustrates this pattern with research from my laboratory. Note that there is a slight increase with age in a cognitive product measure of word knowledge but a large monotonic decline in a cognitive process measure of the ability to infer abstract relations.

Most research concerned with aging and cognition has focused on decline aspects. There are probably three major reasons for this emphasis. The first is an assumption that there is nothing to explain when there is stability. That is, if there is no age-related change, then there may be no phenomenon in need of explanation because lack of change is the default state, and it could be argued that only deviations from the default state require an explanation. A second possible reason for the lack of more research concerned with the relation be-

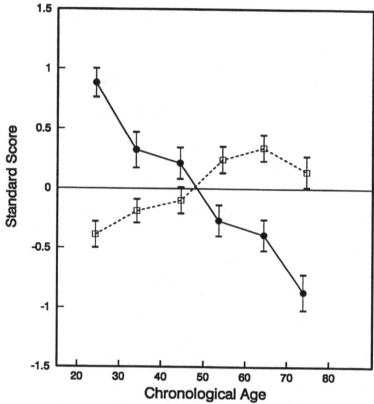

Figure 1. Means and standard errors by decade of scores on a cognitive product measure of vocabulary (open boxes) and a cognitive process measure of inductive reasoning (i.e., Raven's Progressive Matrices; solid circles). For the multiple-choice vocabulary test, $N = 449$, $r = .22$; for Raven's Progressive Matrices, $N = 221$, $r = -.57$. Data are from cross-sectional studies by Salthouse.

tween age and cognitive product measures is that knowledge is typically expected to increase as a function of experience, and consequently, stable or increasing relations between age and knowledge would not be surprising from the perspective of cumulative learning. A third likely reason why relatively little research has focused on the relations between age and product measures of cognition is a belief that the declining (cognitive process) aspects reflect the individual's current level of functioning, which is frequently of greater interest than his or her status at some prior time (as reflected by cognitive product measures).

Regardless of the reasons for the unequal allocation of research devoted to the two types of cognition, however, it is important to realize that even though the bulk of the research in aging and cognition has focused on decline, there is a major type of cognition that does not exhibit this pattern. Furthermore, it is quite possible that this other—product, or crystallized—type of cognition is of greater importance for many activities in everyday life than the process, or fluid, type of cognition, which has received the most attention of researchers.

In the remaining sections of this chapter, I briefly review the major categories of explanations that have been proposed to account for age-related declines in process aspects of cognition and then discuss possible implications of the age–cognition relations that have been reported. The research to be discussed includes that based on standardized tests traditionally classified as psychometric as well as research with experimental tasks created by cognitive psychologists.

Why Is There Age-Related Cognitive Decline?

Two major categories of explanation have been proposed to account for age-related declines in process measures of cognition. *Distal* explanations focus on factors in the past that affect performance at the current time, whereas *proximal* explanations concentrate on characteristics of processing at the time of assessment that are responsible for the observed level of performance.

Distal Determinants

In the current context, *distal* refers to temporally distant in the sense that a person's level of performance at age 60 is influenced by events or experiences that occurred many years earlier in his or her life. One way in which distal influences have been investigated involves examining different generations (cohorts) of people, who can be assumed to have had different experiences and different types of exposure to education and broad aspects of culture. If these groups vary in characteristics that have changed over time, then they might be expected to exhibit different patterns of age relations. For example, if particular types of educational experiences, such as rote memorization, affect performance on certain cognitive tests, then some of the performance differences between young and old adults in tests of process aspects of cognition may be attributable to the different types of educational experiences the adults received when they were children. To the extent that an interpretation such as this is plausible, one might expect age trends to vary across different generations or across cultural groups, who were likely to have had different educational and other experiences.

Although some small variations in the pattern of age relations have been reported, age trends in various measures of cognitive performance have generally been found to be quite similar across different historical periods in this century in the United States and at the same point in time across different countries (e.g., see Salthouse, 1991, for a review). These findings suggest that gross educational or cultural factors are probably not responsible for much, if any, of the age-related cognitive differences that have been reported.

Another manner in which distal interpretations have been investigated consists of examining the same individuals in longitudinal comparisons. If declines in cross-sectional comparisons (i.e., people of different ages tested at the same point in time) are primarily attributable to different early experiences across cohorts, then few or no age relations might be expected in comparisons of the same people tested at different ages. Some early reports suggested that this appeared to be the case, but these studies frequently involved small, unrepresentative samples, and often did not include many measures of age-sensitive process aspects of cognition. More recent studies suggest that although selective attrition and practice can lead to smaller, and possibly delayed, age-related effects in longitudinal than in cross-sectional comparisons, significant age-related declines in process measures are apparent in longitudinal studies (e.g., Arenberg, 1988; Hultsch, Hertzog, Small, McDonald-Miszczak, & Dixon, 1992; Schaie, 1996; Zelinski & Burnight, 1997).

A third procedure that has been used to investigate experientially based interpretations of age-related cognitive differences involves comparisons of age trends across groups that share similar types of interests or experiences. For example, a variety of comparisons have involved individuals from the same occupations. This procedure does not necessarily control the nature of early experiences, but members of the same occupation are nevertheless likely to share many educational and occupational experiences during their adult years. Among the occupations in which process aspects of cognitive performance have been compared across different age groups are architects (e.g., Salthouse, Babcock, Skovronek, Mitchell, & Palmon, 1990), business executives (e.g., Schludermann, Schludermann, Merryman, & Brown, 1983), college professors (Shimamura, Berry, Mangels, Rusting, & Jurica, 1995; Sward, 1945), physicians (Powell, 1994), nuns (Erber, 1974), pilots (Szafran, 1970), and teachers (Lachman, Lachman, & Taylor, 1982). Several of these samples have been rather small, and consequently, the age trends have been somewhat variable, but most of the results from comparisons of members of the same occupation are similar to those found in unselected samples. At least based on the available evidence, therefore, it does not appear that adult age differences in process measures of cognition are attributable to variations in the nature of one's experiences as an adult.

Only very crude investigations of distal factors have been reported thus far, and consequently, it is premature to conclude that distal factors are not important contributors to adult age differences in process measures of cognition. In fact, from a certain perspective, it is necessarily the case that factors occurring at earlier ages are responsible for characteristics observed at later ages because it is implausible to suggest that those characteristics appeared spontaneously, with no precursors at younger ages. The problem is that researchers have not yet been able to identify the nature of the early factors that contribute to cognitive functioning at a later time. This lack of success at identifying important distal influences may be one of the reasons why most of the contemporary research in process aspects of cognition has had a proximal focus. An implicit assumption seems to have been that progress in understanding distal influences may be facilitated once a clearer characterization is available of exactly what has been affected.

Proximal Determinants

As noted earlier, proximal interpretations of the relations between age and cognition focus on factors that are operating at the time of assessment. That is, proximal explanations are concerned with the question of whether we can identify characteristics of processing that are responsible for the current level of performance, regardless of how, or when, those characteristics originated.

One proximal factor concerns *strategies*, which can be defined as one of several possible approaches to performing a task. Strategic variations are potentially important because if the procedure used to perform the task is not the same for all people, then at least some of the observed performance variations may be attributable to factors related to strategy selection or use. Furthermore, conclusions about quantitative differences may not be very meaningful if everyone is not performing the task in the same manner. As a very simple illustration, comparisons of the speed of repetitive addition would not be interpretable if some individuals used multiplication on some of the problems while other individuals always carried out a series of addition operations.

Some research has found evidence that poor-performing older adults may use less effective strategies than better-performing young adults. However, before age-related differences in cognitive performance can be attributed to strategic variations, it is important to determine what is responsible for the apparent differences in strategy. One possibility is that less effective strategies are used because of lack of knowledge about the existence, or advantages, of alternative strategies. If this is the case, then instructions in the use of the more effective strategy might be expected to eliminate, or at least greatly reduce, the age differences in measures of cognitive performance. However, very few, if any, published reports have confirmed this expectation. An alternative interpretation is that less effective strategies were used because the person was no longer capable of consistently using the most effective, but perhaps the cognitively most demanding, strategies. To the extent that this is the case, then individual and age-related differences in strategy use might be more appropriately viewed, not as a cause of the performance differences, but rather as another manifestation of some more fundamental age-related change.

A second type of proximal interpretation of age–process relations has focused on the possibility that deficits in specific processing components contribute to the observed age-related impairments in cognitive functioning. That is, the issue in this perspective is whether low levels of cognitive performance can be attributed to a critical weakness in one or more fundamental components responsible for processes such as encoding, transforming, or retrieving information. Researchers using this approach have designed many clever procedures to attempt to isolate the operation of specific hypothesized processes. For example, the efficiency of particular types of transformation processes has been examined by manipulating the nature and amount of processing required in a task when other aspects of the task remain constant.

Research concerned with specific processing deficits has yielded some evidence for the existence of impaired and spared functioning in measures assumed to reflect distinct cognitive processes. As an illustration, processes associated with conscious recollection, which are postulated to be involved in most deliberate attempts to recall information, have been found to exhibit moderate-to-large age-related differences, whereas processes associated with automatic retrieval, which may operate unconsciously, appear to have minimal age-related effects (e.g., Howard, 1996). Although these dissociation patterns are quite interesting, relatively little research has been conducted to determine whether theoretically similar measures derived from different types of tasks are substantially correlated with one another, as one might expect if they reflect the same kind of processing, and compelling explanations of the reasons for the differential patterns are still lacking.

Another category of proximal explanation emphasizes the role of general impairments on cognitive functioning. These are considered general because rather than postulating deficits in components specialized for a particular type of processing, and hence likely to affect only a limited set of tasks, the age-related influences are assumed to have an impact on a very broad range of cognitive tasks. For example, age-related effects on sensory processes might be considered a general factor if they contribute to problems in registering information from the environment. Age-related increases in visual and auditory problems are well documented (e.g., Kline & Scialfa, 1996), but most of the materials used in cognitive tests are presented well above the sensory thresholds of nearly all adults, and therefore, it has been considered unlikely that the cognitive problems are a consequence of the information simply not being registered in the central nervous system. Problems in processing could still occur if more mental or cognitive effort is devoted to merely registering the information, as when one finds oneself concentrating so hard to hear a speaker in a noisy room that some aspects of comprehension are impaired. However, there currently appears to be little evidence that is directly relevant to this interpretation of age-related deficits in process aspects of cognition.

In recent years, one of the most popular interpretations of age-related differences in process aspects of cognition has been based on the idea that there are reductions with increasing age in some type of general-purpose *processing resource*. The precise nature of the processing resource is seldom explicitly specified, although concepts such as *attention, working memory*, and *processing speed* are frequently mentioned in this connection. The use of these terms is often metaphorical because they all loosely refer to some type of "energy" or "fuel" that is needed for mental processing, but the exact mechanisms by which resources affect cognitive performance are seldom articulated. To go beyond the level of metaphor, a number of researchers have attempted to obtain measures of the hypothesized resource and then to use statistical procedures to hold those measures constant when examining the relation of age on the cognitive variables of interest (e.g., Salthouse, 1991, 1992).

To illustrate, the concept of working memory is assumed to play an important role in many contemporary views of cognition because it is considered analogous to random access memory in a computer and hence corresponds to the "region" where nearly all cognitive processing is assumed to be carried out. A variety of experimental tasks have been used to assess working memory, but because a distinguishing characteristic of working memory relative to other types of memory is that it involves simultaneous storage and processing, most of the tasks have required the research participants to remember information while also carrying out some type of processing.

If all of the participants in a research study are administered tests of working memory in addition to the cognitive tests of primary interest, then various statistical procedures can be used to equate them on the working memory measures. The reasoning is that if age-related differences in working memory are responsible for much of the age-related differences in other cognitive variables, then the differences in the other cognitive variables should be substantially reduced after eliminating the individual differences in working memory.

Results from analyses in which measures of working memory (and of other hypothesized processing resources) have been statistically controlled have frequently revealed a considerable reduction of the age relations in a variety of different cognitive variables (e.g., Salthouse, 1992, 1996). These findings have consequently been interpreted as supporting the view that age-related changes in a small number of cognitive primitives contribute to the age differences observed in many cognitive variables.

Although the processing resource perspective is currently quite popular, a number of important questions need to be answered before this perspective can be fully accepted. For example, there is not yet consensus on (a) the best measures of each hypothesized resource, (b) which type of processing resource is the most primitive or fundamental, (c) how limitations of the resource affect such a wide variety of cognitive tasks, and (d) why the resource diminishes with age.

Another category of proximal explanation for age-related declines in process aspects of cognition has focused on neuroanatomical and neurophysiological factors. One of the motivations for this emphasis has been the existence of parallels between the behavioral effects of aging and of damage to specific neuroanatomical regions, such as the frontal cortex (e.g., West, 1996), or to reduced supplies of certain neurotransmitters, such as dopamine (e.g., Gabrieli, Singh, Stebbins, & Goetz, 1996). One of the implicit goals of this type of research is to determine whether many of the cognitive deficits can be localized to particular neuroanatomical structures or regions or to a specific type of neurotransmitter. A great deal of effort has been devoted to investigating possible links between structural and functional characteristics of the brain and level of cognitive processing across the period of adulthood. However, progress has been slow because of the difficulty of obtaining objective quantifiable measures of neurophysiological or neuroanatomical characteristics, which are necessary to go beyond gross statements of approximate parallels and obtain convincing evidence of genuine links between brain and behavior in the same sample of individuals.

To summarize, although it is a very active area of research, there is still little consensus on the reasons for the age-related declines in process aspects of cognition. A number of intriguing speculations have been proposed, but satisfying and widely accepted explanations do not yet exist at either the proximal or distal levels of explanation.

Implications for Functioning

Before discussing the implications of age-related differences in cognitive functioning, it is important to first consider the magnitude of age-related effects in measures of cognitive performance. We have seen that age-related declines in healthy normal adults have frequently been reported in certain types of memory, abstract reasoning, and novel problem solving. The magnitude of these age-related differences varies across measures and samples, but there is often a shift of at least 1 standard deviation across a period of 40 years, such as that between 25 and 65 years of age. This magnitude of difference means that if the average 65-year-old was evaluated relative to the distribution of 25-year-olds, he or she would perform at about the 16th percentile of that distribution. Alternatively, if the average 25-year-old were evaluated relative to a distribution of 65-year-olds, he or she would perform at about the 84th percentile of the older adult distribution. These are relatively large differences, and they could have potentially important consequences in situations such as occupational selection because hiring decisions are frequently based at least partially on cognitive performance scores.

However, there is enormous variability at all ages, and if anything, changes associated with aging may lead to greater amounts of between-person variability. The extent of interindividual variability is illustrated in Figure 2 with a

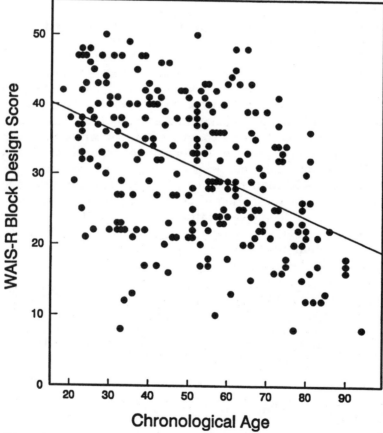

Figure 2. Plot of individual scores on the Wechsler Adult Intelligence Scale (WAIS–R) Block Design test as a function of age. ($r = -47$. The regression line represents the best estimate of the average score at each age. Cross-sectional data are from Salthouse, Fristoe, & Rhee, 1996.)

scatterplot of scores on the Wechsler Block Design test from a recent study involving 259 adults ranging between 18 and 94 years of age (Salthouse, Fristoe, & Rhee, 1996). The regression line in this figure represents the best estimate of the average score at each age, but it is apparent that there is a great deal of variation above and below the line, and all of that variability is unrelated to age. In fact, in these data, only 21.9% of the total variance in the scores was associated with age, which means that more than 75% of the between-person variability was unrelated to age.

Just as it is impossible to specify the score of a particular individual when given information about the mean and standard deviation of scores from a sample of individuals, it is also impossible to specify the effects of aging on a single individual when given information about the relation of the scores to age. This does not mean that the age-related effects are not real or large, but rather that there are many factors that contribute to cognitive functioning, of which aging is only one. We are therefore not yet in a position to predict the effects of aging in a given individual, and we are far from being able to specify how any negative effects can be prevented from occurring.

Minimizing the Consequences

Despite this uncertainty, it is nevertheless possible that consequences of these changes might be minimized by combinations of adaptation and accommodation. In other words, it is possible that the consequences of age-related changes might be minimized by reducing one's exposure to deficit-revealing situations. A prototypical example in the domain of sensory and motor abilities may be the tendency for many older adults to avoid driving at night. This shift in behavior does not eliminate the age-related declines in dark adaptation, sensitivity to glare, or reaction time, but it does reduce the likelihood that these factors will place the individual, and others, in a dangerous situation.

Similar types of adaptation and accommodation may occur with respect to cognitive abilities. For example, as the ability to comprehend rapidly presented information declines, an older adult may prefer various print (e.g., newspaper and magazine) rather than electronic (e.g., radio and television) media as the primary source of his or her information. There may also be a shift in the type of activities one chooses for enjoyment. As one illustration, late in his life, B. F. Skinner noted that his reading for pleasure had changed from serious books to light novels and mysteries (Skinner, 1983).

Another intriguing possibility, but about which very little is currently known, is that as people become more experienced and knowledgeable in a particular domain, their performance in that domain may be increasingly determined by product rather than process aspects of cognition. In other words, as people acquire greater amounts of experience, their competence in that area may be more a function of their knowledge of what has happened in similar situations that they have encountered in the past rather than of their ability to solve novel problems.

When Do the Problems Become Serious?

When is age-related cognitive decline severe enough to be a problem? There is some agreement among researchers and clinicians that three criteria need to be considered when evaluating the severity of cognitive changes. One criterion indicative of a serious problem is if there has been a dramatic change in the person's level of cognitive functioning over a relatively short period, such as several months or a few years. Any rapid alteration in mental status needs to be carefully examined because normal age-related changes tend to occur gradually over a period of decades.

A second criterion that should be considered in evaluating the severity of age-related changes concerns the person's level of performance relative to his or her age peers. The problems may be serious when the individual's performance is consistently two or more standard deviations below the mean of his or her age group. Although low levels of performance are not indicative of a pathology by themselves, they are a cause for concern if prior levels of performance were considerably higher.

Finally, the age-related changes are obviously serious if they affect normal activities and if neither adaptation nor accommodation is possible to maintain functioning in daily life. Fortunately, this does not seem to occur until extreme old age, if at all during normal aging. However, if it does happen before the age of 70, then it is highly likely that one or more pathological conditions are present.

Conclusion

This chapter has briefly reviewed research concerned with the relation between age and cognitive functioning during the adult years. At least two types of cognition have been distinguished, product measures reflecting accumulated knowledge and process measures reflecting efficiency or effectiveness of processing at the time of assessment. Increased age is associated with stable or increasing levels of performance in product cognition, but with moderate-to-large declines in process cognition. Although much research has attempted to investigate the reasons for age-related declines in process aspects of cognition, no consensus has yet been reached about why those differences occur. Little is also currently known about the practical consequences of these differences because they may be offset by increases in product aspects of cognition or various adaptations or accommodations may be used. Finally, the cognitive declines should probably be considered serious when they are large enough to affect daily functioning, and have occurred over a relatively short period of time.

References

Arenberg, D. (1988). Analysis and synthesis in problem solving and aging. In M. L. Howe & C. J. Brainerd (Eds.), *Cognitive development in adulthood* (pp. 161–183). New York: Springer-Verlag.

Erber, J. T. (1974). Age differences in recognition memory. *Journal of Gerontology, 29*, 177–181.

Gabrieli, J. D. E., Singh, J., Stebbins, G. T., & Goetz, C. G. (1996). Reduced working memory span in Parkinson's disease: Evidence for the role of a frontostriatal system in working and strategic memory. *Neuropsychology, 10*, 322–332.

Howard, D. V. (1996). The aging of implicit and explicit memory. In F. Blanchard-Fields & T. M. Hess (Eds.), *Perspectives on cognitive change in adulthood and aging* (pp. 221–254). New York: McGraw-Hill.

Hultsch, D. F., Hertzog, C., Small, B. J., McDonald-Miszczak, L., & Dixon, R. A. (1992). Short-term longitudinal change in cognitive performance in later life. *Psychology and Aging, 7*, 571–584.

Kline, D. W., & Scialfa, C. T. (1996). Visual and auditory aging. In J. E. Birren & K. W. Schaie (Eds.), *The handbook of the psychology of aging* (4th ed., pp. 181–203). San Diego, CA: Academic Press.

Lachman, R., Lachman, J. L., & Taylor, D. W. (1982). Reallocation of mental resources over the productive lifespan: Assumptions and task analyses. In F. I. M. Craik & S. Trehub (Eds.), *Aging and cognitive processes* (pp. 279–308). New York: Plenum.

Powell, D. H. (1994). *Profiles in cognitive aging*. Cambridge, MA: Harvard University Press.

Raven, J., & Court, H. (1989). Manual for Raven's progressive matrices and vocabulary scales. London: H. K. Lewis & Co.

Salthouse, T. A. (1991). *Theoretical perspectives on cognitive aging*. Hillsdale, NJ: Erlbaum.

Salthouse, T. A. (1992). *Mechanisms of age–cognition relations in adulthood*. Hillsdale, NJ: Erlbaum.

Salthouse, T. A. (1996). The processing speed theory of adult age differences in cognition. *Psychological Review, 103*, 403–428.

Salthouse, T. A., Babcock, R. L., Skovronek, E., Mitchell, D. R. D., & Palmon, R. (1990). Age and experience effects in spatial visualization. *Developmental Psychology, 26*, 128–136.

Salthouse, T. A., Fristoe, N., & Rhee, S. H. (1996). How localized are age-related effects on neuropsychological measures? *Neuropsychology, 10*, 272–285.

Schaie, K. F. (1996). *Intellectual development in adulthood: The Seattle Longitudinal Study*. New York: Cambridge University Press.

Schludermann, E. H., Schuldermann, S. M., Merryman, P. W., & Brown, B. W. (1983). Halstead's studies in the neuropsychology of aging. *Archives of Gerontology and Geriatrics, 2*, 49–172.

Shimamura, A., Berry, J. M., Mangels, J. A., Rusting, C. L., & Jurica, P. J. (1995). Memory and cognitive abilities in university professors. *Psychological Science, 6*, 271–277.

Skinner, B. F. (1983). Intellectual self-management in old age. *American Psychologist, 38*, 239–244.

Sward, K. (1945). Age and mental ability in superior men. *American Journal of Psychology, 58*, 443–479.

Szafran, J. (1970). The effects of ageing on professional pilots. In J. H. Price (Ed.), *Modern trends in psychological medicine II* (pp. 24–52). New York: Appleton-Century-Crofts.

Wechsler, D. (1981). Manual for the Wechsler Adult Intelligence Scale—revised. New York: The Psychological Corporation.

West, R. L. (1996). An application of prefrontal cortex theory to cognitive aging. *Psychological Bulletin, 120*, 272–292.

Zelinski, E., & Burnight, K. (1997). Sixteen-year longitudinal and time-lag changes in memory and cognition in older adults. *Psychology and Aging, 12*, 503–513.

5

Psychoanalysis and the Life Course: Development and Intervention

Bertram J. Cohler

This chapter reviews the problems and prospects posed by the extension of psychoanalysis as a means for the study of wish and intent from early childhood through later life. The understanding that psychoanalysis provides regarding the course of development across the course of life is founded on a unique mode of understanding experience—that of the relationship between 2 persons, analyst and analysand, collaborating in the process of understanding the analysand's particular construction of lived experience. Clinical psychoanalytic study has highlighted the importance of studying the manner in which past experiences might influence present understanding of self and others and, more generally, the influence of the remembered past on the experienced present and anticipated future. Findings from clinical psychoanalytic study of a number of persons provide insights, which may then be generalized to the study of lives within our own society, additionally informed by findings reported in systematic study of the course of life.

From Past to Present in Psychoanalytic Developmental Study

Since the Enlightenment, it has been believed that early life events shape the experiential world of later life. Nowhere has this view been more thoroughly accepted than in the genetic point of view within psychoanalysis (Rapaport & Gill, 1959). Freud (1913/1958) observed that "not every analysis of psychological phenomena deserves the name of psychoanalysis. The latter implies more than the mere analysis of composite phenomena into simpler ones. It consists of tracing back one psychological structure to another which preceded it in time and out of which it developed" (pp. 182–183).

Recognizing that memories of our past are rearranged and transformed over a lifetime, Freud emphasized the importance of studying the presently recounted life history, particularly the manner in which wish and experience of the past might play a role in lived experience. Further, childhood wishes, particularly those related to the parents experienced at about the time of the transformation from early to middle childhood, live on in the adult, not destroyed but merely overlaid by time and age. This perspective on the study of the psychological past led Freud (1913/1958) to conclude that before all else, psychoanalysis is a genetic psychology and that a defining characteristic of the psychoanalytic perspective must show this tie of present psychological to past lived experience.

This concern with development seeks to understand why, in the past, persons adopted one means of dealing with these wishes and their consequences and why, in adulthood, particular aspects of lived experience may still evoke a powerful personal response. At the same time, Freud was fully aware that the life history recounted in the consulting room by an adult was not the same kind of account as one provided by observing a person's life over time. Freud (1920/1955) noted sagely that by reviewing a person's life backward from the present, the person and the psychoanalyst emerge with a sense of a continuous story, which adequately explains the experiences of a lifetime.

However, starting the reverse way, making inferences about a person's life then observing how things turn out, matters become far more complex. In other words, it is easier to make sense of a story of lived experience than it is to predict forward to the future. The problem in approaching the study of development from a psychoanalytic perspective is the tendency to confuse study of a coherent life story with prediction about the future. We have all had the experience of making predictions about friends or family members on the basis of previous experience, only to later find out how wrong we are.

We know little about the reasons why one person is able to manage personal or collective adversity, whereas others, less resilient, experience great personal distress, overwhelming and defeating any ability to cope with the situation. It is as important to understand how people remain resilient over time as it is to know why they succumb to psychological symptoms (Lewis, 1997). Further, some people are able to be resilient at one point in their life but are vulnerable to distress at another point. Finally, some means of mastering conflict are problematic at one point in the course of life but adaptive at another. For example, in studies reported by psychologists David Gutmann (1987), studying gender roles in later adulthood, and Morton Lieberman and Sheldon Tobin (1983), studying adjustment to relocation to long-term care, those older adults living in long-term care who were unpleasant, suspicious of others, and difficult to accommodate tended to live longer than those who were more compliant and prosocial.

Another problem has been the use of more traditional psychological methods to study certain issues presumed important in the analysand's and analyst's construction of a story of the past or the use of findings from such studies to modify assumptions about development influencing the analyst's and analysand's effort to understand the analysand's personal past (Schafer, 1992). For example, psychoanalysis has always placed great stock in the memories of the past that are reported by the analysand. However, inspired in part by a recent focus on reports of childhood abuse and efforts to determine the truth of these memories, studies by experimental psychologists have shown that these memories may be influenced by present circumstances in such a manner that people come to believe a story about the past that has been fabricated for the study and never took place (Brennis, 1997).

Understanding the significance of recollected events of the past is an issue that has proven difficult for psychoanalysis from the outset (Singer & Salovey,

1993). Present efforts to conclude, on the basis of such evidence as an incompletely understood dream or a shadowy memory evoked by a presumably linked present experience, that some abuse actually occurred during early childhood, perhaps before the child could remember such experiences, may be the result of the analyst's more or less intentional effort to induce this memory or to assume on the basis of other evidence that abuse had occurred.

Psychoanalytic Perspectives on the Life Course

The (epi)genetic point of view regarding psychological development (Abrams, 1977; Erikson, 1950/1963; Hartmann & Kris, 1945; Rapaport & Gill, 1959) presumes a necessary, causal connection between earlier and later states. However, this rigid connection has been called into question by both clinical and systematic studies of lives over time. For example, imprinting plays a minimal role in human learning and development: Ethological models are largely irrelevant to the study of human infant development (Cohler, 1987; Kagan, 1980). Longitudinal studies of personality from childhood through middle and late life demonstrate that lives are less continuous and predictably ordered than is assumed in epigenetic models (Emde 1981, 1985; Kagan, 1980; Neugarten, 1969).

Personality development may be better conceived in terms of abrupt transformations than in terms of linear continuity or predictable epigenetic transitions, with much of what happens over time a consequence of maturational and social factors, together with unexpected, often adverse experiences. A major task, therefore, across the life course, involves efforts to maintain a sense of coherence when confronted by precisely these sorts of experiences. Additionally, since historical understanding itself holds within it this dimension of fostering coherence among the disparate data of the past, persons continually rewrite their own life story in such a manner as to show connectedness between past and present (Schafer, 1992).

Although there is some variation in the felt coherence of this developmental narrative resulting from efforts to fashion a narrative out of the presently experienced course of development, with the task inherently more difficult for some persons than for others, virtually all people attempt to maintain a coherent narrative of their own life, if not in the concrete sense of telling the story of their life, then at least in the sense of maintaining some semblance of self-consistency. Much of what is assumed to be developmental continuity may be a reflection of this concern with maintaining a narrative that is consistent with prevailing values and standards, including those regarding self, at particular points across the course of life, and which adequately accounts for the presently remembered past (Galatzer-Levy & Cohler, 1993).

Understanding the Life Course: Linear Progression or Transformation?

First psychoanalytic discussion of adult lives from a developmental perspective (Abraham, 1919/1951) presumed that much of personality development was realized across the years of early childhood and resolution of issues of competition and jealousy within the family. From this perspective, adult lives largely reflected the experience anew of these issues first salient in early childhood. However, developmental study of the course of life has suggested that lives may be less predictable and continuous over time than earlier assumed (Emde, 1985; Kagan, 1980). Both experience of expectable life changes and also encounter with early, off-time life changes have an impact on the experience of self and others and also the course of life itself. Issues of social timing (Hagestad, 1990) affect the experience of both time and memory of the past. Indeed, lived experience might better be portrayed as a number of transformations of time and memory than as a linear progression, with the past always influencing the present in the stepwise manner portrayed by Erikson (1963, 1982).

Four transformations over the course of life have been portrayed in psychoanalytically influenced study of development. Each of these four transformations, affecting different perspectives both on time (past, present, and future) and on memory (forgetting and remembering), have been described to date, although it is possible that subsequent study, and the continuing interaction of history with life history, will lead to identification of different points in the course of life as the source of transformation. The first transformation, accompanying the change from early to middle adulthood, is characterized by the emergence and resolution of a set of related wishes, portrayed by Freud (1900, 1910) as the *family romance* and reflecting the classic story of Sophocles' drama, *Oedipus the King*. Resolution of this struggle with competing wishes leads to forgetting the past, portrayed by Freud as *infantile amnesia*, and a focusing on present time, which facilitates a shift of energy in school into learning the skills necessary for adult success and realization of a family like that of parents.

This first transformation, from early to middle childhood, reflected in a changed focus on time and memory, is the ideal type of transformation across the course of life. Evocation and at least partial resolution of wishes within the family circle are reflected in the forgetting of these personally and socially disruptive wishes of the preschool years, focusing instead on the present and on gaining those skills that will help the child one day to satisfy those wishes associated with the family romance within his or her own family. A major problem in the psychoanalytic study of adult lives has been to portray the continuing influence, out of awareness, of wishes stemming from this first epoch of life while acknowledging the influence of subsequent life changes across the years of adolescence and adulthood. The course of life leads to distinctive challenges to the experience of self and personal integrity, resulting both from expectable transitions into and out of major adult social roles and also as a consequence of unexpected, often adverse, life changes, such as job loss or the illness or death of spouse or offspring.

A second transformation of time and memory takes place with the shift from middle childhood to adolescence, when the focus in time shifts from present to future and the child realizes more appropriate goals than were possible in middle childhood. As Cottle and Klineberg (1974) and Greene (1990) have observed, if middle childhood was focused on the present, adolescence becomes a time for considering the future.

A third transformation takes place with realization of midlife, a time when there is most often increased experience of personal loss through death of parents and loved ones, increased recognition of the finitude of life, and realization that there is less time to be lived than has been lived already. This third transformation of time and memory leads to a shift away from concern with the future to increased psychological use of the past, first in the service of mastery (Lieberman & Falk, 1971) and later as a means for uniting the loose strands of life through what Butler (1963) termed the *life-review*.

A fourth transformation, in the sense of time and use of memory across the course of life, may be a result of being a survivor of a generation. This fourth transformation is characterized by living in the present, taking each day as it comes, while relying on reminiscence as a means of providing solace in response to the loss of family members and friends.

It should be emphasized that these transformations are not explicitly age connected. Although some discussion of the life course (i.e., Levinson, 1978) assumes the correspondence of age and stage of life course, such views tend to confuse chronological and social age. As Freud first suggested in the "Three Essays" (1905/1953), efforts at connecting age and stage of life may emphasize a degree of precision not actually observed in experience over time. Rather, there appears to be a range of time within which transformations are expectable. With the attainment of adulthood, and when social rather than maturational processes are primarily responsible for changes in the sense of self, there is increased variation in the age at which particular transformations may be observed.

The Nuclear Conflict and the Transition From Early to Middle Childhood

From the outset, Freud struggled with the problem of wishes and deeds. Fantasy is not the same thing as action in the world, although it may help to inspire such action. The question then is the foundation of wishes. Freud's (1900/1948) discovery was a simple but limited one: At least within Western culture, little boys develop an intense relationship with their primary caregiver, their mother, across the first few years of life. Increasing awareness that where there were two, now there are three—mother, father, and oneself (and perhaps brothers and sisters as well)—leads to feelings of resentment and enhanced effort to maintain the love and affection of mother as the primary caregiver. Other family members, particularly the father in the bourgeois family of the West, become the source of feelings of rivalry and enmity.

The little boy struggling with the *nuclear conflict* leading to the transformation from early to middle childhood both wishes to maintain the exclusive tie with his mother and also fears his father's possible retaliation. In part because of the intense pleasure that his genitals provide him, the little boy comes to fear that his father will retaliate for this nuclear wish and mutilate him. In response, the child first offers himself to his father as a source of sexual satisfaction, to forestall this mutilation, then adopts his father's talents and skills, to get a woman for himself like his mother (Freud, 1909/1955).

According to Freud, the compelling quality of Sophocles' tragedy is its gripping power to remind each person of her or his own destiny. Later, referring to this nuclear wish, in deference to Jung's terminology, Freud (1909a, 1910) portrayed the family romance of this entire period before the transition from early to middle childhood as the *Oedipus complex*. Further, because this complex referred to a psychological conflict between wish and fear that the wish might come true, seen so well in preschoolers' night terrors, Freud portrayed this as an infantile neurosis in the sense that anxiety led to symptoms (phobias, obsessions) just as in the manner of the adult psychological conflict.

Over time, this nuclear conflict is partially resolved as the boy adopts an identification with the parent of the same gender and renounces wishes for the parent of the opposite gender. This conflict is partially resolved as the boy gives up the wish to have mother and replaces it with a wish to find a woman outside the family like his mother and the boy is propelled into the school years, where he is able to learn those instrumental skills, at home and in the community, that will permit him to realize this goal. The conflict of this point in the course of life is nuclear because it leads to the first transformation of time and memory across the course of life. Further, it is assumed that this conflict includes sexual wishes toward other family members, which the child regards as reprehensible (as does society), represses out of awareness, and knows later only through enactments such as dreams and creative activity, which represent partial satisfaction of wishes enduring across the course of life in ways that are socially acceptable.

There are two obvious problems with the nuclear conflict as primary for the subsequent course of life. The first is that it emerged from Freud's own self-analysis in the months after his father's death, when Freud was already a middle-aged man. Freud regarded this awareness of ambivalent feelings toward his father as his single greatest discovery, and as the foundation for all of psychoanalytic psychology, he then sought verification for his discovery from the personal recollections of others and from analysands such as the young child Hans (Freud, 1909b). Hans was the 3-year-old son of one of Freud's collaborators. His analysis was carried out principally by his father, with advice from Freud regarding appropriate interpretations. It is ironic that there has been so little effort to verify this discovery through systematic developmental study, although there have been a number of supporting case reports of the analysis of young children.

The other problem is that Freud had difficulty relating his discovery to the experiences of little girls. The little boy is able to enjoy his mother's continual love and affection while adopting a competitive relationship with his father. However, the little girl is faced with the problem that her source of life and affection and her prime rival are the same. Later, as Freud (1925) argued that anatomy is destiny, he struggled with the development of little girls. Because the boy abandoned competition in favor of becoming like his father, he adopted his father's skills and values, together with the prohibition against incest. As a result, the little boy was able to adopt a strong moral sense. However, the little girl, not fearing genital mutilation, because she believed that she already had been castrated by a jealous mother, had not such impetus for the development of morality. Psychoanalysis continues to struggle with issues of feminine development and the impact of the nuclear conflict of early childhood on the lives of women through later life (Benjamin, 1995; Chodorow, 1989).

From Middle Childhood to Adolescence: Discovery of the Future

No period in the course of life has been subject to as much discussion, but also stereotyping, as the adolescent epoch. If a central task of the transformation from early to middle childhood is to forget the past and the feelings of competition of the previous years, which had led the child to learn parental competencies in order to realize similar goals, the task of adolescence is to learn the future. Family resources and interests, problems in learning particular competencies, competition from peers, and the ever present reality of social status all demand that adolescents develop a more realistic life plan.

Although in former times, the task of learning adulthood was less of a concern when parents indentured their young children into employment or sent children off to boarding school to learn the skills necessary to participate in the father's business, across the present century, we have increasingly stressed personal choice of career, placing additional burdens on young people to make a reasonable life plan. Social scientist John Clausen (1993) showed that variation in adolescent capacity for planful competence largely determines later life feelings of satisfaction and accomplishments. Those teenagers who are able to make realistic plans and to follow along with these plans in an organized manner seem to be better able to manage adulthood as a whole through later life. Indeed, emergence and management of the concern with futurity are among the most central of the tasks of adolescence (Greene, 1990).

Closely related to the issue of futurity is that of identity. First popularized by the psychoanalyst Erik Erikson (1958) in his comparative study of college-age youth seen in psychiatric treatment, and such historical figures as Martin Luther, resolution of identity issues has become a central focus in virtually every discussion of adolescence. Erikson was never able to provide a clear definition of *identity*. This term has been used in a variety of contexts by a number of authors. Perhaps the best way of portraying this concept is as a feeling of continuity with the personal and collective past, knowing who and what one is. Clearly, knowing where one is headed in life, along with being at home with one's own body and sexuality, is central to the feeling of having resolved issues of who and what one is.

Erikson noted that this experience of enhanced personal congruence was not possible apart from some struggle. He further noted that, ideally, young people suspend all decisions about the future and are able to explore a number of identities. After this period of experimentation or psychosocial moratorium, there may be an enhanced sense of personal congruence and a more appropriate appraisal of future goals than was possible before adolescence. This period of moratorium was best characterized in Erikson's (1958) portrayal of young Martin Luther, who, like other young people of the sixteenth century, often lived between the walls of a nearby monastery and the community while they struggled with the possibility of adopting the religious life. Erikson saw college, at least during the 1950s and early 1960s, as a contemporary equivalent.

One outcome of this time of experimentation might be a prolonged struggle with these issues, never able to consolidate identity and develop a coherent sense of self. Another outcome might be a foreclosed identity, that is, declaring a set of life interests and goals before giving oneself time to experiment and try on a number of possible roles. A third outcome might be a negative identity, that is, phrasing one's life primarily in terms of what one is not. Optimally, however, a young person will permit herself or himself the opportunity to struggle with what she or he is not, before deciding who and what she or he is.

This concept of identity struggle presumes that adolescence must inevitably be a time of personal turmoil, beginning with the high school years and leading to renewed vitality and coherence in young adulthood. In the first place, not all young people report the need for such personal questioning. The struggle with a changing body image, including often quite dramatic growth surges and sexual maturation leading to the experience of desire, need not lead to renouncement of preadolescent interests and concerns. Many adults who have never been able to attain a sense of coherence in their own lives may look back with regret at their own adolescence and subtly encourage the rebellion of youth at the same time that they decry such rebellion. It is only from hearing a particular account of a particular young person that it is possible to differentiate more and less successful outcomes. One adolescent may feel at home with the values and attitudes of the family, whereas another young person may seek rebellion.

Later in adolescence, young people begin to make a life for themselves, still behaving as a part of the family and interdependent, but with perhaps a different, generationally shaped, lifestyle. Living apart from the family need not mean rejection of family values. On the contrary, it is striking to see young people replicating important family values as they begin their own adult lives. There are invisible loyalties within the family that transcend generationally shaped lifestyle differences. Too often, parents and offspring alike become entangled with these lifestyle issues, leading to friction without due consideration for underlying similarities in values and attitudes.

Adulthood and the Midlife Transformation

There is some question of whether the advent of parenthood may lead to reorganization of memory and sense of time, which are the distinctive features of the several transformations taking place across the course of life. In this manner, it may be possible to break into a multigenerational cycle of particular enactments, which lead children in the next generation to experience their upbringing as not good enough, or particular conflicts, such as overly high expectations for offspring without taking into account the offspring's distinctive manner of negotiating lived experience.

Although the advent of parenthood provides unique satisfaction, at least within contemporary American families, the transition into parenthood, as well as the birth of each additional child, may present unique problems (Cohler, McLanahan, & Adams, 1984). Findings regarding this role transition, for which there can be little preparation (Cohler et al., 1984), suggest that new mothers and fathers experience enhanced distress that lasts for periods of as long as 2 years after the baby's birth. Having a child demands responsibilities previously unknown for most couples. No amount of anticipation can prepare for the reality of assuming total care for the young child. Finally, note that it is not just with the birth of the first child, but across the years of active parenting that women in particular report lowered morale.

Whereas married, still childless men and women show high levels of life satisfaction, with the birth of the first child, there is a decline in morale, which is at its lowest point when all children are preschoolers but improves for both mothers and fathers when children begin school. However, until all children are grown, women still report lowered levels of life satisfaction as compared with men. Findings reported from an epidemiological study of an American urban community (Weissman & Meyers, 1978) showed that as many as two thirds of the resident women reported at least moderate depression; other studies showed that beginning in adolescence, girls report lowered morale as contrasted with boys. Although women who choose to remain single are the next happiest group, followed by married men, married women, and single men, society extracts some toll on the morale of women who are expected to be kinkeepers and caregivers for the family.

Because marriage and parenthood are transitions taking place at somewhat later ages than in the past, particular issues are presented within the analytic situation itself. With the advent of parenthood among men and women in their 40s (Daniels & Weingarten, 1982), both new opportunities and challenges are presented for men and women more settled at work than earlier in their career, in terms of the relationships with spouse and children. The problems and benefits of remarriage and the reconstituted family pose distinctive issues for analysis.

Shared understanding of the expectable duration of life and of one's own place within the finitude of life, with the increased personalization of death as adults encounter the deaths of parents, brothers and sisters, and friends, expectably leads middle-aged adults to confront their own mortality within an immediacy not experienced earlier across the adult years (Marshall, 1986; Munnichs, 1966; Neugarten, 1979; Neugarten & Datan, 1974). Sometime in the early 50s among men, and the later 50s or early 60s among women, there is increased realization that there is less time to be lived than has been lived already. This recognition of the finitude of life fosters a new perspective on the past (Tobin, 1991).

Colarusso and Nemiroff (1979) and Nemiroff and Colarusso (1985) suggested that personality development processes across the second half of life may not be simply a linear continuation of earlier life experiences. Earlier discussion within psychoanalysis assumed that little psychological development took place across the adult years. However, following Erikson's (1963) initial discussion of personality development and change across the adult years, Vaillant's (1993) elaboration of Erikson's portrayal of the adult years, and Abrams's (1977) portrayal of the developmental perspective, as contrasted with the genetic point of view portrayed within earlier discussion of adult personality change (Abraham, 1919/1951), Colarusso and Nemiroff maintained that such issues as the increased possibility of loss through death of older parents and friends, retirement, and widowhood all reflect issues unique to middle and older adulthood.

Issues of competition with others at work, and within the family, including both one's parents and offspring, may reflect continuing impact of the nuclear neurosis of early childhood, with attendant issues of competition, guilt, and inhibition. However, issues of competition and guilt are rendered less intense than in childhood as a result of other interests, concerns, and satisfactions, such as with work attainments or with friends, and are interwoven with appropriate concerns regarding generativity and enhanced realization of the finitude of life and enhanced sense of purpose of one's own life, which may help to place these issues within a larger perspective in regard to the meaning of life (Jung, 1933).

Just as the transformation from early to middle childhood leads to emphasis on the present at the expense of the past and adolescence shifts experience of time and memory to include a more realistic picture of the future, the transformation of midlife may lead to increasing use of the past, first in the service of solving problems in living and, much later in life, in providing solace and replacing continuing contact with spouse, friends, and parents no longer alive. Further, for most men, attainment of midlife signals attainment of career peak. As the late social psychologist Daniel Levinson (1978) observed, attainment of midlife signals the end of the dream, in the sense that possibilities are foreclosed that formerly seemed possible. For the scientist, most contributions have already been made, and it is necessary to make peace with the reality that there may be no Nobel Prize. For the businessman seeking to become company president, this dream remains unfulfilled. Finally, with children launched into the world, their own attainments and career interests may diverge from parental aspirations for them.

Midlife is a time of "taking stock," of making peace with possible limitations on activity imposed by health problems, with own offspring career attainments, and, perhaps, with diminished hopes and increased fears regarding the quality of life in retirement. Early retirements, and even loss of jobs held for many decades, so common in the late twentieth century as a result of corporate reorganization, pose problems of grief and mourning. There is some evidence that men in their early 50s may experience increased anxiety and diminished morale (Cohler & Lieberman, 1979). Similar issues are posed for most women a decade or so later, because women, whose work life is more often interrupted by active parenthood, return to full-time work later in life than men. However, midlife can pose a unique opportunity for change and enhanced life satisfaction. The decision to quit a successful professional practice, to realize the goal of becoming a teacher or cleric, or to return to college or graduate school, may first be possible at midlife as children grow to adulthood and no longer require parental financial assistance.

Late Life and the Issue of Survivorship

Persons over age 85 presently represent the most rapidly growing segment of the population. This population will continue to increase as the baby boom generation reaches later life. It is ironic that much less is known about aging than about other points in the course of life and that much of what is known is based on earlier studies of adults who lifelong have had less education and less adequate health care. Later life becomes the point at which experiences of a lifetime become particularly relevant in determining level of functioning. It is also ironic that as compared with other points in the course of life, much of the discussion of aging focuses on a tension between decline and successful aging (Cohler & Nakamura, 1996).

At no other point in the course of life has so much of the discussion regarding self and lived experience focused on issues of loss and decline. Indeed, adults who continue to use intellectual skills are less likely to show cognitive decline in later life than adults who do not continue to read, write, and seek intellectual stimulation. The present generation of elders is more healthy than any preceding generation. Indeed, studies have suggested that it is only after adults reach the mid-70s that there is any change in health status. In their 70s, adults are less able than younger adults to perform certain cognitive tasks rapidly. However, older adults make up in accuracy what they lose in speed in performing cognitive tests.

Clinical Psychoanalysis and the Middle-Aged and Older Analysand

There has been considerable controversy regarding both the value and the contributions of the intensive psychodynamic psychotherapy or psychoanalysis of older adults and also regarding possible differences in such analyses as contrasted with the analysis of much younger adults. Freud had been terrified of his own aging and believed that he would die young. His own early life experiences with somewhat older, religious governesses also apparently frightened him (Gay, 1988). Wylie and Wylie (1987) noted that Freud believed that psychoanalysis would be impossible across the second half of life; he maintained that older adults could not successfully be treated in analysis. Relying on stereotypes emerging from studies of prior generations of elders, he claimed that older adults were too rigid in their beliefs and prejudices to be open to change. In fact, there is little evidence that older adults are more rigid or stereotyped than younger counterparts. The reality of an aging population, with recognition that well-educated, healthy older adults are no less flexible than younger counterparts, has changed psychoanalytic conceptions of intervention across the second half of life (Tobin, 1991).

Freud's own distaste for aging has had an impact on the hesitance of analysts to work with older adults. Even among those analysts willing to work with older analysands, issues posed by middle and later life may be too readily understood in terms of the nuclear neurosis (Miller, 1985, 1987). Freud (1900) had suggested that fear of death was itself merely another expression of the castration complex. Some analysts believe that those older adults previously analyzed might be able to profit from further analysis in later life but do not believe that older adults never before in analysis can make use of this mode of enhanced self-understanding. Earlier formulations of aging placed particular emphasis on the reverberations of the nuclear conflict across the course of life. The older adult struggling to face the loss of the work role through retirement was presumed to be experiencing anew conflicts first engendered 6 or 7 decades earlier with parents, during the transition from early to middle childhood. The loss of a spouse through death was similarly assumed to be the enactment anew of the nuclear conflict of early childhood.

However, there is nothing from the perspective of the developmental psychology of later life to suggest that older adults are any less cognitively competent or any less able than younger counterparts to engage readily in the analytic process. Indeed, often more introspective and more involved in refashioning the meaning of their life than younger counterparts, older adults may be in an ideal position to profit from psychoanalytic intervention, which could foster the process of rewriting the narrative of life, to attain an enhanced sense of personal integrity in facing their own mortality (Nemiroff & Colarusso 1990). Further, because many older adults may have as much as a third of their life remaining after retirement, psychoanalysis could help these older adults to realize later life with an enhanced sense of integrity and vitality (Miller, 1987).

Nemiroff and Colarusso (1985) reviewed much of the literature on psychoanalysis and the clinical study of later life. Although first clinical reports were enthusiastic in regard to the positive outcome of psychoanalytic intervention in work with older adults (Abraham, 1919/1951), the approach in this early study was explicitly informed by a traditional view of nuclear neurosis reenacted in a form not modified through later experience as the foundation of psychoanalytic intervention. More recent reports by analysts reporting on psychoanalytic intervention with older adults (Kahana, 1978; Sandler, 1978) are considerably more optimistic regarding the possibility of changes taking place across the course of the later adult years.

Although Erikson's (1982) focus on the course of life as a whole has helped to shift the terms of discussion from childhood to the course of life from childhood through oldest age, continued reliance on an epigenetic rather than transformational view of the course of life maintains undue emphasis on childhood, as contrasted with adult experiences, in understanding the particular experiences of the adult years. Even in the work of Gould (1993) and Vaillant (1993), the concurrent, coactive impact of early childhood experiences is presumed to echo across the adult years in a manner not necessarily modified by adult experiences. A number of pioneering publications (Colarusso, 1998; Colarusso & Nemiroff, 1979; Nemiroff & Colarusso, 1985, 1990) have systematically reconsidered this earlier perspective.

Although recognizing the significance, not necessarily the primacy, of issues stemming from earlier life experience for adult lives, these pioneer investigators of psychoanalysis and adult development also recognize the significant and transforming contributions of the adult years to the experience of self and others. Their seven basic hypotheses regarding adult psychological development (Colarusso & Nemiroff, 1979, 1985) emphasize that the adult past is as significant as the early childhood past in understanding the manner in which middle-aged and older adults experience self and others. Expected and eruptive adverse changes across the adult years are particularly significant as factors shaping the course of adult personality development, as is the experience of changes on body image and physical health (Miller, 1987).

Issues of rivalry and competition reflecting incomplete resolution of the nuclear conflict accompanying the transformation from early to middle childhood may become evident within the psychoanalytic situation. For example, an 80-year-old man in analysis may express feelings of jealousy about his 40-year-old analyst and a young woman analysand of the hour preceding his own hour and may envision competition with the analyst for the affections of this analysand. On the other hand, just as Dr. Borg ruminated on choices made across a lifetime and their consequences (Erikson, 1978), other analysands may be very much focused on the analyst as sibling, spouse, or offspring.

Reworking and integrating into consistent memories the experiences of a lifetime are particularly difficult tasks. The analyst becomes important as a source of affirmation regarding choices made and opportunities lost. Most significantly, the analyst may be viewed as a source of continued self-affirmation and self-completion as a twin or even as a part of oneself. In each case, it is assumed that the analyst would be completely attuned and absorbed into the analysand's own life, so that even the most minute failure to understand the analysand was experienced as a particular breach, a cruel reminder that analysand and analyst are separate.

The impact of the changing experience of life's duration is often problematic in psychoanalysis or psychoanalytical psychotherapy, where older patients present material at least some of which is difficult for younger therapists to understand (Nemiroff & Colarusso, 1985). Although all therapists have experienced transformations from early to middle childhood and from middle childhood to adolescence and are at least potentially able to respond to the patient's distress with empathy grounded in personal experience, not all therapists have experienced the transformation from early- to mid-adult years or even, in some instances, from adolescence to young adulthood. For this reason, it is sometimes hard for younger therapists to understand transferences in which they are experienced, for example, as a grandchild.

Clearly, the analytic experience of the older analysand depends to some extent on the age of the analyst. However, younger analysts often fail to realize that chronological age becomes irrelevant as the analytic process unfolds. A 40-year-old analyst may be endowed by the analysand with the qualities of the analysand's own mother or father, whereas a 70-year-old analyst may be endowed with the qualities of a less than sympathetic offspring regarding the analysand's continued difficulties. The analyst who is unable to deal with his or her own feelings about growing older may find it particularly difficult to remain empathic with the personal struggles of older analysands, because the analyst's own anxiety intrudes into the process of tasting and experiencing the analysand's own subjectivity. Such issues as the increasing reality of one's own mortality pose a challenge to analyst and analysand alike (Wylie & Wylie, 1987).

The older analyst's own struggles with such issues as the life review may be a problem interfering in being able to remain empathic with the analysand. The middle-aged analyst encountering problems in the care of her or his own older parents may also find it difficult to work with older analysands. The illness and impending death of parents and such decisions as who will care for older parents all become issues implicitly raised in work with older analysands. Just as in the analysis of younger adults, each point in the course of life poses its own unique challenges to the analyst's experience of self and others, with important implications for remaining empathic and able to foster the analysand's further understanding of the manner in which others remain psychologically important for the analysand.

Continuing enactment of wishes stemming from unresolved aspects of the nuclear conflict of early childhood and the repetition of yet to be mastered issues arising across the course of childhood and youth are important as factors related to experience of personal coherence and vitality among adults across the middle and later years of life. Whereas earlier reports had focused primarily on the repetition of the nuclear neurosis in the enactments of older analysands toward their analysts, as Nemiroff and Colarusso (1985), Galatzer-Levy and Cohler (1993), and others have noted, additional issues are posed across the course of life. Enactments of older adults toward their analysts reflect expectable changes in the experience of self and others, including such issues as the life review (Butler, 1963), enhanced personalization of death (Neugarten & Datan, 1974), and also the crisis of survivorship (Myerhoff, 1979). The psychoanalyst Pearl King (1980) noted also that enactments of older patients reflect concerns regarding issues of loss of function, enhanced awareness of own aging, and concern for the welfare of offspring. King emphasized the significance of enactments reflecting experiences with others over as many as five generations.

Particularly in the analysis of middle-aged men and women, King (1980) maintained that issues stemming from adolescence are once again salient. For example, the experience of leaving home as an adolescent may be enacted anew as one's young adult offspring prepare to live independently (Blos, 1967), and losses experienced as a result of the death of parents and friends may also evoke struggles of loss and change experienced across the years of middle and late adolescence. Further, Greene (1990) noted, midlife shares with adolescence a point in the course of life at which concepts of time and memory are reorganized. If adolescence represents a time at which a realistic connection between an expectable future and past is first attained, middle age in our society represents a time at which the past disappointments are acknowledged and in which this new peace with the past may first be attained.

Persons entering analysis across the second half of life bring to the analysis not only the enactments repeated from efforts to solve the nuclear conflicts of early childhood but also those experiences of a lifetime with spouse or partner and children. The analyst may now be experienced as a child or even as a grandchild, in addition to being experienced as the parent of one's own childhood. In addition, as analyst and analysand come to share increasing complementarity in their place within the expectable course of adult life, additional issues are posed for each with the therapeutic relationship. Just as for the analysand, the analyst faces issues regarding the finitude of life and personalization of death (Jaques, 1993). Health problems may become increasingly real for analyst as for analysand, and concerns regarding the loss of youthful vitality may also be an issue.

Depending on the anxiety that these issues evoke for the analyst, there may be interference in assisting the analysand's own efforts to make peace with lived experience. Fearing his or her own aging, the analyst may find it difficult to maintain an empathy when confronted with such potentially anxiety-inducing issues. However, shared experience may foster enhanced capacity to understand the analysand's experiences and to enter ever more effectively into helping the analysand to maintain sense of personal integrity. Recognizing anxiety induced by the analysand's idealization of the analyst's own wisdom about aging, the analyst may be able to permit the analysand to use this idealization in the service of his or her own enhanced vitality even while confronting issues of finitude.

Additional enactments observed across the course of analysis, such as the grandchild transference of an older adult analysand working with a much younger analyst (Rappaport, 1958), must be understood as more than another enactment stemming from the Oedipal neurosis. Indeed, increased recognition of finitude of life, portrayed in the work of Munnichs (1966) and of Marshall (1986), represents a fundamental shift in our understanding of self and experience across the adult years. Shared understanding regarding the expectable course of human life generally leads to increased awareness of the finitude of life and to the personalization of death (Neugarten & Datan, 1974). This enhanced awareness of finitude leads to a shift in the experience of self and place in the world, fostering the life review (Butler, 1963). Whereas experiences taking place earlier in life may indeed color the manner in which integration of past within present is understood, distinctive and unique experiences across the adult years further influence this life review.

Conclusion

The concept of wish or intention, often out of awareness, informs psychoanalytic study of the course of life. Recognition of wishes that were personally and socially reprehensible was presumed by Freud as founded in the family romance of early childhood, in which the child experienced desire for the parent of the opposite gender. Issues of competition and fear of possible harmful consequences led the child in time to abandon rivalry for the attentions of the desired parent in favor of identification with the parent of the same gender, to realize these wishes outside the family.

Freud observed that before all else, psychoanalysis was a genetic psychology concerned with the manner in which earlier experiences were formative for later experiences. However, Freud also realized that it was easier to look backward and to make sense of the course of life on the basis of present understanding of the past than to predict the past. Further, much of the understanding of the manner in which the past was experienced is founded in the enaction by the analysand of wishes first founded in early childhood anew within the context of the psychoanalytic situation. A psychoanalytic psychology of the life course is confronted with the task of showing both the continuing significance of wish or intention, first arising within the family romance of the preschool years, and also the impact of those expectable and eruptive, often adverse, life changes arising over the course of life, as factors related to present experience of self and personal integrity.

First efforts to show the relevance of psychoanalysis to the study of adult lives, using the nuclear conflict marking the transformation from early to middle childhood as a model, led in time to emphasis on a number of points across the adult years that may be associated with subsequent transformations of memory and sense of time. This study of changes over time in the experience of self and others both has benefited from systematic study of the expectable course of life and has made contributions to such study. This focus on the course of life beyond childhood also has informed the psychoanalytic situation itself.

Study of the expectable course of adult lives has shown that important enactments directed toward the analyst may refer not only to the repetition and continuing effort to gain satisfaction of the nuclear conflict of early childhood but also to the effort to resolve issues necessarily arising across the years of youth and adulthood with a first focus on a realistic future. The transformations of middle childhood to young adulthood and across the adult years, perhaps as a consequence of the growing awareness of the finitude of life, led to increasing focus on remembering the past rather than anticipating the future and, within later adulthood, or survivorship, on remembering the past as a source of solace after the losses of later life, but also on living in the present and taking each day as it comes.

Understanding the manner in which people experience the course of life through clinical psychoanalysis provides important understanding of the manner in which life circumstances come to have an impact on the integrity of self and life story and also in the experience of relations with others. Systematic study of the course of expectable lives over time provides understanding of the context of lived experience. Together, clinical psychoanalytic study and systematic reports of lives studied over time will foster enhanced understanding of the impact of past on present lived experience.

References

Abraham, K. (1951). The applicability of psycho-analytic treatment to patients at an advanced age. *Selected papers on psychoanalysis* (pp. 323–325). New York: Basic Books. (Original work published 1919)

Abrams, S. (1977). The genetic point of view: Antecedents and transformations. *Journal of the American Psychoanalytic Association, 25,* 417–425.

Benjamin, J. (1995). *Like subjects, like objects: Essays on recognition and sexual difference.* New Haven, CT: Yale University Press.

Blos, P. (1967). The second individuation process of adolescence. *Psychoanalytic Study of the Child, 22,* 162–186.

Brennis, B. (1997). *Recovered memories of trauma: Transferring the present to the past.* Madison, CT: International Universities Press.

Butler, R. (1963). The life-review: An interpretation of reminiscence in the aged. *Psychiatry, 26,* 65–76.

Chodorow, N. (1989). *Feminism and psychoanalytic theory.* New Haven, CT: Yale University Press.

Clausen, J. (1993). *American lives: Looking back at the children of the Great Depression.* New York: Free Press–Macmillan.

Cohler, B. (1984). Parenthood, psychopathology, and child-care. In R. Cohen, B. Cohler, & S. Weissman (Eds.), *Parenthood: A psychodynamic perspective* (pp. 119–148). New York: Guilford Press.

Cohler, B. (1987). Approaches to the study of development in psychiatric education. In S. Weissman & R. Thurnblad (Eds.), *The role of psychoanalysis in psychiatric education: Past, present and future* (pp. 225–270). New York: International Universities Press.

Cohler, B., & Lieberman, M. (1979). Personality change across the second half of life: Findings from a study of Irish, Italian and Polish-American men and women. In D. Gelfand & A. Kutznik (Eds.), *Ethnicity and aging* (pp. 227–245). New York: Springer.

Cohler, B., & Nakamura, J. (1996). Self and experience across the second half of life. In L. Sadovay, L. Lazarus, L. Jarvik, & G. Grossberg (Eds.), *Comprehensive review of geriatric psychiatry* (2nd ed., pp. 153–196). Washington, DC: American Psychiatric Press.

Colarusso, C., & Nemiroff, R. (1979). Some observations and hypotheses about the psychoanalytic theory of adult development. *International Journal of Psychoanalysis, 60,* 59–71.

Colarusso, C. (1998). Development and treatment in late adulthood. In G. Pollock & S. Greenspan (Eds.), *The course of life. Vol. VII. Completing the journey* (pp. 285–317). Madison, CT: International Universities Press.

Cottle, T., & Klineberg, S. (1974). *The present of things future.* New York: Free Press–Macmillan.

Daniels, P., & Weingarten, K. (1982). *Sooner or later: The timing of parenthood in adult lives.* New York: Norton.

Emde, R. (1981). Changing the models of infancy and the nature of early development: Remodeling the foundation. *Journal of the American Psychoanalytic Association, 29,* 179–219.

Emde, R. (1985). From adolescence to midlife: Remodeling the structure of adult development. *Journal of the American Psychoanalytic Association, 33*(Suppl.) 59–112.

Erikson, E. (1978). Reflections on Dr. Borg's life cycle. In E. Erikson (Ed.), *Adulthood* (pp. 1–33). New York: Norton.

Erikson, E. H. (1958). *Young man Luther: A study in psychoanalysis and history.* New York: Norton.

Erikson, E. H. (1963). *Childhood and society* (Rev. ed.). New York: Norton.

Erikson, E. (1982). *The life-cycle completed: A review.* New York: Norton.

Freud, S. (1953). Three essays on the theory of sexuality. In J. Strachey (Ed. and Trans.), *The standard edition of the complete psychological works of Sigmund Freud* (Vol. 7, pp. 130–243). London: Hogarth Press. (Original work published 1905)

Freud, S. (1955). Analysis of a phobia in a five-year-old boy. In J. Strachey (Ed. and Trans.), *The standard edition of the complete psychological works of Sigmund Freud* (Vol. 10, pp. 5–147). London: Hogarth Press. (Original work published 1909)

Freud, S. (1955). The psychogenesis of a case of homosexuality in a woman. In J. Strachey (Ed. and Trans.), *The standard edition of the complete psychological works of Sigmund Freud* (Vol. 18, pp. 147–172). London: Hogarth Press. (Original work published 1920)

Freud, S. (1957). Five lectures on psychoanalysis. In J. Strachey (Ed. and Trans.), *The standard edition of the complete psychological works of Sigmund Freud* (Vol. 11, pp. 3–55). London: Hogarth Press. (Original work published 1910)

Freud, S. (1958). The claims of psychoanalysis to scientific interest. In J. Strachey (Ed. and Trans.), *The standard edition of the complete psychological works of Sigmund Freud* (Vol. 13, pp. 165–192). London: Hogarth Press. (Original work published 1913)

Freud, S. (1958). The interpretation of dreams. In J. Strachey (Ed. and Trans.), *The standard edition of the complete psychological works of Sigmund Freud* (Vols. 4–5). London: Hogarth Press. (Original work published 1900)

Freud, S. (1959). Family romances. In J. Strachey (Ed. and Trans.), *The standard edition of the complete psychological works of Sigmund Freud* (Vol. 9, pp. 235–244). London: Hogarth Press. (Original work published 1909)

Freud, S. (1959). Some psychical consequences of the anatomical distinction between the sexes. In J. Strachey (Ed. and Trans.), *The standard edition of the complete psychological works of Sigmund Freud* (Vol. 20, pp. 173–179). London: Hogarth Press. (Original work published 1925)

Freud, S. (1985). *The complete letters of Sigmund Freud to Wilhelm Fliess, 1897–1904* (J. M. Masson, Ed. and Trans.). Cambridge, MA: Harvard University Press.

Galatzer-Levy, R., & Cohler, B. (1993). *The essential other: A developmental psychology of the self.* New York: Basic Books.

Gay, P. (1988). *Freud: A life for our times.* New York: Norton.

Gould, R. (1993). Transformational tasks in adulthood. In G. H. Pollock & S. Greenspan (Eds.), *The course of life: Vol. VI. Late adulthood* (pp. 23–68). Madison, CT: International Universities Press.

Greene, A. L. (1990). Great expectations: Constructions of the life-course during adolescence. *Journal of Youth and Adolescence, 19,* 289–306.

Gutmann, D. (1987). *Reclaimed powers: Towards a psychology of men and women in later life.* New York: Basic Books.

Hagestad, G. (1990). Social perspectives on the life course. In R. Binstock & L. K. George (Eds.), *Handbook of aging and the social sciences* (3rd ed., pp. 151–168). New York: Academic Press.

Hartmann, H., & Kris, E. (1945). The genetic approach in psychoanalysis. *The Psychoanalytic Study of the Child, 1*, 11–30.

Jaques, E. (1993). The midlife crisis. In S. Greenspan & G. Pollock (Eds.), *The course of life: V. Early adulthood* (pp. 201–232). Madison, CT: International Universities Press.

Jung, C. C. (1933). *Modern man in search of a soul*. New York: Harcourt, Brace.

Kagan, J. (1980). Perspectives on continuity. In O. G. Brim, Jr., & J. Kagan (Eds.), *Constancy and change in human development* (pp. 26–74). Cambridge, MA: Harvard University Press.

Kahana, R. (1978). Psychoanalysis in later life: Discussion. *Journal of Geriatric Psychiatry, 11*, 37–49.

King, P. (1980). The life cycle as indicated by the nature of the transference in the psychoanalysis of the middle-aged and elderly. *International Journal of Psychoanalysis, 61*, 153–160.

Levinson, D. (1978). *The seasons of a man's life*. New York: Knopf.

Lewis, M. (1997). *Altering fate: Why the past does not predict the future*. New York: Guilford Press.

Lieberman, M., & Falk, J. (1971). The remembered past as a source of data for research on the life cycle. *Human Development, 14*, 132–141.

Lieberman, M., & Tobin, S. (1983). *The experience of old age: Stress, coping and survival*. New York: Basic Books.

Marshall, V. (1986). A sociological perspective on aging and dying. In V. Marshall (Ed.), *Later life: The social psychology of aging* (pp. 125–146). Thousand Oaks, CA: Sage.

McLanahan, S., & Adams, J. (1987). Parenthood and psychological well-being. *Annual Review of Sociology, 5*, 237–257.

Miller, E. (1985). The development of intimacy at age fifty. In R. Nemiroff & C. Colarusso (Eds.), *The race against time: Psychotherapy and psychoanalysis in the second half of life* (pp. 121–142). New York: Plenum.

Miller, E. (1987). The Oedipus complex and rejuvenation fantasies in the analysis of a seventy-year-old woman. *Journal of Geriatric Psychiatry, 20*, 29–51.

Munnichs, J. (1966). *Old age and finitude: A contribution to psychogerontology*. New York: Karger.

Myerhoff, B. (1979). *Number our days*. New York: Dutton.

Nemiroff, R., & Colarusso, C. (Eds.). (1985). *The race against time: Psychotherapy and psychoanalysis in the second half of life*. New York: Plenum.

Nemiroff, R., & Colarusso, C. (1990). Frontiers of adult development in theory and practice. In R. Nemiroff & C. Colarusso (Eds.), *New dimensions in adult development* (pp. 97–124). New York: Basic Books.

Neugarten, B. (1969). Continuities and discontinuities of psychological issues into adult life. *Human Development, 12*, 121–130.

Neugarten, B. (1979). Time, age, and the life-cycle. *American Journal of Psychiatry, 136*, 887–894.

Neugarten, B., & Datan, N. (1974). The middle years. In S. Arieti (Ed.), *American handbook of psychiatry* (Vol. 1, pp. 592–606). New York: Basic Books.

Rapaport, D., & Gill, M. (1959). The points of view and assumptions of metapsychology. *International Journal of Psychoanalysis, 40*, 153–162.

Rappaport, E. (1958). The grandparent syndrome. *Psychoanalytic Quarterly, 27*, 518–538.

Sandler, A. M. (1978). Psychoanalysis in later life: Problems in the psychoanalysis of an aging narcissistic patient. *Journal of Geriatric Psychiatry, 11*, 5–36.

Schafer, R. (1992). *Retelling a life: Narration and dialogue in psychoanalysis*. New York: Basic Books.

Singer, J., & Salovey, P. (1993). *The remembered self: Emotion and memory in personality*. New York: Free Press.

Tobin, S. (1991). *Personhood in advanced old age: Implications for practice*. New York: Springer.

Vaillant, G. (1993). *The wisdom of the ego*. Cambridge, MA: Harvard University Press.

Weissman, M., & Meyers, J. (1978). Affective disorders in a U.S. urban community. *Archives of General Psychiatry, 35*, 1304–1311.

Wylie, H., & Wylie, M. (1987). The older analysand: Countertransference issues in psychoanalysis. *International Journal of Psychoanalysis, 68*, 343–352.

6

Physical Changes in the Aging Individual: Clinical Implications

Susan Krauss Whitbourne

The physical aging process occurs against a backdrop of a lifetime of accumulated experiences in which the individual has come to know and understand the functioning and appearance of his or her unique body. In this chapter, the most significant age-related changes in physical functioning are summarized and analyzed in terms of their impact on the person's sense of self as well as their clinical implications. The concept of *physical identity* as used here refers to the person's self-perception of the body's appearance, competence, and limitations. A model of the aging of physical identity is presented and used as the backdrop for discussion of age-related changes in specific areas of functioning. Implications for health professionals also are discussed in the context of these changes.

In this chapter, I stress that the physical changes associated with the aging process are complex, multifaceted, and multidirectional. Individuals age in their own unique ways, due to their genetic inheritance and lifestyle choices. Of particular importance is the necessity of distinguishing between the processes of normal aging and alterations in functioning that are the result of specific diseases. Although it is true that older people are at heightened risk of developing chronic health problems such as arthritis, cardiovascular disease, cancer, and diabetes, these are diseases rather than normal age-related changes. Clinicians should be aware that they need to persist in the treatment of an older client rather than assume that the symptoms of chronic disease represent inevitable losses due to aging.

The Multiple Threshold Model of Physical Aging and Identity

The aging process is a constant challenge to the maintenance of a stable sense of identity over time. The multiple threshold model of aging (Whitbourne, 1996a) relates age changes to identity, coping processes, and adaptational outcomes. The term *threshold* in this model refers to the point at which an age-related change is recognized by the individual. Before this threshold is reached, the individual does not think of the self as aging or old, or even perhaps as having the real potential to be aging or old. After crossing the threshold, the person recognizes the possibility that functions may be lost through aging (or disease) and begins to adapt to this possibility by changing identity accordingly.

The term *multiple* in this model refers to the fact that the aging process involves potentially every system in the body, so that there is in actuality no single threshold leading into the view of the self as aging. The individual may feel old in one domain of functioning, such as mobility, but feel middle-aged or possibly young in other domains, such as intellectual functioning. Whether a threshold is crossed depends in part on the aging process itself as well as the salience of the area to the person. Mobility may not be as important to an individual whose major source of pleasure is derived from sedentary reading activities. Changes in mobility are less relevant to the individual's adaptation to the environment or to identity than changes in vision. It is assumed that changes in areas important to adaptation and competence have the greatest potential to affect identity.

Furthermore, changes in valued functions are watched for most carefully by the individual and early signs of age-related changes are most apparent in these areas. The increased vigilance for areas of functioning central to identity theoretically heightens the impact of age changes. However, with increased vigilance may come increased motivation to take advantage of control activities that reduce the impact of aging. The adult who values being in peak physical shape will work devotedly each day to avoid loss of muscle strength and aerobic capacity.

There are hypothesized variations in the reactions that individuals have to the crossing of an aging threshold. Some individuals attempt to deny or distort evidence that their bodies are aging; conversely, others overreact to even small indications that an aging threshold has been crossed. The consequences of denial or minimization of age-related changes, on the one hand, versus overreaction or discouragement, on the other, are explored within each relevant area discussed below. The concepts of the multiple threshold model are used as the basis for suggesting clinical implications. The underlying assumption is not that the aging process must or should be slowed, but that the person's adaptation to the aging process can be maximized by working within this model. Ultimately, the value of these interventions can be measured in terms of improved physical health and an improved or perhaps more realistic outlook on the part of the person toward the aging process.

Effects of Age on Appearance and Mobility

Skin

Age changes. A variety of changes contribute to the phenomena of wrinkling and sagging, the most apparent age-related effects on the skin. The epidermis, the outer layer of the skin, becomes flattened, and as cells in the epidermis are replaced through cell renewal processes, their patterns become less organized, and their arrangement less regular. These changes at the microscopic level are reflected in visible changes of the geometric furrows visible on the surface of exposed areas of the skin. Many of the changes in the skin's appearance and structure can be explained by *photoaging*, or exposure to the ultraviolet rays of the sun—changes that are most apparent in the facial skin (Takema, Yorimoto, Kawai, & Imokawa, 1994). Throughout the body, wrinkling and sagging occur due to changes in the middle, dermal layer of the skin, notably a decrease in the connective tissue collagen. Elastin fibers become more brittle, so that the ability of the skin to conform to movement of the bones is compromised. The subcutaneous fat on the limbs decreases and instead collects in areas of fatty deposits, such as around the waist and hips. A decrease in muscle mass, as is discussed later, further adds to the loss of firmness in the skin's appearance.

There are also significant changes in the sweat and oil-producing glands within the dermis that maintain body temperature and lubricate the skin surface particularly in the summer months (Inoue, Nakao, Araki, & Murakami, 1991; Kurban & Bhawan, 1990). In areas such as the palms and underarms, the sweat glands become less active. The sebaceous glands that lubricate the skin with their secretions diminish in activity, and consequently, the skin becomes rougher, dryer, and more vulnerable to surface damage. These changes lead to heightened risk of medical problems such as dermatitis and pruritis (excessive itching), as well as to general discomfort (Kligman, 1989). Age-related alterations also occur in the coloring of the skin. There are fewer melanocytes, and those that remain develop irregular areas of dark pigmentation.

Psychological and clinical implications. Age-related changes in the skin and skin-related structures alter the skin's protective functions as well as its appearance. There is less insulation provided against extremes of temperature and less of a barrier against environmental agents that can irritate the skin and cause dermatitis. Even if the person is not particularly concerned about the effects of age on appearance, these changes in comfort level can trigger the crossing of an aging threshold. However, for many people, particularly in middle age (Whitbourne, 1996b), age changes in the skin that lead to wrinkling are very noticeable and can have an impact on the individual's identity. In particular, comparisons of present appearance with pictures or memories of youth can have negative effects in older people who valued this image of the self (Kleinsmith & Perricone, 1989).

Having crossed this threshold in terms of appearance, there are many steps that older people can take to slow, compensate for, or correct the changes in appearance caused by aging of the skin (Fenske & Albers, 1990). The primary method of prevention is for fair-skinned people to avoid direct exposure to the sun and to use sunblocks when exposure cannot be avoided. There are also many ways for the individual to compensate for age-related changes in the skin once they have become manifest. To counteract the fragility, sensitivity, and dryness of the skin, the individual can use sunscreens, emollients, and fragrance-free cosmetics (Ditre et al., 1996). Although there is considerable skepticism in the academic community toward the bold claims of facial care advertisers, there is some evidence of restorative effects resulting from the continual use of facial massages (Iida & Noro, 1995) and the application of vitamin E (Nachbar & Korting, 1995). Regular participation in aerobic exercise may also offset age-related changes in sweat gland production (Tankersley, Smolander, Kenney, & Fortney, 1991). If a client raises concerns about these aspects of appearance, interventions here, as with hair color (see below), must attempt to strike a judicious balance between intrusiveness into matters of personal taste and the concerns of preventive practice.

Hair

Age changes. With increasing age in adulthood, for men and women, the hair on the head and body loses pigmentation and takes on a white appearance due to a decrease in melanin production in the hair follicles. The rate at which hair color changes varies from person to person due to variations in the onset and rate of melanin production decrease across the surface of the scalp. Gradual and general thinning of scalp hair occurs in both sexes over the years of adulthood, although loss of hair is popularly regarded as a concern of men. Hair loss results from destruction or regression of the germ centers that produce the hair follicles underneath the skin surface. Men may also experience thinning of the hair in their whiskers and a growth of coarse hair on the eyebrows and inside the ear. Patches of coarse terminal hair may develop on the face in women, particularly around the chin.

Psychological and clinical implications. As is true for wrinkles, the threshold for age-related changes in the hair, at least for graying, appears to be crossed at some point in the 30s or 40s (Whitbourne, 1996b). Compared with wrinkles, gray hairs are relatively easy to detect; however, unlike wrinkles, gray hairs can be returned to virtually their original state through the use of hair dye. Changes in hair thickness, however, are not so easily reversed. The desire to disguise or stop the apparent signs of aging through surgery or the wearing of hairpieces is widespread, as is evident in the many advertisements for hair loss replacement processes.

There are many ways in which clinical intervention can be of use when changes in hair amount and color become a concern. Apart from providing information about commercial products, interventions can focus on ways the person can learn to reframe age changes in the hair's appearance in a reasoned manner. Because there are no practical implications of hair loss or hair graying, interventions in this area can be entirely at the discretion of the client and clinician. Unlike cardiovascular functioning, in which denial of age-related changes can prove fatal, the denial of changes in the hair does not have severe health consequences.

Body Build

Age changes. Over adulthood, standing height is reduced (de Groot, Perdigao, & Deurenberg, 1996), particularly after the 50s and particularly in women (Shephard, 1978). The major cause is loss of bone mineral content in the vertebrae, which leads them to collapse and cause compression in the length of the spine. Changes in the joints and flattening of the arches of the feet can further contribute to height loss. Total body weight increases from the 20s until the mid-50s, after which total body weight declines. Most of the weight gain in middle adulthood is due to an accumulation of body fat, particularly around the waist and hips. The weight loss that occurs in the later years of adulthood is due to a loss of lean body mass consisting of muscle and bone (Baumgartner, Heymsfield, & Roche, 1995). Consequently, very old adults may have very thin extremities but fatty areas in the chin, waist, and hips. Although increases in adiposity are found in men (Grinker, Tucker, Vokonas, & Rush, 1995), middle-aged and older women are particularly likely to experience this accumulation of body fat around the torso, with a gain of abdominal girth amounting to 25%–35% across the adult years, compared with 6%–16% for men over a comparable time period (Shephard, 1978). There are secular trends, however, in these patterns. Cohorts of older women are showing a decrease rather than an increase in body fat (Rico, Revilla, Hernandez, Gonzalez-Riola, & Villa, 1993), possibly related to changes in lifestyle and dietary habits. Conversely, more recent cohorts of older men are more likely to be heavier than earlier cohorts of men at comparable ages (Grinker et al., 1995).

Psychological and clinical implications. Changes in body fat that lead to the appearance of a sagging or heavier body shape can result in increased identification of the self as moving away from the figure of youth. The development of "middle-age spread" is one of the first occurrences to trigger recognition of the self as aging, perhaps even before the first gray hairs have sprouted. Indeed, awareness of changes in body composition can occur surprisingly early in adulthood, perhaps by the 30s (Whitbourne, 1996b). Fortunately, the crossing of the body fat threshold may be readily compensated, and before the individual gives up on trying to slow down this particular process, there are many activities that the clinician can promote if this is an area of concern. Participation in exercise training programs can be of value even for middle-aged and older adults who were sedentary throughout their lives. By engaging in vigorous walking, jogging, or cycling for 30–60 minutes a day for 3–4 days a week, the sedentary adult can expect to achieve positive results in a period as short as 10–20 weeks (Whitbourne, 1996a). Resistance training also can promote loss of body fat in middle-aged and older adults (Campbell, Crim, Young, & Evans, 1994; Fielding, 1995). Furthermore, the same activities that a middle-aged person might engage in to combat body fat changes also can have very positive cardiovascular and general health benefits. Thus, vanity might actually serve a protective function in this area.

Changes in body height are less easily compensated, but the threshold appears to be less relevant for most adults unless they have always felt too short. Clinical interventions here may focus on the maintenance of bone strength through weight resistance training, and although these activities might not have an enhancing effect on height, they can be very important in promoting mobility (see below), another major concern for many older adults.

Mobility

Age changes. Changes in the muscles, bones, and joints result in movement that is more difficult, painful, and less effective with each passing year. Between ages 40 to 70, there is a loss of muscle strength amounting to approximately 10% to 20% (Skelton, Greig, Davies, & Young, 1994), with more severe losses of 30% to 40% after age 70 to 80—losses that are more pronounced in the muscles of the lower extremities (McArdle, Katch, & Katch, 1991). However, there are individual variations that can lead to important deviations from such a general pattern of decline. The extent to which aging affects loss of muscle strength depends in part on which gender is being tested, the individual's activity level, the particular muscle group being tested, and whether the type of muscle strength being assessed is static (isometric) or dynamic.

Similarly, the overall course of bone development in adulthood is toward loss of bone strength (Currey, Brear, & Zioupos, 1996), ranging from 5% to 12% per decade from the 20s through the 90s (McCalden, McGeough, Barker, & Court-Brown, 1993), with the loss more pronounced in women. Loss of bone strength is generally explained as a function of the loss of bone mineral content, meaning that the bone becomes increasingly porous and unable to support the loads it must bear (Dargent & Breart, 1993). Microcracks develop in response to stress placed on the bones and heighten the likelihood of fracture (Courtney, Hayes, & Gibson, 1996). Genetic factors also play a role (Dargent & Breart, 1993) as does lifestyle—including factors such as physical activity, smoking, alcohol use, and diet—which can account for 50%–60% of the variation in bone density (Krall & Dawson-Hughes, 1993) and can also influence the rate of fractures (Seeley, Kelsey, Jergas, & Nevitt, 1996). African American women have higher bone mineral density than do White women, although women in both races are at risk of bone fracture due to reduced density (Perry et al., 1996). There are also hormonal influences on bone mass. Bone mineral loss in women proceeds at a higher rate in postmenopausal women, who are no longer producing estrogen in monthly cycles (Garnero, Sornay Rendu, Chupuy, & Delmas, 1996). In men, testosterone levels are positively related to several measures of bone mineral formation (Clarke et al., 1996).

Although the aging of joints is most commonly associated with the later years of life, degenerative processes that reduce the functional efficiency of the joints begin even before the person reaches skeletal maturity. Restrictions of movement and discomfort are therefore potential problems for adults of any age, but they occur with increasing frequency as age progresses. The decline in joint functioning can be accounted for by age losses in virtually every structural component of the joint. Starting in the 20s and 30s, the arterial cartilage begins to thin, fray, shred, and crack. Unprotected by cartilage, the underlying bone eventually begins to wear away. At the same time, outgrowths of cartilage develop, and these interfere with the smooth movement of the joint (Ralphs & Benjamin, 1994). Age-related weakening of the muscles further contributes to restrictions in range of movement due to changes in the joints themselves (Vandervoort et al., 1992).

Psychological and clinical implications. Changes in the structures that support movement have many pervasive effects on the person's life, resulting in restrictions in activity and pain, which can interfere with the individual's psychological adaptation and sense of well-being (Hughes, Edelman, Singer, & Chang, 1993). One of the most serious outcomes of reduced muscle strength, bone strength, and joint mobility is the heightened susceptibility of older people, particularly women, to falls (Dargent & Breart, 1993). If a broken hip results, for example, the person is more likely to suffer long-term disability and dependency (Roberto, 1992). Unfortunately, individuals might overreact to falls by developing a fear of falling or lowered sense of self-efficacy regarding the ability to avoid a fall (Tinetti & Powell, 1993). As a result, they become less stable on their feet and avoid physical activities that might benefit their strength and stability. Understandably, these individuals are vulnerable to feelings of depression and anxiety.

This summary of age-related changes in mobility describes a fairly downhill process, but there are many interventions clinicians can pursue that will have practical advantages. As has been mentioned already, it is important to structure an intervention around the nature of the individual's identity processes, particularly as balanced against his or her actual age-related losses and possibilities for compensation. Given such an assessment, older individuals can be encouraged to participate in a variety of physical exercises that can prove to be extremely helpful in maintaining or restoring mobility. A regular program of exercise can help the middle-aged and older adult compensate substantially for the loss of muscle fibers (Taaffe, Pruitt, Pyka, Guido, & Marcus, 1996), even in persons as old as 90 years (Fiatarone et al., 1990). The same is true of bone loss. Older individuals can benefit from resistance training exercises that, within limits, increase the stress placed on the bone (Sinaki, 1996). Supplement of the diets of older women with vitamin D also has been shown effective in retarding the process of bone loss (Dawson Hughes, 1996). Although degenerative changes in the joints are not reversible, it is possible for older individuals to benefit from exercise training, particularly if it is oriented toward promoting flexibility (Jirovec, 1991); strengthening the muscles that support the joints; increasing the circulation of blood to the joints, thereby promoting the repair of injured tissues; and decreasing risk of injury (Stamford, 1988). Finally, balance training can be an effective intervention to minimize the risk of falls in older women (Province et al., 1995), as can Tai Chi (S. L. Wolf et al., 1996), which includes balance and flexibility exercises.

There has been a great deal of attention within recent years on supplementation with growth hormone as a treatment for various age-related changes in muscle and bone. Unfortunately, consumers are misled by the exaggerated claims of advertisers into believing that growth hormones will reverse or retard the aging process. The research on which the original claims for the effectiveness of hormone therapy are based was conducted on individuals (not necessarily elderly) with growth hormone deficiency. The majority of findings fail to support the advertised benefits of this form of intervention (Taaffe, Jin, Vu, Hoffman, & Marcus, 1996), and there are indications that such treatments may have harmful side effects (M. Riedel, Brabant, Rieger, & von zur Muhlen, 1994).

Effects of Age on Vital Functions

Cardiovascular System

Age changes. The aging process results in serious limitations of the heart's functional requirement to pump blood continuously through the circulatory system at a rate that adequately perfuses the body's cells. Although a distinct entity in terms of underlying processes, fatal cardiovascular diseases do become more probable with advancing age in adulthood. These diseases can have widespread effects on daily life in addition to providing constant sources of reminders of the individual's mortality. For example, the chest pains associated with angina, a chronic cardiac illness, are not only uncomfortable but provide clear warning signals of the heart's impending failure.

The reduction in the heart's pumping capacity is due to a variety of changes affecting the structure and function of the heart muscle walls, particularly the left ventricle, which becomes progressively thicker and less elastic with each decade in adulthood and less elastic (Kitzman & Edwards, 1990) as the number of myocardial cells decreases and the remaining cells become hypertrophied (Olivetti, Melissari, Capasso, & Anversa, 1991). The decreased capacity of the ventricle walls to expand results in a reduced and delayed filling of the left ventricle and the ejection of less blood into the aorta (Arrighi et al., 1994).

Effects of aging on the arteries further compromise the system's ability to distribute blood to the body's cells. Although it is difficult to separate the effects of aging from those of atherosclerosis (a disease in which the arteries become rigid and narrowed by fatty accumulation), the aging process itself appears to cause changes in the aorta and arteries (Shimojo, Tsuda, Iwasaka, & Inada, 1991). The wall of the aorta becomes less flexible, so that the blood leaving the left ventricle of the heart is faced by more resistance and cannot travel as far. The walls of the arteries throughout the body become thicker and less flexible. Impedence of blood flow through the arteries is further increased by the accumulation of lipids in the blood (Heiss et al., 1980).

Although age-related changes in the heart and arteries reduce the amount of blood available to the cells of the body, under normal conditions these changes are not particularly pronounced or noticeable. The effects of aging of the circulatory system are most apparent while the individual is engaging in aerobic exercise, when there is a reduction both in maximum oxygen consumption (aerobic capacity) and the maximum attainable heart rate (Lakatta, 1987). Aerobic capacity decreases in a linear fashion throughout the adult years, so that the average 65-year-old has 30%–40% of the aerobic capacity of the young adult (McArdle et al., 1991). This decrease is significantly lower, however, in very active people, amounting to 5% to 7% per decade (Trappe, Costill, Vukovich, Jones, & Melham, 1996).

Psychological and clinical implications. Although not as apparent in its effects on identity as appearance, the functioning of the cardiovascular system is an important influence on the individual's feelings of well-being and identity. The efficiency of the cardiovascular system is essential to life, so that threats to the integrity of this system are perceived as highly dangerous. Awareness of reduced cardiovascular efficiency can therefore serve as a reminder of one's own personal mortality.

There is a wealth of research pointing to the effectiveness of exercise in slowing or reversing the effects of the aging process. The results of research on the effectiveness of exercise training have consistently revealed improved functioning in long-term endurance athletes, master athletes, exercisers, and previously sedentary adults (Whitbourne, 1996a). Even moderate- or low-intensity exercise can have beneficial effects on healthy sedentary older people (Hamdorf, Withers, Penhall, & Haslam, 1992). That exercise can have such positive effects on physical functioning in old age, even if it is begun after a lifetime of sedentary patterns, provides strong evidence in favor of the view that the rate of the aging process can be significantly altered through active lifestyle choices made by the individual. A word of caution, however, as noted above, even highly trained individuals nevertheless lose aerobic capacity by the time they reach their 60s (Trappe et al., 1996).

In addition to the advantages of exercise training for the cardiovascular system, it is well established that adults who become involved in aerobic activities experience a variety of positive effects on mood, anxiety levels, and particularly feelings of mastery and control, leading to enhanced feelings of self-esteem (Hill, Storandt, & Malley, 1993). Although some researchers have demonstrated there to be positive effects of exercise on cognitive functioning (Chodzko-Zajko, Schuler, Solomon, Heinl, & Ellis, 1992), this effect is not consistently observed (Hill et al., 1993). Nevertheless, it appears clear that older adults who enter exercise training programs feel better and that this improvement in mood may be translated into other areas of functioning (Strawbridge, Cohen, Shema, & Kaplan, 1996).

A great deal has been written in the area of behavioral medicine on strategies for increasing the compliance of cardiac patients with dietary and exercise controls over the progress of their disease. In terms of the normal aging process, similar interventions might be suggested. Those individuals who deny the effects of aging must be brought to recognize that they will risk physical harm if they either fail to engage in preventative behaviors or engage in strenuous activities without proper supervision or training. In contrast, middle-aged and older individuals who overreact to what they have heard about the effects of aging on cardiovascular functioning, or perhaps to the appearance of slight symptoms, need to be given assurance that they can nevertheless continue to engage in exercise activities and that, indeed, such activities are necessary for the prevention of further and more serious health limitations. There is evidence that a diagnosis of cardiovascular disease may serve as a prompt for individuals to engage in more favorable health behaviors than do those who have no diagnosed heart condition (Fuchs, Heath, & Wheeler, 1992). It may be inferred that individuals who are able to adopt a flexible approach to their cardiovascular functioning in the absence of disease will be able to engage in positive health behaviors without going to the extremes of either denial or despondency.

Respiratory System

Age changes. The airways in the respiratory system permit gas exchange between the blood and air, making it possible for the body's cells to receive support for their metabolic activities. Aging's primary effect is to reduce the quality of gas exchange in the lungs, so that less oxygen from the outside air reaches the blood (Kenney, 1989). Aging also reduces *vital capacity*, the amount of air that is moved into and out of the lungs at maximal levels of exertion

(Reddan, 1981), and *forced expiratory volume*, the amount of air that can be breathed out during a short amount of time (W. D. F. Smith, Cunningham, Patterson, Rechnitzer, & Koval, 1992). These reductions in respiratory functioning result from changes in pulmonary structures that reduce the amount of air that can be brought into and out of the lungs, particularly under conditions of exertion (Teramoto, Fukuchi, Nagase, Matsuse, & Orimo, 1995).

Psychological and clinical implications. Age changes in respiration can lead to dyspnea and fatigue associated with exertion, sensations that can approach the intensity of a panic attack. Adding to age effects on cardiovascular functioning, changes in the respiratory system can lead the aging individual to avoid strenuous activities, a consequence that further impairs his or her cardiovascular and respiratory efficiency. Because both of these functions are so crucial to life and because shortness of breath is so frightening, the person might prematurely conclude that death waits just around the corner.

The effects of exercise training on respiratory functioning are encouraging (Blumenthal et al., 1989) but not as dramatic as are the effects on the cardiovascular system. Equally, if not more, beneficial to the respiratory function is the avoidance of cigarette smoking (Hermanson, Omenn, & Kronmal, 1988).

Taking these factors into account, clinicians may wish to treat instances of dyspnea leading to panic as overreactions and try to bring the individual to a more adaptive state through recognizing the fact that some age-related changes in breathing capacity are in fact inevitable. On the other hand, for individuals who deny the importance of factors that impede respiratory efficiency, notably cigarette smoking, steps need to be taken to increase the recognition that this behavior can accelerate the deleterious effects of aging on respiratory efficiency and feelings of comfort during exercise.

Effects of Age on Regulatory Systems

Excretory System

Age changes. There are significant and widespread changes in the structure of the kidneys, as reflected in cross-sectional studies in impaired efficiency across adulthood on every measure of renal functioning studied (Rowe, Shock, & DeFronzo, 1976); these findings are confirmed by more recent investigations (Saltzman, Kowdley, Perrone, & Russell, 1995). The loss of renal functions over the adult years is estimated at 6% per decade from age 20 and continuing into the 90s, a loss that exists in longitudinal studies as well (Shock et al., 1978). The cause of the aging of the kidney is loss of structure and function of the basic cell of the kidney, the nephron (McLachlan, Guthrie, Anderson, & Fulker, 1977). There are also independent losses in mechanisms within the kidney responsible for concentrating urine (Rowe, 1982).

The effects of aging on the bladder are of great importance to the individual's conscious experience of aging. Adults past the age of 65 years experience a reduction in the total amount of urine they can store before feeling a need to void, and more urine is retained in the bladder after the individual has attempted to empty it. These phenomena appear to be related to age changes in the connective tissue of the bladder causing the organ to lose its expandability and contractility somewhat like that which is seen in the lung. Furthermore, the recognition of the need to void may not occur until the bladder is almost or even completely filled. This means that the individual has less or perhaps no time to reach a lavatory before leakage or spillage occurs.

The most significant effect of age on the bladder is on patterns of urinary incontinence, estimated to affect 19% of women and 8% of men over the age of 60 (Herzog, Diokno, Brown, Normolle, & Brock, 1990). Women are more likely to suffer from *stress* incontinence, which refers to loss of urine at times of exertion, such as when one is laughing, sneezing, lifting, or bending, and is the result of weakness of the pelvic muscles. *Urge* incontinence, which is more prevalent in men, involves urine loss after an urge to void or lack of control over voiding with little or no warning; it is related to prostatic disease or incomplete emptying of the bladder. Among the community-dwelling elderly, each of these conditions, particularly urge incontinence, is reversible and may disappear within a year or two of its initial development (Herzog et al., 1990).

Psychological and clinical implications. Age-related changes in the bladder can be important threshold phenomena in later adulthood (Whitbourne, 1996a). Incontinence can be highly disruptive to the older individual's everyday life, causing distress and embarrassment (Hunskaar & Vinsnes, 1991). Not only do such occasions involve shame, but they feed into the association in many people's minds between "senility" and urinary incontinence. Given the many associations to urinary continence, it would not be unreasonable to suppose that even a single episode of stress incontinence could create a painful if not traumatic threshold experience. Advertisers prey on this vulnerability of older adults in commercials for adult diapers that suggest these changes to be expectable and unpreventable. Clinicians need to go to great lengths to dispel these myths. On the positive side, once identified, incontinence is a condition that in many cases can be managed if the individual is able to learn new behavioral strategies. Through behavioral techniques, sometimes involving only very simple exercises, the problem can be held in check if not reversed (Burns et al., 1993).

Age effects on renal functioning significantly affect the older person's ability to excrete medications, a fact that can be of great importance clinically. When an older person is given the same dosage of medication appropriate for a younger adult, more of the drug will remain in the bloodstream over the period of time between doses. With repeated dosages of the drug, it is more likely that toxic levels will build in the blood. Unless the dosage is adjusted, drugs may have an adverse impact instead of their intended benefits (Montgomery, 1990).

Digestive System

Age changes. The documented effects of aging on digestion in the empirical literature are remarkably minor compared with the lavish attention devoted by the popular media to the supposed inefficiencies of digestive processes in older adults. One change with age that may have implications for digestive functioning is a reduction in the metabolism of certain nutrients in the stomach and small intestine, but other structures such as the esophagus, liver, pancreas, and large intestine appear to be relatively spared by the aging process (Whitbourne, 1996a). More important than aging per se are the beliefs that people hold as communicated through the media, the social context in which food is eaten, other physical and cognitive deficiencies, and the individual's lifelong patterns of nutrition (Costello & Moser-Veillon, 1992).

Psychological implications. Changes in the digestive system at the physiological level due to aging are not likely to propel the individual over an aging threshold (Whitbourne, 1996b). Yet, so many older people have been exposed to inaccurate conceptions in the media about the aging digestive system that clinicians have an important psychoeducational role to play. In the area of digestion and, particularly, elimination, embarrassment may lead the older individual to avoid discussions of anxiety-provoking issues that if discussed and allayed, could ease these very uncomfortable feelings. Furthermore, questions about food intake are essential for clinicians to explore, because inadequate nutrition may lead to symptoms that mimic those of psychological or cognitive impairment disorders. Unchecked, a vicious circle may be created, as depression can lead to loss of interest in food and food preparation (Rosenbloom & Whittington, 1993). Conversely, the establishment of healthy dietary patterns can serve to compensate for declines in other areas of physiological functioning (Sone, 1995).

Another clinical issue related to digestion concerns fecal incontinence. Although, at least for women, there are changes in the anal sphincters that can eventually lead to incontinence (Haadem, Dahlstrom, & Ling, 1991), this condition does not affect the majority of the older population. However, older adults, particularly those who overreact to this threshold, may associate irregularities in defecation with feared diseases and the prospects of institutionalization in later life (Wald, 1990). Older persons who believe that senility is an inevitable feature of aging may regard with alarm any indication that their patterns of elimination are changing, seeing in such changes a more ominous significance that can risk putting them over the threshold. The anxiety created by this concern may contribute further to gastrointestinal problems, so that what originates as a temporary problem comes to have a more prolonged course. Interventions by clinicians that involve sensitive discussion of this very personal and potentially frightening area of daily life can be extremely beneficial to the aging individual.

Immune System

Age changes. There is substantial evidence of reduced immune system functioning across age groups of adults. T cells, which destroy antigens (foreign substances that enter the body), lose effectiveness over the adult years (Bloom, 1994; Trebilcock & Ponnappan, 1996), in part due to changes in the thymus gland. Autopsy studies have revealed that the deterioration of the thymus gland begins shortly after sexual maturity is reached, so that by the time the individual is 45–50 years old, the thymus retains only 5% to 10% of its peak mass. As a result of these changes, there are more immature T cells present both within the thymus gland and in the bloodstream. Other immune system cells, including NK cells, K cells, and macrophages, do appear to retain their functioning into old age (Bloom, 1994; Kutza, Kaye, & Murasko, 1995), and there is some evidence that the remaining T cells are able to produce an enhanced response despite their smaller numbers (Born et al., 1995).

Psychological and clinical implications. Recent investigations have been stimulated by progress in psychoneuroimmunology, a field in which the intricate connections are examined among affective states such as stress and depression, nervous system functioning, and the operation of the immune system (Kiecolt Glaser & Glaser, 1995). For example, older people with high levels of life stress have been found to experience lower T cell functioning (McNaughton, Smith, Patterson, & Grant, 1990). Conversely, social support has been demonstrated to be positively related to immune system competence measured in terms of lymphocyte numbers and response to mitogens (Thomas, Goodwin, & Goodwin, 1985). Stress also seems linked to the release of beta-endorphin, an opioid peptide released from the pituitary gland that has an analgesic effect. This process may play an important role in mediating the effects of emotions on the immune system (Antoni, 1987).

Apart from changes in the immune system that interact with psychological functioning, the lowered effectiveness of the immune system in older adults has important implications for health. The aging immune system has been linked to increased vulnerability to influenza, infections, cancer, and certain age-associated autoimmune disorders such as diabetes and atherosclerosis. A less competent immune system can put the older individual at higher risk at least to certain forms of cancer and influenza (Ershler, 1990; Miller, 1993). Clearly, the development of severe health problems can have significant effects on the individual's psychological well-being.

There are many ways in which clinicians can take advantage of the potential interactions between psychological variables and immune system functioning. The crossing of an aging threshold in any salient area of functioning, to the extent that it triggers a stressful reaction, can lead to deleterious effects on immune functioning. The individual then becomes more susceptible to immune-related conditions, further accentuating the effects of crossing the threshold. Various methods of stress reduction can help older individuals who have become overly preoccupied with changes in their body's functioning, so that more harmful effects on overall health status can be avoided.

Effects of Age on the Reproductive System and Sexuality

Female Reproductive System

Throughout her 40s, a woman's reproductive capacity becomes gradually reduced until, by the age of 50–55, it ceases altogether. Associated with the ending of the monthly phases of ovulation and menstruation is a diminution of the hormones estrogen and progesterone. Other changes in sexual functioning are related to aging of the tissues in other bodily systems, causing changes in wrinkling, body weight, and fat distribution. Changes also occur in the female genitals—changes that are significant not only for their effects on sexual functioning but also for their effects on the woman's enjoyment of sexual intercourse. The older woman may experience discomfort during intercourse due to changes in the genitals and uterus.

Despite changes in the reproductive system, the conclusion reached by Masters and Johnson nearly 30 years ago is still generally accepted: Older women are limited in their sexual gratification more by their attitudes, values, and accessibility to partners than they are by physical changes involved in aging. The sexual response cycle might be slowed down somewhat in the older woman, but the possibility of achieving orgasm is not reduced (Masters & Johnson, 1966).

Male Reproductive System

Just as women gradually lose reproductive capacity, men experience a climacteric of sorts, in which there is a reduction in the number of viable sperm they produce due to degenerative changes in the seminiferous tubules of the testes (Harman, 1978). With increasing age, men may experience changes in the prostate gland that lead to a reduction of the volume and pressure of semen expelled during ejaculation. Overgrowth or hypertrophy may occur of the glandular and connective tissue in the parts of the prostate that surround the prostatic urethra. This condition, called *benign prostatic hypertrophy*, is increasingly prevalent in men past 50 years, rising to an estimated 50% of men 80 years and older. The adjacent penile urethra may become constricted due to this overgrowth, and urinary retention may ensue. Discomfort and embarrassment may result from difficulties in urination and from the occurrence of involuntary penile erections (Masters & Johnson, 1966).

A physiological index of reproductive function that has a decidedly noticeable effect on the older man's sense of his own sexuality is that of penile erectility. Older men experience fewer nightly episodes of penile erections than do younger men (Karacan, Williams, Thornby, & Salis, 1975). By contrast, there are inconsistencies in the findings regarding increase in penile circumference during erection, with some decreases noted across age groups (Solnick & Birren, 1977), and no age differences are observed in other research (Schiavi & Schreiner-Engel, 1988).

As is true for aging women, there is a general slowing down in aging men of the progression through the human sexual response cycle. Compared with that of young adult men, orgasm is shorter and involves fewer contractions of the prostate and ejection of a smaller amount of seminal fluid (Masters & Johnson, 1970). These findings may carry some negative implications for the aging man's sexual relations. However, the gains for the older man's ability to enjoy sexuality are also compelling. He may feel less driven toward the pressure to ejaculate, be able to prolong the period of sensual enjoyment before orgasm, and have the control to coordinate his pleasure cycle to correspond more to his partner.

A man's pattern of sexuality in the earlier years of adulthood is a strong predictor of his sexuality in old age (George & Weiler, 1985), second only to health and the presence of physical disease or use of medications (Segraves & Segraves, 1995). The sexually active middle-aged man, given good health, has the potential to remain sexually active well into his later years.

Psychological and Clinical Implications

The impact of menopause depends heavily on how the woman interprets the significance of this transition, which may be met with relief or as a reminder of the inevitability of aging and mortality. Although the aging man is likely to be less preoccupied by his diminished (but not lost) reproductive capacity, he may also find age-related changes to have a negative impact on his enjoyment of sexual relations. He may overreact to aging changes, believing that his masculine prowess has failed. Furthermore, the changes he perceives in his sexual functioning may be interpreted as movement toward deterioration and death. As is true for any man (regardless of age), depression, heavy alcohol use, or career pressures may also interfere with the aging man's ability to enjoy sexual relations. Difficulties in adjusting to age changes in the sexual response cycle may present a problem if the partners are unfamiliar with the fact that sexual responsivity naturally becomes altered in later adulthood. The woman may worry that she has lost her orgasmic capacity because it takes her longer to become aroused, excited, and stimulated. The aging male may be at high risk for developing symptoms of secondary (nonphysiological) impotence.

As is true of other sensitive areas of physical functioning, the clinician's responsibility in these areas is to explore in a calm and careful manner the level of concern the individual or couple may have about their functioning. Given cohort differences in attitudes toward sexuality, it is likely that the average older person finds it difficult to discuss specific details about problems in sexual functioning. The general level of anxiety associated with sexual matters can lead to heightened potential reactions to actual age changes in physiological functioning. Furthermore, in this area perhaps more so than in any other, it might be necessary for the professional's own attitudes toward sexuality in the aged to become an area of personal focus and reflection before proceeding to the level of intervention.

Effects of Age on the Nervous System

Central Nervous System

Age changes. In the central nervous system (CNS), as in the other major organ systems, changes that are due to aging alone are difficult to separate from changes that are the result of disease (Morris & McManus, 1991). Neurofibrillary tangles and amyloid plaques are deleterious changes observed in the brains of people with Alzheimer's disease but are also found to a lesser extent in normal aging (Price, Davis, Morris, & White, 1991). There are reported decreases in acetylcholine levels in the hippocampus of normal aging individuals (E. K. Perry, Piggott, Court, Johnson, & Perry, 1993)—changes that are generally associated with Alzheimer's disease. Although there have been earlier reports of a decline in the number of neurons in the hippocampus (Ball, 1977), more recent evidence on normal aging calls these findings into question (Davies, Horwood, Issacs, & Mann, 1992). Similarly, decreased amounts of dopamine in the substantia nigra–basal ganglia pathway are reported in conjunction with the normal aging process (Cruz-Sanchez, Cardozo, & Tolosa, 1995), but these changes are hallmarks of Parkinson's disease. It is not clear whether these losses occur normally in later life and are exaggerated in the case of disease or whether they constitute discrete phenomena. Furthermore, conflicting results abound in this rapidly emerging field, such as contradictory data on age-related changes in the nucleus basalis of Meynert, a subcortical area of the brain thought to be a major contributor to age-related cortically based memory losses (Baloyannis, Costa, Psaroulis, Arzoglou, & Papasotiriou, 1994). New findings on larger samples (Leuba & Kraftsik, 1994) are also challenging some of the previously established conclusions regarding the effect of aging on cortical structures (Devaney & Johnson, 1980), such as in the primary visual cortex. As knowledge of the brain and the quality of measurement techniques continue to become refined, these contradictory findings may become resolved. For example, regional variations in neurotransmitter levels and neuron numbers may be found that account for apparent discrepancies between investigations (Mozley et al., 1996).

There are also some intriguing relationships being pursued by researchers working in the field of psychoneuroimmunology, pointing to the interaction of life experiences with age-related developmental changes in the brain. In one such investigation, it was suggested that chronic stress may lead to damage in hippocampal cells through the mediating effects of adrenal glucocorticoids (M. A. Smith, 1996).

The most significant new contributions to the literature on aging, however, are emerging from investigations using measures of brain structure and function in living individuals. Obviously, not only is it possible to relate behavioral measures to such indices but also the use of brain scans averts the many technical problems and methodological confounds that are associated with staining techniques in microscopic brain tissue samples. One of the key conclusions emerging from these studies is that there is considerable interindividual variability in patterns of brain changes. Whereas in previous studies on neuron counts throughout brain regions, researchers focused on mean changes across decades, more recent investigators using brain scans are documenting variation as well as mean changes. Thus, in one large study using magnetic image resonancing (MRI) techniques, percentages of atrophy ranging from 6% to 8% per year were reported, but it was also noted that individuals varied widely both in patterns of cortical atrophy and in ventricular enlargement (Coffey et al., 1992). Some of this variability may very well be accounted for by health status of the individual, as indicated by contrasting findings from two MRI studies of temporal lobe volume in which the declines found in one study (Convit, de Leon,

Hoptman, & Tarshish, 1995) were not observed in a second investigation of individuals selected on the basis of their excellent health (DeCarli et al., 1994). There also may be significant gender variations, as indicated in the finding of greater reductions in both the frontal and temporal lobes in men compared with women (Cowell et al., 1994). Conversely, men may be relatively spared, compared with women, in the case of the hippocampus and parietal lobes (Murphy, DeCarli, McIntosh, & Daly, 1996).

In studies of the frontal lobes using both MRI and positron-emission tomography scans, age reductions appear to be more conclusively demonstrated than in studies of other cortical areas, amounting, perhaps, to 1% per decade (DeCarli et al., 1994; De Santi, de Leon, Convit, & Tarshish, 1995). Such findings, in conjunction with alterations in the limbic system with age, are interpreted as providing a neurological basis for the behavioral observations of memory changes in older adults (Nielsen Bohlman & Knight, 1995).

Psychological and clinical implications. Aging of the CNS has direct effects on a variety of sensory, motor, and cognitive capacities and behaviors, including perception, short-term memory, fine motor coordination, and large muscle control. However, the view of the aging brain as a degenerating system does not take into account what is known about the compensatory processes of redundancy and plasticity (Diamond, 1990). The impact of these processes is most likely to occur in the association areas of the cerebral cortex, where higher order abstract thinking processes are mediated. In fact, these abilities may improve in the later years of adulthood, as the individual stores more experiences into the long-term memory association areas on which decisions and judgment are based.

Clinically, it is essential that those working with older people are knowledgeable about and sensitive to the symptoms of Alzheimer's disease, particularly as these differ from those other forms of cognitive impairment or depression. Clinicians must also be aware of the extent to which older people fear the onset of Alzheimer's disease and interpret even minor changes in cognitive functions as signs that the end is in sight. Overreactions to age changes in the cognitive domain can prove extremely damaging to the older adult's identity as a sentient being, and vigilance in this area toward any signs of deterioration is likely to be high. Conversely, serious problems may result when an individual who is experiencing early symptoms of Alzheimer's disease denies the memory or judgment problems that are interfering with daily life activities. Media attention to Alzheimer's disease, though positive in the sense of educating the public, may backfire in this domain, leaving many older people (and clinicians) with the erroneous impression that the disease is an inevitable outcome of the aging process.

Autonomic Nervous System

Age changes. Although in many aspects the autonomic nervous system (ANS) operates without significant age-related alterations throughout adulthood, there are important effects of aging on two functions served by the ANS that have a considerable impact on the individual's daily life: bodily temperature control and sleep patterns.

Individuals over the age of 65 years are known to have impaired adaptive responses to extremely hot and cold outside temperatures. The diminished response of older people to cold appears to be due to a diminished perception that the core body temperature is low (Taylor, Allsopp, & Parkes, 1995) and to an impaired vasoconstrictor response (Budd, Brotherhood, Hendrie, & Jeffery, 1991). Responses to extremes of heat are impaired due to decreased secretion by the sweat glands in the skin (Inoue et al., 1991). However, well-trained older men with greater aerobic power seem to be less susceptible to hyperthermia (Tankersley et al., 1991). Older adults also appear to be less likely to drink water under conditions of heat stress due mainly to reduced thirst sensitivity (Phillips, Bretherton, Johnston, & Gray, 1991), a phenomenon that could contribute to less efficient behavioral responses to overheating.

Older adults spend more time in bed relative to time spent asleep, due to longer time taken to fall asleep, more periods of wakefulness during the night, and time spent lying awake before arising in the morning (Bliwise, 1992). The primary causes of sleep disturbance include sleep apnea (Ancoli-Israel & Kripke, 1991), periodic leg movements, heartburn, and frequent needs to urinate (Friedman et al., 1992). Electroencephalograph sleep patterns show some corresponding age alterations, including a rise in Stage 1 sleep and a large decrease in Stage 4 sleep. By the 60s and 70s, REM sleep starts to diminish, as do the observable behaviors associated with REM sleep. Perhaps related to changes in sleep patterns is the preference for (Atkinson & Reilly, 1995) and actual superiority of (Harma, 1996) work performed in the morning by older adults.

Psychological and clinical implications. The knowledge gained from personal experience and media exposure that one's aging body is less adaptable to outside temperatures means that adults living in geographical areas with cold winters and hot summers may restrict their outdoor activities and spend more time at home. An overreaction to this information can reduce the well-being of the older adult who may unnecessarily feel forced to remain indoors even on days when the temperature would not pose a threat. Conversely, for the older adult to ignore completely actual age changes in temperature control can lead to deleterious effects when the older adult does not take precautions during physical exertion or when venturing out into a very hot or very cold day. Fortunately, the changes in the ANS described here occur gradually over a period of years. Consequently, there are many opportunities for the individual to learn to adjust to the effects of aging and find new behavioral accommodations as these become necessary.

Similarly, the function of sleep in everyday life is clearly crucial to the individual's sense of well-being, and there is a strong relationship between quality of sleep and psychological symptoms (Hays, Blazer, & Foley, 1996). Given the sensitivity of sleep patterns to psychological distress, this is an area where identity–age change relationships might very profitably be discussed in therapy. Older adults who overreact to slight sleep change patterns are perhaps the ones fated to experience the most significant changes in their ability to get a good night's sleep. They need to be given the information that a night's sleep need not consist of more than 7 hr and that the longer the time spent in bed awake, the harder it will be to develop a normal nightly rhythm based on this more realistic sleep requirement. It is also important for the older individual to develop healthy sleep habits (B. W. Riedel, Lichstein, & Dwyer, 1995) and, especially, to avoid daytime naps, because these interfere with nighttime sleep (Hays et al., 1996).

Effects of Age on Sensory Functioning

Vision

Age changes. The effects of normal aging on the retina, lens, and vitreous humor have a cumulative effect of reducing the clarity of the visual image reaching the retina. Changes in the lens decrease its capacity to accommodate to necessary changes in focus as objects move closer or further away. In addition to becoming denser, the lens fibers become harder and less elastic (Paterson, 1979), and the nucleus of the lens moves forward in the capsule (Cook, Koretz, Pfahnl, Hyun, & Kaufman, 1994). The loss of accommodative power of the lens due to these changes, referred to as *presbyopia*, is a condition that typically requires correction between the ages of 40 to 50. By the age of 60, the lens is completely incapable of accommodating to focus on objects at close distance (Moses, 1981). The lens also yellows due to an accumulation of yellow pigment; as a result, the older adult is less able to discriminate colors in the green–blue–violet end of the spectrum (Mancil & Owsley, 1988).

Visual acuity is particularly poor at low levels of illumination, such as when driving at night and when tracking moving objects (Kline, 1994). Dark adaptation is reduced, so that older adults have greater difficulty adjusting to movement from bright to dim lighting and have lower absolute levels of ability to see in the dark (McFarland, Domey, Warren, & Ward, 1960). There is also a reduction in the individual's ability to react to sudden exposure to bright light, such as a flashbulb or the headlights of an oncoming car at night (E. Wolf & Gardiner, 1965). *Stereopsis*, the perception of three-dimensional space resulting from the varying input that reaches the two eyes, is stable, at least up to age 65 years (Yekta, Pickwell, & Jenkins, 1988).

Psychological and clinical implications. Presbyopia, although reached after a gradual process of changes in the lens, is often perceived with relative suddenness by the individual (Carter, 1982). The immediacy of this apparent change, given the association that many people have between presbyopia and the infirmities of age, makes it more likely that the change will be negatively interpreted. The necessity of wearing bifocals adds the complication of requiring the individual to adjust to a new and awkward way of using corrective lenses.

Difficulties in depth perception and dark adaptation can heighten the older adult's vulnerability to falls (McMurdo & Gaskell, 1991), exacerbating changes in bone fragility and stiffness. Visual losses can increase the individual's dependence on others, interfering with the ability to complete basic tasks of living, such as driving, housekeeping, grocery shopping, and food preparation (Rudberg, Furner, Dunn, & Cassel, 1993). Age changes in vision can also detract from the older adult's ability to enjoy leisure and aesthetic activities, and even to choose appropriate clothes (Morgan, 1988). Although not a serious problem compared with difficulties in driving, such changes can be annoying and perhaps lead to derision by others. Other leisure activities involving the perception of color and fine detail may be interfered with, such as needlepoint, gardening, word puzzles, and painting. Loss of the ability to enjoy these activities adds further to the threshold experience that may be crossed each time a new visual function is altered or affected by aging.

A number of changes in visual functioning can, fortunately, be compensated by corrective lenses, increases in the ambient lighting, efforts to reduce glare and heighten contrast between light and dark, and corrective surgery for cataracts (Brenner, Curbow, Javitt, Legro, & Sommer, 1993). The success of these efforts depends on the individual's willingness to persist in trying new solutions, a process that might be enhanced through clinical intervention. Nevertheless, a point may be reached within each sphere of functioning in which the individual's range of movement becomes compromised. Furthermore, the situation may not permit compensation, as is true for night driving. Again, clinical sensitivity plays an important role in helping the older person accommodate to age-related changes in these valued functions.

Hearing

Age changes. Presbycusis, the general term used to refer to age-related hearing loss, includes several specific subtypes reflecting different changes in the auditory structures. The most common form of presbycusis reduces sensitivity to high-frequency tones earlier and more severely than sensitivity to low-frequency tones (Van-Rooij & Plomp, 1990), a loss that is particularly pronounced in men (Lebo & Reddell, 1972). Speech perception is affected both by the various forms of presbycusis operating at the sensory level and by changes in the central processing of auditory information at the level of the brain stem and above (Van-Rooij & Plomp, 1992). Age effects begin to appear even as early as 40 years in the understanding of sentences under a variety of distorting conditions, particularly when the speech signal is interrupted (Bergman et al., 1976). Other conditions that impair speech perception in older people include higher rate of presentation, deletion of parts of the message, competition from background noise or competing messages, and reverberation (Neils, Newman, Hill, & Weiler, 1991).

Psychological and clinical implications. Hearing deficits greatly interfere with interpersonal communication, leading to strained relationships and greater caution by the older person, in an attempt to avoid making inappropriate responses to uncertain auditory signals. They also reduce the older person's ability to hear noises such as a siren or a door knock (Gatehouse, 1990).

Furthermore, hearing deficits can indirectly affect cognitive processes. Listening is more effortful for the older adult with hearing loss and, consequently, is more draining of cognitive resources (Pichora-Fuller, Schneider, & Daneman, 1995). These changes are almost impossible to avoid noticing (Slawinski, Hartel, & Kline, 1993), and it is perhaps for this reason that hearing loss forms a threshold for a large percentage of individuals over the age of 70 and particularly those in their 80s (Whitbourne, 1996b). There is evidence linking hearing loss to impaired physical functioning (Ives, Bonino, Traven, & Kuller, 1995) and psychological difficulties including loneliness (Christian, Dluhy, & O'Neill, 1989) and depression (Kalayam, Alexopoulos, Merrell, & Young, 1991).

Clinicians and others who interact with hearing-impaired older people can benefit from learning ways to communicate that lessen the impact of age-related changes (Slawinski et al., 1993). Modulating one's tone of voice, particularly for women, so that it is not too high and avoiding distractions or interference can be important aids to communicating clearly with older adults (Souza & Hoyer, 1996). The clinician can also use observations of the older client's reaction to communication difficulties in therapy as the basis for clinical recommendations. For example, a client who denies the existence of an obvious hearing deficit should be made aware of this problem through sensitive clinical intervention.

Balance

Age changes. A number of age-related changes in the vestibular system combine to produce increased dizziness and vertigo in older people (Toglia, 1975). Not only are these sensations unpleasant but also they can increase the likelihood of accidental falls. Dizziness may also be exacerbated or caused by psychological disorders, use of certain medications, and physical illnesses including cardiac and vascular problems (Anderson, Yolton, Reinke, & Kohl, 1995).

Psychological and clinical implications. Balance is an essential element of moving about effectively in the environment. Aging of the vestibular system brings with it the potential for the individual to feel insecure in moving, particularly under conditions that are less than ideal, such as sloping, steep, or uneven surfaces. Fear of falling due to other changes in mobility can increase the individual's anxiety and perhaps exacerbate any true deficits in vestibular functioning (Maki, Holliday, & Topper, 1991; Myers et al., 1996). Conversely, individuals who ignore signs of dizziness and vertigo may place themselves in danger, as they may not be able to avoid a fall when and if they do lose their balance. There are social consequences of aging of the vestibular system as well. The older adult who experiences dizziness and vertigo may fear appearing disoriented in front of other people, perhaps due to concern about appearing intoxicated or mentally confused. A desire to avoid such embarrassment may lead the individual to avoid leaving the home, creating unnecessary limitations on social opportunities.

Nevertheless, vestibular dysfunction is not an inevitable consequence of the aging of the vestibular system, and compensation is possible if the individual is able to adapt other sensory systems to make up for vestibular losses (Lord, Clark, & Webster, 1991). Such compensation seems to be more likely to occur if the individual is able to react in a constructive manner to the experience of dizziness or vertigo. The clinician can encourage the older individual to benefit from the coping strategies that involve seeking other cues, such as those provided by the somesthetic system. During episodes of dizziness or vertigo, the individual can learn to pay attention to stance and bodily orientation, learning to judge the position of the lower body limbs to make better use of feedback in adjusting posture (Hu & Woollacott, 1994a, 1994b). Balance training and Tai Chi, mentioned earlier in the context of changes in mobility, can also be of great value in fall prevention (Province et al., 1995; Wolfson et al., 1996).

Taste and Smell

Age changes. Nutritional concerns are of particular importance for older adults, who are at risk for health problems due to altered functioning in a variety of bodily systems. Age-related changes in taste present the risk of lowering the older individual's enjoyment of food and therefore the motivation to eat a balanced diet. Although there are general decreases in taste sensitivity across age groups of older adults, there is nevertheless wide variability across individuals and within the same individual among the four primary tastes (Stevens, Cruz, Hoffman, & Patterson, 1995). Similarly, although there are general cross-sectional decreases in the ability to recognize and detect odors, individuals vary in odor detection due to differences in the older population in health status (Weiffenbach & Bartoshuk, 1992). Different odors also show differential sensitivity to age effects (Wysocki & Gilbert, 1989).

Contributing to the observed age differences in sensitivity to taste and smell are apparent cognitive differences in the ability to identify odors and food tastes (Corwin, 1992; Russell et al., 1993). Age effects in these higher order cognitive and perceptual processes may lead to a distorted picture of the effects of aging on the sensory processes involved in taste and smell.

Psychological and clinical implications. The ability to enjoy food is vitally important not only to the individual's health but also to the ability to enjoy the sensory pleasures associated with the experience of eating. Thus, to the extent that the individual suffers age-related changes in taste and smell, a potentially satisfying aspect of daily life is lost. The real or perceived effects of aging on digestive functioning can further accentuate any sensory losses. On the other hand, age changes in taste and smell are neither inevitable nor universal, and there is tremendous variation among older adults based on their health habits and past eating patterns. Furthermore, laboratory studies of functioning in the areas of taste and smell, involving threshold levels of detection, may present an exaggerated picture of age losses as they are experienced in everyday life.

Age-related changes in smell, in particular, may have another set of implications for the individual's daily functioning. Older adults who have lost olfactory sensitivity may not be able to detect the presence of dangerous odors in the home, due, for example, to leakage of natural gas from a faulty heating system or stove. Similarly, they may fail to be sensitive to the foul taste of spoiled food (Whitbourne, 1996a). Again, most older individuals are able to detect smells that are above threshold levels; precipitous losses occurring in this area of functioning may signal a more serious underlying medical condition in need of clinical attention.

Conclusion

In this chapter, a number of age-related changes have been described that occur throughout the body's organ systems and sensory processes. The multiple threshold model postulates that an individual's reactions to these changes vary according to how central the area of functioning is to identity as well as how the individual approaches the age change. Older adults who overreact to physical changes may experience an unnecessary and potentially harmful sense of discouragement or despair. Conversely, those who deny or minimize the presence of age-related limitations in physical functioning may place themselves at risk due to overexertion or failure to take preventative actions.

Authors in the field of gerontology have, for years, advised professionals to examine their own age biases and attitudes toward older people. This admonition definitely applies with regard to the aging of the body, because professionals who are a product of Western culture have undoubtedly acquired a number of negative attitudes toward the loss of functioning that is so generally associated with old age. Less well recognized, though, is the need for the clinician to examine his or her own personal aging thresholds and take these into account when dealing with older individuals.

Finally, it is crucial for clinicians to recognize the independence, autonomy, and vitality of spirit seen in many older people, even those with severe losses or age-related limitations. They are coping daily with physical changes that would daunt the younger professional or specialist. Gerontologists who condescend to older people or patronize them (perhaps as a result of their own fears of aging) are missing important opportunities for intervention as well as important opportunities to learn from the wisdom of their elders.

References

Ancoli-Israel, S., & Kripke, D. F. (1991). Prevalent sleep problems in the aged. *Biofeedback and Self Regulation, 16*, 349–359.

Anderson, D. C., Yolton, R. L., Reinke, A. R., & Kohl, P. (1995). The dizzy patient: A review of etiology, differential diagnosis, and management. *Journal of the American Optometric Association, 66*, 545–558.

Antoni, M. H. (1987). Neuroendocrine influences in psychoimmunology and neoplasia: A review. *Psychology and Health, 1*, 3–24.

Arrighi, J. A., Dilsizian, V., Perrone Filardi, P., Diodati, J. G., Bacharach, S. L., & Bonow, R. O. (1994). Improvement of the age-related impairment in left ventricular diastolic filling with verapamil in the normal human heart. *Circulation, 90*, 213–219.

Atkinson, G., & Reilly, T. (1995). Effects of age and time of day on preferred work rates during prolonged exercise. *Chronobiology International, 12*, 121–134.

Ball, M. J. (1977). Neuronal loss, neurofibrillary tangles and granuovacuolar degeneration in the hippocampus with ageing and dementia. *Acta Neuropathologica, 37*, 111–118.

Baloyannis, S. J., Costa, V., Psaroulis, D., Arzoglou, L., & Papasotiriou, M. (1994). The nucleus basalis of Meynert of the human brain: A Golgi and electron microscope study. *International Journal of Neuroscience, 78*, 33–41.

Baumgartner, R. N., Heymsfield, S. B., & Roche, A. F. (1995). Human body composition and the epidemiology of chronic disease. *Obesity Research, 3*, 73–95.

Bergman, M., Blumenfeld, V. G., Cascardo, D., Dash, B., Levitt, H., & Margulies, M. K. (1976). Age-related decrement in hearing for speech: Sampling and longitudinal studies. *Journal of Gerontology, 31*, 533–538.

Bliwise, N. G. (1992). Factors related to sleep quality in healthy elderly women. *Psychology and Aging, 7*, 83–88.

Bloom, E. T. (1994). Natural killer cells, lymphokine-activated killer cells, and cytolytic T lymphocytes: Compartmentalization of age-related changes in cytolytic lymphocytes? *Journal of Gerontology: Biological Sciences, 49*, B85–B92.

Blumenthal, J. A., Emery, G. F., Madden, D. J., George, L. K., Coleman, R. E., Riddle, M. W., McKee, D. C., Reasoner, J., & Williams, R. S. (1989). Cardiovascular and behavioral effects of aerobic exercise training in healthy older men and women. *Journal of Gerontology: Medical Sciences, 44*, M147–M157.

Born, J., Uthgenannt, D., Dodt, C., Nunninghoff, D., Ringvolt, E., Wagner, T., & Fehm, H. L. (1995). Cytokine production and lymphocyte subpopulations in aged humans: An assessment during nocturnal sleep. *Mechanisms of Ageing and Development, 84*, 113–126.

Brenner, M. H., Curbow, B., Javitt, J. C., Legro, M. W., & Sommer, A. (1993). Vision change and quality of life in the elderly: Response to cataract surgery and treatment of other chronic ocular conditions. *Archives of Ophthalmology, 3*, 680–685.

Budd, G. M., Brotherhood, J. R., Hendrie, A. L., & Jeffery, S. E. (1991). Effects of fitness, fatness, and age on men's responses to whole body cooling in air. *Journal of Applied Physiology, 71*, 2387–2393.

Burns, P. A., Pranikoff, K., Nochajski, T. H., Hadley, E. C., Levy, K. J., & Ory, M. G. (1993). A comparison of effectiveness of biofeedback and pelvic muscle exercise treatment of stress incontinence in older community-dwelling women. *Journal of Gerontology: Medical Sciences, 38*, M167–M174.

Campbell, W. W., Crim, M. C., Young, V. R., & Evans, W. J. (1994). Increased energy requirements and changes in body composition with resistance training in older adults. *American Journal of Clinical Nutrition, 60*, 167–175.

Carter, J. H. (1982). Predicting visual responses to increasing age. *Journal of the American Optometric Association, 53*, 31–36.

Chodzko-Zajko, W. J., Schuler, P., Solomon, J., Heinl, B., & Ellis, N. R. (1992). The influence of physical fitness on automatic and effortful memory changes in aging. *International Journal of Aging and Human Development, 35*, 265–285.

Christian, E., Dluhy, N., & O'Neill, R. (1989). Sounds of silence: Coping with hearing loss and loneliness. *Journal of Gerontological Nursing, 15*, 4–9.

Clarke, B. L., Ebeling, P. R., Jones, J. D., Wahner, H. W., Riggs, B. L., & Fitzpatrick, L. A. (1996). Changes in quantitative bone histomorphometry in aging healthy men. *Journal of Clinical Endocrinology and Metabolism, 81*, 2264–2270.

Coffey, C. E., Wilkinson, W. E., Parashos, I. A., Soady, S. A., Sullivan, R. J., Patterson, L. J., Figiel, G. S., Webb, M. C., Spritzer, C. E., & Djang, W. T. (1992). Quantitative cerebral anatomy of the aging human brain: A cross-sectional study using magnetic resonance imaging. *Neurology, 42*, 527–536.

Convit, A., de Leon, M. J., Hoptman, M. J., & Tarshish, C. (1995). Age-related changes in brain: I. Magnetic resonance imaging measures of temporal lobe volumes in normal subjects. *Psychiatric Quarterly, 66*, 343–355.

Cook, C. A., Koretz, J. F., Pfahnl, A., Hyun, J., & Kaufman, P. L. (1994). Aging of the human crystalline lens and anterior segment. *Vision Research, 34*, 2945–2954.

Corwin, J. (1992). Assessing olfaction: Cognitive and measurement issues. In M. J. Serby & K. L. Chobor (Eds.), *Science of olfaction* (pp. 335–354). Berlin, Germany: Springer-Verlag.

Costello, R. B., & Moser-Veillon, P. B. (1992). A review of magnesium intake in the elderly. A cause for concern? *Magnesium Research, 5*, 61–67.

Courtney, A. C., Hayes, W. C., & Gibson, L. J. (1996). Age-related differences in post-yield damage in human cortical bone: Experiment and model. *Journal of Biomechanics, 29*, 1463–1471.

Cowell, P. E., Turetsky, B. I., Gur, R. C., Grossman, R. I., Shtasel, D. L., & Gur, R. E. (1994). Sex differences in aging of the human frontal and temporal lobes. *Journal of Neuroscience, 14*, 4748–4755.

Cruz Sanchez, F. F., Cardozo, A., & Tolosa, E. (1995). Neuronal changes in the substantia nigra with aging: A Golgi study. *Journal of Neuropathology and Experimental Neurology, 54*, 74–81.

Currey, J. D., Brear, K., & Zioupos, P. (1996). The effects of ageing and changes in mineral content in degrading the toughness of human femora. *Journal of Biomechanics, 29*, 257–260.

Dargent, P., & Breart, G. (1993). Epidemiology and risk factors of osteoporosis. *Current Opinions in Rheumatology, 5*, 339–345.

Davies, D. C., Horwood, N., Isaacs, S. L., & Mann, D. M. (1992). The effect of age and Alzheimer's disease on pyramidal neuron density in the individual fields of the hippocampal formation. *Acta Neuropathologica Berlin, 83*, 510–517.

Dawson-Hughes, B. (1996). Calcium and vitamin D nutritional needs of elderly women. *Journal of Nutrition, 126*, 1165s–1167s.

DeCarli, C., Murphy, D. G., Gillette, J. A., Haxby, J. V., Teichberg, D., Schapiro, M. B., & Horwitz, B. (1994). Lack of age-related differences in temporal lobe volume of very healthy adults. *American Journal of Neuroradiology, 15*, 689–696.

de Groot, C. P., Perdigao, A. L., & Deurenberg, P. (1996). Longitudinal changes in anthropometric characteristics of elderly Europeans. SENECA Investigators. *European Journal of Clinical Nutrition, 50*, 2954–3007.

De Santi, S., de Leon, M. J., Convit, A., & Tarshish, C. (1995). Age-related changes in brain: II. Positron emission tomography of frontal and temporal lobe glucose metabolism in normal subjects. *Psychiatric Quarterly, 66*, 357–370.

Devaney, K. O., & Johnson, H. A. (1980). Neuron loss in the aging visual cortex in man. *Journal of Gerontology, 35*, 836–841.

Diamond, M. C. (1990). An optimistic view of the aging brain. In A. L. Goldstein (Ed.), *Biomedical advances in aging* (pp. 441–449). New York: Plenum.

Ditre, C. M., Griffin, T. D., Murphy, G. F., Sueki, H., Telegan, B., Johnson, W. C., Yu, R. J., & Van Scott, E. J. (1996). Effects of alpha-hydroxy acids on photoaged skin: A pilot clinical, histologic, and ultrastructural study. *Journal of the American Academy of Dermatology, 34*, 187–195.

Ershler, W. B. (1990). Influenza and aging. In A. L. Goldstein (Ed.), *Biomedical advances in aging* (pp. 513–521). New York: Plenum.

Fenske, N. A., & Albers, S. E. (1990). Cosmetic modalities for aging skin: What to tell patients. *Geriatrics, 45*, 59–60.

Fiatarone, M. A., Marks, E. C., Ryan, N. D., Meredith, C. N., Lipsitz, L. A., & Evans, W. J. (1990). High-intensity strength training in nonagenarians: Effects on skeletal muscle. *Journal of the American Medical Association, 263*, 3029–3034.

Fielding, R. A. (1995). The role of progressive resistance training and nutrition in the preservation of lean body mass in the elderly. *Journal of the American College of Nutrition, 14*, 587–594.

Friedman, L. F., Bliwise, D. L., Tanke, E. D., & Salom, S. R. (1992). A survey of self-reported poor sleep and associated factors in older individuals. *Behavior, Health, and Aging, 2*, 13–20.

Fuchs, R., Heath, G. W., & Wheeler, F. C. (1992). Perceived morbidity as a determinant of health behavior. *Health Education Research, 7*, 327–334.

Garnero, P., Sornay Rendu, E., Chapuy, M. C., & Delmas, P. D. (1996). Increased bone turnover in late postmenopausal women is a major determinant of osteoporosis. *Journal of Bone and Mineral Research, 11*, 337–349.

Gatehouse, S. (1990). Determinants of self-reported disability in older subjects. *Ear and Hearing, 11*(Suppl.) 575–655.

George, L. K., & Weiler, S. J. (1985). Sexuality in middle and late life. In E. Palmore, J. Nowlin, E. Busse, I. Siegler, & G. Maddox (Eds.), *Normal aging III*. Durham, NC: Duke University Press.

Grinker, J. A., Tucker, K., Vokonas, P. S., & Rush, D. (1995). Body habitus changes among adult males from the normative aging study: Relations to aging, smoking history and alcohol intake. *Obesity Research, 3*, 435–446.

Haadem, K., Dahlstrom, J. A., & Ling, L. (1991). Anal sphincter competence in healthy women: Clinical implications of age and other factors. *Obstetrics and Gynecology, 78*, 823–827.

Hamdorf, P. A., Withers, R. T., Penhall, R. K., & Haslam, M. V. (1992). Physical training effects on the fitness and habitual activity patterns of elderly women. *Archives of Physical Medicine and Rehabilitation, 73*, 603–608.

Harma, M. (1996). Ageing, physical fitness and shiftwork tolerance. *Applied Ergonomics, 27*, 25–29.

Harman, S. M. (1978). Clinical aspects of the male reproductive system. In E. L. Schneider (Ed.), *Aging: Vol. 4. The aging reproductive system.* New York: Raven Press.

Hays, J. C., Blazer, D. G., & Foley, D. J. (1996). Risk of napping: Excessive daytime sleepiness and mortality in an older community population. *Journal of the American Geriatrics Society, 44*, 693–698.

Heiss, G., Tamir, I., Davis, C. E., Tyroler, H. A., Rifkind, B. M., Schonfeld, G., Jacobs, D., & Frantz, I. D. J. (1980). Lipoprotein–cholesterol distributions in selected North American populations: The Lipid Research Clinics Program Prevalence Study. *Circulation, 61*, 302–315.

Hermanson, B., Omenn, G. S., & Kronmal, R. A. (1988). Beneficial six-year outcome of smoking cessation in older men and women with coronary artery disease. *New England Journal of Medicine, 24*, 1365–1392.

Herzog, A. R., Diokno, A. C., Brown, M. B., Normolle, D. P., & Brock, B. M. (1990). Two-year incidence, remission, and change patterns of urinary incontinence in noninstitutionalized older adults. *Journal of Gerontology: Medical Sciences, 45*, M67–M74.

Hill, R. D., Storandt, M., & Malley, M. (1993). The impact of long-term exercise training on psychological function in older adults. *Journal of Gerontology: Psychological Sciences, 48*, P12–P17.

Hu, M.-H., & Woollacott, M. H. (1994a). Multisensory training of standing balance in older adults: I. Postural stability and one-leg stance balance. *Journal of Gerontology: Medical Sciences, 49*, M52–M61.

Hu, M.-H., & Woollacott, M. H. (1994b). Multisensory training of standing balance in older adults: II. Kinetic and electromyographic postural responses. *Journal of Gerontology: Medical Sciences, 49*, M62–M71.

Hughes, S. L., Edelman, P. L., Singer, R. H., & Chang, R. W. (1993). Joint impairment and self-reported disability in elderly persons. *Journal of Gerontology: Social Sciences, 48*, S84–S92.

Hunskaar, S., & Vinsnes, A. (1991). The quality of life in women with urinary incontinence as measured by the Sickness Impact Profile. *Journal of the American Geriatrics Society, 39*, 378–382.

Iida, I., & Noro, K. (1995). An analysis of the reduction of elasticity on the ageing of human skin and the recovering effect of a facial massage. *Ergonomics, 38*, 1921–1931.

Inoue, Y., Nakao, M., Araki, T., & Murakami, H. (1991). Regional differences in the sweating responses of older and younger men. *Journal of Applied Physiology, 71*, 2453–2459.

Ives, D. G., Bonino, P., Traven, N. D., & Kuller, L. H. (1995). Characteristics and comorbidities of rural older adults with hearing impairment. *Journal of the American Geriatrics Society, 43*, 803–806.

Jirovec, M. M. (1991). The impact of daily exercise on the mobility, balance and urine control of cognitively impaired nursing home residents. *International Journal of Nursing Studies, 28*, 145–151.

Kalayam, B., Alexopoulos, G. S., Merrell, H. B., & Young, R. C. (1991). Patterns of hearing loss and psychiatric morbidity in elderly patients attending a hearing clinic. *International Journal of Geriatric Psychiatry, 6*, 131–136.

Karacan, I., Williams, R. L., Thornby, J. I., & Salis, P. J. (1975). Sleep-related penile tumescence as a function of age. *American Journal of Psychiatry, 132*, 932–937.

Kenney, A. R. (1989). *Physiology of aging* (2nd ed.). Chicago: Yearbook Medical.

Kiecolt Glaser, J. K., & Glaser, R. (1995). Psychoneuroimmunology and health consequences: Data and shared mechanisms. *Psychosomatic Medicine, 57*, 269–274.

Kitzman, D. W., & Edwards, W. D. (1990). Age-related changes in the anatomy of the normal human heart. *Journal of Gerontology: Medical Sciences, 45*, M33–M39.

Kleinsmith, D. M., & Perricone, N. V. (1989). Common skin problems in the elderly. *Clinics in Geriatric Medicine, 5*, 189–211.

Kligman, A. M. (1989). Psychological aspects of skin disorders in the elderly. *Cutis, 43*, 498–501.

Kline, D. W. (1994). Optimizing the visibility of displays for older observers. *Experimental Aging Research, 20*, 11–23.

Krall, E. A., & Dawson-Hughes, B. (1993). Heritable and life-style determinants of bone mineral density. *Journal of Bone Mineral Research, 8*, 1–9.

Kurban, R. S., & Bhawan, J. (1990). Histologic changes in skin associated with aging. *Journal of Dermatology and Surgical Oncology, 16*, 908–914.

Kutza, J., Kaye, D., & Murasko, D. M. (1995). Basal natural killer cell activity of young versus elderly humans. *Journal of Gerontology: Biological Sciences, 50A*, B110–B116.

Lakatta, E. G. (1987). Why cardiovascular function may decline with age. *Geriatrics, 42*, 84–94.

Lebo, C. P., & Reddell, R. C. (1972). The presbycusis component in occupational hearing loss. *Laryngoscope, 82*, 1399–1409.

Leuba, G., & Kraftsik, R. (1994). Changes in volume, surface estimate, three-dimensional shape and total number of neurons of the human primary visual cortex from midgestation until old age. *Anatomy and Embryology Berlin, 190*, 351–366.

Lord, S. R., Clark, R. D., & Webster, I. W. (1991). Physiological factors associated with falls in an elderly population. *Journal of the American Geriatrics Society, 39*, 1194–1200.

Maki, B. E., Holliday, P. J., & Topper, A. K. (1991). Fear of falling and postural performance in the elderly. *Journal of Gerontology: Medical Sciences, 46*, M123–M131.

Mancil, G. L., & Owsley, C. (1988). "Vision through my aging eyes" revisited. *Journal of the American Optometric Association, 59*, 288–294.

Masters, W. H., & Johnson, V. E. (1966). *Human sexual response*. Boston: Little, Brown.

Masters, W. H., & Johnson, V. E. (1970). *Human sexual inadequacy*. Boston: Little, Brown.

McArdle, W. D., Katch, F. I., & Katch, V. L. (1991). *Exercise physiology: Energy, nutrition, and human performance* (3rd ed.). Philadelphia: Lea & Ferbiger.

McCalden, R. W., McGeough, J. A., Barker, M. B., & Court-Brown, C. M. (1993). Age-related changes in the tensile properties of cortical bone: The relative importance of changes in porosity, mineralization, and microstructure. *Journal of Bone and Joint Surgery, 75*, 1193–1205.

McFarland, R. A., Domey, R. G., Warren, A. B., & Ward, D. C. (1960). Dark adaptation as a function of age: I. A statistical analysis. *Journal of Gerontology, 15*, 149–154.

McLachlan, M. S. F., Guthrie, J. C., Anderson, C. K., & Fulker, M. J. (1977). Vascular and glomerular changes in the aging kidney. *Journal of Pathology, 121*, 65–78.

McMurdo, M. E., & Gaskell, A. (1991). Dark adaptation and falls in the elderly. *Gerontology, 37*, 221–224.

McNaughton, M. E., Smith, L. W., Patterson, T. L., & Grant, I. (1990). Stress, social support, coping resources, and immune status in elderly women. *Journal of Nervous and Mental Disease, 178*, 460–461.

Meltzer, D. E. (1996). Body-mass dependence of age-related deterioration in human muscular function. *Journal of Applied Physiology, 80*, 1149–1155.

Miller, R. A. (1993). Aging and cancer—Another perspective. *Journal of Gerontology: Biological Sciences, 48*, B8–B9.

Montgomery, S. A. (1990). Depression in the elderly: Pharmacokinetics of antidepressants and death from overdose. *International Clinical Psychopharmacology, 5*, 67–76.

Morgan, M. W. (1988). Vision through my aging eyes. *Journal of the American Optometric Association, 59*, 278–280.

Morris, J. C., & McManus, D. Q. (1991). The neurology of aging: Normal versus pathologic change. *Geriatrics, 46*, 47–48.

Moses, R. A. (1981). Accommodation. In R. A. Moses (Ed.), *Adler's physiology of the eye*. St. Louis, MO: Mosby.

Mozley, P. D., Kim, H. J., Gur, R. C., Tatsch, K., Muenz, L. R., McElgin, W. T., Kung, M. P., Mu, M., Myers, A. M., & Kung, H. F. (1996). Iodine-123-IPT SPECT imaging of CNS dopamine transporters: Nonlinear effects of normal aging on striatal uptake values. *Journal of Nuclear Medicine, 37*, 1965–1970.

Murphy, D. G. M., DeCarli, C., McIntosh, A. R., & Daly, E. (1996). Sex differences in human brain morphometry and metabolism: An in vivo quantitative magnetic resonance imaging and positron emission tomography study on the effect of aging. *Archives of General Psychiatry, 53*, 585–594.

Myers, A. M., Powell, L. E., Maki, B. E., Holliday, P. J., Brawley, L. R., & Sherk, W. (1996). Psychological indicators of balance confidence: Relationship to actual and perceived abilities. *Journal of Gerontology: Medical Sciences, 51*, M37–M43.

Nachbar, F., & Korting, H. C. (1995). The role of vitamin E in normal and damaged skin. *Journal of Molecular Medicine, 73*, 7–17.

Neils, J., Newman, C. W., Hill, M., & Weiler, E. (1991). The effects of rate, sequencing, and memory on auditory processing in the elderly. *Journal of Gerontology: Psychological Sciences, 46*, P71–P75.

Nielsen Bohlman, L., & Knight, R. T. (1995). Prefrontal alterations during memory processing in aging. *Cerebral Cortex, 5*, 541–549.

Olivetti, G., Melissari, M., Capasso, J. M., & Anversa, P. (1991). Cardiomyopathy of the aging human heart: Myocyte loss and reactive cellular hypertrophy. *Circulation Research, 68*, 1560–1568.

Ouslander, J. G., & Abelson, S. (1990). Perceptions of urinary incontinence among elderly outpatients. *Gerontologist, 30*, 369–372.

Paterson, C. A. (1979). Crystalline lens. In R. E. Records (Ed.), *Physiology of the human eye and visual system*. New York: Harper & Row.

Perry, E. K., Piggott, M. A., Court, J. A., Johnson, M., & Perry, R. H. (1993). Transmitters in the developing and senescent human brain. *Annals of the New York Academy of Science, 695*, 69–72.

Perry, H. M., III, Horowitz, M., Morley, J. E., Fleming, S., Jensen, J., Caccione, P., Miller, D. K., Kaiser, F. E., & Sundarum, M. (1996). Aging and bone metabolism in African American and Caucasian women. *Journal of Clinical Endocrinology and Metabolism, 81*, 1108–1117.

Phillips, P. A., Bretherton, M., Johnston, C. I., & Gray, L. (1991). Reduced osmotic thirst in healthy elderly men. *American Journal of Physiology, 261*, R166–R171.

Pichora-Fuller, M. K., Schneider, B. A., & Daneman, M. (1995). How young and old adults listen to and remember speech in noise. *Journal of the Acoustical Society of America, 97*, 593–608.

Price, J. L., Davis, P. B., Morris, J. C., & White, D. L. (1991). The distribution of tangles, plaques and related immunohistochemical markers in healthy aging and Alzheimer's disease. *Neurobiology of Aging, 12*, 295–312.

Province, M. A., Hadley, E. C., Hornbrook, M. C., Lipsitz, L. A., Miller, J. P., Mulrow, C. D., Ory, M. G., Sattin, R. W., Tinetti, M. E., & Wolf, S. L. (1995). The effects of exercise on falls in elderly patients: A preplanned meta-analysis of the FICSIT Trials. *Journal of the American Medical Association, 273*, 1341–1347.

Ralphs, J. R., & Benjamin, M. (1994). The joint capsule: Structure, composition, ageing and disease. *Journal of Anatomy, 184*, 503–509.

Reddan, W. G. (1981). Respiratory system and aging. In E. L. Smith & R. C. Serfass (Eds.), *Exercise and aging: The scientific basis* (pp. 89–107). Hillsdale, NJ: Erlbaum.

Rico, H., Revilla, M., Hernandez, E. R., Gonzalez-Riola, J. M., & Villa, L. F. (1993). Four-compartment model of body composition of normal elderly women. *Age and Ageing, 22*, 265–268.

Riedel, B. W., Lichstein, K. L., & Dwyer, W. O. (1995). Sleep compression and sleep education for older insomniacs: Self-help versus therapist guidance. *Psychology and Aging, 10*, 54–63.

Riedel, M., Brabant, G., Rieger, K., & von zur Muhlen, A. (1994). Growth hormone therapy in adults: Rationales, results, and perspectives. *Experimental and Clinical Endocrinology, 102*, 273–283.

Roberto, K. (1992). Coping strategies of older women with hip fractures: Resources and outcomes. *Journal of Gerontology: Psychological Sciences, 47*, P21–P26.

Rosenbloom, C. A., & Whittington, F. J. (1993). The effects of bereavement on eating behaviors and nutrient intakes in elderly widowed persons. *Journal of Gerontology: Social Sciences, 48*, S223–S229.

Rowe, J. W. (1982). Renal function and aging. In M. E. Reff & E. L. Schneider (Eds.), *Biological markers of aging* (NIH Publication No. 82-2221) Bethesda, MD: National Institutes of Health.

Rowe, J. W., Shock, N. W., & DeFronzo, R. A. (1976). The influence of age on the renal response to water deprivation in man. *Nephron, 17*, 270–278.

Rudberg, M. A., Furner, S. E., Dunn, J. E., & Cassel, C. K. (1993). The relationship of visual and hearing impairments to disability: An analysis using the longitudinal study of aging. *Journal of Gerontology: Medical Sciences, 48*, M261–M265.

Russell, M. J., Cummings, B. J., Profitt, B. F., Wysocki, C. J., Gilbert, A. N., & Cotman, C. W. (1993). Life span changes in the verbal categorization of odors. *Journal of Gerontology: Psychological Sciences, 48*, P49–P53.

Saltzman, J. R., Kowdley, K. V., Perrone, G., & Russell, R. M. (1995). Changes in small-intestine permeability with aging. *Journal of the American Geriatric Society, 43*, 160–164.

Schiavi, R. C., & Schreiner-Engel, P. (1988). Nocturnal penile tumescence in healthy aging men. *Journal of Gerontology, 43*, M146–M150.

Seeley, D. G., Kelsey, J., Jergas, M., & Nevitt, M. C. (1996). Predictors of ankle and foot fractures in older women. *Journal of Bone and Mineral Research, 11*, 1347–1355.

Segraves, R. T., & Segraves, K. B. (1995). Human sexuality and aging. *Journal of Sex Education and Therapy, 21*, 88–102.

Shephard, R. J. (1978). *Physical activity and aging.* Chicago: Yearbook Medical.

Shimojo, M., Tsuda, N., Iwasaka, T., & Inada, M. (1991). Age-related changes in aortic elasticity determined by gated radionuclide angiography in patients with systemic hypertension or healed myocardial infarcts and in normal subjects. *American Journal of Cardiology, 68*, 950–953.

Sinaki, M. (1996). Effect of physical activity on bone mass. *Current Opinions in Rheumatology, 8*, 376–383.

Skelton, D. A., Greig, C. A., Davies, J. M., & Young, A. (1994). Strength, power and related functional ability of healthy people aged 65–89 years. *Age and Ageing, 23*, 371–377.

Slawinski, E. B., Hartel, D. M., & Kline, D. W. (1993). Self-reported hearing problems in daily life throughout adulthood. *Psychology and Aging, 8*, 552–562.

Smith, M. A. (1996). Hippocampal vulnerability to stress and aging: Possible role of neurotrophic factors. *Behavioural Brain Research, 78*, 25–36.

Smith, W. D. F., Cunningham, D. A., Patterson, D. H., Rechnitzer, P. A., & Koval, J. J. (1992). Forced expiratory volume, height, and demispan in Canadian men and women aged 55–86. *Journal of Gerontology: Medical Sciences, 47*, M40–M44.

Solnick, R. L., & Birren, J. E. (1977). Age and male erectile responsiveness. *Archives of Sexual Behavior, 6*, 1–9.

Sone, Y. (1995). Age-associated problems in nutrition. *Applied Human Science, 14*, 201–210.

Souza, P. E., & Hoyer, W. J. (1996). Age-related hearing loss: Implications for counseling. *Journal of Counseling and Development, 74*, 652–655.

Stamford, B. A. (1988). Exercise in the elderly. In K. B. Pandolf (Ed.), *Exercise and sports sciences reviews* (Vol. 16). New York: Macmillan.

Stevens, J. C., Cruz, L. A., Hoffman, J. M., & Patterson, M. Q. (1995). Taste sensitivity and aging: High incidence of decline revealed by repeated threshold measures. *Chemical Senses, 20*, 451–459.

Strawbridge, W. J., Cohen, R. D., Shema, S. J., & Kaplan, G. A. (1996). Successful aging: Predictors and associated activities. *American Journal of Epidemiology, 144*, 135–141.

Taaffe, D. R., Jin, I. H., Vu, T. H., Hoffman, A. R., & Marcus, R. (1996). Lack of effect of recombinant human growth hormone (GH) on muscle morphology and GH-insulin-like growth factor expression in resistance-trained elderly men. *Journal of Clinical Endocrinology and Metabolism, 81*, 421–425.

Taaffe, D. R., Pruitt, L., Pyka, G., Guido, D., & Marcus, R. (1996). Comparative effects of high- and low-intensity resistance training on thigh muscle strength, fiber area, and tissue composition in elderly women. *Clinical Physiology, 16*, 381–392.

Takema, Y., Yorimoto, Y., Kawai, M., & Imokawa, G. (1994). Age-related changes in the elastic properties and thickness of human facial skin. *British Journal of Dermatology, 131*, 641–648.

Tankersley, C. G., Smolander, J., Kenney, W. L., & Fortney, S. M. (1991). Sweating and skin blood flow during exercise: Effects of age and maximal oxygen uptake. *Journal of Applied Physiology, 71*, 236–242.

Taylor, N. A., Allsopp, N. K., & Parkes, D. G. (1995). Preferred room temperature of young vs aged males: The influence of thermal sensation, thermal comfort, and affect. *Journal of Gerontology: Medical Sciences, 50*, M216–M221.

Teramoto, S., Fukuchi, Y., Nagase, T., Matsuse, T., & Orimo, H. (1995). A comparison of ventilation components in young and elderly men during exercise. *Journal of Gerontology: Biological Sciences, 50A*, B34–B39.

Thomas, P. D., Goodwin, J. M., & Goodwin, J. W. (1985). Effect of social support on stress-related changes in cholesterol, uric acid level, and immune function in an elderly sample. *American Journal of Psychiatry, 142,* 735–737.

Tinetti, M. E., & Powell, L. (1993). Fear of falling and low self-efficacy: A cause of dependence in elderly persons. *Journals of Gerontology, 48,* 35–58.

Toglia, J. U. (1975). Dizziness in the elderly. In W. Fields (Ed.), *Neurological and sensory disorders in the elderly.* New York: Grune & Stratton.

Trappe, S. W., Costill, D. L., Vukovich, M. D., Jones, J., & Melham, T. (1996). Aging among elite distance runners: A 22-yr longitudinal study. *Journal of Applied Physiology, 80,* 285–290.

Trebilcock, G. U., & Ponnappan, U. (1996). Evidence for lowered induction of nuclear factor kappa B in activated human T lymphocytes during aging. *Gerontology, 42,* 137–146.

Vandervoort, A. A., Chesworth, B. M., Cunningham, D. A., Paterson, D. H., Rechnitzer, P. A., & Koval, J. J. (1992). Age and sex effects on mobility of the human ankle. *Journal of Gerontology: Medical Sciences, 47,* M17–M21.

Van-Rooij, J. C., & Plomp, R. (1990). Auditive and cognitive factors in speech perception by elderly listeners: II. Multivariate analyses. *Journal of the Acoustical Society of America, 88,* 2611–2624.

Van-Rooij, J. C., & Plomp, R. (1992). How much do working memory deficits contribute to age differences in discourse memory? *Journal of the Acoustical Society of America, 91,* 1028–1033.

Wald, A. (1990). Constipation and fecal incontinence in the elderly. *Gastroenterological Clinics of North America, 19,* 405–418.

Weiffenbach, J. M., & Bartoshuk, L. M. (1992). Taste and smell. *Clinics in Geriatric Medicine, 8,* 543–555.

Whitbourne, S. K. (1996a). *The aging individual: Physical and psychological perspectives.* New York: Springer.

Whitbourne, S. K. (1996b, August). *Identity processes and perceptions of physical functioning in adults: A test of the multiple threshold model.* Paper presented at the 104th Annual Convention of the American Psychological Association, Toronto, Ontario, Canada.

Wolf, E., & Gardiner, J. S. (1965). Studies on the scatter of light in the dioptric media of the eye as a basis of visual glare. *Archives of Opthalmology, 74,* 338–345.

Wolf, S. L., Barnhart, H. X., Kutner, N. G., McNeely, E., Coogler, C., & Xu, T. (1996). Reducing frailty and falls in older persons: An investigation of Tai Chi and computerized balance training. *Journal of the American Geriatrics Society, 44,* 489–497.

Wolfson, L., Whipple, R., Derby, C., Judge, J., King, M., Amerman, P., Schmidt, J., & Smyers, D. (1996). Balance and strength training in older adults: Intervention gains and Tai Chi maintenance. *Journal of the American Geriatrics Society, 44,* 498–506.

Wysocki, C. J., & Gilbert, A. N. (1989). The National Geographic smell survey: Effects of age are heterogenous. *Annals of the New York Academy of Sciences, 561,* 12–28.

Yekta, A. A., Pickwell, L. D., & Jenkins, T. C. (1988). Binocular vision, age and symptoms. *Opthalmic Physiological Optics, 9,* 115–120.

7

Coping With Aging: Individuality as a Key to Understanding

Richard S. Lazarus

It seems to me that research on the psychological characteristics of aging and old age has largely failed to promote a properly informed and wise approach to the subject. Despite the relative meaninglessness of chronological age, most research has overemphasized small differences between people who differ in age. The findings, reported as means or medians without much or any attention given to the manifold individual variations, do not describe any particular individual's aging experience. The typical research approach needs to be changed radically if we are to gain the necessary understanding, and there is much we need to learn.

I do not intend to review this research, even that which deals specifically with stress, emotion, and coping. This has recently been done well by Aldwin (1994) and authors of book chapters edited by Magai and McFadden (1996). In this essay, I try to defend my opening criticism and go beyond it. My focus is stress and emotion, especially the coping process, both in general and as it applies to aging. I begin by laying the intellectual groundwork for my later recommendations, proceed to the question of whether aging can be explained developmentally, discuss the coping process in general and misapprehensions about it, and examine methodological issues, which segue into thoughts about the most useful direction of research in the future.

Four Metatheoretical Perspectives

In accordance with the mission of clinical geropsychology, if we wish to provide services for those who are aging and to do research that can better advance our understanding of the aging process, it would be helpful to draw on four abstract metatheoretical perspectives about mind and behavior. They formalize theses I have been expressing for a long time and suggest principles for mounting future research. The perspectives deal with (a) structure and process, (b) individual differences, (c) subjectivism, and (d) relational meaning.

Structure and Process

All sciences understand the world by means of structure and process. *Structure* refers to relatively stable attributes; *process* refers to functions and change. To draw on two analogies that have didactic value, an automobile engine is made up of parts, which are organized into a complex mechanical structure that converts fuel into motion (process). A mountain range is a geological structure that directs the flow of wind and water (process), which, in turn, slowly change and erode the mountains themselves (process).

Some geological changes are slow, so over our short lifetime, we do not notice them, except perhaps temporarily in acute events, such as hurricanes, floods, volcanos, and earthquakes. The changes in an automobile engine are much more rapid—the structures wear out in short order, forcing us to replace the parts and ultimately to replace the engine. This sounds a bit like what we say about illness in old age and the constant need for preventive maintenance and bodily repair. In any event, structures and processes are interdependent, and each affects the other.

Psychological traits, which are formed earlier in life, are the structures by means of which we engage in the processes of thinking, feeling, acting, and adapting. Unlike geological and mechanical analogies, psychological structures are not observed directly, but inferred. Our theories represent reasoned, observation-based speculations about the structures and processes of the mind.

Structures and processes are opposite sides of the same coin. Each addresses a different but related question. Consider, for example, coping traits and processes. When structure dominates, the way a person copes is relatively stable over time and across different circumstances, and change is minimal; when process dominates, coping is unstable and stability is minimal. To evaluate stability and change empirically, we must use research designs that allow us to study the same persons over time and across diverse kinds of stressful encounters (intraindividual comparisons), as in longitudinal research.

Coping traits (or *styles*) refer to relatively stable dispositions to manage stress in particular ways. If the consistency of the coping process is very high, however, we can speak of the person as coping in a rigid way, which suggests defensiveness and neuroticism. Coping flexibility, which is manifest when people attune what they think, feel, and do under conditions of harm, threat, and challenge with respect to the requirements of those conditions, probably makes for the most efficacious coping.

Because the stress emotions involve life encounters whose short- or long-term status is unsatisfactory, the dominant pull under stressful conditions of life is for change. Therefore, the psychology of coping is properly biased toward processes that alter the conditions a person under stress wants to change. Strong evidence supports the position that people cope in very different ways with different harms, threats, and challenges (Folkman, Lazarus, Dunkel-Schetter, DeLongis, & Gruen, 1986; Folkman, Lazarus, Gruen, & DeLongis, 1986).

Coping also changes over time within stressful encounters (see, e.g., Folkman & Lazarus, 1985, on changes during the stages of a college examination). To use an illustration more closely related to aging and illness, as the status of a deadly cancer worsens, the person begins to cope differently and experiences a changed emotional state as the probability of death becomes a more serious prospect. Conversely, if a cancer is brought under control or reversed, the coping process changes accordingly, along with the dominant emotional state.

A process emphasis is essential to geropsychology because coping can change during the course of aging, but whether it does change for the average person is quite uncertain because of methodological problems in research on aging, which I identify later. If coping does change with age, for example, from middle to old age, we need to discover why. Even an accurate and full empirical description of patterns of psychological change does not help us understand what accounts for the change or how we get from one point in life to another. Therefore, only a process formulation allows us to address the why of change.

Individual Differences

Even under the same or very similar life circumstances, what is stressful and how we cope with it vary from person to person and group to group. Yet scientific knowledge tends to be defined normatively, in the epidemiological tradition of a search for causal variables and mechanisms in health, morale, and social functioning in various populations—defined, say, by age, gender, social class, marital status, and whether one is still working. However, even within these population subgroups, individual differences are ubiquitous and substantial.

Psychology has always been ambivalent about individual differences because, in their effort to be scientific, psychologists believe that variations among persons undermine the main tenet of science, which is to search for simplifying general principles. Individual differences suggest confusion and unpredictability and are, therefore, threatening. I regard the usual approach to psychological science as entirely too narrow, because good research also requires accurate and rich description of phenomena in all their manifestations. Kurt Lewin (1946) understood the problem well and tried to reconcile both outlooks:

> The problems of general laws and individual differences frequently appear to be unrelated questions which follow somewhat opposite lines. Any prediction, however, presupposes a consideration of both types of questions . . . problems of individual differences . . . and of general laws are closely interwoven. A [scientific] law is expressed in an equation which relates certain variables. Individual differences have to be conceived of as various specific values which these variations have in a particular case. In other words, general laws and individual differences are merely two aspects of one problem; they are mutually dependent on each other and the study of one cannot proceed without the study of the other. (p. 794)

Some years ago, while writing about psychological stress and coping in aging, Lazarus and DeLongis (1983) wrote the following about individual differences:

> To date, most of the research . . . has addressed the . . . question of whether people of different chronological ages vary in sources of stress, degree of stress, and patterns of coping. The evidence of age effects produced by this

research is relatively meager and difficult to interpret. *Aging is a highly individualized process.* (p. 245; italics added)

Nothing much has changed roughly 15 years later. I find it personally astonishing and somewhat disconcerting that at 76 years of age, and from a commonly expressed gerontological outlook, I am not merely aging but old. Most of my elderly neighbors and I feel our age in many similar ways but in many different ways too. It is a grave mistake to speak glibly about who and what are old or the way people in general age. To do so implies that a norm exists that applies to everyone, or at least most of us, defining how we should be at a given age, as if what happens when we reach the 60s, 70s, and 80s can be predicted with any precision from chronological age.

Subjectivism

Individual differences in the aging process oblige us to confront the third metatheoretical principle—namely, the need for a subjective approach to properly understand stress, coping, and emotion in aging and in life in general. Whatever we think, feel, and do is based on how we, as distinct individuals, facing our own versions of life, construe and evaluate our ongoing and changing relationships with the physical and social environment. Shakespeare expressed this dictum in the famous line spoken by Hamlet (act 2, scene 2): "There is nothing either good or bad, but thinking makes it so."

For those interested in history, in much of modern North American and British psychology, subjective approaches have been anathema. Their rejection was exacerbated from the 1920s to the 1970s by the dominance of radical behaviorism and its love affair with positivism, and to some extent even today, long after this epistemic nonsense has gone out of favor.

The change in outlook was gradual, but it began as early as the 1930s with the writings of an illustrious group of personality and social psychologists, which included Gordon Allport, Kurt Lewin, Henry Murray, and Edward Tolman. There were also important European dissident movements, such as the individual psychology of William Stern, Gestalt psychology, existentialism, phenomenology, and psychoanalysis, all of which influenced American and British thought in subsequent years.

The more recent protagonists of these movements, to name some of the most visible, include Solomon Asch, Harry Harlow, Fritz Heider, George Kelly, David McClelland, Gardner Murphy, Julian Rotter, Mutzafer Sherif, and Robert White, whose main work took place in the 1950s. The so-called New Look movement in the late 1940s and 1950s, illustrated by the work of Jerome Bruner, added to the crescendo of protest against the epistemic confines of radical behaviorism and positivism.

All this intellectual discontent paved the way for what is often referred to as the *cognitive revolution*, which was no revolution at all, because all it did was restore psychology to its long-standing emphasis, from the time of Aristotle, on rationalism and the doctrine of cognitive mediation, which are epistemologically favorable to a subjective outlook. *Cognitive mediation* means, basically, that thought or, more broadly speaking, mind (which also includes motivation and emotion) stands between the environmental stimulus and the reaction and that it shapes that reaction.

With respect to aging, well-known psychologically oriented gerontologists, such as Butler (1975), have emphasized that aging people, more than young ones, try to make sense out of what has happened in their life and try to achieve a sense of order and continuity. This struggle centers on divergent personal beliefs about self and world and highly individual goal commitments, which influence our appraisals of transactions with the environment and our ways of coping with them.

Appraisal is the central construct of cognitive mediation (for a history, see Lazarus, 1998). I define it as an evaluation of the significance of what is happening for our well-being. We are all constantly engaged in appraising and, therefore, distinguishing among conditions of harm, threat, challenge, and benefit. Doing this provides the opportunity to anticipate adaptational problems and cope successfully, thereby helping us to survive and flourish. I use the noun form, *appraisal*, to refer to the evaluative product and the gerund form, *appraising*, for the process of making the evaluation.

Psychology still suffers from considerable residual behaviorism and remains overcommitted to two narrow research methods: the laboratory experiment and the large-sample survey. The latter is the prime research methodology of epidemiology, which, although very useful in exploring variables affecting health, is inimical to a clinical concern with the individual mind. There is, fortunately, a growing movement in most of the social sciences to broaden the research approaches and the models of human social and cultural existence— both changes compatible with a subjective approach (see Jessor, 1996).

When I speak of *subjectivism*, the reader should not assume that my version is that of classical phenomenology, which suggests that what people wish is tantamount to their reality. Such an outlook is much too solipsistic. My view is that when we evaluate what is happening in our life, we negotiate between two points of view: wanting to understand how things actually are and wanting to see the objective realities in the most favorable light possible, so as not to lose sanguinity or hope. Along with coping, appraising has been a central theme of my research and thought and serves as a bridge to the final metatheoretical perspective.

Relational Meaning

Psychologists generally acknowledge that person variables interact with environmental variables to influence mind and action (e.g., Magnusson & Stattin, 1996). Interaction by itself, however, leaves out what I consider the most important theme in our emotional lives: the person–environment relationship and, above all, the personal meaning that is constructed by an individual about that relationship by means of the process of appraising.

Our emotions and the conditions of life that bring them about depend on and express relational meanings. It is not merely that the person influences the environment and vice versa. Relational meaning takes our understanding to a higher level of abstraction than when we separate, for the purpose of analysis, the environmental and personality components of a *transaction*, which is a term I prefer to *interaction* (see Lazarus, 1997; Lazarus & Folkman, 1987; also Pervin & Lewis, 1978).

Science is usually defined as a search for elemental, causal variables, which are component parts of a larger unit or system. In separating complex phenomena into smaller components, we lose a sense of the whole system. The confluence of the two sets of variables, environment and person, which are the main components of the person–environment relationship, results in what Dewey and Bentley (1949) called a *synthesis*. *To synthesize* is the theoretical act of putting the parts back together into an integrated whole.

We must draw on both analysis and synthesis (Lazarus, 1997) to understand individual persons' life goals; beliefs about self and world; sense of past, present, and future; and the personal meanings they construct about ongoing and changing person–environment relationships. We must also cease avoiding the difficult task of studying meaning in human affairs and develop a new conceptual language. This language should be less focused on separate components of the total system, such as the person and the environment, and instead should focus more on the person–environment relationship and its meaning for the individual.

Explaining Age Differences in Stress, Emotion, and Coping

Having laid the intellectual groundwork for our look at aging, permit me now to approach the topic of coping with aging by considering what old people must face in their lives. We must ask how age differences in stress, emotion, and coping—assuming they can be empirically demonstrated—should be explained.

The great majority of those who explore changes in our intellectual and emotional life from adulthood to old age try to explain age differences developmentally. The developmental approach assumes a progression from infancy to adulthood, beginning with a relatively primitive psychological status in utero or at birth and proceeding to a more advanced one. The changes observed proceed from a less organized condition of mind toward increasing structure and function.

From this standpoint, it seems unsound to interpret most of the changes of aging in developmental terms, because they do not reflect this principle of increasing structure and function. Rather, what typically occurs is an effort to prevent regression, that is, to preserve endangered functions as much as possible in the face of increasing physical and mental losses.

Aside from efforts to sustain morale, much of coping with aging is an attempt to slow down or compensate for inevitable loss of structure and function and to actualize some goal commitments while abandoning others as no longer attainable or worthwhile—in other words, to cope with an inevitable spiral downward toward increasing entropy and approaching death. This process should not be viewed as development; to do so waters down the meaning of development to any change, regardless of its functional significance. Regression, yes, which is the enemy to be fought; development, no.

What I have just said does not negate the possibility that new creative functions could emerge in old age, fueled, in part, by efforts to cope with the stressful demands imposed by losses. Basically, however, the process of coping with aging is a holding action designed to actualize personal values and goals that still remain viable. We should also acknowledge the potential for increased wisdom with age, which might help aging persons accept the realities of their fate without despair, although we still do not know how best to characterize and measure wisdom.

I am confident that there must be a viable sense of a past, present, and future to experience satisfaction at this advanced time of life. We cannot live totally in the past, even if it was glorious. The past alone seldom sustains us; one wants the possibility of an encore. It is the present, and especially the immediate future, however limited it may be, that counts. Otherwise, life is likely to seem empty, a matter of just waiting for death.

There is nothing absolute about the losses brought on by aging, except they are likely to be more common as we age. The rates of such losses and their exact forms vary greatly from individual to individual. In many instances, significant psychological changes are not obvious even near the point of death, as in people who work or socialize effectively until the end. Many old people hope death, when it comes, will be quick rather than slow with prolonged debilitating struggles or dysfunction.

The Coping Process

The reader interested primarily in aging might well perceive a general discussion of coping at this point to be a digression from the main topic. However, research on coping in aging requires a sound approach to theory and measurement, and I believe I would be remiss not to address this topic. Describing, measuring, and conceptualizing coping in any population are no simple matters. If the reader wants to do research on coping with aging, or to evaluate research being done, a knowledge of coping and how it should be conceived and studied should be an important resource, which is why I feel obliged to include it here. In addition to my work on coping (Lazarus, 1966, 1981, 1983, 1985, 1991, 1993a, 1993b; Lazarus & Commentators, 1990; Lazarus, Averill, & Opton, 1974; Lazarus & Folkman, 1984; Lazarus & Launier, 1978), my colleagues and I have also directed some attention to coping with aging (Folkman, Bernstein, & Lazarus, 1987; Folkman, Lazarus, Pimley, & Novacek, 1987; Lazarus, 1996; Lazarus & DeLongis, 1983).

The growth of research on coping in recent years has been phenomenal. There are now three recent major books on the subject, Gotlieb's (1997) edited volume on coping with chronic stress, Aldwin's (1994) monograph dealing with coping over the life course, and an ambitious *Handbook of Coping*, edited by Zeidner and Endler (1996). In this handbook, Carver (1996) pointed out that "the vast majority of the work done in this area has occurred within the past two decades" (p. xi). A chapter by Costa, Somerfield, and McCrae (1996) illustrates the growth of the topic. They noted that 113 articles were published on coping in 1974, 183 in 1980, and 639 in 1984, with no end in sight to this expansion, although quantity is no guide to quality or importance.

There are three common misapprehensions about the coping process, which, unfortunately, are indigenous to much of coping research and evolved, I believe, from the tendency to analyze coping in the typically reductive fashion of science. They include (a) treating the functions of coping as distinctive action types, (b) divorcing coping from the person who is doing it, and (c) separating coping from emotion. These misapprehensions should be understood and avoided by those who would themselves do research on coping with aging or draw on the research of others in their professional work.

Treating Functions of Coping as Distinct Action Types

There are a number of coping functions, but my colleagues and I have emphasized two: the *problem-focused* function, which involves actions designed to alter the troubling realities of the person–environment relationship, and the *emotion-focused* function, which involves cognitive coping strategies designed to reduce or manage emotional distress without trying to change the realities of the stressful encounter. This function is mainly accomplished by *avoidance* and reappraisals that make use of either denial of the threatening significance of what is happening or engagment in the process of psychological distancing.

An unfortunate tendency characterizes a great deal of research, which pits one coping function against the other (for some examples, see McQueeney, Stanton, & Sigmon, 1997), and I have probably contributed to this tendency inadvertently. It is often suggested, for example, that problem-focused coping has a more favorable adaptational outcome than emotion-focused coping, even though some solid research had found that when the conditions of stress are unchangeable, problem-focused coping is associated with poorer outcomes than emotion-focused coping (e.g., Collins, Baum, & Singer, 1983; and Solomon, Mikulincer, & Flum, 1988).

This poses several problems. Separating the functions can be a problem because it is often difficult to assess which function is operating in a complex coping process, especially if we fail to examine carefully the total context in which coping takes place. In addition, most coping thoughts and actions have multiple functions. Thus, using diazepam to reduce the distress and bodily disturbance of performance anxiety, as in being evaluated for a job or taking a test, seems to emphasize the emotion-focused function, but it also has the effect of improving performance, which seems to emphasize the problem-focused function. The performer probably wants to do both.

The most important mistake in pitting one function against another, however, is that both are part of a complex, integrated effort at coping. As in efforts at positive thinking or maintaining hope, the emotion-focused function may provide crucial support for the decision to take some action about one's plight, whether or not it seems likely to be successful. Often it is successful, however, despite initial doubts on the part of the person who tries, thereby justifying the effort. Psychologists who emphasize the positive value of optimism in adaptation probably have this paradox in mind.

The key point is that people draw on more than one coping function, and not to recognize this disavows the complex and integrated nature of coping. The functions of coping should never be separated except for didactic purposes, and we should try to see how they combine and contribute to the total coping process.

Divorcing Coping From the Person Who Is Doing It

This happens when coping is measured superficially, for example, in questionnaires that were never designed to assess personality dispositions important in coping choice, such as goals, situational intentions, beliefs about self and world, cognitive styles, and personal resources and limitations. These personality variables influence appraisals and the relational meanings derived from them.

Of all the personality variables that influence coping, the most overlooked are a person's goals and situational intentions. In this connection, I have often cited Laux and Weber's (1991) research on anxiety-producing and anger-producing transactions of married couples. The evidence suggests that if the main threat in a spousal argument, as appraised by one or both partners, is the dissolution of the marriage, the expression of anger will be inhibited in favor of efforts to protect the relationship. But if the most important threat is appraised as wounded self-esteem, then retaliation and escalation of anger are apt to be chosen as the coping strategy.

I have also cited Folkman, Chesney, and Christopher-Richards's (1994) observations of caregiving partners of men dying of AIDS, in which the deeper relational meaning of this tragedy carries the main weight of the struggle to cope. Thus, if the caregiver understands that he is soon to lose his partner, this is bound to be a major chronic threat with which he must cope. And if the dying process is interpreted by the caregiver as what he is likely himself to experience in the future, especially if he has the HIV virus or believes he will probably contract it, he is likely to view this drawn out and miserable death as a forecast of his own dismal future. He is then likely to feel a mixture of hope and despair about whether, when his time comes, he will be cared for as he is now caring for his partner.

My reservations about the superficial measurement of coping also apply to my own Ways of Coping Questionnaire (Folkman & Lazarus, 1988). We have always regarded it as more useful for large-scale, epidemiologically focused research than for clinical work with individuals. Questionnaire measures have provided a good beginning for coping research and still have their uses but should not be considered the final or best way to assess the coping process.

To gain an adequate understanding of the threats involved in protracted stressful transactions requires that questionnaire data be supplemented by repeated in-depth interviews that reveal changes over time and across different stressful conditions. A number of farsighted researchers have been approaching coping from this in-depth, personality-centered perspective (e.g., Folkman, 1987; Stein, Folkman, Trabasso, & Richards, 1997).

Separating Coping From Emotion

One of the perplexing features of most cognitive-mediational approaches to the emotion process is that the importance of coping is often underestimated, and coping and emotion are often treated as if they were independent entities. Coping is incorrectly said to be brought into play only after a person has experienced negative emotions, that is, as a strategy for managing emotions that have already been aroused by harms, threats, or challenges.

The reality, however, is that coping is an integral part of the emotion process right from the beginning, even at the stage when an emotion is first being aroused, thereby influencing that arousal. In effect, the appraisal of the personal significance of what is happening always includes an evaluation of the options for coping. Thus, if the provocation to anger is made by someone who can be defeated in an argument or fight, we allow ourselves to feel and express anger. But if we see ourselves as too vulnerable to mount a successful attack, the main emotion is more likely to be anxiety and lead either to the concealment of anger or to mollifying acts to appease the person who provoked us.

I am suggesting that the options for coping, and the constraints against them, shape our appraisals and the emotions that ensue. It may be useful to separate coping from emotion for clear discourse, or to analyze its role in the emotion process, but to do so distorts the emotion process as it actually occurs in nature. The three concepts—stress, emotion, and coping—form a conceptual unit, which operates in a part–whole relationship, the emotion process constituting the whole.

There would be no argument against the idea that coping is important in the *stress* emotions, such as anxiety, anger, guilt, shame, sadness, envy, jealousy, and disgust. When we take into account the part coping plays in our emotions, however, it might surprise the reader if I say we also cope with positively toned emotions and the conditions that bring them about. To suggest, as I do, that coping is often—if not always—important even in the so-called positively toned emotions would raise many skeptical eyebrows.

Not infrequently, positive emotional states also involve harms and threats. For example, *relief* results from a harmful or threatening situation that has disappeared or abated. *Hope*, more often than not, stems from a situation in which we must prepare for the worst while hoping for better. So coping is always involved in these emotions, and we could even regard hope as a form of coping.

Even *happiness*, *pride*, *love*, *gratitude*, and *compassion* are frequently, although not always, associated with harm or threat. Consider, for example, the following scenarios: Although *happy*, we may experience the fear that the happy feeling will soon fade, and coping may consist of trying to avoid this. Or we may fear that having things this good will expose us to the hostile reactions of others who resent our good fortune, so we disguise or soft pedal our happiness. Similarly, the feeling of *pride* may be threatening because it is often regarded by others as unseemly, as in the biblical aphorisms "pride goeth before a fall" and "overweening pride."

Love is commonly viewed as a positive emotional state, but when it is unrequited or associated with uncertainty about the lover's commitment, it is stressful and calls for coping to change what is happening or to reappraise it. *Gratitude* may require coping if it is based on social pressure, yet displaying it is onerous or grudging. And *compassion* is aversive when we share the suffering of another person too keenly. The case seems logically strong that coping applies not only to the stress emotions but also, in many instances, to the circumstances surrounding positively toned emotions.

For a long time, I have had mixed feelings about diagrams and flowcharts designed to help readers visualize a model, although I have experimented with such charts before, for example, in Lazarus and Folkman (1984) and Lazarus (1991). What makes me uneasy is that the simplified presentation often creates the illusion of understanding and that arrows showing recursive influences, which are essential in a feedback system, always leave too much out that is essential. However, I am persuaded that one might be useful here for readers unfamiliar with my stress, coping, and emotion theory, as long as they understand its limitations. The visualization is a gross oversimplification designed only to show the main sources of influence and the proposed flow of events. The model I have diagramed in Figure 1 takes into account some of what I have said in this chapter.

Methodological Problems in Research on Aging

Most aging research uses cross-sectional research designs, which suffer from the fatal defect that we cannot determine whether functional differences associated with chronological age have anything to do with getting older or are merely cohort effects (see also Lazarus & DeLongis, 1983). The age-defined cohorts used in such research have grown up during different sociocultural periods, when the dominant issues and outlooks also differed—for example, during the Great Depression of the 1930s, right after World War II, or in the 1980s—thereby confounding age-caused variations with cohort effects. Allow me to illustrate with two studies, one of my own on stress and coping in aging, which was published by Folkman, Lazarus, et al. (1987) as part of the Berkeley Stress and Coping Project, and a more recent one by Carstensen, Graff, Levenson, and Gottman (1996).

In my study, we compared two cohorts of men and women, one between 35 and 45 years of age and the other between 65 and 75 years of age, once a month over a 12-month period, with respect to their coping patterns as measured by the Ways of Coping Questionnaire/Interview and the sources of stress they reported on the Hassles Scale. We found modest differences between the two age groups. For example, the younger cohort reported using more confrontive coping (except with respect to health issues), more planful problem solving, and more social support seeking for major stresses than the older cohort, which reported more distancing (and humor), accepting more responsibility for what had gone wrong, and making more positive reappraisals. Gender effects were minor, as had been found earlier by Folkman and Lazarus (1980) and many others later.

The coping differences between the two cohorts impressed us as fitting their respective sources of stress, which, although overlapping, were not the

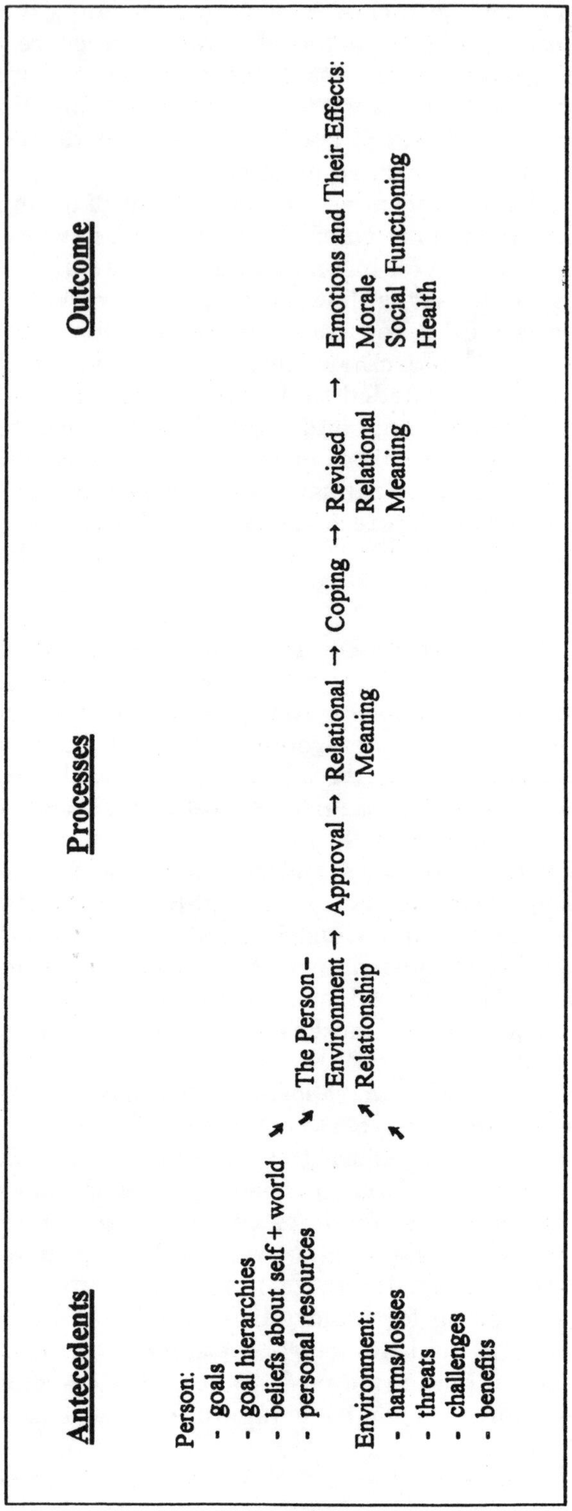

Figure 1. A Model of Coping.

same. The younger cohort reported more hassles in the domains of finance, work, personal life, family, and friends. The older cohort reported more hassles having to do with the environment, social issues, home maintenance, and health.

I cite the second study, reported by Carstensen et al. (1996), because of the unusual and interesting methodology of directly observing people with marital conflicts in a laboratory setting. Each couple discussed the events of the day for 15 min, then returned separately to consider videotapes of their conversations.

Using ratings by the observers, the authors reported that the marital problems of older couples were less severe than middle-aged couples, who disagreed more than older couples about children, money, religion, and recreation. Older couples derived more pleasure from talking about children and grandchildren, doing things together, dreams, and vacations. They also showed better emotion regulation (coping)—as evidenced by lower levels of anger, disgust, belligerence, and whining—and higher levels of affection. No gender differences were found between the two cohorts, but wives in both cohorts verbalized more emotion than husbands, both positive and negative. Husbands stonewalled, or refused to talk about conflicts, more than wives.

The provocative findings of both these studies could be important and relevant to aging, but the interpretations of age differences are totally vitiated by the fact that the research designs are cross-sectional. Unfortunately, therefore, we cannot say whether the differences in coping are the result of growing older or merely a cohort effect. In addition—and this applies to a high proportion of research comparing different age groups—the differences reported, although statistically significant, were not large enough to characterize adequately the participants at the two chronological ages.

Cross-sectional research designs can be useful in a preliminary effort to learn whether age differences might be promising for follow-up study. But if we really want to evaluate and carefully document these differences, and to determine their sources, the only sure way is to do longitudinal research in which the same persons are studied over a substantial period of time and comparisons are made of changes as they grow older. Unfortunately, longitudinal research is not common because of its high cost in resources and time.

Long-term longitudinal studies are needed to assess the effects on the emotional life of illnesses, such as cancer and heart disease, which are slow to develop. What many psychologists do not realize, however, is that a longitudinal research design also can be conducted over a relatively brief period, such as a year, or even just one research session, as in an argument between two people or a therapeutic session in which the changing psychodynamics of interest to the researcher take place rapidly. The process of emotional arousal, its unfolding, and the coping that takes place can best be studied in a brief time frame rather than over long periods. Because the research design is intraindividual, however, it meets the fundamental criteria of a longitudinal study.

Two additional methodological problems are common in aging research. One is that although they deal with similar constructs, researchers commonly use extremely diverse approaches to observation and measurement, for example, projective tests, clinical type interviews, and questionnaire measures of coping. Researchers also use very different variables to study stress, emotion, and coping as a function of age. Because of this chaos of variables and measurement preferences, studies in this field are often difficult to compare in the search for valid generalizations about aging (see Lazarus, 1996, for a review and analysis), though this has not prevented researchers from overstating what is known.

The second methodological problem is the tendency to report age difference as central tendencies, with the usual finding of small but statistically significant mean differences. As I said at the outset, little or no documentation is provided about individual or subgroup variations, and the large overlap among the age-related data being compared is usually ignored. What is worse, conclusions are blithely drawn about differences between older and younger people, as if these differences reflect what most people are like at each chronological age.

If as much attention were given to ubiquitous individual differences as is typically given to small differences in central tendencies, comparing more than one age level would have more utility. Statistically reliable differences as a function of age have value mainly in identifying variables that might influence the aging process, but if the differences are modest, as they usually are, it is not a sound way of describing the actual lives of older and younger people.

It would be more useful to group people into clusters in such research by means of correlational analysis on the basis of shared sources of stress and patterns of coping. I believe the inductive effort to organize the potentially rich descriptions of coping and the emotional life could yield more insight into the most frequent problems of aging and processes of coping with them than is being achieved solely by chronological-age-based comparisons, especially when so many of these studies are cross-sectional.

Thoughts About the Future

The four metatheoretical principles I espoused earlier, and the methodological confusions indigenous to so much aging research, should encourage us to try something new. My recommendation is to document the relational meanings elderly persons construct from their shared and diverse circumstances. We need to know how they cope with these circumstances by compensating for loss, or the threat of loss, while managing nevertheless to have comparatively vigorous, productive, and satisfying lives.

This theme could suggest a number of major agendas for research on aging. It also overlaps substantially with the view of successful aging presented by Baltes and Baltes (1990), which, as I see it, breathes a valuable dose of fresh air into a research field that has all but stagnated. They suggest that successful aging depends on the acquisition of attitudes and coping processes that permit an aging person, despite increasing deficits or the threat of them, to remain independent, productive, and socially active for as long as possible. Although they do not use the word, they are basically talking about *coping* with aging.

Permit me to quote from Baltes and Carstensen (1996), who made many points that are similar to those I have made in this chapter:

> We suggest that understanding the *processes* [sic] that people use to reach their goals under increasing limitations in resources, be they social, psychological, or biological, will lead to additional insights and progress in the field. . . . The proposed model defines success as the attainment of goals which can differ widely among people and can be measured against diverse standards and norms. The three processes identified in the model—namely, selection, compensation and optimization—in concert, provide a way to conceptualize the strategies older people use to age well even in the face of loss. We cannot predict what any given individual's successful ageing will look like until we know the domains of functioning and goals . . . that individual considers important, personally meaningful, and in which he or she feels competent. (p. 399)

The environments of old persons are increasingly being designed to reduce the danger of injury and to maximize functioning in diverse ways, for example, the use of walkers and canes; safety bars, especially in the bathroom; transportation to and from the market; delivery of food and medicine when ordered by phone; and the tendency to restrict driving to relatively safe areas. I see some of this in the elderly community of over 9,000 persons in which my wife and I live, where the average age is 77.

Some years ago, I was entranced by the distinguished psychologist B. F. Skinner's (1983) observations about how he compensated for the expectable problems of memory. I notice that Baltes and Carstensen (1996) mentioned this too. By then quite old, he spoke of hanging his umbrella on the doorknob the moment the thought occurred to him so he would not forget to take it with him when he went to his office. Skinner, by the way, also argued against a developmental interpretation of aging losses and the ways people handle them.

Many older persons I know often joke about the fact that they cannot remember the name of a public figure who they can clearly see in their mind's eye. They are mystified; what could not be recalled is not forgotten but cannot be retrieved when they want to call it up, yet it will suddenly pop into their heads when not needed. They are also frustrated by the tendency to lose the thread of what they wanted to say just a few moments ago. When elderly professors lecture, they learn to write the names of those they want to cite on their notes, lest they be embarrassed by obviously intending to announce the name but being unable to come up with it. In the process of writing, they often require much extra time trying to find the name of the person who said this or that and the reference to it, when years before this information would come to mind quickly.

Nevertheless, the degree of the deficits, the age at which they become evident, the strategies for dealing with them, the emotions connected with them, and the situations in which they arise are still remarkably variable. This applies to the other inevitable problems of growing old, such as one's psychological outlook about death and dying.

To study aging fruitfully, we need to catalogue the full range of coping strategies old people use and examine how they work, and how well, with re-

spect to the main adaptational outcomes of coping, namely, morale, social functioning, and somatic health. We also need to identify the person variables that
influence these outcomes—for example, skills and their lack, resources and
liabilities, high or low energy, available social supports or their absence—and
the environmental conditions that interact with them.

A research project, for example, might center on older persons who are still
working at something, whether or not they are officially retired. A research
question might be to identify the problems they face in doing this work and to
explore in depth how they cope with them—in effect, a more formal version of
Skinner's (1983) personal account. Such a study should also have a comparison
group of those with comparable demographics, who are not functioning as they
would like.

To make such a study both representative and inclusive of important variables, the researcher might select people in diverse fields, types of activities,
and might group together for further study those who shared similar problems
or diseases, such as Parkinson's disease, heart disease, arthritis, or myasthenia
gravis. I am not sure I like classifications that are based only on diseases,
because their psychological properties are only partly related to the bodily ailment, but there are very interesting psychological questions here that should
not be foreclosed.

Nevertheless, this kind of in-depth study of sources of difficulty in sustaining productive engagement during later life, and the patterns of coping with
these problems, could, I think, be very fruitful. This would be especially true
if such a study were done longitudinally to identify when the problems began
and when and why people stopped working. Perhaps they could no longer cope,
but we need to know more about this. The motivation for the study should not
be merely to demonstrate what older people can do, although this would be
useful, but should also include those who cannot seem to establish any productive engagements. This research could analyze the extent to which the failures (if that is what they are) are intractable or could be ameliorated either by
suitable coping efforts or clinical assistance.

I have the impression that the most difficult coping problems of aging are
the existential ones—that is, a lack of motivation to seek a satisfying commitment. Younger people with existential neuroses are very discouraging to work
with clinically because they complain that they know they should be working
toward a goal but lack the motivation. Although they often say "Show me how
to want to engage myself in something," it is all but impossible to impose motivation from the outside.

By the same token, many aging persons, who know well that they need to
have sustaining interests and activities, can find no way to initiate them. Although cause-and-effect here are difficult to disentangle, these persons often
struggle with an unrelenting, low level but debilitating depression, although
this state of mind is not always clinically apparent. Helping aging persons cope
with the losses and handicaps of aging is probably easier to manage clinically
and is apt to be a more satisfying challenge for the clinician to tackle than
motivational deficits. And if we had more knowledge about how diverse individuals are coping successfully, or failing to cope in a satisfactory way, with the
problems of aging, practical help might be more available too.

It makes sense, as I see it, to try to discover by means of repeated interviews the life values and goals that seem unreachable to patients and to assess whether coping strategies they are not drawing on could increase the fruitfulness and meaningfulness of their lives. But I have no direct experience with clinical geropsychological work with aging patients, and I feel diffident about making suggestions about how clinicians who regularly deal with aging people should do their job.

Still, if it is not being done, the kind of research questions I indicated above could be pursued with individual patients, especially if their malaise seems related to coping inadequacies, leading to frustration in seeking social connections or productive work activities. Such exploration, if it is not already being pursued clinically, might uncover counterproductive attitudes and ineffectual modes of coping that could be worked on or changed. Nevertheless, my main objective is to promote the position that the more we have a research basis for interventions having to do with coping, the stronger the case would be for this kind of clinical effort.

Before I sign off, permit me to quote from a source that deals with aging with considerable wisdom, realistically but with a positive outlook. Five or so years ago my wife and I named our boat *Indian Summer* because of an article written by Edwin Shneidman (1989) about the gifted sample studied many years earlier by Terman and others at Stanford University. He spoke almost poetically of septuagenarians as at the "Indian Summer" of their lives:

> Indian Summer is not real summer. During the Indian Summer of life there are premonitions of the imminent winter in which it is embedded, and there is a painful awareness of one's inescapable death-bound plight. (Our plight is that we know our fate, and we feel the turbulent catabolic air-bumps before the inevitable crash). For this reason, a pleasant stretch of weather in the late fall is doubly welcome, and we enjoy the rays of the sun while they last, suppressing our certain knowledge of the threat of what lies beyond the turn. (Shneidman, 1989, p. 693)

If you will indulge me a bit more, let me borrow again from Shneidman, who quoted Oliver Wendell Holmes from a radio broadcast he gave on his 90th birthday, which I like because I too am work oriented:

> The riders in a race do not stop short when they reach the goal. There is a little finishing canter before coming to a standstill. There is time to hear the kind voice of friends and to say to one's self: "The work is done." But just as one says that, the answer comes: "The race is over, but the work is never done while the power to work remains." The canter that brings you to a standstill need not be only coming to rest. It cannot be, while you still live. For to live is to function. That is all there is in living. (Schneideman, 1989, p. 693)

I think we can do better than we have been doing in portraying what aging is like, both in its negative and positive aspects, and how different types of individuals cope with it. The reason for wanting to do so is the promise, or at least the hope, that if we have described well what is out there and fully understand what we have described, we can substantially improve the services we provide for aging persons who need help.

References

Aldwin, C. M. (1994). *Stress, coping, and development: An integrative perspective*. New York: Guilford Press.

Baltes, P. B., & Baltes, M. M. (1990). Psychological perspectives on successful aging: The model of selective optimization with compensation. In P. B. Baltes & M. M. Baltes (Eds.), *Successful aging: Perspectives from the behavioral sciences* (pp. 1–34). New York: Cambridge University Press.

Baltes, M. M., & Carstensen, L. L. (1996). The process of successful ageing. *Aging and Society*, *16*, 397–422.

Butler, R. N. (1963). The facade of chronological age: An interpretative summary. In B. L. Neugarten (Ed.), *Middle age and aging* (pp. 235–242). Chicago: University of Chicago Press.

Carstensen, L. L., Graff, J., Levenson, R. W., & Gottman, J. M. (1996). Affect in intimate relationships: The developmental course of marriage. In C. Magai & S. H. McFadden (Eds.), *Handbook of emotion, adult development, and aging* (pp. 227–247). San Diego, CA: Academic Press.

Carver, C. S. (1996). Foreword. In M. Zeidner & N. S. Endler (Eds.), *Handbook of coping: Theory, research, applications* (pp. xi–xiii). New York: Wiley.

Collins, D. L., Baum, A., & Singer, J. E. (1983). Coping with chronic stress at Three Mile Island: Psychological and biochemical evidence. *Health Psychology*, *2*, 149–166.

Costa, P. T., Somerfield, M. R., & McCrae, R. R. (1996). Personality and coping: A reconceptualization. In M. Zeidner & N. S. Endler (Eds.), *Handbook of coping: Theory, research, applications* (pp. 44–61). New York: Wiley.

Dewey, J., & Bentley, A. E. (1949). *Knowing and the known*. Boston: Beacon Press.

Folkman, S. (1997). Introduction to the special section: Use of bereavement narratives to predict well-being in gay men whose partners died of AIDS—Four theoretical perspectives. *Journal of Personality and Social Psychology*, *72*, 851–854.

Folkman, S., Bernstein, L., & Lazarus, R. S. (1987). Stress processes and the misuse of drugs in older adults. *Psychology and Aging*, *2*, 366–374.

Folkman, S., Chesney, M. A., & Christopher-Richards, A. (1994). Stress and coping in caregiving partners of men with AIDS. *Psychiatric Clinics of North America*, *17*, 35–53.

Folkman, A., & Lazarus, R. S. (1980). An analysis of coping in a middle-aged community sample. *Journal of Health and Social Behavior*, *21*, 219–239.

Folkman, S., & Lazarus, R. S. (1985). If it changes it must be a process: A study of emotion and coping during three stages of a college examination. *Journal of Personality and Social Psychology*, *48*, 150–170.

Folkman, S., & Lazarus, R. S. (1988). *Manual for the Ways of Coping Questionnaire*. Palo Alto, CA: Consulting Psychologists Press (now named MIND GARDEN).

Folkman, S., Lazarus, R. S., Dunkel-Schetter, C., DeLongis, A., & Gruen, R. (1986a). The dynamics of a stressful encounter: Cognitive appraisal, coping, and encounter outcomes. *Journal of Personality and Social Psychology*, *50*, 992–1003.

Folkman, S., Lazarus, R. S., Gruen, R., & DeLongis, A. (1986b). Appraisal, coping, health status, and psychological symptoms. *Journal of Personality and Social Psychology*, *50*, 572–579.

Folkman, S., Lazarus, R. S., Pimley, S., & Novacek, J. (1987). Age differences in stress and coping processes. *Psychology and Aging*, *2*, 171–184.

Gotlieb, B. H. (1997). *Coping with chronic stress*. New York: Plenum.

Holmes, O. W. (1962). The race is over. In O. W. Holmes (Ed.), *The occasional speeches of Justice Oliver Wendell Holmes* (p. 178). Cambridge, MA: Harvard University Press. (Original work published 1931)

Jessor, R. (1996). Ethnographic methods in contemporary perspective. In R. Jessor, A. Colby, & R. A. Shweder (Eds.), *Ethnography and human development: Context and meaning in social inquiry* (pp. 3–14). Chicago: University of Chicago Press.

Laux, L., & Weber, H. (1991). Presentation of self in coping with anger and anxiety: An intentional approach. *Anxiety Research 3*, 233–255.

Lazarus, R. S. (1966). *Psychological stress and the coping process*. New York: McGraw-Hill.

Lazarus, R. S. (1981). The stress and coping paradigm. In C. Eisdorfer, D. Cohen, A. Kleinman, & P. Maxim (Eds.), *Models for clinical psychopathology* (pp. 177–214). New York: Spectrum.

Lazarus, R. S. (1983). The costs and benefits of denial. In S. Breznitz (Ed.), *The denial of stress* (pp. 1–30). New York: International Universities Press.

Lazarus, R. S. (1985). The trivialization of distress. In J. C. Rosen & L. J. Solomon (Eds.), *Preventing health risk behaviors and promoting coping with illness: Vol. 8. Vermont Conference on the Primary Prevention of Psychopathology* (pp. 279–298). Hanover, NH: University Press of New England.

Lazarus, R. S. (1991). *Emotion and adaptation*. New York: Oxford University Press.

Lazarus, R. S. (1993a). Coping theory and research: Past, present, and future. *Psychosomatic Medicine, 55*, 234–247.

Lazarus, R. S. (1993b). From psychological stress to the emotions: A history of changing outlooks. In L. W. Porter & M. R. Rosenzweig (Eds.), *Annual review of psychology* (pp. 1–21). Palo Alto, CA: Annual Reviews.

Lazarus, R. S. (1996). The role of coping in the emotions and how coping changes over the life course. In C. Malatesta-Magai & S. H. McFadden (Eds.), *Handbook of emotion, adult development, and aging* (pp. 289–306). New York: Academic Press.

Lazarus, R. S. (1998). *Fifty years of research and theory by R. S. Lazarus: Perennial historical issues*. Mahwah, NJ: Erlbaum.

Lazarus, R. S., Averill, J. R., & Opton, E. M., Jr. (1974). The psychology of coping: Issues of research and assessment. In G. V. Coehlo, D. A. Hamburg, & J. F. Adams (Eds.), *Coping and adaptation* (pp. 249–315). New York: Basic Books.

Lazarus, R. S., & Commentators. (1990). Theory-based stress measurement. *Psychological Inquiry, 1*, 3–51.

Lazarus, R. S., & DeLongis, A. (1983). Psychological stress and coping in aging. *American Psychologist, 38*, 245–254.

Lazarus, R. S., & Folkman, S. (1984). *Stress, appraisal, and coping*. New York: Springer.

Lazarus, R. S., & Folkman, S. (1987). Transactional theory and research on emotions and coping. In L. Laux & G. Vossel (Guest Eds.), Personality in biographical stress and coping research. *European Journal of Personality* (Special Issue), *1*, 141–169.

Lazarus, R. S., & Launier, R. (1978). Stress-related transactions between person and environment. In L. A. Pervin & M. Lewis (Eds.), *Perspectives in interactional psychology* (pp. 287–327). New York: Plenum.

Lewin, K. A. (1946). Behavior and development as a function of the total situation. In L. Carmichael (Ed.), *Manual of child psychology* (pp. 918–970). New York: Wiley.

Magai, C., & McFadden, S. H. (1996). *Handbook of emotion, adult development, and aging*. San Diego, CA: Academic Press.

Magnusson, D., & Stattin, H. (1996). Person–context interaction theories. *Reports from the Department of Psychology, Stockholm University* (Report No. 824).

McQueeney, D., Stanton, A. L., & Sigmon, S. (1997). Efficacy of emotion-focused and problem-focused group therapies for women with fertility problems. *Journal of Behavioral Medicine, 20*, 313–331.

Pervin, L. A., & Lewis, M. (1978). Overview of the internal–external issue. In L. A. Pervin & M. Lewis (Eds.), *Perspectives in interactional psychology* (pp. 1–22). New York: Plenum.

Shneidman, E. (1989). The Indian summer of life: A preliminary study of septuagenarians. *American Psychologist, 44*, 684–694.

Skinner, B. F. (1983). Intellectual self-management in old age. *American Psychologist, 38*, 239–244.

Solomon, Z., Mikulincer, M., & Flum, H. (1988). Negative life events, coping responses, and combat-related psychopathology: A prospective study. *Journal of Abnormal Psychology, 97*, 302–307.

Stein, N., Folkman, S., Trabasso, T., & Richards, T. A. (1997). Appraisal and goal processes as predictors of psychological well-being in bereaved caregivers. *Journal of Personality and Social Psychology, 72*, 885–891.

Zeidner, M., & Endler, N. S. (Eds.). (1996). *Handbook of coping: Theory, research, applications*. New York: Wiley.

Part II

Challenges and Practical Issues

8

Caregiving to Adults: A Life Event Challenge

John C. Cavanaugh

Caregiving for adults by adults within a family context is generally associated with anxiety and stress. Although the nature and definition of caregiving are difficult to state categorically, and vary across racial, ethnic, and cultural lines, it typically involves providing a wide range of services to someone that go well beyond just being there (Query & Flint, 1996). In the realm of caregiving, anxiety in the marital context often involves anxiety associated with caring for one's spouse, whereas anxiety in an intergenerational context is experienced either as fear or concern over the need to care for older parents, termed *filial anxiety* (Cicirelli, 1988), or as the anxiety accompanying actual caregiving.

Considerable research clearly documents the phenomena (e.g., see Aneshensel, Pearlin, Mullan, Zarit, & Whitlach, 1995). As will be described below, the vast majority of individuals who are currently engaged in caring for a spouse or parent experience anxiety at some point during the process, making anxiety, along with depressive symptoms, one of the most common feelings reported by caregivers (Aneshensel, Pearlin, Mullan, Zarit, & Whitlach, 1995). At a practical level, anxiety associated with caregiving presents significant challenges not only for caregivers but also for their families. Most important, such feelings have the potential to create a significant burden on the caregiver, as well as place a strain on relationships with other family members who are not assisting with the primary caregiving.

One key point is that caregivers' reports of anxiety have been documented across a variety of racial and ethnic groups (e.g., Hennessy & John, 1996; Wu, Zhang, He, & Yu, 1995). Also important are the large gender differences—at least 75% of caregivers are women (Query & Flint, 1996). In order of frequency, caregivers are most likely to be a spouse, daughter, sister, daughter-in-law, niece, granddaughter, or friend of the person needing care. Most often, family caregivers tend to be of moderate financial means, and about one third are poor (Query & Flint, 1996).

Caregiving Contexts and Anxiety

As indicated earlier, the two most common contexts for anxiety in marital and intergenerational relationships are a spouse caring for a partner and an adult child caring for a parent. Key issues leading to feelings of anxiety are different in each type.

Caring for a Spouse

Caring for a chronically ill spouse presents major challenges. Spousal caregivers usually assume this role after decades of shared responsibilities in the marriage. Often without warning, the division of labor that had worked for years must be readjusted. Such change inevitably puts stress on the relationship, producing numerous types of psychological distress. This is especially true in cases involving Alzheimer's disease or other dementias because of the dynamically changing cognitive and behavioral consequences of the disease.

Studies of caregivers assisting spouses with Alzheimer's disease typically show that marital satisfaction is much lower for these couples than it is for healthy couples. Spousal caregivers report a loss of companionship and intimacy over the course of caregiving (Williamson & Schulz, 1990; Wright, 1991). Marital satisfaction is also an important predictor of spousal caregivers' reports of anxiety and depressive symptoms; the better the perceived quality of the marriage, the fewer symptoms caregivers report.

Most spousal caregivers are forced to respond to a life challenge (their partner's illness) that they did not choose, adopting the caregiver role out of necessity. Once they adopt the role, however, caregivers assess their ability to carry out the duties required. Research indicates that how caregivers perceive their ability to provide care at the outset of caregiving may be important (Aneshensel et al., 1995). Caregivers who perceive themselves as competent try to rise to the occasion; data indicate that they report fewer and less intense caregiving hassles than do spousal caregivers who see themselves as less competent. In addition to trying at times to tackle problems head-on in order to solve them and dealing with one's feelings about caregiving, many spousal caregivers also use religion as a means of coping with their situation.

Caring for a Parent: Filial Anxiety

As the number of older adults continues to increase, concern over the possibility that one may have to provide care for one's parents has increased saliency. Given the fact that the research literature clearly documents that actual caregiving typically comes at a psychological price, such concerns have a basis in reality. Indeed, there is growing evidence that such concerns regarding one's appropriate filial responsibility occur well in advance of the actual need for providing care (Brody, Johnsen, & Fulcomer, 1984). Cicirelli (1988) termed these concerns *filial anxiety* and defined this as anxiety over the anticipated care of older parents. Filial anxiety may affect people's response to the actual caregiving situation when it arises. Filial anxiety is most likely to occur during the period in which one is attaining the developmental stage of viewing one's parents as individuals who may be in need of support (termed *filial maturity*); furthermore, filial anxiety may be an indication of difficulty in achieving this stage (Murray, Lowe, & Horne, 1995). Women tend to report higher levels of filial anxiety (e.g., Murray et al., 1995), which is most likely a reflection of the much higher incidence of daughters who actually become caregivers.

Because of the relation between filial anxiety and filial maturity, there should be developmental differences in the specific types of concerns individuals have. Myers and Cavanaugh (1995) confirmed this hypothesis; they reported generational differences in the factor structure of the Filial Anxiety Scale reflecting different concerns of younger and middle-aged women.

An important point in this research is the consistent finding that poorer perceptions of family relationships are related to increased expression of filial anxiety (e.g., Murray et al., 1995; Myers & Cavanaugh, 1995). This is consistent with the findings that strained relations with the care-recipient in general interfere with the quality of care that is actually provided by caregivers.

Caring for a Parent: Being a Caregiver

Actually caring for an older parent comes at a price. Living with one's parent after decades on one's own is usually not done by choice; generally, each party would just as soon live apart. The potential for conflict over daily routines and life styles is high. Overall, stress (often expressed as feelings of anxiety) about caregiving by an adult child results primarily from two sources (Robinson & Thurnher, 1979). First, adult children may have trouble coping with declines in their parents' functioning, especially when the declines involve cognitive abilities. If caregivers do not understand why their parents are declining, such lack of knowledge may result in feelings of anxiety, ambivalence, and antagonism toward their parents. Second, when the caregiving situation is perceived as confining, or seriously infringes on the adult childrens' other roles (e.g., spouse, parent, employee), the caregiving situation is likely to be perceived negatively. This, in turn, is likely to lead to mixed feelings of anger and guilt in addition to anxiety and depression.

The psychological cost for caring for one's parent can be high. Even the most devoted adult-child caregiver feels anxious, depressed, resentful, angry, and guilty at times. Anxiety over financial pressures is especially serious for those caring for parents with chronic conditions, such as Alzheimer's disease, that require services that are not covered by medical insurance. In some cases, adult children may even need to quit their jobs to provide care because adequate alternatives, such as adult day care, are unavailable. Although caring for parents is stressful for all adult children, adult daughters' stress levels are especially affected (Mui, 1995).

Addressing the Stress and Anxiety of Caregiving

As this brief overview attests, being concerned about the potential role of caregiving and actually providing care to a partner or parent is anxiety producing. In addition to traditional means of treating anxiety discussed elsewhere in this volume, several options directly related to caregiving are available. Many of these options can be viewed from the perspective of uncertainty reduction theory (URT), which explains how people can reduce levels of uncertainty during interactions and makes predictions about their communication behavior (Query & Flint, 1996). Because the principal stressors in caring for a person with dementia concern cognitive impairment and behavior management issues, interventions that address these problems are especially effective.

Family-Based Strategies

One of the aspects of caregiving that is especially difficult is the challenge to the caregiver's past roles. The need for role redefinition, a process sufficiently challenging in its own right, becomes more difficult if the caregiving situation necessitates the creation of a multigenerational household (Query & Flint, 1996). In such cases, families are likely to feel the pressures of many competing demands, most notably when the caregiver is an adult daughter with children who are living at home.

Among the various strategies that have been shown to be effective, those with the most empirical support are (a) open and honest communication with all household members, (b) scheduled, uninterrupted time with one's spouse and children away from caregiving duties and responsibilities, (c) if possible, a specific schedule devoted exclusively to the care-recipient when it is least disruptive to the family, and (d) an established source of social support outside the family. Although none of these strategies is perfect, adopting these and others tailored to the situation can lower the likelihood of conflicts.

External Strategies

The two most important contexts for creating external support mechanisms for caregivers are the employment arena and the social network. In terms of employment, the growing availability of employee assistance programs means that workers have wider access to information sessions, support groups, and "buddy systems" at their place of employment. Such programs make it easier to learn about the diseases and problems faced by care-recipients, as well as specific caregiving techniques and intervention strategies that may help reduce anxiety and other stress-related outcomes.

Formal and informal support groups are the most widely available external means of support. Frequently organized in the United States by chapters of the Alzheimer's Association, senior centers, nursing homes, and churches, these groups provide a nonjudgmental forum for caregivers to seek help with difficult caregiving or personal issues and to find information about the diseases they confront. Research results indicate that caregivers usually find these support groups very helpful (Query & Flint, 1996).

Respite care represents a third external strategy involving short-term care, from a few hours to a month, that allows family members to get a break from caregiving. Respite care programs range from adult day care centers to short-term residential placements. Empirical evidence to date indicates that caregivers who use respite care report numerous benefits, including better psychological and physical health (Query & Flint, 1996).

Conclusion

Anxiety in the context of marital and intergenerational relationships most often concerns anticipated or actual caregiving for a relative. In the case of anticipated care, filial anxiety can pose a serious challenge to some individuals. In the case of providing care, anxiety is a common outcome of the stresses associated with caregiving. Several family-based and external strategies are available that have been developed specifically to address the needs of caregivers. Taking advantage of these opportunities can greatly reduce levels of anxiety and overall reports of burden relating to caregiving.

References

Aneshensel, C. S., Pearlin, L. I., Mullan, J. T., Zarit, S. H., & Whitlach, C. J. (1995). *Profiles in caregiving: The unexpected career.* San Diego: Academic Press.

Brody, E. M., Johnsen, P. T., & Fulcomer, M. C. (1984). What should adult children do for elderly parents? Opinions and preferences of three generations of women. *Journal of Gerontology, 39,* 736–746.

Cicirelli, V. G. (1988). A measure of filial anxiety regarding anticipated care of elderly parents. *The Gerontologist, 28,* 478–482.

Hennessy, C. H., & John, R. (1996). American Indian family caregivers' perceptions of burden and needed support services. *Journal of Applied Gerontology, 15,* 275–293.

Mui, A. C. (1995). Caring for frail elderly parents: A comparison of adult sons and daughters. *The Gerontologist, 35,* 86–93.

Murray, P. D., Lowe, J. D., & Horne, H. L. (1995). Assessing filial maturity through the use of the Filial Anxiety Scale. *Journal of Psychology, 129,* 519–529.

Myers, E. G., & Cavanaugh, J. C. (1995). Filial anxiety in mothers and daughters: Cross-validation of Cicirelli's (1988) Filial Anxiety Scale. *Journal of Adult Development, 2,* 137–145.

Query, J. L., Jr., & Flint, L. J. (1996). The caregiving relationship. In N. Vanzetti & S. Duck (Eds.), *A lifetime of relationships* (pp. 455–483). Pacific Grove, CA: Brooks/Cole.

Robinson, B., & Thurnher, M. (1979). Taking care of aged parents: A family cycle transition. *The Gerontologist, 19,* 586–593.

Williamson, G. M., & Schulz, R. (1990). Relationship orientation, quality of prior relationship, and distress among caregivers of Alzheimer's patients. *Psychology and Aging, 5,* 502–509.

Wright, L. K. (1991). The impact of Alzheimer's disease on the marital relationship. *The Gerontologist, 31,* 224–237.

Wu, W., Zhang, M., He, Y., & Yu, Q. (1995). Burden and associated factors in caregivers of old people with dementia. *Chinese Mental Health Journal, 9,* 49–52.

9

Friendships and Social Networks Among Older People

John C. Cavanaugh

Having a group of people with whom one can relate and on whom one can rely is an essential part of a person's overall practical and emotional support system, irrespective of his or her age. Indeed, among the many benefits of relationships is that having a well-functioning and intact support system is a key component in dealing with many types of personal challenges (Duck & Vanzetti, 1996).

Despite the central importance of personal relationships, however, little research has directly examined the processes by which *social networks* (one's collection of personal relationships) in general, or friendships in particular, help people cope with practical issues, anxiety, depression, and so forth. This is in contrast to related research on marital and intergenerational family relationships, summarized elsewhere in this volume.

Social Networks

Social support can be defined as support that is accessible to people through social ties to others (i.e., one's social network). One primary function of social support is to facilitate coping when an individual is experiencing stress (Pearson, 1996). Research supports the view that the more social support a person receives, the greater the protection or buffering from stressors.

How social networks are formed changes somewhat across the adult life span. Carstensen (1995) proposed that changes in social behavior observed in later life reflect a complicated and important process. Specifically, she described a life-span theory of *socioemotional selectivity*, which argues that social contact is motivated by a variety of goals, including *information seeking, self-concept*, and *emotional regulation*. Each of these goals is presumed to be differentially salient at different points of the life span and to result in very different social behavior. For example, when information seeking is the goal, such as when a person is trying to figure out how he or she fits in, meeting many new people is a major part of the process. With a goal of emotional regulation, though, people tend to become much more selective in their choice of social partners and prefer to be with people much like themselves. Carstensen (1995) believes that emotional regulation is the primary goal for older adults. Her research supports this view; people become increasingly selective in their choice of people with whom they want to have contact.

Although women tend to have more extensive social networks than do men and are more likely to receive support from multiple sources, it is the quality rather than the quantity of one's social network that is most strongly related to well-being (Antonucci & Akiyama, 1987). For example, older adults who receive several "friendly visitor" calls per day to check on them may not be as satisfied as those who receive one or two calls from "special friends" each day (Pearson, 1996). Moreover, women are more likely to qualify their support than are men, who are likely to view all forms of social support as roughly equivalent (Pearson, 1996).

In considering the potential for social networks to function as resources for individuals experiencing stressors such as anxiety-related problems, it is important to realize that social support does not provide uniformly positive outcomes. Hansson, Jones, and Fletcher (1990) observed that "negative interactions within support networks may overshadow many positive effects of support" (p. 451). Indeed, some older adults may resent or be offended when they are offered help, which is interpreted by them as a statement that they cannot cope by themselves.

Such feelings of loss of independence are important and strike deeply for many older adults. In this sense, social support, even though well-intentioned, may create more problems than it solves. Clinicians must exercise caution in applying stereotypic beliefs that older adults are willing recipients of support and must take the time to thoroughly assess their clients' support systems as well as their clients' likely interpretation of gestures of support.

Friendships

Across ethnic-group lines, older adults' life satisfaction depends more on the quality and quantity of contacts with friends than it does on contacts with younger members of their own family (Antonucci, 1985). This importance is due in part to older adults' concern that they not become a burden to their families and their subsequent use of friends as a way to remain independent, and in part to the sheer fact that friendships tend to be fun. In general, older adults tend to have fewer relationships with other people than younger adults have, which is typically viewed as a reflection of increased experiences of loss with age (Carstensen, 1995).

Gender differences in friendships have been well documented across the adult life span (Rawlins, 1992). Women tend to base friendships on intimacy and emotional sharing; men tend to base them on shared activities. Thus, women are more likely than men to get together for the purpose of providing emotional or personal support; such confiding is more difficult for men. The evidence indicates that from childhood, women are socialized to engage in more intimate sharing; in contrast, the social pressure on men to suppress their feeling may actually inhibit their ability to form close friendships (Rawlins, 1992). Extrapolating from research examining the normative course of friendships across the adult life span, one would expect that women would be in a better position than men to create the requisite social support systems needed to address emotional and behavioral problems, as well as practical problems.

The longest lasting relationships people normally have are with siblings. The vast majority of older adults report that they feel close to at least one sibling and that this closeness dates to childhood through their shared family experiences.

Gold, Woodbury, and George (1990) identified five central dimensions of sibling relationships: *closeness, involvement with each other, frequency of contact, envy,* and *resentment.* They combined the dimensions to create five types of sibling interactions: *congenial* (characterized by high levels of closeness and involvement, average levels of contact, and relatively low levels of envy and resentment); *loyal* (characterized by average levels of closeness, involvement, and contact and relatively low levels of envy and resentment); *intimate* (characterized by high levels of closeness and involvement and low levels of envy and resentment); *apathetic* (characterized by low levels on all dimensions); and *hostile* (characterized by relatively high levels of involvement and resentment and relatively low levels on all other dimensions).

Congenial and loyal types describe roughly two thirds of older adults' sibling relationships; moreover, older African American siblings have apathetic or hostile relationships roughly five times less often than older European American siblings (Gold, 1990). Sisters have the closest relationships on average (Lee, Mancini, & Maxwell, 1990), and brothers tend to have less frequent contact (Connidis, 1994). Unfortunately, less is known about brother–sister relationships in late life.

An important point for the clinician to consider from this research is that the types of relationships older adults have with their siblings should be assessed to ascertain whether the relationships may be appropriate resources to draw on in addressing practical and emotional problems. One of the most important aspects of sibling relationships is that of providing care and extensive support, especially in situations when a sibling has no other means of care. Most often, siblings who need care from brothers or sisters are *younger,* live alone (were never married or are widowed or divorced), have few if any children, and live in small cities (Cicirelli, Coward, & Dwyer, 1992). Although the notion that siblings may experience anxiety, anger, or depression over anticipated care for a brother or sister would appear reasonable, especially in view of related concerns about a parent, the topic has yet to be researched systematically.

Conclusion

On the basis of normative research, social networks and friendships appear to often represent important potential resources for older adults when confronted with emotional and practical problems. Clinicians would be well advised, however, to ensure that thorough analyses of the nature and extent of the social network, the client's likely interpretation of network-based intervention, and the type of friendships available (especially with siblings) are conducted. Otherwise, even well-intentioned intervention strategies may be misperceived.

What is also clear is that considerably more research is needed to address more directly the potential of social networks and friendships in regard to emotional and behavioral problems. Although the speculations made here would appear reasonable, the findings are based on normative samples and do not address the unique challenges involving all forms of emotional and behavioral problems. Thus, clinicians should exercise some caution in using social networks and friendships as primary tools in helping older adults cope with such problems.

References

Antonucci, T. C. (1985). Personal characteristics, social support, and social behavior. In R. H. Binstock & E. Shanas (Eds.), *Handbook of aging and the social sciences* (2nd ed., pp. 94–128). New York: Reinhold.

Antonucci, T. C., & Akiyama, H. (1987). Social networks in adult life and a preliminary examination of the convoy model. *Journal of Gerontology, 42*, 519–527.

Carstensen, L. L. (1995). Evidence for a life-span theory of socioemotional selectivity. *Current Directions in Psychological Science, 4*, 151–156.

Cicirelli, V. G., Coward, R. T., & Dwyer, J. W. (1992). Siblings as caregivers for impaired elders. *Research on Aging, 14*, 331–350.

Connidis, I. (1994). Sibling support in older age. *Journal of Gerontology: Social Sciences, 49*, S309–S317.

Duck, S., & Vanzetti, N. (1996). An introduction to personal relationships. In S. Duck & N. Vanzetti (Eds.), *A lifetime of relationships* (pp. 4–22). Pacific Grove, CA: Brooks/Cole.

Gold, D. T. (1990). Late-life sibling relationships: Does race affect typological distribution? *Gerontologist, 30*, 741–748.

Gold, D. T., Woodbury, M. A., & George, L. K. (1990). Relationship classification using grade of membership analysis: A typology of sibling relationships in later life. *Journal of Gerontology: Social Sciences, 45*, S43–S51.

Hansson, R. O., Jones, W. H., & Fletcher, W. L. (1990). Troubled relationships in later life: Implications for support. *Journal of Social and Personal Relationships, 7*, 451–463.

Lee, T. R., Mancini, J. A., & Maxwell, J. W. (1990). Sibling relationships in adulthood: Contact persons and motivation. *Journal of Marriage and the Family, 52*, 431–440.

Pearson, J. C. (1996). Forty-forever years? Primary relationships and senior citizens. In S. Duck & N. Vanzetti (Eds.), *A lifetime of relationships* (pp. 383–405). Pacific Grove, CA: Brooks/Cole.

Rawlins, W. K. (1992). *Friendship matters*. Hawthorne, NY: Aldine de Gruyter.

10

Sexuality and Aging

Jørgen Bruun Pedersen

Sexual behavior and sexual desire in older people previously were assumed to be rare. This is now known to be untrue (Brecher, 1984; Kivelä, Pahkala, & Honkakoski, 1986; Persson, 1980; Starr & Weiner, 1981). It was earlier assumed that biological factors, such as menopause among women, represented nature's signals to the person that the time in life had come where sexual activity ought to stop. However, sexuality in older people is not just biologically determined, it is multidetermined. Sexuality is a lifelong force, and there are qualitative and quantitative changes that occur with age, as they do in other areas of human activity. Recent sexological studies point to the importance of sociocultural and psychological factors in determining the fate of sexuality among older people.

Although Kinsey, Pomeroy, and Martin (1948) and Kinsey et al. (1953) provided much information on adult sexual behavior, little was added to the knowledge of sexuality in older people, because less than 200 respondents over the age of 60 were included in their sample of more than 11,000 people. And their observation that 75% of men 80 or more years of age were impotent was based on a sample of 4. Masters and Johnson (1966) added some information on the physiological changes in older people during sexual activity, but again, the number of people over 60 years of age was limited (and only 6 men and 3 women were over 70 years of age).

Continuing Methodological Difficulties

It is somewhat difficult to compare current survey data because of differing definitions of *sexuality* and *aging*. Some studies have limited the definition of *sexual behavior* to intercourse (in the missionary position) and have excluded other manifestations. Sexuality, in other studies, has been measured in terms of erection, lubrication capacity, or orgasm frequency. Still other studies have used a broader definition, including touching, caressing, masturbation, intimacy, sensuality, dreaming, and fantasizing.

Likewise, *older people* has been defined differently. In some studies, people over 60 are considered older people (thereby ignoring cohort differences within the older population). Other studies use broad age categories, such as 60–74 years and 75 years and older, which is better but still blurs developmental trends. It is most useful when older samples are at least divided into young old (55–65 years of age), middle old (66–75 years), and old old (76 years and over). This produces meaningful results, which can be drawn on over time.

Finally, the representativeness of samples in most studies of sexuality among older people is weak. Most research samples comprise individuals with a better social status, higher than average economic status, higher education, better general health, more positive attitudes toward sex, and greater willingness to talk about their own sexuality than the majority of the population. Thus, estimates of sexual activity in older people that are based on recent studies may present a somewhat overoptimistic picture of such interests, desire, and behavior.

Normal Sexual Aging

Nonetheless, two common trends are obvious: (a) Older people are more sexually active than previously assumed, and (b) there is a decline, for both men and women, in sexual activity, even in populations of healthy older people.

Kivelä et al. (1986) sent a questionnaire to 1,529 people who were 60 to 90+ years old, residing in a semi-industrialized rural community in Finland. Seventy-two percent of the men and 38% of the women were married, and 14% of the men and 47% of the women were widowed. Two aspects of this study are particularly valuable: The educational level was low (which suggests a more representative sample), and the return rate was high: 89%. The questionnaire comprised questions about health and life conditions in general, with two questions about sexual intercourse and sexual desire: "Do you have sexual intercourse?" and "Do you currently experience feelings of sexual desire?" Among men, sexual intercourse at least once a month was affirmed by 53% of those in their 60s, 22% of men in their 70s, and 5% of those in their 80s. The corresponding figures for women were 26%, 5%, and 0%. However, in addition to actual behavior, there were sexual interest and sexual desire. Sixty-four percent of the men in their 60s, 54% of those in their 70s, and 35% of those in their 80s sometimes felt sexual desire. The corresponding figures for women were 39%, 16%, and 2%.

Other Scandinavian studies where effort was taken to secure more representative samples also have found a similar progressive decrease in sexual activities with further movement into old age, as well as evidence that a minority of older people remain sexually active. A Danish study (Nielsen et al., 1986) of 179 70-year-old women found that 22% of the group still had intercourse once or twice a month and 44% periodically felt sexual desire. A Swedish study of a carefully drawn sample of 70-year-old from Göteborg found that 76% of the men and 16% of the women still were having intercourse. The difference between men and women was primarily due to women being younger than their husbands and to 26% being widows, compared with 11% of the men being widowers (Persson, 1980).

A cross-sectional study, using both interview and questionnaire data from a representative sample of married U.S. adults 65 years of age and older, found age to be a significant predictor of sexual activity (Marsiglio & Donnelly, 1991). Among respondents 60–65 years of age, 65% reported having sex at least once during the previous month. This figure fell to 45% in the 71–75-year age group and to 24% among respondents 76 years of age and older.

Masturbation is still a delicate subject with current older samples, and most earlier studies omitted questions about this form of sexuality. In the Nielsen et al. (1986) study, only 64% of the 70-year-old women found masturbation acceptable, whereas 10% found it unacceptable under any circumstances. Recent surveys have included questions on this subject, but the rate of refusal to answer is often high. The most consistent impression is that older men masturbate considerably more than older women. This is illustrated in the Bergström-Walan and Høpfner-Nielsen study (1990) of 60–80-year-olds, where 12% of the men but none of the women masturbated at least once per week, although nearly 33% of the women masturbated at least once per year.

Attitudes toward sex and sexual behavior changed strikingly during the 1960s, after the development of oral contraceptives and more liberal abortion legislation. This will influence the sexual habits of new cohorts of older people. Thus, further research will be needed to track how these earlier attitudinal changes result in behavior changes in old age as these cohorts age. This more liberal attitude already has started to show up in young old samples (von Sydow, 1996), whereas the current old old tend to preserve the sexual lifestyle and attitude of their younger years. Stability in sexual habits is a prominent feature found in several studies. Martin (1981) found, for example, that individual differences in sexual functioning before middle age are likely to be maintained past middle age and that it is the persistence of these differences between individuals from the same cohort that accounts for much of the observed variation in current frequencies. Kontula and Haavio-Mannila (1994) compared sexual activity in 1971 and in 1992 in a nationally representative group of adults in Finland and found that in 1971 only 1% of the women in age group 40–44 years had more than 10 sexual partners in their life but that the parallel percentage in the same age group had risen to 20% by 1992. When women in their 40s today reach old age, they will have had a much longer and more varied sexual history than earlier generations of older women, and one may assume that this will influence their sexual behavior, interest, and satisfaction.

Sexual Problems in Old Age

For Men

Men may experience a significant delay in attaining an erection, and the erection may not be as full as that to which they are accustomed. Generally, the older the man is, the longer it takes to achieve full penile erection, regardless of the effectiveness of the stimulative techniques used. Full penile erection frequently is not attained until just before ejaculation. This slowed sexual response can lead to performance anxiety and fears, as seen in the results of Bretschneider and McCoy (1988). They asked a group of healthy, upper-middle-class 80–102-year-old men with sexual partners about most frequently experienced problems in a sexual situation. The six most frequent responses from men were fear of poor performance (37%), inability to maintain an erection (33%), inability to reach an erection (28%), inability to reach orgasm (28%), not enough opportunities for sexual encounters (23%), and partner's vaginal pain or lack of lubrication (23%).

It has long been suspected that much of the decline in sexual behavior in advancing years could be explained by a decrease in circulating androgen levels, but a recent review of the existing data does not support this hypothesis (Segraves & Segraves 1995). In this study, and in several others, what is found is a clear association between decline in sexual behavior and diabetes mellitus, heart disease, hypertension, urinary incontinence, and the use of sedatives. Unfortunately, a sizable minority of cases of impotence are caused by surgical or medical treatments for other disease states (e.g., radical prostatectomy, medication with antihypertensive therapy, and a number of psychiatric drugs).

For Women

Investigations of the biological barriers for sexual activity in older women have focused on the impact of menopause, suspecting that the decline of estrogen and progesterone might cause a decline in sexual activity. The results are inconclusive. A minority of women do report some decline in sexual activity with menopause, but the majority do not, suggesting that the fall in circulating estrogen and progesterone levels may not be the only factor in the prediction of sexual interest and activity after menopause. Studies of hormone replacement in postmenopausal women have yielded inconclusive findings concerning the effects of estrogen replacement on libido (Segraves & Segraves 1995). The effects of disease on female sexuality are less well studied, but there is compelling reason to suspect that physical disease and medical treatment have parallel effects to those observed in aging men.

Partner availability is a problem, and social customs and cultural attitudes are serious barriers for active sexuality in older women. They tend to marry men older than themselves and, therefore, to be widowed when they grow old. It is more difficult for an older woman to find a new sexual partner, because of both cultural attitudes and fewer available partners (Segraves & Segraves 1995).

Practical Perspectives

Sexual issues and problems for older people are multidetermined. Biological, social, and psychological factors can contribute to creating specific sexual problems. The risk is that a problem in one area (e.g., erectile difficulties) leads to a psychological reaction, or a chain of psychological reactions, which eventually leads to an unnecessary termination of all sexual activity.

The biological factors may disappear with new and better medical treatment, and social and attitudinal barriers may diminish as a result of a change in the cultural climate. Most important now, and in the future, is to develop a realistic view and a solid knowledge base on sexuality and aging, to better inform coming cohorts of older people about the avoidable and unavoidable changes in sexual responsiveness and behavior.

Note that the normal trends in sexual development will show the same trend as found in other areas of functioning (e.g., psychomotoric or cognitive development): (a) a reduction in frequency from young old to old old, (b) a slowing down in reaction time or responsivity, (c) a diminishing in strength and endurance, (d) a need for stronger sensory stimuli to elicit a reaction, (e) a continuing inter- and intraindividual variability, and (f) a serious difficulty in separating the effects of aging per se from the specific consequences (e.g., injury, disease, the gradual degenerative processes that may occur with the passage of time, cultural changes, or social changes).

It is possible to compensate for these changes in sexual development if one does not panic and engage in a struggle to continue sex in exactly the same way as in the younger years or cling to traditional sex roles. The task instead is to find new ways to obtain the same goal. When the *allegro molto* is impossible, an *andante* can be a satisfactory alternative, as shown in several studies, where older people found their sex life satisfactory in spite of a reduction in frequency and strength.

References

Bergström-Walan, M. B., & Høpfner-Nielsen, H. (1990). Sexualitet hos 60–80 - åringar [Sexuality in 60–80-year-olds]. *Nordisk Sexologi, 8,* 137–144.

Brecher, E. M. (1984). *Love, sex, and aging: A consumer's union report.* Boston: Little, Brown.

Bretschneider, J. G., & McCoy, N. L. (1988, April). Sexual interest and behavior in healthy 80- to 102-year-olds. *Archives of Sexual Behavior, 17,* 109–129.

Kinsey, A. C., Pomeroy, W. B., & Martin, C. R. (1948). *Sexual behavior in the human male.* Philadelphia: W. B. Saunders.

Kinsey, A. C., Pomeroy, W. B., Martin, C. R., & Gebhard, P. H. (1953). *Sexual behavior in the human female.* Philadelphia: W. B. Saunders.

Kivelä, S. L., Pahkala, K., & Honkakoski, A. (1986). Sexual desire, intercourse, and related factors among elderly Finns. *Nordisk Sexologi, 4,* 18–27.

Kontula, O., & Haavio-Mannila, E. (1994). Sexual behavior changes in Finland during the last 20 years. *Nordisk Sexologi, 12,* 196–214.

Marsiglio, W., & Donnelly, D. (1991). Sexual relations in later life: A national study of married persons. *Journal of Gerontology, 46,* 338–344.

Martin, C. E. (1981). Factors affecting sexual functioning in 60–79-year-old married males. *Archives of Sexual Behavior, 10,* 399–420.

Masters, W. H., & Johnson, V. E. (1966). *Human sexual response.* Boston: Little, Brown.

Nielsen, I. L., Fog, E., Larsen, G. K., Madsen, J., Garde, K., & Kelstrup, J. (1986). 70-å kuiders seksuelle adford, oplevelse, viders og holdning. [Sexual behavior, experience, knowledge, and attitudes in 70-year-old women.] *Ugeskrift for Læger, 198,* 2863–2866.

Persson, G. (1980). Sexuality in a 70-year-old urban population. *Journal of Psychosomatic Research, 24,* 335–342.

Segraves, R. T., & Segraves, K. B. (1995). Human sexuality and aging. *Journal of Sex Education and Therapy, 21,* 88–102.

Starr, B. D., & Weiner, M. B. (1981). *The Starr–Weiner report on sex & sexuality in the mature years.* New York: McGraw-Hill.

von Sydow, K. (1996). Female sexuality and historical time: A comparison of sexual biographies of German women born between 1895 and 1936. *Archives of Sexual Behavior, 25,* 473–493.

11

Employment and Potential Midlife Career Crisis

Harvey L. Sterns and Jennifer H. Gray

The concept of midlife crisis as a life event has been advanced in developmental theory (Erikson, 1963; Levinson, Darrow, Klein, Levinson, & McKee, 1978; Levinson & Levinson, 1996) as well as in popular literature (Sheehy, 1976, 1995). Whereas the experience of such a crisis has been widely accepted as a normative occurrence, more recent literature and empirical evidence have questioned this acceptance. Issues such as (a) a more complex conceptualization of the structure of adulthood (e.g., Sheehy's, 1995, idea of a second adulthood), (b) evidence of continuity of personality during the midlife period (Costa & Mc-Crae, 1989), (c) the status of chronological age as a meaningful predictor (Lachman & James, 1997), and (d) data illustrating different perceptions of midlife (Lachman, Lewkowicz, Marcus, & Peng, 1994) have undermined the normative status of midlife crisis. This chapter reviews conceptualizations of midlife and crisis, considers the frequency of the phenomena, and explores connections between midlife and midcareer experiences.

Conceptualizations of Midlife

Erikson (1963) conceptualized psychosocial development as associated with age and predicted stage-related changes in adult personality primarily based on internal factors. The developmental issue at midlife was viewed in terms of *generativity* versus *stagnation*. Successful resolution of this life period was characterized by a shift in focus to a concern for the larger social structure and the development of the younger generation. Unsuccessful resolution of this developmental dilemma was believed to result in self-absorption and potentially hinder resolution of the subsequent stage.

Levinson (Levinson et al., 1978; Levinson & Levinson, 1996) also viewed developmental stages as connected to specific age periods. In Levinson's theory, the midlife transition was described as a period of self-evaluation, spanning ages 40 to 45, and was emphasized as a universal experience. This transition was conceptualized as a time of severe crisis brought about by tensions and discrepancies between a person's actual and desired achievements. Although specific external stresses were thought to be an influence, internal events were considered to drive the developmental crisis. The self and increasing individ-uation were thought to be the focus during this life period.

Levinson's original work was specifically based on the male experience at midlife. More recently, Levinson and Levinson (1996) suggested that both men and women experience the same periods of adult development at the same ages. The general structural framework of development was thought to be similar, but the specific life circumstances, available resources, and existing constraints were considered as potentially differing by gender.

Popular literature has often addressed the issue of midlife crisis with Sheehy (1976, 1995) being one such translator of adult developmental issues. Sheehy (1976) used broad markers of chronological age to define life stages and has more recently (Sheehy, 1995) reported that the meaning of age ranges has shifted upward. That is, people currently in midlife tend to view middle age differently than previous cohorts. Included in her discussion of midlife is the shift from first adulthood (ages 30–45) to second adulthood (ages 45–85+), with a predictable transition occurring between these stages. This transition may potentially have both positive and negative resolutions. Issues considered in this conceptualization of midlife include (a) coming to terms with disparities between earlier generation's notions of middle age and how one actually sees oneself at middle age, (b) leaving first adulthood, and (c) actively engaging in creating second adulthood. A major proposition of transitioning to second adult-hood is constructing a new identity and developing a sense of mastery.

In addressing gender issues, Sheehy (1995) suggested that men and women negotiate this period differently. Particular issues and concerns confronted may differ by gender, and a potential asynchrony within couples may result. The subsequent tensions within relationships may produce either growth or nega-tive consequences (e.g., divorce).

It is interesting to note that both Erikson's and Levinson's conceptualiza-tions are stage theories and, in essence, are organismic models in which each stage is represented as being qualitatively different from the preceding stage. These discussions place strong emphasis on periods of transition and the res-olution of developmental issues in order to achieve the next stage (Hultsch & Plemmons, 1979).

In contrast to the stage-based theories, the personality factor analytic ap-proach to adult development has been based on a more empirical tradition (Costa & McCrae, 1989). This approach has examined the structure of person-ality (i.e., the NEO Five Factors of Extraversion, Agreeableness, Conscientious-ness, Neuroticism, and Openness to Experience) across the life span, and the research consistently finds a general pattern of stability extending from the 30s through the 80s (Costa & McCrae, 1989).

Recently, it has also been suggested that chronological age may not be the most useful indicator of midlife (Lachman & James, 1997). Positive relations have been found between respondents' ages and perceived ages of midlife: Older respondents tend to report later entry and exit ages than younger respondents (Lachman et al., 1994). Older adults feel that midlife ranges from ages 40–70, whereas younger adults consider midlife to range from ages 30–55. The point in time when an individual feels that she or he is middle-aged may be a sub-jective experience and is likely to vary across individuals and cohorts. Furthermore, respondents perceive middle age as a time of many responsibilities, increased stress in several life domains, and little time for leisure, as well as a time of peak competence, ability to handle stress, sense of control, purpose in life, and productivity (Lachman et al., 1994).

Crisis and Development

Developmental theories emphasizing periods of transitions, particularly midlife transitions, also necessitate discussion of the meaning or nature of change and crisis. Riegal (1975) conceptualized development by viewing stability and crisis as mutually dependent and not necessarily negative or positive. That is, development incorporates periods of both stability and change, and transition in and of itself is not necessarily a negative experience. In fact, contradictions may be viewed as the basis of development (Riegal, 1975). Similarly, both Levinson and associates (1978, 1996) and Sheehy (1976, 1995) suggested that crises are not necessarily negative, because both benefits and costs may result from such experiences.

The equating of *change* with *crisis* exaggerates the importance of the first and weakens the connotations of the second (Chiriboga, 1989). Furthermore, it blurs the important distinction between constructive contradiction as part of normal development and imbalanced contradiction, which surpasses coping resources and causes deviations from normal development (Riegal, 1975). When an individual is unable to deal with his or her life situation and contradiction surpasses coping resources, the result is a deviation from normal development. Riegal (1975) labeled developmental deviations *catastrophes* and considered these occurrences as pathological deviations from normal, constructive development. This theme of conditions exceeding coping resources surfaces throughout much of the adult development literature.

Prevalence of Midlife Crisis

Empirical evidence and popular literature present very different pictures of the prevalence of midlife crisis as a negative experience. For example, on the basis of a summary of the results of several studies, Chiriboga (1989) suggested that only 2% to 5% of middle-agers may actually experience serious midlife problems. More recently, preliminary findings from the Midlife Project funded by the McArthur Foundation suggest that life evaluations during this period may be common but not a crisis at all (Lachman et al., 1994). Even though many respondents believed there is a midlife crisis, many also reported conceptualizing this period as an opportunity for growth and development as opposed to difficulty (Lachman & James, 1997). Similarly, within the framework of the NEO Five Factors, the empirical data indicate continuity of personality. In general, consistent, replicated evidence of changes in mean level or relative standing of personality factors is rarely found over time (Costa & McCrae, 1989). In contrast, popular literature (i.e., Sheehy, 1976, 1995) and case-study-oriented work (i.e., Levinson et al., 1978; Levinson & Levinson, 1996) both suggest the

occurrence of universal, predictable transition periods, with the majority of individuals reporting crises experiences. Although empirical findings suggest consistency in general, this does not rule out the possibility of specific instances
of change. Change may be an intrinsic characteristic of some individuals, and
others may have had long-standing problems rather than just experiencing difficulties at their current stage (Costa & McCrae, 1989; Lachman & James,
1997; Lachman et al., 1994). For example, individuals who have developed immature, as opposed to mature, coping styles may experience difficulties
throughout the life span (Valliant, 1977).

Evidence of stability may also be contingent on the individual-differences
variable under investigation. Empirical investigations have typically focused
on personality traits, which, by definition, are expected to be enduring. Different traits may differ in terms of stability, and, furthermore, this stability may
differ depending on the stage of the life span or environmental circumstances
(Costa & McCrae, 1989). In some instances, specific personality traits have
been found to be related to change. For example, Neuroticism has been found
to predict midlife crises, and Openness to Experience to predict frequent midcareer shifts (Costa & McCrae, 1989).

Personality stability may also be due in part to a stable and unchanging
environment. This suggests the possibility that environmental factors might be
related to changes or crises. Multiple factors are likely to influence midlife
development (Lachman & James, 1997), and vectors of influence (e.g., career-
and family-related issues and individual differences) may come together to affect individuals in a unique and nonnormative manner.

Midcareer and Midlife

Traditional linear career models bring together midcareer and midlife by tying
career stages to chronological age. This conceptualization has reinforced the
interconnectedness of midcareer and midlife experiences. In contrast, life-span
theory recognizes that career changes and events may take place at any point
throughout the life span. Because career stages are not necessarily tied to any
particular age, midcareer and midlife may potentially coincide. Life-span theory, however, does not require a co-occurrence of these events. This conceptualization suggests that non-age-specific organizational, career, and individual
variables may act together in influencing either midlife or midcareer experiences, or both. These events may act as stressors that have the potential to
overwhelm individuals' coping resources.

Changes in organizational systems have repercussions for individuals
within these systems. As organizations undergo downsizing and restructuring
in transitioning from pyramid to flatter, more streamlined, configurations, em-
ployees may experience job loss, job plateauing, skills obsolescence, and the
need for career self-management (Farr, Tesluk, & Klein, 1998; Sterns & Miklos,
1995). Additionally, slow company growth may lead to less opportunity for ad-
vancement and the need for career self-management (Farr et al., 1998). These
events potentially lead to changes in the nature of work, which may be perceived as threatening to middle-aged and older workers (Farr et al., 1998). Note

that depending on age of career entry, middle-aged workers may be more likely to occupy the midlevel managerial positions that are often the focus of downsizing and restructuring strategies. The experiences of those who are downsized, as well as the survivors, may trigger careful self-evaluations of one's situation and opportunities.

In terms of midlife and work, Levinson et al. (1978) suggested that only 10% to 20% of middle-aged individuals experience moderate-to-high work satisfaction and that 20% to 30% receive minor gratification. In comparison, the largest group of individuals (i.e., 50%) were thought to experience work as demeaning, empty, or damaging to the self. Although both women and men were presumed to be represented in all three groups, Levinson et al. (1978) felt that women were likely to be disproportionately found in the last group, as opposed to the first two.

In contrast to the potentially negative midlife work experiences suggested by Levinson et al. (1978), Chiriboga (1989) highlighted evidence that the middle years are often viewed as a time of challenge and reward in regard to work life. Furthermore, the positive relation between age and job satisfaction indicates that midlife can be a time of positive work experiences (Farr et al., 1998).

Whether individuals experience work and career events as stressful or as opportunities for growth and challenge may depend on individual resources as well as external factors. An example of a potential individual resource is *organization-based self-esteem* (OBSE), or the degree to which an individual perceives he or she can satisfy needs through organizational membership (Pierce, Gardner, Cummings, & Dunham, 1989). High OBSE is characterized by perceiving oneself as important, meaningful, effectual, and worthwhile as an organizational member.

As organizations restructure, worker experiences of uncertainty, overload, and unsupportive environments may become more common. These types of work-related events may be more likely to impact individuals with low as compared with high OBSE (Pierce, Gardner, Dunham, & Cummings, 1993). For example, people with low OBSE tend to have lower achievement satisfaction under conditions of role ambiguity and role overload. Low-OBSE individuals also tend to have lower achievement satisfaction and job performance when the work environment and supervisors are perceived as being unsupportive rather than supportive (Pierce et al., 1993). Individuals with high OBSE may be less vulnerable to these situations than those with low OBSE. High OBSE may be a potential coping resource for maintaining employment, promoting career growth as opposed to plateauing, and proactively maintaining and updating competencies.

Along with individual resources, external factors also have the potential to facilitate or disrupt career development. Sterns and Dorsett (1994) reviewed ways in which organizations can foster competence and enhance employee motivation to update skills. These factors include providing challenging work coupled with security, interaction between peers and management, flexibility in keeping pace with job changes, organizational support and commitment, and reward systems. Factors that may derail career development include stereotypes of older workers and fewer training and updating opportunities (Farr et al., 1998; Sterns & Dorsett, 1994).

Conclusion

Qualitative research (i.e., that of Levinson) has tended to support the concept of midlife crisis as a normative occurrence. In addition, this literature suggests that career and work-related events are included in this age-initiated self-evaluation period. In contrast, quantitative research (e.g., Costa & McCrae, 1989) has found little evidence of a normative experience of mid-life crisis. Furthermore, life-span approaches to understanding careers have emphasized the potential disconnection between midlife and midcareer and the opportunity for continued development and growth at midlife and beyond. We recognize that difficulties at midlife may be nonnormative occurrences related to unique individual experiences, such as having a history of adjustment difficulties, having developed immature coping styles, or experiencing organizational events that exceed one's coping resources.

In conclusion, viewing midlife as a normative period of crisis may lead to an overreadiness to address surface issues and not identify the bases of experienced difficulties (Chiriboga, 1989). Midlife may be experienced as a period of recommitment and reevaluation, and many people find this period highly satisfying and rewarding. Some people, however, may experience difficulties due to external or internal influences triggering the need for intervention and support. Practitioners and researchers need to be aware of these multiple factors and avoid diagnosis and conclusions primarily based on life stage.

References

Chiriboga, D. A. (1989). Mental health at the midpoint: Crisis, challenge, or relief? In S. Hunter & M. Sundel (Eds.), *Mid-life myths: Issues, findings, and practice implications* (pp. 116–144). Newbury Park, CA: Sage.

Costa, P. T., & McCrae, R. R. (1989). Personality continuity and the changes of adult life. In M. Storandt & G. R. VandenBos (Eds.), *The adult years: Continuity and change* (pp. 41–77). Washington, DC: American Psychological Association.

Erikson, E. H. (1963). *Childhood and society*. New York: Norton.

Farr, J. L., Tesluk, P. E., & Klein, S. R. (1998). Organizational structure of the workplace and the older worker. In K. W. Schaie & C. Schooler (Eds.), *Impact of work on older individuals* (pp. 143–185). New York: Springer.

Hultsch, D. F., & Plemmons, J. K. (1979). Life events and life-span development. In P. B. Baltes & O. G. Brim, Jr. (Eds.), *Life-span development and behavior* (pp. 1–36). New York: Academic Press.

Lachman, M. E., & James, J. B. (1997). Charting the course of midlife development: An overview. In M. E. Lachman & J. B. James (Eds.), *Multiple paths of midlife development* (pp. 1–17). Chicago: University of Chicago Press.

Lachman, M. E., Lewkowicz, C., Marcus, A., & Peng, Y. (1994). Images of midlife development among young, middle-aged and older adults. *Journal of Adult Development, 1*, 201–211.

Levinson, D. J., Darrow, C. N., Klein, E. B., Levinson, M. L., & McKee, B. (1978). *The seasons of a man's life*. New York: Knopf.

Levinson, D. J., & Levinson, J. D. (1996). *The seasons of a woman's life*. New York: Knopf.

Pierce, J. L., Gardner, D. G., Cummings, L. L., & Dunham, R. B. (1989). Organization-based self-esteem: Construct definition, measurement, and validation. *Academy of Management Journal, 32*, 622–648.

Pierce, J. L., Gardner, D. G., Dunham, R. B., & Cummings, L. L. (1993). Moderation by organizational-based self-esteem of role condition–employee response relationships. *Academy of Management Journal, 36*, 271–288.

Riegel, K. F. (1975). Adult life crises: A dialectic interpretation of development. In N. Datan & L. H. Ginsberg (Eds.), *Life-span developmental psychology: Normative life crises* (pp. 99–128). New York: Academic Press.

Sheehy, G. (1976). *Passages*. New York: Dutton.

Sheehy, G. (1995). *New passages: Mapping your life across time*. New York: Random House.

Sterns, H. L., & Dorsett, J. G. (1994). Career development: A life span issue. *Experimental Aging Research, 20,* 257–264.

Sterns, H. L., & Miklos, S. M. (1995). The aging worker in a changing environment: Organizational and individual issues. *Journal of Vocational Behavior, 47,* 248–268.

Valliant, G. E. (1977). *Adaptation to life*. Boston: Little, Brown.

12

Retirement and Retirement Planning in Old Age

Raymond Bossé

Retirement from the labor force is a relatively recent life-cycle event in the industrialized world. Consider that in 1900, life expectancy at birth was 47, so few workers lived long enough to retire. Those who stopped working were likely to do so because of injury or poor health. National pension plans were just beginning to appear in two or three European countries. Private pensions were provided only to a small upper-class minority or to select occupations such as civil servants.

By 1930, life expectancy at birth had increased to 63.7 years and by 1950 to 68.0 years, due to medical advances. Increasing longevity along with the deprivation and suffering caused by the Great Depression underscored the need to provide for unemployment in general and financial security in the later years. By the 1950s, national and private pension plans made it possible for older workers not only to retire but to do so at specified mandatory ages, generally at or near age 65.

Effect of Retirement Legislation on Workforce Participation

The availability of pensions had a gradual but eventually very pronounced effect on workforce participation. In the year 1900, for instance, in the United States, 68.4% of men age 65 years or older were still in the workforce and 9.1% of women (they tended to be housewives). In 1936, the Social Security system was initiated. Four years later, in 1940, the number of men and women age 65 years or older in the workforce had declined to 41.8% and 6.1%, respectively. In 1994, those percentages had declined to 16.8% for men and increased to 9.2% for women. (Comparable numbers are presented for European countries in Jacobs, Kohli, & Rein, 1991). These low percentages of workforce participation by those age 65 years or older are now prompting governments in many countries to delay the age for pension eligibility or to eliminate a mandatory retirement age. The hope is that this action will encourage older workers to remain in the workforce and thus relieve the strain on national pension systems.

The Paradox of Retirement and Health

Despite the persistent withdrawal of older workers from the workforce, the myth prevails in medical and psychosocial circles that retirement is harmful to physical and emotional health. Three distinct arguments have been made to support this notion. A *deductive* argument states that because humans spend most of their adult years in the workforce, individuals construct their identity and that of others on occupation (Crawford, 1972, 1973; Palmore, Burchett, Fillenbaum, George, & Wallman, 1985, chap. 4). Therefore, loss of the work role means loss of identity, which generates stress, which in turn leads to health declines. The fallacy of this reasoning is in the premises, namely, the equating of work with identity and its loss as stressful.

The second argument is *observational* (McMahan & Ford, 1955; Tyhurst, Salk, & Kennedy, 1957). It concludes that retirement is harmful because some retirees are or become ill and die. The error of this reasoning is in attributing causality to the event of retirement because it appears to precede illness or death. In fact, illness is just as likely to have preceded and precipitated the retirement event. In addition, retirement is a life event that occurs at older ages, when humans tend to be more frail and more susceptible to illness.

The third argument may be viewed as *historical* or *dogmatic* (Barron, Streib, & Suchman, 1952; MacBride, 1976). It is based on the belief that work is divinely mandated. Work is professed to be the salubrious norm for the majority, and retirement, the unhealthful exception. The fallacy of this view is its dogmatization of an empirical question. At best, it is a hypothesis transformed into a conclusion.

The preceding views are not to be taken lightly, because they have been held by many and have influenced not only individual behaviors but also legislation and scientific investigation. It behooves us, therefore, to examine the true health consequences of retirement.

Physical Health

Studies that focus exclusively on retirees conclude that retirement harms health. However, note that retirees tend to be older and more likely to be sick. A more legitimate approach is to compare the health of retirees with that of workers within the same age range or to study the health of retirees longitudinally within the first years of retirement, along with comparably aged workers. Studies that have done this generally have failed to find a significant physical health effect of retirement (Ekerdt, Baden, Bossé, & Dibbs, 1983; Mor-Barak, Scharlach, Birba, & Sokolov, 1992). Hence, despite the persisting belief that retirement harms health, there is little evidence to support this idea except for a minority of retirees.

Mental Health

As with physical health, those who believe that retirement harms mental health have even implicated retirement in the higher rates of suicide among older men (Heikkines, Aro, & Lönnqvist, 1992). Also, several case studies of Second World War and Korean War veterans have linked retirement with the onset of posttraumatic stress disorder (PTSD) in previously asymptomatic veterans (Hierholzer, Munson, Peabody, & Rosenberg, 1992; Van Dyke, Zilberg, & McKinnon, 1985). Other studies have indicated a variety of limited short-term effects of retirement for specific individuals (Bossé, Aldwin, Levenson, & Ekerdt, 1987; de Grâce, Joshi, Pelletier, & Beaupré, 1994; Midanik, Soghikian, Ransom, & Tekawa, 1995).

Thus, research into the physical and mental health consequences of retirement suggests that retirement may constitute a problem for specific minorities as in the cases of PTSD or short-term effects such as loneliness, depression, and anxiety. These cases prompt us to investigate the stressfulness of retirement possibly due to the many losses incurred, such as loss of identity, income, or social support.

The Stressfulness of Retirement

The fact that retirement has been included consistently in stressful life events inventories indicates that to retire has been considered stressful (Aldwin, 1990). Studies that have used such investories, however, have not found retirement to be stressful except for a very specific minority. In regard to, first, the stressfulness of retirement compared with other stressful life events, Matthews, Brown, Davis, & Denton, 1982 found that retirement ranked 28th among 34 stressful life events. Mattila, Joukamaa, and Salokangas, (1989) reported similar findings, whereas Bossé, Aldwin, Levenson (1991) found that retirement scored 30th in stressfulness from a list of 31 events. Spouse's retirement ranked 31.

As for the proportion of retirees who find retirement stressful, Bossé et al. (1991) found 30% of retirees reporting retirement to be stressful. In addition, Bossé, Spiro, and Kressin (1996) referenced several other studies that consistently reported between 30% and 33% of retirees who described a variety of negative feelings about being retired. Please note that at a national level, reports that some 30% of retirees find retirement stressful are not trivial and suggest the need to better understand the factors that make retirement stressful for this minority.

Characteristics of Stressed Retirees

Research has identified several factors that may be related to retirement stress in specific cases (for a review of published research, see Bossé et al., 1996). Among the numerous factors found to be related to retirement stress are the circumstance of retiring early, unexpectedly, or for reasons of health; socioeconomic status; white- versus blue-collar occupation; a combination of daily hassles; the experience of other stressful life events at about the time of retirement. In general, these multiple factors may be reduced to three: health, income, and retiring unexpectedly. Poor health that is related to retirement stress usually occurs before the retirement and tends to precipitate the event such that it too coincides with the retirement being unexpected, which in turn leads to loss of income.

Other factors that have been hypothesized to cause retirement stress are loss of social support, work saliency, whether one experienced stress at work, and certain dimensions of personality. The evidence for these factors, however, is very inconsistent.

A unique factor that is sometimes related to retirement stress is the marital relationship, because of what is sometimes called "the husband underfoot syndrome" due to his invasion of the wife's domain. The evidence indicates that the opposite is just as likely, namely, that couples enjoy each other's company more and that the real outcome depends more on the quality of the relationship than on the event of retirement. Stressed marriages may be further stressed by the event and vice versa.

Conclusion

Defining Retirement

To understand retirement and its potential effects, it is essential to stop treating it as a yes or no situation. It has become almost impossible today to define retirement. There are possibly a dozen different combinations of work and retirement that must be taken into consideration, to understand and properly deal with retiree problems. To provide proper counseling, one must consider not only the possible stressful circumstances described earlier but also the various combinations of new full-time or part-time work after retirement, along with a variety of private and public pensions that a retiree may or may not receive.

A Normative Life Event

Retirement at or about age 65 became an expected occurrence starting in the 1930s with the introduction of government and private pensions. Within the next few years, many workers began to retire as soon as possible. For the earliest cohorts that experienced mandatory retirement, the event may have been stressful and have led to health declines. It appears that retirement quickly became a normative life event, such as going to school, learning to drive, getting married, or going to work. Therefore, contrary to expectations, only a minority of retirees tend to find retirement stressful or to experience physical or mental health declines. The principal characteristics of that minority are (a) they retired unexpectedly due to such factors as poor health or business failures or (b) they now experience financial problems.

References

Aldwin, C. M. (1990). The Elders Life Stress Inventory (ELSI): Egocentric and nonegocentric stress. In M. A. P. Stephens, S. E. Hobfoll, J. H. Crowther, & D. L. Tennenbaun (Eds.), *Stress and coping in late life families* (pp. 49–69). New York: Hemisphere.

Barron, M. L., Streib, G., & Suchman, E. A. (1952). Research on the social disorganization of retirement. *American Sociological Review, 17,* 479–482.

Bossé, R., Aldwin, C. M., Levenson, M. R., & Ekerdt, D. J. (1987). Mental health differences among retirees and workers: Findings from the Normative Aging Study. *Psychology and Aging, 2,* 383–389.

Bossé, R., Aldwin, C. L., Levenson, M. R., & Workman-Daniels, K. (1991). How stressful is retirement? Findings from the Normative Aging Study. *Journal of Gerontology, 46,* 9–14.

Bossé, R., Spiro, A., III, & Kressin, N. R. (1996). The psychology of retirement. In R. T. Woods (Ed.), *Handbook of the clinical psychology of ageing* (pp. 141–157). London: Wiley.

Crawford, M. (1972). Retirement as a psycho-social crisis. *Journal of Psychosomatic Research, 16,* 375–380.

Crawford, M. (1973). Retirement: A rite de passage. *Sociological Review, 21,* 447–461.

de Grâce, G. R., Joshi, P., Pelletier, R., & Beaupré, C. (1994). Consequences psychologique de la retraite en fonction du sexe et du niveau occupationnel antérieur. *Canadian Journal on Aging, 13*(2), 149–168.

Ekerdt, D. J., Baden, L., Bossé, R., & Dibbs, E. (1983). The effect of retirement on physical health. *American Journal of Public Health, 73,* 779–783.

Heikkines, M., Aro, H., & Lönnqvist, J. (1992). The partners' view on precipitant stressors in suicide. *Acta Psychiatrica Scandinavica, 85,* 380–384.

Hierholzer, R., Munson, J., Peabody, C., & Rosenberg, J. (1992). Clinical presentation of PTSD in World War II combat veterans. *Hospital and Community Psychiatry, 43,* 816–820.

Jacobs, K., Kohli, M., & Rein, M. (1991). The evolution of early exit: A comparative analyses of labor force participation patterns. In M. Kohli, M. Rein, A.-M. Guillemard, & J. Van Gunsteren (Eds.), *Time for retirement: Comparative studies of early exit from the labor force* (pp. 36–66). Cambridge, England: Cambridge University Press.

MacBride, A. (1976). Retirement as a life crisis: Myth or reality? *Canadian Psychiatric Association Journal, 21,* 547–556.

Matthews, A. M., Brown, K. H., Davis, C. K., & Denton, M. A. (1982). A crisis assessment technique for the evaluation of life events: Transition to retirement as an example. *Canadian Journal on Aging, 1*(3 & 4), 28–39.

Mattila, V. J., Joukamaa, M. I., & Salokangas, R. K. R. (1989). Retirement, aging, psychosocial adaptation and mental health. *Acta Psychiatrica Scandinavica, 80,* 356–367.

McMahan, C. A., & Ford, T. R. (1955). Surviving the first five years of retirement. *Journal of Gerontology, 10,* 212–215.

Midanik, L. T., Soghikian, K., Ransom, L. J., & Tekawa, I. S. (1995). The effect of retirement on mental health and health behaviors: The Kaiser Permanente Retirement Study. *Journal of Gerontology: Social Sciences, 50B*(1), S59–S61.

Mor-Barak, M. E., Scharlach, A. E., Birba, L., & Sokolov, J. (1992). Employment, social networks, and health in the retirement years. *International Journal of Aging and Human Development, 35*(2), 145–159.

Palmore, E. B., Burchett, B. M., Fillenbaum, G. G., George, L. K., & Wallman, L. M. (1985). *Retirement causes and consequences.* New York: Springer.

Tyhurst, J. S., Salk, L., & Kennedy, M. (1957). Mortality, morbidity and retirement. *American Journal of Public Health, 47,* 1134–1144.

Van Dyke, C., Zilberg, J. J., & McKinnon, J. A. (1985). Posttraumatic stress disorder: A thirty-year delay in a World War II veteran. *American Journal of Psychiatry, 142,* 1070–1073.

13

Domestic Elder Abuse and Neglect

Rosalie S. Wolf

Elder abuse and *neglect* can be defined, in their simplest terms, as acts of commission and omission that cause unnecessary suffering to older persons, carried out by individuals with whom the older persons have a trusting relationship. Although such behaviors can be manifested in many ways, they are usually divided into four categories: *physical* abuse (i.e., the infliction of physical pain or injury), *psychological* abuse (i.e., the infliction of mental anguish), *financial* abuse (i.e., the misuse of money and other assets), and *neglect* (the refusal or failure to fulfill a caretaking obligation). Whether an act is considered abusive or neglectful may depend on its intentionality, severity, intensity, frequency, and consequences. Casework with subpopulations suggests that the older person's perception of the behavior and the cultural context may be the salient factors for case identification and treatment (Moon & Williams, 1993).

Prevalence and Incidence

Although the prevalence of elder abuse in the United States has been estimated to range from 4% to 10% of the population 65 years of age and older, worldwide studies based on community surveys reveal about a 5% to 6% rate. Only four prevalence studies have been reported in the literature. Using a methodology that was validated previously in two national family violence surveys, a research team surveyed over 2,000 noninstitutionalized elders living in the metropolitan Boston area (Pillemer & Finkelhor, 1988). They found that 2.0% had experienced physical abuse; 1.1%, psychological abuse; and 0.4%, neglect, since they had reached 65 years of age. The overall prevalence rate was 3.2%. Abuse by the spouse (58%) was more prevalent than abuse by adult children (24%), the proportion of victims was roughly equally divided between men and women, and economic status and age were not related to the risk of abuse.

A similar survey of Canadian elders, with an additional question on financial exploitation, showed that 4.0% had been abused, of which the predominant type was financial abuse (2.5%; Podnieks, 1992). Among older people in one semi-industrialized Finnish town, 5.4% reported having been the victim of abuse, neglect, or exploitation since they had reached retirement age (Kivelä, Köngäs-Saviaro, Kesti, Pahkala, & Ijäs, 1992). The fourth study, based on a poll of British residents, indicated that 5.0% of persons age 65 years and over recently had been psychologically abused by a close family member or relative;

2.0%, physically abused; and 2.0%, financially abused (Ogg, 1993). Because all four surveys were based on self-reporting and, except for the Boston project, excluded those who could not respond to a survey question, the percentages are considered to be an underestimation of the problem.

Risk Factors

Although many theoretical explanations for elder mistreatment have been proposed, rigorous scientific studies to test them are lacking. Instead, attention has focused on *risk factors*, characteristics or attributes that are associated with the increased probability of victimization but are not necessarily causal agents. The factors that seem the most predictive at this time include (a) the abuser's dependence on the victim, especially for financial support, which is more often associated with physical abuse and financial exploitation than with neglect; (b) the abuser's psychological state (e.g., substance abuse or history of mental illness), which is also associated with physical and psychological abuse; (c) the victim's poor physical and cognitive state, which is more likely to be identified with neglect than other forms of mistreatment; and (d) family social isolation, which is more apt to occur with neglect and financial abuse cases than with physical or psychological mistreatment. So far, evidence regarding stressful life events and history of violence, two factors that are closely associated with child and spouse abuse, is inconclusive. Stressful life events may decrease the family's resistance and increase the likelihood of abuse (Lachs & Pillemer, 1995); a history of violence early in a spousal relationship may foretell elder mistreatment in later life.

Consequences

The elder abuse literature contains little if any empirical data on the consequences of elder mistreatment, although clinical records document the severe emotional distress experienced by mistreated older persons. In several case control studies, proportionately more abused elders were found to suffer from depression than nonabused elders. Because of the cross-sectional nature of the methodology, however, it was not possible to determine whether depression was an antecedent or an outcome. Other problems such as learned helplessness, alienation, withdrawal, distrust, guilt, shame, fear, and posttraumatic stress syndrome have all been suggested as a response to abuse, but further research is needed to confirm their role.

Whereas emergency room statistics have been used to show the impact of domestic violence on the health of battered women, no such relationship has been demonstrated for mistreated elders. The data have not been available, and the methods for easily differentiating between the effects of disease and the consequences of abusive actions are not well defined. However, one team, comparing mortality rates of abused and nonabused elders, found a significant relationship between abuse and death. They matched a sample of elders from one of the National Institute on Aging's established populations for epidemiologic studies of the elderly (EPESE) sites with adult protective services agency reports of abuse over a multiyear period (Lachs, 1996). The mortality rates of three groups within the sample were tracked: those who had been physically abused or neglected, those who had been investigated for other complaints (mainly self-neglect), and the rest of the cohort. No difference in mortality rates was found in the first few years, but by the 13th year, 36% of the noninvestigated group were still alive, 20% of the self-neglect groups, and 11% of the abused group. Further investigation is under way to identify the variables that affect mortality.

Abusive Situations and Interventions

The three situations profiled below are representative of elder abuse cases.

The Elder Parent and the Abusive Adult Child

Although the Boston prevalence study indicated more abuse by the spouse than abuse by adult children, reports made to U.S. state adult protective service systems consistently show adult children, more often sons than daughters, as the most frequent abusers of older persons in domestic settings. A comparison of cases in which spouses and adult children were the perpetrators revealed that children were more likely to commit acts of abuse (most often psychological) and neglect with more severe ramifications than were spouses (who were more often guilty of physical abuse). The adult children were more likely to have money problems, to be financially dependent on their elderly parents, and to have a history of mental illness and alcoholism (Wolf & Pillemer, 1989). In a study of adult offspring who had abused their elderly parents (Anetzberger 1988), the mistreatment was traced to (a) certain pathological personality characteristics, (b) the acute stress in their lives and their social isolation, (c) the vulnerability of the elderly parents, and (d) the "prolonged and profound" (p. 97) intimacy between the adult offspring and the parent.

Of course, the safety of the victim is a priority in these cases. Obtaining a restraining order or order of protection from the courts, calling the police, or pressing charges may serve to stop the violence, but often the victim will not agree to such interventions or leave the home. At the least, the victim may need help in overcoming the sense of shame or guilt or the emotional dependency on the adult child. The caseworker may refer the perpetrator to mental health, alcohol treatment, vocational counseling, job placement, housing assistance, and financial support programs, but often the perpetrator is not present, denies the problem, or refuses the services.

The Aggressive Alzheimer's Patient and Family Caregiver

A small body of research with Alzheimer's patients and their caregivers has attempted to unravel the relationship of cognitive impairment, caregiver stress, dependency, and elder abuse (Paveza et al., 1992). The results show that (a) abusive, aggressive, or violent behavior (physical or psychological) is more prevalent in caring situations involving Alzheimer's patients than in the general population; (b) abusive behavior includes both caregiver-to-patient and patient-to-caregiver aggression; (c) the relationship of cognitive impairment to abuse is mixed: Some studies indicate that there is a relationship, but others do not; (d) the relationship of dependency of the older person on the caregiver, often measured in terms of functional status, presents a similar ambiguous picture; (e) the patient's aggressive behavior may trigger aggressive behavior by the caregiver; and (f) the nature of the premorbid caregiver–patient relationship is the most consistent predictive factor.

Even though additional research is necessary to clarify the prevalence of abusive behavior in Alzheimer's patient–caregiver relationships, to understand the nature of the abusive behavior by both the caregiver and care recipient, and to learn the best methods for helping both, the preliminary studies suggest a number of preventive techniques, including (a) training caregivers in behavior management techniques, to lessen the disruptive and violent behavior of the patient; (b) providing psychological, medical, and social services to caregivers, to treat depressive symptoms and improve self-esteem and coping skills; (c) making respite, day care, and other support services available to families, to reduce the number of hours of caregiving per day; and (d) helping the caregiver through alcohol abuse, anger management, and stress reduction programs; and (e) offering counseling services, to assist families in placing their family members in a residential facility when caregiving tasks become overwhelming.

The Older Person and Abusive Spouse

A comparison of abusive and nonabusive couples from the National Family Violence Resurvey showed that more than half of the physically abused spouses over 60 years of age had been mistreated for many years (Harris, 1996). As for the other physically abused spouses, the abusive behavior might have come about after a significant life change such as a second marriage or mental or physical illness. Older people are said to remain in these abusive relationships for many of the same reasons as those found in cases with younger victims: low self-esteem, passive interpersonal style, strong sense of loyalty, social isolation, and limited social and job skills. Poor health status and disinclination to divorce are further constraints against separation.

Assisting elderly victims of spouse abuse is difficult particularly because so much of it is undetected and unreported. With strong support from the American Medical Association, health care professionals are being trained to recognize the signs and symptoms and to ask their patients directly about mistreatment.

Battered women's shelters have been the primary source of help for younger women, but relatively few have been able to accommodate older victims. A 1993 national survey identified only 16 specialized services for older battered women (American Association of Retired Persons Women's Initiative, 1994). The state of Wisconsin has had the most extensive program, with a network of support groups provided through domestic violence organizations. One of the objectives of the U.S. Administration on Aging (AoA) has been to bring about a more coordinated approach by protective services, aging organizations, and agencies concerned with domestic violence, on behalf of older battered women. Six projects were funded by AoA to create these partnerships and to develop education, legal advocacy, public awareness, and safe housing programs and other specialized services for this underserved population.

Conclusion

First described 20 years ago in British medical literature (Burston, 1975) as a social problem, elder abuse is now recognized as a worldwide phenomenon. Much of what is known, however, has been based on small samples without the rigorous methodology required to achieve valid and reliable results. Building a solid knowledge base is the challenge in the years ahead.

References

American Association of Retired Persons Women's Initiative. (1994). *Survey of services for older battered women*. Washington, DC: American Association of Retired Persons.

Anetzberger, G. J. (1988). *The etiology of elder abuse by adult offspring*. Springfield, IL: Thomas.

Burston, G. R. (1975, September 6). Granny battering. *British Medical Journal*, 592.

Harris, S. B. (1996). For better or for worse: Spouse abuse grown old. *Journal of Elder Abuse & Neglect, 8*(1), 1–33.

Kivelä, S. L., Köngäs-Saviaro, P., Kesti, E., Pahkala, K., & Ijäs, M. L. (1992). Abuse in old age: Epidemiological data from Finland. *Journal of Elder Abuse & Neglect, 4*(3), 1–18.

Lachs, M. (1996). *The Paul Beeson physician faculty scholars in aging research program, 1996*. New York: American Federation for Aging Research.

Lachs, M., & Pillemer, K. (1995). Abuse and neglect of elderly persons. *New England Journal of Medicine, 332*, 437–443.

Moon, A., & Williams, O. (1993). Perceptions of elder abuse and help-seeking patterns among African-Americans, Caucasian Americans, and Korean-American women. *Gerontologist, 33*, 386–395.

Ogg, J. (1993). Researching elder abuse in Britain. *Journal of Elder Abuse & Neglect, 5*(2), 37–54.

Paveza, G. J., Cohen, D., Eisdorfer, C., Freels, S., Semla, T., Ashford, J. W., Gorelick, P., Hirshman, R., Luckins, D., & Levy, P. (1992). Severe family violence and Alzheimer's disease: Prevalence and risk factors. *Gerontologist, 32*, 493–497.

Pillemer, K., & Finkelhor, D. (1988). The prevalence of elder abuse: A random sample survey. *Gerontologist, 28*, 51–57.

Podnieks, E. (1992). National survey on abuse of the elderly in Canada. *Journal of Elder Abuse & Neglect, 4*(1/2), 5–58.

Wolf, R. S., & Pillemer, K. (1989). *Helping elderly victims: The reality of elder abuse*. New York: Columbia University Press.

14

Insomnia in Older Adults

Geir Høstmark Nielsen, Inger Hilde Nordhus, and Gerd Kvale

Insomnia (i.e., the subjective complaint that one's sleep is unsatisfactory in quantity or quality) represents a major public health problem in most Western countries. In addition to considerable subjective distress, the symptoms of chronic insomnia are associated with increased morbidity and mortality (Neckelmann, 1996). Findings from epidemiological studies indicate that between 20% and 30% of the adult population experience some sleep disturbance (Cartwright, 1991). There is evidence that the prevalence of sleep problems increases with age and that women report such difficulties more often than men (Kales & Kales, 1984). In a recent Norwegian study, 3% of the male respondents in the 20–29 years age group reported that they suffered from an inadequate amount of sleep often or every night. For women over 80, the corresponding figure was 20% (Holmen et al., 1990).

Not surprisingly, the prevalence of sleep problems among people who consult for medical assistance is higher than among the general population. In Germany, Hohagen et al. (1994) reported that among 330 general practice patients 65 years of age or older, 23% suffered from severe insomnia, 17% from moderate insomnia, and 17% from mild insomnia. More than 80% of the patients reported having suffered from insomnia for 1 to 5 years, or longer. Only 41% of the sample did not complain of any sleep problems. Among the patients suffering from severe insomnia, women prevailed by far over men. In Great Britain, Brabbins et al. (1993) assessed 1,070 persons (aged 65+ years) for prevalence of perceived insomnia. Of the participants, 35% (twice as many women as men) reported having trouble sleeping.

Insomnia as a severe health problem is also underscored by the population's high consumption of drugs. In the Hohagen et al. (1994) study, more than half of the severe insomniacs age 65 or older took prescribed hypnotic drugs habitually. In a Norwegian study, it was found that among older patients under rehabilitation in a public geriatric hospital, 42% used hypnotics on a regular basis. The sections that follow describe typical sleep changes in older people, address diagnostic issues and etiological factors in insomnia, and point to current treatment alternatives.

Sleep Physiology and Normal Changes With Age

Sleep manifests itself as a cyclical, usually rhythmical, psychophysiological state with reduced physical and mental activity. It is common to divide normal sleep into five different stages, on the basis of all-night polysomographic re-cordings of the electrical signals generated by the brain (electroencephalogram [EEG]), postural muscles (electromyogram [EMG]), and eye movement activi-ties (electrooculogram [EOG]). In more advanced laboratory studies, additional parameters such as heart rate, body temperature, respiration, and airflow also are monitored.

The five stages are usually designated as *Stage 1* (drowsy and transitional), *Stage 2, Stage 3, Stage 4* (deep sleep), and *rapid eye movement (REM)* sleep. Whereas REM sleep represents an activated brain (similar to the awake state), the other four stages (nonrapid eye movements [NREM]) are indicative of a quiescent brain, characterized by a general slowing of physiological processes.

With advancing age (60+ years), characteristic changes can normally be observed in sleep physiology and sleep patterns. Summarizing recent literature in the field, Hoch, Buysse, Monk, and Reynolds (1992) especially pointed to decreased sleep continuity, with numerous transient microarousals (of 3–15-s duration); decreased amounts of Stage 3 and 4 sleep, with correspondingly in-creased Stage 1 and 2 sleep; slightly decreased absolute amounts of REM sleep; shorter REM periods; and a tendency for REM sleep to occur earlier in the night. The result of these changes is that the older person's sleep becomes more fragmented and of reduced quality.

Several studies indicate that the age-related physiological changes in sleep are more pronounced in men than in women. Older men tend to have more impaired sleep maintenance and less delta (deep) sleep. Despite this, women tend to report more sleep difficulties, and they consume more sleeping pills. Hoch et al. (1992) suggested that an explanation of these seemingly paradoxical findings may be caused by gender-related differences in sleep perception and effects of sleep disruption on mood, making older women more sensitive to sleep quality and sleep loss.

The subjective impression produced by changes in objective sleep pa-rameters may be highly unsatisfying sleep. However, such complaints tend to be most strongly correlated with frequent awakenings and less with objective changes in slow-wave sleep and REM sleep (Bonnet & Johnson, 1978). Because identical or similar symptoms may have different causes, a thorough diagnostic assessment needs to be made in each case.

Diagnostic Considerations

In clinical work with older people, it may be easy to overlook or underestimate the severity of the patient's sleep problems. This was clearly demonstrated in the Hohagen et al. (1994) study, which showed that general practitioners had failed to identify severe sleep disorders in nearly half of their cases. Conversely, some patients tend to strongly overrate their needed amount or quality of sleep. Among Hohagen et al.'s respondents, only 21% reported that they would be satisfied with less than 8 hr of sleep. On average, the respondents said that they would prefer to sleep 80 min more than they actually did. About half of them reported the habit of having at least one daytime nap, and there was a positive correlation between the duration of daytime naps and the complaints of severe insomnia.

Insomnia among older people, as with younger age groups, may take different forms. A patient may complain mainly of difficulty initiating sleep (prolonged sleep onset), frequent awakenings during the night, too early awakening, short sleep time, or nonrestorative sleep. Often patients report a combination of prolonged sleep onset and intermittent wakefulness during the night. He or she may also report daytime symptoms resulting from bad sleep, such as physical or mental fatigue, sleepiness, and mood changes. Behavioral symptoms of tenseness, irritability, and preoccupation with oneself can be observed in many patients.

Contemporary diagnostic classification systems define insomnia in somewhat different ways. Common to the most recent version of the *ICD–10 Classification of Mental and Behavioral Disorders* (*ICD–10*; World Health Organization, 1992) and the *Diagnostic and Statistical Manual of Mental Disorders* (*DSM–IV*; American Psychiatric Association, 1994) is a differentiation between *primary* insomnia and insomnia that occurs during the course of another sleep disorder or mental disorder. Whereas the *DSM–IV* applies separate categories for such combined disorders, the *ICD–10* requires that one use "(nonorganic) insomnia" as the primary diagnosis if insomnia symptoms dominate the picture, regardless of the concurrent existence of another mental disorder. If, however, other symptoms or complaints (e.g., anxiety or depression) tend to predominate over the patient's sleep difficulties, these other symptoms should determine the primary diagnosis. (See Exhibit 1 for a direct comparison of the diagnostic criteria proposed for a definite diagnosis of insomnia according to the *DSM–IV* and the *ICD–10*, respectively.)

In the assessment of insomnia, a comprehensive and precise clinical anamnesis is of utmost importance (Kayed, 1995). The anamnesis should include not only information about the patient's sleep difficulties but also information about his or her more general life situation and health condition. In addition, one should ask the patient to keep a sleep diary for 2–3 weeks before one starts treatment. This may give the therapist a more differentiated picture of the patient's difficulties and may be a useful guide with regard to treatment strategy and selection of specific intervention techniques. A systematically kept sleep diary might also assist the therapist and the patient in monitoring treatment progress. Finally, it has been found that the keeping of a sleep diary, in and of itself, often contributes to positive treatment effects by increasing the patient's motivation (Leimand, 1993). An example of a clinically useful sleep diary may be found in Morin (1993).

Easily administered questionnaires such as the Sleep Questionnaire and Assessment of Wakefulness (Miles, 1982) or the Basic Nordic Sleep Questionnaire (Partinen & Gislason, 1995), psychological tests like the Minnesota Multiphasic Personality Inventory, and in some cases polysomnography (i.e., EEG, EMG, and EOG) also are recommended as supplementary assessment devices. However, polysomnographic equipment, although useful in laboratory research and hospital settings, may be impractical to administer as part of ambulatory treatment.

Exhibit 1. Criteria for (Primary) Insomnia According to the *DSM–IV* and (Nonorganic) Insomnia According to the *ICD–10*

DSM–IV

The predominant complaint is difficulty initiating or maintaining sleep, or nonrestorative sleep, for at least one month.

The sleep disturbance (or associated daytime fatigue) causes clinically significant distress or impairment in social, occupational, or other important areas of functioning.

The sleep disturbance does not occur exclusively during the course of Narcolepsy, Breathing-Related Sleep Disorder, Circadian Rhythm Sleep Disorder, or a Parasomnia.

The disturbance does not occur exclusively during the course of another mental disorder (e.g., Major Depressive Disorder, Circadian Rhythm Disorder, Generalized Anxiety Disorder, a delirium).

The disturbance is not due to the direct effects of a substance (e.g., a drug of abuse, a medication) or a general medical condition.

ICD–10

The complaint is either difficulty falling asleep or maintaining sleep, or poor quality of sleep.

The sleep disturbance has occurred at least three times per week for at least one month.

There is preoccupation with sleeplessness and excessive concern over its consequences at night or during the day.

The unsatisfactory quantity and/or quality of sleep either causes marked distress or interferes with ordinary activities in daily living.

Note. From *Diagnostic and Statistical Manual of Mental Disorders* (p. 557), by the American Psychiatric Association, 1994, Washington, DC: Author, and the *ICD–10 Classification of Mental and Behavioral Disorders* (p. 183), by the World Health Organization, 1992, Geneva, Switzerland: Author.

Etiological and Correlated Factors

Insomnia (generally defined; i.e., not restricted to primary insomnia) may have a variety of causes and is most often a result of multiple factors (Buysse & Reynolds, 1990). The causes can be organic, psychophysiological, or psychological, and insomnia may be secondary to both physical and mental disorders. Among the latter, anxiety disorders and affective disorders (depression) seem to play a particularly significant role (Benca, Obermeyer, Thisted, & Gillin, 1992). Typically, a patient's first episode of insomnia develops at a time of increased life stress, most often related to family life (Gagne, Bastien, & Morin, 1997).

Among factors that should be considered are the patient's need for nocturnal urination, pains, nocturnal respiratory dysfunction, biological rhythm alterations, sleep habits, inactivity and daytime naps, current stressors, known

physical illness, medication (including prescribed hypnotics), caffeine and nicotine, abuse of drugs or alcohol, periodic nocturnal leg movements (so-called
restless legs), dementia, and, not to be neglected, psychosocial factors such as
loneliness and concern about one's financial situation (Bjørndal, 1993).

A particularly interesting and consistent finding is the high comorbidity of
insomnia with other mental disorders (Billiard, Partinen, Roth, & Shapiro,
1994). A meta-analysis of 177 individual studies containing data from more
than 7,000 psychiatric patients and control participants (Benca et al., 1992)
revealed that significantly less amounts of sleep and sleep effectiveness were
reported in most diagnostic groups, compared with the controls. Further analyses of the data, with particular regard to sleep patterns, revealed that perceived insomnia was strongly related to decreased Stages 3 and 4 NREM sleep,
whereas REM sleep was relatively intact in all groups. All sleep parameters
considered, it was found that patients with affective disorders differed most
from the controls. Similarly, Brabbins et al. (1993) found that the prevalence
of insomnia in older people (age 65+) correlated strongly with clinically rated
seriousness of depression.

Numerous studies have demonstrated increased prevalence of insomnia in
older patients with dementia (Alzheimer's disease). Compared with elderly
healthy persons and patients with a diagnosis of "pseudodementia," a relatively
consistent finding is that the Alzheimer patients have more transient awakenings during the night, less REM sleep time and REM activity, irregular and
indeterminate NREM sleep, and also less Stage 3 and Stage 4 sleep. In addition, Alzheimer patients have significantly more sleep-disordered breathing,
more daytime naps, and, concurrent with advancing dementia, a gradual but
progressive loss of the ordinary phasic activity (Hoch et al., 1992).

Of course, the high comorbidity between insomnia and other mental disorders does not tell us much about cause and effect relationships. Most probably, it is a question of complex interactions among several factors, suggesting
that a circular model of causality may be the most adequate one with regard
to effective treatment planning. In any event, there is a strong need for more
(methodologically sophisticated) research before more specific and precise
causal connections can be identified.

Treatment for Insomnia: Pharmacological Therapy

Pharmacological therapy ideally should be delayed until other forms of intervention have been tried without expected success (Shapiro, 1993; Spar &
La Rue, 1990). Despite such recommendations, it seems that pharmacological
treatment (particularly benzodiazepines and various antidepressants) is still
by far the most common treatment offered to older insomniacs (Engle-Friedman
& Bootzin, 1991).

There is strong evidence that continuous use of hypnotics (first and fore-
most benzodiazepines) is potentially harmful for the chronic insomniac (Grad,
1995). Note also that most hypnotics deprive a patient of REM sleep and produce a marked REM rebound on subsequent nights. The result is often nights
spent in restless dreaming, nightmares, and fitful sleep. Several other negative

side effects are also well documented. With particular regard to older persons, Engle-Friedman and Bootzin (1991) cited states of confusion, psychomotor performance deficit, nocturnal falls, dysphoric mood, impaired intellectual functioning, and daytime sleepiness.

Considering these and other possible hazardous effects of hypnotic drugs, Kayed (1995) proposed the following indications for their continuous use:

- transient insomnia;
- clear-cut psychophysiological insomnia;
- particular anxiety disorders with insomnia as a predominant symptom;
- periodic nocturnal leg movements or restless legs;
- insomnia directly caused by pain;
- when other forms of treatment, for example, specific behavioral interventions or psychotherapy, have been tried without success. Even in such cases, hypnotics should be prescribed on a low-dosage and intermittent basis.

In Norway, two nonbenzodiazepine hypnotics (zopiclone and zolpidem) with short-elimination half-lives have recently been introduced for clinical use. Compared with benzodiazepines, such drugs have an advantage in terms of decreased risk of accumulation. They might, therefore, represent a promising alternative drug treatment in cases of transient sleep-onset difficulties. However, because of their short-term effects, they probably are less suitable for cases of sleep maintenance difficulties and early awakening (Kayed, 1995).

Another promising biologically based treatment approach that might be considered as an alternative to hypnotics is bright light (2,500–3,000 lux) therapy (Mishima, Hishikawa, Hozumi, & Takahashi, 1994), that is, exposing the patient to artificial daylight. Bright light exposure is assumed to yield its positive effects by compensating for disruptions of the biological (circadian) rhythms and the deprivation of natural daylight stimulation often reported by older patients (Neckelmann, 1996).

Behavioral and Psychological Treatment Methods

With the growing awareness of hazardous side effects associated with drug (particularly benzodiazepine) treatment of insomnia in older people, many therapists have become more attentive to behavioral and psychological treatment alternatives. During the last 20–25 years, a number of well-documented behavioral principles for good sleep (sleep hygiene) have been described, and particular forms of brief, or short-term, behavioral and psychological therapies have become available. Clinical interest in the possible effectiveness of such approaches has been stimulated also by the fact of high comorbidity between insomnia and other forms of mental disorders, usually responsive to psychological approaches. One can roughly classify the various techniques into three different categories: behaviorally based educative methods, relaxation techniques, and formal psychotherapy.

Educative Methods

The main goal for these techniques is to help the patient reduce the amount of time spent in bed without sleeping, that is, increased sleep effectiveness. This is done by teaching the patient stimulus control and good sleep hygiene. In short, *stimulus control* aims "to strengthen the bed as a cue for sleep, and to weaken it as a cue for activities that might interfere with sleep" (Engle-Friedman & Bootzin, 1991, p. 287). The following self-instructions have been proposed to facilitate treatment goals: (a) go to bed only when you are sleepy; (b) do not use your bed for anything but sleep, for example, for reading, watching TV, or eating; (c) if sleep doesn't come, get up, go to another room, and don't return to your bed until you feel sleepy; (d) get up at about the same time every morning, regardless of how much you have slept during the night; and, finally, (e) avoid daytime naps.

Sleep hygiene refers to interventions that consist of a smaller number of direct behavioral instructions to the patient, on the basis of his or her history, such as to involve him- or herself in more physical or mental activity during the day, to keep the bedroom temperature at a moderate level (high body temperature interferes with sleep), to use a good mattress, to avoid excessive lighting or noise, and to avoid large amounts of coffee or heavy food just before bedtime (Morin, 1993).

A third technique that also belongs to this group is *sleep restriction*, that is, having the patient intentionally restrict the time spent in bed to no more than his or her estimated hours of actual sleep the previous week. This controlled sleep deprivation is assumed to facilitate sleep onset. As the amount of sleep starts to go up, the allowed number of hours spent in bed also increases. Thus, sleeping may become a positive reinforcer for more sleep (a benign circle).

Independent of the specific technique used in a particular case, treatment should always proceed within an atmosphere of emotional support and encouragement. It is also essential to didactically inform the patient about normal age-related changes in sleep.

Despite their seeming simplicity, these techniques all have been proven to be highly effective in both case studies and controlled evaluations (Morin, Culbert, & Schwartz, 1994). With individually tailored adaptations, they seem to be practically applicable with older adults (Neckelmann, 1996).

Relaxation Techniques

Among relevant methods under this category are progressive muscle relaxation, briefer forms of autogenic training, and various forms of self-hypnosis. Common to these approaches is that when appropriately done, they provide muscle relaxation and thereby facilitate sleep onset. Because the patient has to spend a certain amount of time practicing (homework), these approaches require a substantial amount of motivation.

Holte (1989) developed a simple technique that combines (taped) relaxation and sleep-inducing suggestions with respiration exercises. In controlled experiments with younger adults, this technique has proven very effective and might very well be applied and systematically evaluated also with older persons.

Psychotherapy

Formal psychotherapy of relatively long duration is seldom recommended as a treatment of choice for patients with insomnia as their main complaint. However, more active, briefer forms of psychotherapy (cognitive or psychodynamic) can be very beneficial in individual cases, particularly if a patient's sleep difficulties occur in combination with marked anxiety or depression (Nielsen, 1990). Among others, Morin (1993) has proposed that especially briefer forms of cognitive therapy, that is, interventions that directly address both the patient's dysfunctional sleep-related beliefs and attitudes and underlying emotional stress, might profitably be included in one's therapeutic toolbox.

References

American Psychiatric Association. (1994). *Diagnostic and statistical manual of mental disorders* (4th ed.). Washington, DC: Author.

Benca, R. M., Obermeyer, W. H., Thisted, R. A., & Gillin, C. (1992). Sleep and psychiatric disorders. *Archives of General Psychiatry, 49,* 651–670.

Billiard, M., Partinen, M., Roth, T., & Shapiro, C. (1994). Sleep and psychiatric disorders. *Journal of Psychosomatic Research, 38,* 1–2.

Bjørndal, A. (1993). Er det nå så farlig med sovemidler til eldre? [Are hypnotics for the elderly really that dangerous?]. *Journal of the Norwegian Medical Association, 113,* 326–327.

Bonnet, M. H. & Johnson, L. C. (1978). Relationship of arousal threshold to sleep stage disturbance and subjective estimates of depth and quality of sleep. *Sleep, 1,* 161–168.

Brabbins, C. J., Dewey, M. E., Copeland, J. R., & Davidson, I. A. (1993). Insomnia in the elderly: Prevalence, gender differences and relationships with morbidity and mortality. *International Journal of Geriatric Psychiatry, 8,* 473–480.

Buysse, D. J., & Reynolds, C. F. (1990). Insomnia. In M. J. Thorpy (Ed.), *Handbook of sleep disorders* (pp. 373–431). New York: Dekker.

Cartwright, R. D. (1991). Development of a program for sleep disorders. In J. J. Sweet, R. H. Rosensky, & S. M. Tovian (Eds.), *Handbook of clinical psychology in medical settings* (pp. 455–471). New York: Plenum.

Engle-Friedman, M., & Bootzin, R. R. (1991). Insomnia as a problem for the elderly. In P. A. Wisocki (Ed.), *Handbook of clinical behavior therapy with the elderly client* (pp. 273–298). New York: Plenum.

Gagne, A., Bastien, C. H., & Morin, C. M. (1997). Precipitating events of insomnia. *APSS Abstracts Search Results* [On-line], 6–7. Available: HTTP: Hostname: www.websciences.org Directory cftemp

Grad, R. M. (1995). Benzodiazepines for insomnia in community-dwelling elderly: A review of benefit and risk. *Journal of Family Practice, 41,* 473–481.

Hoch, C., Buysse, D. J., Monk, T. H., & Reynolds, C. F. (1992). Sleep disorders and aging. In J. E. Birren, R. B. Sloane, & G. D. Cohen (Eds.), *Handbook of mental health and aging* (2nd ed., pp. 557–581). New York: Academic Press.

Hohagen, F., Käppler, C., Schramm, E., Rink, K., Weyerer, S., Riemann, D., & Bergen, M. (1994). Prevalence of insomnia in elderly general practice attenders and the current treatment modalities. *Acta Psychiatrica Scandinavica, 90,* 102–108.

Holmen, J., Midthjell, K., Bjartveit, K., Hjorth, P. F., Lund-Larsen, P. G., Moum, T., Naess, S., & Waaler, H. T. (1990). *The Nord-Trøndelag Health Survey 1984–86* (Report No. 4). Oslo, Norway: National Institute of Public Health.

Holte, A. (1989). The Holte sleeping technique: An experimental study. *Scandinavian Journal of Psychology, 30,* 46–51.

Kales, A., & Kales, J. D. (1984). *Evaluation and treatment of insomnia.* Oxford, England: Oxford University Press.

Kayed, K. (1995). Insomni og hypnotika [Insomnia and hypnotica]. *Journal of the Norwegian Medical Association, 115*, 1087–1090.

Leimand, R. (1993). Ikke-medikamentell behandling av søvnløshet [Nonpharmacological treatment of insomnia]. *Psykolog Nyt, 48*, 235–236.

Miles, L. (1982). Sleep Questionnaire and Assessment of Wakefulness (SQAW). In C. Guilleminault (Ed.), *Sleeping and waking disorders: Indications and techniques* (pp. 383–411). Reading, MA: Addison-Wesley.

Mishima, K., Okawa, M., Hishikawa, Y., Hozumi, S., & Takahashi, K. (1994). Morning bright light therapy for sleep and behavior disorders in elderly patients with dementia. *Acta Psychiatrica Scandinavica, 89*, 1–7.

Morin, C. M. (1993). *Insomnia: Psychological assessment and management.* New York: Guilford Press.

Morin, C. M., Culbert, J. P., & Schwartz, S. M. (1994). Nonpharmacological interventions for insomnia: A meta-analysis of treatment efficacy. *American Journal of Psychiatry, 151*, 1172–1180.

Neckelmann, D. (1996). *Behandling av kronisk insomni* [Treatment of chronic insomnia with special emphasis on problems in the elderly]. *Journal of the Norwegian Medical Association, 116*, 854–859.

Nielsen, G. (1990). Brief integrative dynamic psychotherapy for insomnia: Systematic evaluation of two cases. *Psychotherapy and Psychosomatics, 54*, 187–192.

Partinen, M., & Gislason, T. (1995). Basic Nordic Sleep Questionnaire (BNSQ): A quantitated measure of subjective sleep complaints. *Journal of Sleep Research* (Suppl. 1), 150–155.

Shapiro, C. M. (Ed.). (1993). *ABC of sleep disorders.* London: British Medical Journal Publishing Group.

Spar, J. E., & La Rue, A. (1990). *Concise guide to geriatric psychiatry.* Washington, DC: American Psychiatric Press.

World Health Organization. (1992). *The ICD–10 classification of mental and behavioural disorders.* Geneva, Switzerland: Author.

15

Death, Dying, and Bereavement

Reidun Ingebretsen and Per Erik Solem

A fundamental, and often repeated, truth is that we all are going to die. However, older people, in general, have a shorter remaining life than younger people. Older people experience more losses of contemporary family and friends. In these ways, they are closer to death. Thus, loss, bereavement, and mourning play a significant part in the lives of most older people. In addition, many experience loss of roles and functions. Illness is a reminder of death, and it may threaten values of independence. Multiple losses over a short period of time may exacerbate grief.

Incidence and Prevalence

Mortality increases with age. Growing old means that the risk of dying in any given year increases. At the same time, the probability of living beyond one's at-birth mean life expectancy also increases.

The at-birth life expectancy in the Nordic countries is about 74 years for men and 80 years for women. In the United States, these numbers are 73 and 79, respectively. Modern industrialized countries have much the same life expectancy, with Japan at the top (77 and 83 years, respectively). Some developing countries have life expectancies below 50 years for both men and women, with Uganda at the bottom (40 years for both men and women).

However, those who have survived to the age of 65 live beyond the mean life expectancy in all countries. Both in the United States and in the Nordic countries, a 65-year-old man has on average about 15 remaining years to live, whereas 19 years remain for a woman of the same age.

The probability of dying in any given year after age 65 also increases as one ages. Among the *young old* (65–69 years of age), this risk, however, is only about 2.5% a year for men and 1% for women (in the Nordic countries). This rises to about 4% and 2% in the age group 70–74 years, 7% and 4% for 75–79 years, and 11% and 7% for 80–84 years and continues to increase until it is about 41% and 35% for above 95 years of age.

As mortality increases, so does the prevalence of widowhood. In the Nordic countries, approximately 12.5% of men over 60 years of age are widowers, whereas about 40% of women are widows. In the United States, 11% of men and 42% of women over 60 years of age have had their partner die.

Over the years, the face of death has gotten increasingly wrinkled. It has not always been the case that it was mostly older people who die. In the Nordic countries, for example, more than 80% of those who die each year are over 65 years of age (for 1993, 82.1%). Similar proportions are found in other industrialized countries (in Britain for 1986, 79%; Sidell, 1993). However, a hundred years ago, less than one third of annual deaths were older people. Children's deaths were common. Often, over 30% of annual deaths were people under 15 years of age; however, today, this age group accounts for less than 1% of annual deaths.

Attitudes About Death and Dying

Although death today is statistically connected to old age, the thanatology literature has primarily concentrated on death at younger ages—mainly, death caused by cancer or, more recently, by AIDS. This is also true in terms of the portrayal of death in the media, where it also focuses on younger persons. Death in old age attracts little attention, even in research.

Attitudes toward death seem to change over the life span. Cameron, Stewart, and Biber (1973) found that older people were the most occupied with thoughts about death, followed by adolescents, whereas young adults (18–25 years of age) were the least occupied with death. Other studies confirm that older people think and talk more about death and that this is in a generally calm manner, without anxiety. Fear of death seems to diminish with increasing age (Marshall & Levy, 1990). Younger adults think less about death, but when they do talk about it, it seems to provoke more anxiety than in older persons. This may create problems in communication between older people and their younger relatives and caregivers.

Older people's attitudes toward death are influenced by their whole life and how they summarize it when the end is approaching. Butler (1963) elaborated on this in his theory on *life review*, the active reorganization of past experience as a response to awareness of finitude or impending death. Butler illustrated this with the double-faced Janus. When one face is looking forward on death, the other is looking back on life. This may prepare one for death, mitigating one's fears. Or it may create agony over old, unresolved matters and cause depression.

To accept death is not the same as to welcome the end of life. Most older people still prefer to live. According to Jung, belief in an afterlife helps to cope with fear of death. Numerous studies confirm that religiousness is correlated with less fear of death, whereas other studies find least fear of death among the deeply religious and the deeply irreligious and the greatest fear among those uncertain or uncommitted to religion (Kalish, 1985).

Individual control over one's death is increasingly supported by the general public. Public opinion polls in a number of countries show increasing numbers favoring voluntary euthanasia, with between 60% and 80% of the public in different Western countries in favor of such options. Older people are less in favor than the younger (Waller, 1986), which may be due to more traditional attitudes about death or may be because older persons are closer to death.

Emotional Reactions Related to Loss

Grief over the loss of significant others seems to be universally felt, although the cultural manifestations of grief may vary. The most stressful and disruptive losses are those of a spouse, child, or parent by death (Raphael, 1983).

In general, bereavement reactions and adjustment among older people follow the same patterns as for young and middle-aged people. However, older people in grief are found to have a lower level of help-seeking activity, compared with younger populations (Brown, 1978). Although some authors (e.g., Parkes, 1964) suggest that older people experience milder stress reactions, more indirect ways of grieving, and grief underlying somatic concerns, Sable (1991) found that elderly women showed more intense grief than younger women.

Adjustment after bereavement is characterized by more similarities than differences between men and women (Lund, Caserta, & Dimond, 1986). Higher mortality is found among widowed persons compared with married persons, especially for older men (Stroebe & Stroebe, 1987). Results from a large Finnish sample (Martiainen & Valkonen, 1996) also showed that mortality was higher among men than among women, but higher among younger rather than older bereaved persons. The possible explanations discussed are related to stress, coping with stress, and loss of social support. Men usually have fewer confidants and rely more on their spouse for support than do women.

Fatigue, various bodily symptoms, and loss of energy are associated with grief. When the bereaved person misinterprets such reactions as age-related deterioration, pessimism about the future may add further sadness over one's own aging, on top of the grief reaction related to the lost loved one. The same is true when grief-related social withdrawal is misinterpreted as evidence of aging.

Positive emotions, like feelings of relief and pride about being able to cope, may exist side by side with sadness. According to Arbuckle and de Vries (1995), bereavement is a multidimensional process affecting the individuals both psychologically, physiologically, socially, economically, and spiritually. The meaning and the consequences of the loss may differ by the timing of the death in the life course. It seems more easy to accept and cope with life changes that are "on time." The death of an older spouse is more on time than the death of a younger partner. However, on a personal level, a death may be "off time" even for an older spouse. Even if the older person is prepared for the separation, the actual death often tends to strike at the wrong time or in a wrong way. When death comes after a long period of illness, some grief may already be worked through in an anticipatory way. In other cases, a long period of illness may bring the spouses closer together, isolate the caregiver from other relationships, and increase vulnerability to loss.

Feeling lonely is often the most persistent problem among older widows and widowers. In old age the processes of grief over close, often lifelong, relationships and retrospective glances on one's life are mingled. An actual bereavement may also reactivate old losses. On the other hand, a static idealized picture of the deceased or long-lasting avoidance of memories may hamper the process of life review.

For an older widow or widower, keeping the bonds with the deceased may represent important aspects of meaning and continuity. Experiences of closeness to the deceased, illusions of the person as still being there, and hallucinations of the deceased are common (Ingebretsen, 1988). Such experiences are often considered helpful and are mostly associated with feelings of security. They may coexist with acceptance of the loss and are not per se contrary to social adaptation. Grimby (1993) found, however, that early in the grief process, hallucinations are most frequent among people suffering from severe loneliness, crying, and memory problems.

Prevention and Intervention

Many of the losses and life transitions described here seem inevitable and are related to a natural life course and the existential conditions of mankind. These conditions can lead to surrender and passivity when thinking about what to do. Confronted with losses in old age, practitioners should consider such relevant questions as, Is this loss inevitable, and if so, can something be done to moderate the traumatic character of the situation? If nothing can be done to moderate the situation, a relevant question would still be how to support the person coping and prevent needless disruptive reactions.

Some older people will need professional help or guidance related to overwhelming acute reactions, long-lasting emotional problems, inhibited or delayed grief reactions, managing negative and ambivalent feelings, and problems of coping with new tasks on their own (Ingebretsen, 1988). Zisook and Shuchter (1993) found that bereavement is complicated for persons with a history of major depressive episodes. The life histories of the bereaved, not just their recent loss, must be taken into account. Unresolved reactions to previous losses are often activated.

Miller et al. (1994) concluded that interpersonal psychotherapy appears to be an effective short-term treatment for bereavement-related depression in older people. Rosenblatt et al. (1991) offered a family perspective on grief: It will frequently be beneficial to work with families rather than individuals, to put the difficulties in perspective and help the family members to deal with the sources and consequences of the difficulties. Loss of a child or a grandchild has great implications for the whole family. The same is true for problems related to illness and dependency among older family members.

References

Arbuckle, N. W., & de Vries, B. (1995). The long-term effects of later life spousal and parental bereavement on personal functioning. *Gerontologist, 35,* 637–647.

Brown, B. B. (1978). Social and psychological correlates of help-seeking behavior among urban adults. *American Journal of Community Psychology, 6,* 425–439.

Butler, R. N. (1963). The life review: An interpretation of reminiscence in the aged. *Psychiatry, 26,* 65–76.

Cameron, P., Stewart, Z., & Biber, H. (1973). Consciousness of death across the life span. *Journal of Gerontology, 28,* 92–95.

Grimby, A. (1993). Bereavement among elderly people: Grief reactions, post-bereavement hallucinations and quality of life. *Acta Psychiatrica Scandinavica, 87*, 72–80.

Ingebretsen, R. (1988). *Not entirely alone even so* (Report No. 6/88). Oslo, Norway: Norwegian Institute of Gerontology.

Kalish, R. A. (1985). The social context of death and dying. In R. H. Binstock & E. Shanas (Eds.), *Handbook of aging and the social sciences* (2nd ed., pp. 149–170). New York: Van Nostrand Reinhold.

Lund, D. A., Caserta, M. S., & Dimond, M. F. (1986). Gender differences through two years of bereavement among the elderly. *Gerontologist, 26*, 314–320.

Marshall, V. W., & Levy, J. A. (1990). Aging and dying. In R. H. Binstock & L. K. George (Eds.), *Handbook of aging and the social sciences* (3rd ed., pp. 245–260). San Diego, CA: Academic Press.

Martiainen, P., & Valkonen, T. (1996). Mortality after the death of a spouse: Rates and causes of death in a large Finnish cohort. *American Journal of Public Health, 86*, 1087–1093.

Miller, M. D., Frank, E., Cornes, C., Imber, S. D., Anderson, B., Ehrenpreis, L., Malloy, J., Silberman, R., Wolfson, L., Zaltman, J., & Reynolds, C. F. (1994). Applying interpersonal psychotherapy to bereavement-related depression following loss of a spouse in late life. *Journal of Psychotherapy Practice and Research, 3*, 149–162.

Parkes, C. M. (1964). The effect of bereavement on physical and mental health: A study of case records of widows. *British Medical Journal, 2*, 274–279.

Raphael, B. (1983). *The anatomy of bereavement.* New York: Basic Books.

Rosenblatt, P. C., Spoentgen, P., Karis, T. A., Dahl, C., Kaiser, T., & Elde, C. (1991). Difficulties in supporting the bereaved. *Omega, 23*, 119–128.

Sable, P. (1991). Attachment, loss of spouse, and grief in elderly adults. *Omega, 23*, 129–142.

Sidell, M. (1993). Death, dying, and bereavement. In J. Bond, P. Coleman, & S. Peace (Eds.), *Aging in society* (pp. 151–179). London: Sage.

Stroebe, W., & Stroebe, M. S. (1987). *Bereavement and health: The psychological and physical consequences of partner loss.* New York: Cambridge University Press.

Waller, S. (1986). Trends in public acceptance of euthanasia world-wide. *The Euthanasia Review, 1*, 33–47.

Zisook, S., & Shuchter, S. R. (1993). Uncomplicated bereavement. *Journal of Clinical Psychiatry, 54*, 365–372.

16

Cognitive Dysfunction and Dementia

Pia Fromholt and Peter Bruhn

Dementia is a brain syndrome caused by widespread structural and neurochemical damage to cortical and subcortical structures. As a coarse generalization, primarily to be used for diagnostic purposes, the syndrome is characterized by impairment (relative to the premorbid level) of various aspects of memory as well as other cognitive domains, aspects of personality, and behavior. According to *Diagnostic and Statistical Manual of Mental Disorders* (American Psychiatric Association, 1994) criteria, a diagnosis of dementia involves memory impairment and at least one of the following disturbances: aphasia, apraxia, agnosia, or disturbance in executive functioning.

Etiology of Dementia

A great number of diseases and conditions may be responsible for the development of dementia. The most frequent etiology of dementia, however, is *Alzheimer's disease* (AD), accounting for as much as 50% to 70% of cases of dementia in the aged. In this condition, parts of the limbic memory system (especially the hippocampus) as well as various regions of cortical secondary and tertiary association cortices are affected by the disease process. *Cerebrovascular disease* is the second most common etiology of dementia, either in the form of widespread small vessel disease or due to multiple minor and major ischemic injuries (infarctions) of the cerebral hemispheres. Other dementias may primarily be due to disease processes affecting *fronto-temporal* regions (e.g., Pick's disease) or *subcortical* nuclei (the subcortical dementing diseases, e.g., Huntington's chorea, Parkinson's disease, progressive supranuclear palsy, and Wilson's disease). For a more detailed overview of subcategories of dementia, see, for example, Cummings and Benson (1992).

The Dementia Syndrome

Dementia exists in various degrees of severity. In all stages, the pattern of relatively preserved versus impaired cognitive domains is extremely heterogeneous, as various cortical and subcortical structures are affected differentially in individual cases (Waldemar et al., 1994) and in various diseases (Cummings & Benson, 1992). Further, although the cognitive decline is considered a sine qua non for diagnostic purposes, cognition is not the only mental area affected. In most cases, a variety of behavioral disturbances, not to be derived directly from the cognitive problems, coexist (Patterson & Bolger, 1994; Reisberg et al., 1987). Finally, the patient's awareness of being sick and his or her perception of the cognitive and behavioral dysfunctions suffer in most demented individuals (McGlynn & Kaszniak, 1991). Thus, as a primary consequence of the disease process in the brain, the current neuropsychological status must be conceptualized as the interaction of at least four factors: (a) the stage of progression of the disease process, (b) the pattern of spared and impaired cognitive capacities, (c) the behavioral (noncognitive) disturbances, and (d) the level of awareness.

Stages of Dementia

Dementia appears at all levels of severity, from subtle subjective experiences of diminished efficiency to a virtually vegetative (mute and immobile) state. Life expectancy in most degenerative dementias, from the appearance of the first symptoms to death, may be as long as 10 to 15 years. The patient's experiences of herself or himself, the burdens on relatives, and the challenges for caregivers and other professionals are widely different during this protracted development. Accordingly, the demented person, the relatives, and the caregivers are faced with changing coping tasks over time.

Patterns of Cognitive Impairment

The characteristic cognitive dysfunctions of dementia constitute a progressive decline of memory, accompanied by deterioration of basic cognitive functions such as language, spatial skills, attention, judgment, and reasoning. One cognitive domain of specific relevance to daily living has been labeled *executive* functions. This domain refers to mental processes that are involved in the planning, initiation, and regulation of behavior. Intellectual and higher level self-care skills—such as managing finances, transportation, and planning—generally deteriorate at a faster speed than more basic practical abilities (Haley & Pardo, 1989). Procedural activities such as well-established habits and routines are relatively resistant to deterioration and may be preserved even in severely demented stages.

The effects of executive dysfunctions on daily living are considerable, as the patient may become incapable of managing a wide range of daily tasks despite relatively intact basic cognitive skills. These problems are particularly characteristic of patients suffering from frontal lobe and subcortical types of dementia, as well as for AD patients in more advanced stages.

Behavioral Changes

Behavioral disturbances constitute a central, but often neglected, part of the symptomatology of dementia. Whereas the loss of memory and concentration

Exhibit 1.   Behavioral Changes in Dementia

Changes in affect
  Depression
  Anxiety
  Aggression
  Euphoria
Changes in activity
  Apathy
  Agitation
  Restlessness
  Hyperactivity
  Wandering
  Hoarding
Psychotic disturbances
  Hallucinations
  Delusions
  Paranoia
Changes of basic drives
  Hyper- and hyposexuality
  Hyperphagia
  Appetite loss
Changes of diurnal rhythm and sleep
  Sleep disturbances

often poses the biggest problem to the patient, the behavioral pathology represents a major burden to close relatives and a major challenge to those professionals devoted to the care and management of dementia patients. Exhibit 1 summarizes the range of disturbed behaviors most often observed in dementia. Some behavioral symptoms—such as anxiety, suspiciousness, depression, and lack of spontaneity—appear at a frequency of up to 50% of patients with AD, and during the course of progression, at least some behavioral features will appear in all dementia patients.

Level of Awareness

Patients with dementia as well as many other types of brain dysfunction demonstrate variable degrees of awareness of their cognitive and behavioral problems. In the extreme, the patient may not be aware that he or she is ill at all (*anosognosia*). More often, awareness of more circumscribed dysfunctions, the degree of these impairments, and their implications for work, leisure, and social life may be distorted. Although awareness may be compromised even in the initial stages of dementia, the awareness may diminish further when the condition progresses, leading to the clinical paradox that the more impaired the patient is, the less she or he may complain of impaired competency. Distorted perceptions of capacities and deficits have important implications for the patient's acceptance of medical interventions, professional care, and rehabilitation.

This impairment of awareness is considered to be primarily an expression of brain dysfunction rather than a psychodynamic defense mechanism (e.g., denial or repression). In typical AD dementia, an awareness of failing skill is usually present in earlier stages of the disease, presumably until the frontal lobes are affected (Fromholt & Larsen, 1991; Morris, 1994). In frontal lobe dementias, early loss of self-evaluative abilities is prominent, and such patients are consequently less likely to develop compensatory behavior.

Individual Patterns in Dementia

Coping and Compensatory Behavior

For the time being, no medical treatment is available to prevent the development and progression of most brain diseases that cause dementia. Accordingly, initiatives directed to support the patient's ability to preserve self-care behaviors and sustain normal interactions with social surroundings are strongly emphasized.

Modern psychological conceptions of dementia stress the automatic or deliberate efforts in dementia patients to cope with failing competence and changing interpersonal interactions. Compensatory behavior is unlikely to arise, unless the dementia patient has some kind of awareness of the problem (Bäckman, 1992); the efforts may be more or less functional and adaptive, and they may be problem focused (e.g., writing notes to support a failing memory) or emotion focused (e.g., clinging to an intimate person to reduce anxiety).

Illustrative of typical compensatory behavior in early stages of AD dementia are measures taken to conceal autobiographical memory deficits and failing recall of specific knowledge such as names, one's age, and dates. Phrases and diversions replace specific information, such as when asked about age, a diversionary reply could be "How old do you think?" In addition to being considered symptoms of the disease, such efforts will signify, from a more humanistic and psychodynamic perspective, deliberate efforts from the person to adapt to a stressful encounter and to conceal the deficiency as far as possible.

Personality Factors

Although the localization of the brain damage within cortical and subcortical structures has a major impact on cognition and behavior, the great individual variation among demented persons implies that premorbid personality factors play an important role also. Generalizations such as "dementia exaggerates prior personality traits" are hardly justified. A more probable assumption is that predispositions like coping resources, cognitive flexibility, conceptions of self, and temperament will influence the way a particular person reacts to the intrapsychic and interpersonal changes caused by the disease. However, systematic studies of the impact of individual predispositions on dementia are practically nonexistent.

Cognitive Decline in the "Gray Zone" Between Normal Age Changes and Dementia

Several factors may contribute to decreasing cognitive and socioemotional functioning in older persons and produce cognitive changes that are hard to distinguish from symptoms of incipient dementia. Some of these conditions are treatable; therefore, accurate identification of the causes behind failing abilities is essential to avoiding misdiagnosis and inadequate intervention.

The accumulated knowledge of normal age-related changes in basic cognitive skills (see chapter 4 by Timothy A. Salthouse) provides a baseline for assessment of cognitive competence in old age. When cognitive changes become pronounced within a shorter span of time, a suspicion of incipient dementia arises, but other possibilities have to be considered before a diagnosis of dementia is decided.

Depression and dementia are the two most common neuropsychiatric disturbances in old age and share many symptoms, so that the risk of misdiagnosis is considerable. Depression-related symptoms may be common in early stages of AD (Kaszniak & Christenson, 1995). Correct differential diagnosis is important, because depressions can be treated effectively today.

Health problems and some medications are confounding variables of cognitive functioning in older people. Chronic diseases, especially cardiovascular disease and hypertension, have been found to be associated with lower levels of performance. Also, more temporary diseases, such as infectious diseases, may have long-lasting effects on performance in older people. Generally, mental abilities are more confounded with health problems in old age, due to both the higher frequency of health problems in older people and the more vulnerable biology with age (e.g., slower recovery and reduced reserve capacity).

Disuse of mental capacities due to lack of stimulation and social reinforcement to maintain cognitive functions, such as through social interaction, may lead to decreasing capacity. Isolated people are at risk of deficit updating of knowledge and maintenance of mental speed and may be misinterpreted as suffering from dementia. The effects of prolonged isolation and disuse are less understood, such as whether pronounced isolation can lead to irreversible brain changes.

Several studies have documented a relationship between proximity to death and declining cognitive skills (Berg, 1996), the *terminal decline phenomenon*. Thus, the distance from death can be regarded as an overall measure of biological aging. This condition may be characterized by a psychological withdrawal concomitant to the cognitive deterioration before death, and in such cases, care rather than activating interventions is needed. At present, no reliable methods to differentiate between terminal phenomena and confusionable conditions such as incipient dementia are available.

References

American Psychiatric Association. (1994). *Diagnostic and statistical manual of mental disorders.* Washington, DC: Author.

Bäckman, L. (1992). Psychological compensation: A theoretical framework. *Psychological Bulletin, 112*, 259–283.

Berg, S. (1996). Aging, behavior and terminal decline. In J. E. Birren, K. W. Schaie (Eds.), *Handbook of the psychology of aging* (4th ed., pp. 323–337). San Diego, CA: Academic Press.

Cummings, J. L., & Benson, D. F. (1992). *Dementia: A clinical approach.* (2nd ed.). Woburn, MA: Butterworth-Heinemann.

Fromholt, P., & Larsen, S. F. (1991). Autobiographical memory and life-history narratives in aging and dementia (Alzheimer type). In M. A. Conway, D. C. Rubin, H. Spinnler, & W. A. Wagenaar (Eds.), *Theoretical perspectives on autobiographical memory* (pp. 413–426). Dordrecht, The Netherlands: Klüwer Academic.

Haley, W. E., & Pardo, K. M. (1989). Relationship of severity of dementia to caregiving stressors. *Psychology and Aging, 4*, 389–392.

Kaszniak, A. W., & Christenson, G. D. (1995). Differential diagnosis of dementia and depression. In M. Storandt & G. R. VandenBos (Eds.), *Neuropsychological assessment of dementia and depression in older adults: A clinician's guide* (pp. 81–117). Washington, DC: American Psychological Association.

McGlynn, S. M., & Kaszniak, A. W. (1991). When metacognition fails: Impaired awareness of deficit in Alzheimer's disease. *Journal of Cognitive Neuroscience, 3*, 183–189.

Morris, R. G. (1994). Recent developments in the neuropsychology of dementia. *International Review of Psychiatry, 6*, 85–107.

Patterson, M. B., & Bolger, J. P. (1994). Assessment of behavioral symptoms in Alzheimer's disease. *Alzheimer Disease and Associated Disorders, 8*(Suppl. 3), 4–20.

Reisberg, B., Borenstein, J., Salob, S. P., Ferris, S. H., Franssen, E., & Georgotas, A. (1987). Behavioral symptoms in Alzheimer's disease: Phenomenology and treatment. *Journal of Clinical Psychiatry, 48*(Suppl. 5), 9–15.

Waldemar, G., Bruhn, P., Schmidt, E., & Kristensen, M. (1994). Cognitive profiles and regional cerebral blood flow patterns in dementia of the Alzheimer type. *European Journal of Neurology, 1*, 81–89.

17

Substance Use and Abuse in Old Age

Edith S. Lisansky Gomberg and Robert A. Zucker

Biological changes over the life span suggest that the body's response to different drugs will vary with age (Gromberg, 1990). Both the pharmacokinetics (absorption) and the pharmacodynamics (response) can vary with age in relation to the most commonly encountered drugs that have central nervous system (CNS) effects. In this chapter, we consider the use by older people of prescription medicines, alcohol, illegal substances, and nicotine.

A *drug* may be defined as a substance (not food) that may be natural or laboratory-produced that, by its chemical nature, alters the structure or function of an organism. Drugs may be classified in terms of chemical composition or in terms of CNS action; CNS action is produced by *psychoactive* drugs (e.g., alcohol, narcotics, and nicotine). Another classification of drugs might be in terms of social acceptability, which varies widely, from broadly accepted drugs (e.g., caffeine) to banned substances defined by law as Schedule I substances. Substance abuse is deviant usage, diagnosis of which is usually made by the criteria of the *Diagnostic and Statistical Manual of Mental Disorders* (*DSM–IV*; American Psychiatric Association, 1994).

There are several classes of substances involved in use and abuse by older people (Beresford & Gomsberg, 1995). The first class is medication, both prescribed and over-the-counter (OTC); psychoactive medications are of particular interest. The second class is alcohol. The third class is the controlled substances banned by law, including marijuana, heroin, and cocaine—the best known of "street drugs." These are the substances that get a major share of media attention. The final class is nicotine, which is used by all age groups.

Age Changes

Pharmacokinetics is the study of the time course of absorption, tissue distribution, metabolism, and excretion of drugs and their metabolites from the body and the relationship of drug disposition to the duration and intensity of drug effects (Vestal & Dawson, 1985). Although there are apparently insignificant age changes in drug absorption, there are body composition changes that come

Preparation of this work was supported in part by National Institute on Alcohol Abuse and Alcoholism Grant 5 P50 AA07378.

with age that influence drug distribution. There are age changes as well in drug elimination, particularly a decline in renal function.

Studying the effects of age on pharmacokinetics yields information about the mechanism of altered *pharmacodynamics*, the physiological and psychological response to drugs, in older people. The study of pharmacodynamics among older people is directed toward understanding their greater or lesser response to particular drugs, independent of pharmacokinetic effects. There have been observations of age changes in sensitivity to some drugs (e.g., increased sensitivity to drugs acting on the CNS). Different psychoactive drugs may produce different pharmacodynamic effects in older people, for example, there is some evidence that the response of older people to some of the benzodiazepines is enhanced (McCormack & O'Malley, 1986). Susceptibility to adverse drug reactions (ADRs) to psychoactive drugs is apparently increased.

ADRs among older patients can result from multiple drug therapies, drug overdose or misuse, slowing of drug metabolism or elimination; they can be a product of age-related chronic diseases, alcohol intake, and food–drug incompatibilities. ADRs among older patients are more severe than among younger patients. Risk factors for ADRs include being female, living alone, suffering from multiple diseases, ingesting multiple drugs, and practicing poor nutrition. Although only about 3% of people presenting to emergency rooms with drug-related episodes are 55 years of age or older, it is of interest that two thirds of them present with overdose, 10% with chronic effects, and 6% with unexpected reaction (U.S. Department of Health and Human Services [DHHS], Drug Abuse Warning Network, 1996).

Incidence and Prevalence

Medications

In the United States, 12%–13% of the general population is defined as elderly, but they account for 35% of prescription drug expenditure (Health Care Financing Administration, Office of National Cost Estimates, 1990). As people age, there is increased use of prescription drugs for both chronic and acute illness. Older people are also more likely to take OTC drugs (Korrapati & Vestal, 1995). Hale, May, Marks, and Steward (1987) reported that the most commonly prescribed drugs were diuretics, cardiovascular drugs, and sedative–hypnotics. Most commonly purchased OTC drugs were analgesics, vitamins, and laxatives. Data for older persons in other countries are similar (Vestal & Dawson, 1985). Medications used by older Canadians are, in order of reported frequency, cardioactives, vasoactives and diuretics, analgesics and anti-inflammatory drugs, tranquilizers and hypnotics, laxatives, and vitamins (McKim & Mishara, 1987).

The question of psychoactive drug use (tranquilizers, sedatives, and hypnotics) is vexing. In almost every country for which statistics are available, more such drugs are prescribed not only for older patients, but for women in general (Balter, Levine, & Manheimer, 1974; Hansen, 1989). When an older person is seen in an American hospital emergency room, he or she is most likely to present with a misuse of a psychoactive drug (LaRue, Dessonville, & Jarvik, 1985).

Alcohol

After a review of cross-sectional and longitudinal studies of older people's drinking practices and a reanalysis of data from a Epidemiological Catchment Area study (Helzer, Bucholz, & Robins, 1995), epidemiologists Bucholz, Sheline, and Helzer (1995) made the following conclusions: (a) Drinking generally declines with age up to the 80s, (b) there are consistent gender differences, that is, a greater percentage of men drink, and a greater percentage of men drink heavily, (c) there is a decrease in prevalence of alcohol abuse and dependence, (d) the male–female ratio for abuse and dependence increases, and there is a pronounced increase in alcohol abuse and dependence among separated and divorced older people, but not among widowed older people.

The percentage of Americans who drink ranges from 73.1% for the 18–29 years age group down to 49.4% for the 60 years and older age group (National Institute on Alcohol Abuse and Alcoholism, Alcohol and Health, 1997). Heavier drinker percentages range from 7.0% in the youngest group to 1.5% in the oldest group. There is variation by subgroup: Older persons with disrupted marital status are more likely to drink heavily than those in marriages, and older White men report the highest percentage of alcohol-related problems (1.2%), whereas older African American men report 0.8%. There are also regional, socioeconomic, and educational variations.

If we compare the most recent, 1995 rankings of litres of pure alcohol consumed, by country (International Beverage Consumption and Production Trends, 1996; World Drink Trends, 1996), the first 19 ranks are taken by countries in Europe with Luxembourg, France, Portugal, Hungary, and Spain leading the others. Australia, the United Kingdom, and New Zealand rank 20th, 22nd, 21st, and 23rd. Argentina reports the most consumption in South America, Japan in Asia (25th), and South Africa in Africa (34th). Interestingly, the United States ranks 24th and Canada 28th. Consumption of alcohol in English-speaking countries is, therefore, quite similar.

International figures for the prevalence of liver disease and cirrhosis, as indicators of alcohol problems and alcohol use disorders, show the following: The number of deaths in North America are highest for the United States, for China and Japan among the Asian nations, and for Germany in Europe. Again, caution is needed in interpreting the available figures; populations vary and only the number of deaths are reported. A review of the European nations (Harkin, Anderson, & Lehto, 1995) shows many differences in the proportion of adults who drink alcoholic beverages; this review provides the percentages of male and female drinkers and the proportion drinking heavily.

Illegal Substances

It is difficult to get comprehensive figures on the use of illegal drugs among older people. There are some cross-national figures for average daily consumption of various narcotics in defined daily doses per million inhabitants (Addiction Research Foundation, 1994), but these are likely to be prescription use. In America, Canada ranks first, Falkland Islands second, the United States third, and Bermuda fourth. The use of heroin in the United States or elsewhere is at best an estimate; traditionally, the U.S. Federal Bureau of Narcotics has estimated the number of heroin-addicted people in the country to be approximately half a million. Although historically heroin addiction was more likely a phenomenon of youth rather than of old age, there is some evidence that a growing number of heroin addicts are 60 years of age and older. Pascarelli (1985) reported that people age 60+ constituted 0.005% of methadone program patients in 1974 and 2.0% in 1985. DesJarlais, Joseph, and Courtwright (1985) described this elderly cohort and the characteristic behaviors that made them survivors.

The use and abuse of cocaine appears to be relatively infrequent among older people. The 1991 data (Addiction Research Foundation, 1994) show the largest number of cocaine consumers to be in the United States, in the United Kingdom, and in the former Soviet Union.

Cannabis is an illegal drug in the United States but is used legally as hashish, ganja, and bhang in other countries. Information about the extent of usage is sparse. Cannabis has been a banned substance in the United States since 1937, but it is estimated to be the most widely used illegal substance in the country.

Nicotine

Nicotine is mostly used in the form of cigarettes, and cigarette consumption rose in the United States until the 1960s when the surgeon general began a campaign for smoking cessation. From 1974 on, consumption has dropped steadily. In the 1960s, more than 42% of the adult population were smokers; in 1993, this figure dropped to 25% (National Center for Health Statistics, 1996). In 1993 among U.S. men age 65 and older, the percentage of cigarette smokers was 13.5%; among U.S. women age 65 and older, it was 10.5%.

One thing is certain: There are more male than female cigarette smokers in those countries for which statistics are available (e.g., China, Japan, and Southeast Asian countries). In the United States, Australia, and New Zealand, there are more male than female smokers, although the gender gap is not as wide as it is in the other countries of the world.

Implications

Medications

The increase in acute and chronic diseases that appears among older people means greater health care expenditure and more medication for this group. The most widely used prescribed drugs include both general medications— among which cardiovascular medication, diuretics, antibiotics, and analgesics are some of the most frequently prescribed—and psychoactive drugs—among which sedative hypnotics, including benzodiazepines, and psychotherapeutic drugs, such as antidepressants and stimulants, are some of the most frequently prescribed. Although some treatment facilities report sizable patient intake of older persons with drug-associated problems and dependence on psychoactive drugs, the issue has never evoked much research interest or attention. Older persons frequently associate their use of psychoactive drugs with problems such as insomnia or depression; in one study, almost half of those taking such drugs reported that they could not perform their daily activities without the medication (Prentice, 1979).

There are several issues related to the use of prescribed psychoactive medication. Nursing home use of such drugs is a problem; media attention occasionally focuses on such usage. Emergency room patients differ by age: Younger patients are more likely to appear with problems relating to controlled substances (e.g., cocaine), whereas older patients are more likely to present with ADRs to psychoactive drugs. There are also definite gender differences in medication-associated problems: Women are prescribed and use more psychoactive drugs, and this appears at least as a dependency problem more often among older women than older men (Glantz & Backenheimer, 1988). There is a suggestion from several epidemiological sources that older men are more likely to be prescribed antidepressants than older women. If this is true, it might be related to more use of health resources among older men, but it also appears to be a fact of aging that older men show a number of indicators of more depression than older women. In addition to the prescription of antidepressants, older men also have higher rates of alcohol-associated problems than women, and older men have considerably higher suicide rates than older women. Suicide rates for older men rise with age.

Epidemiological surveys of older persons living in the community show widespread usage of psychoactive drugs, and it is clear that older persons receive a disproportionately higher percentage of prescriptions for sedatives, tranquilizers, and so forth (O'Malley, Judge, & Crooks, 1980). Except for pharmacists' educational materials, which warn of the dependency potential for the prescribed psychoactive drugs, this does not appear to be a major social concern, even among older people. Data from the Drug Abuse Warning Network (reports from urban emergency rooms; DHHS, 1996) indicate that older people are likely to present with problems relating to nonbarbiturate sedatives, tranquilizers, barbiturate sedatives, and antidepressants. On all of these drugs, the percentage of women appearing for emergency treatment is greater than the percentage of men.

Older people buy and use a disproportionately larger number of OTC drugs. In the general population, the most commonly used nonprescription drugs are analgesics, nutritional supplements, laxatives, and antacids. Nonnarcotic analgesics are the most commonly reported drugs of purchase by older people both in the United States and in other countries. There is, however, a lack of agreement among investigators: Some believe that older people purchase and use disproportionately more OTC medications than other age groups (Simonson, 1984) but other investigators believe that older people do not use OTC medications excessively. The Food and Drug Administration has suggested that there be age-related labeling on prescribed drugs for persons over 65. Generally, the response to this suggestion has been negative; consensus among investigators seems to be that labeling medications should be done by specific medical conditions.

The question of folk remedies and the growing popularity of alternative medicines may be noted here. Traditionally, folk remedies (e.g., herbs, chicken soup, and chamomile tea) have been used by many people, probably most often by low-income groups. Studies of eating habits or self-medication would be welcome; it is likely that self-medication with home remedies may be the first line of health defense for most people.

Alcohol

Alcoholic beverages may be consumed infrequently, in moderate quantities, or in large quantities, and use of them may produce alcohol abuse or alcohol dependence. To what extent is alcohol used by older people? Data collected over the last decades show that moderate social drinking does decline with age, but there are some data that challenge this generalization. Several reports, one done by the National Health Interview Survey and one in Framingham, MA, suggest modest increases in proportion of drinkers among older persons (Gordon & Kannel, 1983). The issue has not been resolved, but the majority of studies do report a smaller proportion of moderate and heavy drinkers among older people. There may be a number of reasons for this trend: health issues, finances, a specific cohort effect, changing physiological response to alcohol with age, and so forth. The question is whether increased acceptability of drinking among younger persons will produce an older population in the future that will not show a decrease in drinking as they age. This is a complex issue, and one may speculate that the health awareness of the under-60 generation will produce the same decline in drinking as they age.

How much of a health risk is alcohol for older persons? It is true that older people are more likely to manifest acute and chronic illness, and it is also true that this population subgroup takes more medication than younger groups (Maddox, Robins, & Rosenberg 1984). The question of age changes in hepatic blood flow and the capacity of the liver to metabolize alcohol and drugs as it ages is relevant. Older individuals manifest a decrease in body water content, so that the same amount of an alcoholic beverage will produce a higher peak serum ethanol level in older persons and a lower peak serum ethanol level in younger persons. The increased vulnerability of the brain with aging raises questions about confusion, depression, and dementia as they relate to alcohol intake of older persons. The general consensus is that light drinking is not harmful to older persons (Dufour, Archer, & Gordis, 1992) if they are reasonably healthy and take no medications that interact with alcohol.

Although there may be a large number of older adults with psychoactive medication problems, they are infrequently seen in substance abuse services. Older adults who drink heavily or frequently and who have alcohol-related health or family problems are more likely to appear in treatment services, voluntarily or not. In Michigan, substance abuse treatment admissions of patients under 60 years of age include 62% for whom alcohol is the primary substance of abuse; for those age 60 and older, that figure is 86%. In a study done earlier in a Michigan Veterans Hospital, 65% of younger alcoholic men and 80% of older alcohol men chose alcohol as "the substance of first choice" (Gomberg, 1977).

The literature on older people's alcohol problems draws on samples from clinical populations (e.g., hospital wards, arrest records, and clinics) and from community and national surveys. The proportion of older people with alcohol problems in clinical populations is almost always larger than in community studies, but the epidemiological studies in communities may minimize the problem. This is suggested by a recent report of records from all hospital inpatient Medicare Part A beneficiaries age 65 and older: The highest rate of alcohol-related hospitalizations occurs in the 45–64 years age group (94.8 per 10,000 population), but the second highest rate is in the population age 65 years and older (65.1 per 10,000). The alcohol-related disorders include alcohol abuse and dependence, alcoholic liver disease, psychoses, cardiomyopathy, gastritis, and polyneuropathy (Adams, Yuan, Barboriak, & Rimm, 1993).

The issue of screening and diagnosis may be raised. Although there are many good screening instruments (e.g., the Michigan Alcoholism Screening Test; Selzer, 1971, or the CAGE four items; Mayfield, McLeod, & Hall, 1974), the question is the appropriateness of these instruments for older people. Losing time from work, for example, is an appropriate criterion for younger people but not necessarily for the age 65 and older group. Screening instruments specifically designed for older people are beginning to appear (Blow et al., 1992). Another methodological issue is the definition of *heavy* drinking for older people; the same amount of alcohol produces higher peak serum ethanol levels for older persons than for younger ones, and heavy drinking criteria may need to be adjusted.

There is some study of neuropsychological or cognitive impairment as a by-product of heavy or problem drinking. Psychological deficits have been explored in terms of functions impaired, gender differences, the relationship of age to alcohol-impaired cognition, and the effects of moderate drinking on memory and other cognitive activity (Gomberg, 1990). There has been a hypothesis about "premature aging," which posits that premature senescence is brought about by heavy drinking; evidence on this hypothesis has been ambiguous (Tarter, 1995). Cognitive impairment studies focus on specific functions: short-term memory, nonverbal abstracting, the ability to process new information, and so forth. There is a continuing question about the reversibility of cognitive loss (Tarter, 1995). Many clinicians affirm that older heavy drinkers who quit drinking may with time regain a good deal of lost function; the process is apparently slow, and patience is required.

Among older heavy or problem drinkers, interest in differentiated types has produced some research activity. A major distinguishing characteristic among older problem drinkers is between early onset and later onset. Some investigators have defined *later* onset as problem drinking begun around or after age 40, but if we are to associate onset of problem drinking and aging, it would be more useful to divide older heavy or problem drinkers 60 years of age and older into *early* onset versus *recent* onset. Recent onset older problem drinkers constitute as much as one third of older alcohol abusers; recent onset appears to occur more frequently with women than with men, who report more early onset. Is recent onset associated with experienced stress of aging? The literature is quite mixed, and *stress* is apparently a complex and subjective phenomenon, defined differently by different investigators. The apparent stresses of aging, such as losses and decreased status, impact quite differently on different people, depending on gender, general health, socioeconomic status, coping mechanism, and life experience. The available reports do show meaningful comparison between early and recent onset; the early-onset group reports more positive family history, more comorbid diagnoses of antisocial personality, and a poorer prognosis (Atkinson, Tolson, & Turner, 1990; Liberto & Oslin, 1996; Schonfeld & Dupree, 1991).

The clinician should take a drinking history, because there is not only the question of early versus recent onset; there are people with intermittent histories of heavy drinking. At particular points in their lives, these people have tended to solve problems with alcohol, so that, in a sense, although the problem drinking seems to be of recent onset, their history suggests an on-and-off use of alcohol as problem solver (Gomberg, 1982).

The cues to look for include health problems (e.g., hypertension with no previous history); social problems with family and friends (e.g., hassles with other people or withdrawal); some mental status issues, such as disorientation, confusion, or forgetfulness; and problems of coordination, such as falls, injuries, and bruises. Often, heavy drinking by an older person is accompanied by depression, anorexia, psychomotor retardation, or paranoid ideation. The heavy drinkers may show up, drunk or sober, in an emergency room or hospital or in a health caretaker's office; they may show up in housing developments, senior centers, and retirement colonies. Social networks are often impaired, with family and friends angry at the problem drinker. Compared with younger problem drinkers, they tend to drink alone, engage in binges, and get into more accidents. In most ways, however, the patterns of problem drinking and the alcohol-related problems that result are not very different for younger and older problem drinkers (DeHart & Hoffman, 1996). There is not much information about older women problem drinkers, but a recent comparison between men and women in substance abuse treatment for alcohol abuse (Gomberg, 1995) showed the same gender differences found in all age groups: for the women, more marital disruption (more likely widowhood), more recent age of onset, more spousal heavy or problem drinking, less drinking in public places, and more report of dependence on prescribed psychoactive drugs. Comparison of White and African American men in relation to drinking shows an interesting difference: Among low-income men, African Americans have significantly more drinking problems and drinking consequences; however, among affluent men, the difference between African Americans and Whites is not significant. A recent comparison (Gomberg & Nelson, 1995) of African American and White male alcoholic patients in their mid-60s showed a number of differences: African American alcoholic men drank larger quantities, preferred high-alcohol-content beverages, were more likely to drink in public places, and reported more health consequences. The African American alcoholics had used and abused drugs other than alcohol significantly more and reported such use as having occurred earlier in life (the question of availability of such drugs and the consequences of alcohol and drug combination may be raised).

Decades ago in alcohol studies, there was much interest in the chronic drunkenness offender. At that point, a high percentage of arrests for public intoxication was of older men. Several recent changes should be noted. First, the Supreme Court Dewitt Easter decision that permits arrests for antisocial behavior but not for public intoxication per se changed the patterns of detoxification for this group (Kurtz & Regier, 1975; Rubington, 1982, 1995). Second, in many large cities, skid row's population used to be White, male, and elderly, but it has changed into a mix of ethnicities, more women, and different age groups, and this population is now called the "homeless." Third, most alcohol and drug researchers do not include this subgroup in their studies.

Illegal Substances

The occasional social use of drugs like marijuana, hashish, and cocaine probably does occur among older people, but we know little about the use of such substances among ethnic minority older men and women, among retired blue-collar workers, or among the sophisticates in the demimonde. There are apparently heroin users who began using fairly early in life and have survived into old age. One of the widely held beliefs about heroin addicts was that they did not survive to old age: They either died or "matured out" (this belief did not include what may be most common, i.e., a switch to alcohol, an easier addiction to maintain than heroin). There are, however, some older heroin-dependent people who have maintained their habits and lived beyond their 60s. In the mid-1970s, addicts 60 years and older constituted 0.005% of the methadone maintenance population in New York City; 10 years later, their proportion had risen to 2%. DesJarlais and his colleagues (1985) described the behaviors of this older group of heroin addicts who had survived. The Michigan Department of Public Health (1994) reported that for treatment admissions in 1992 and 1993, of those in the age group 60 years and older, heroin was the primary substance of abuse for 3%.

In the DesJarlais et al. (1985) study, the older patients on methadone maintenance had the following behavioral characteristics: Their parents had led long lives, they avoided violence, they were careful about the use of clean needles, they were able to hold their drug supply at times in reserve, and they used other drugs—particularly alcohol—sparingly. These survivors were in reasonable health when compared with same-age people in the general population; ironically, if there were medical problems, they were often related to a smoking history. The use of banned substances is a modest problem for older populations. In 1994 Michigan Department of Public Health statistics, substance abuse treatment admissions for people under age 60 showed twice the percentage of younger patients whose primary substance of abuse was heroin: 6% compared with 3% of those over 60. The contrast was even sharper for those whose primary substance of abuse was cocaine: 18% of those under age 60 versus 2% of those age 60 and older. Data from the criminal justice system suggest a triadic relationship: youth, criminal activity, and illegal drugs. In the older population, the criminal justice system has historically been involved with homeless older people; in recent years, however, arrests for public intoxication have diminished, and the homeless population has become more heterogeneous. Little is known about case findings or treatment practices of older abusers of illegal substances.

Nicotine

Men are more likely to be smokers than women, although the gap between the genders has narrowed in the last 20 years. The U.S. Public Health Service has tracked the marked increase in female smoking, which began during World War II; by the 1960s and 1970s, lung cancer began to rise among women, and by 1985, lung cancer surpassed breast cancer as the chief cause of cancer death among women.

A survey of people age 65 and older in Massachusetts (Branch & Jetter, 1984) showed that those less likely to be current smokers included respondents living alone or with their children, those who reported their health as poor or fair, and "the frail elderly." There has been a recent increase in reports of the relationship between drinking alcoholic beverages and smoking (e.g., Fertig & Allen, 1995). Data collected at the University of Michigan Alcohol Research Center has shown a clear relationship between smoking and alcohol intake among relatively healthy older persons (Gomberg, Walton, Bandekar, Coyne, & Blow, 1997).

The relationship between smoking and several acute and chronic diseases is well documented. A recent review of studies of the metabolism of drugs in older persons concluded that the effects of aging, nicotine, and alcohol are confounded and difficult to separate.

The percentage of American adults who smoke has declined considerably over the past 30 years in every age group, particularly among those with higher educational achievement. Recent interviews with over 2,000 patients of primary care physicians have turned up significant differences between those older men and women who are lifetime abstainers and those with a past history of drinking, moderate or heavy. Among men, 22% of former drinkers and 5% of lifetime abstainers are current smokers; among women, 19% of former drinkers and 6% of lifetime abstainers are current smokers (Gomberg, Hegedus, & Zucker, in press).

Treatment

Diagnosis and Assessment

Substance-related disorders may be at the level of abuse or dependence, as defined by the *DSM–IV*; both involve some loss of control, but substance dependence also commonly includes tolerance and withdrawal as criteria of diagnosis (Kleber, 1990). How useful the diagnostic criteria are for older people has been questioned, and relying on the *DSM–IV* criteria may lead to underdiagnosis and inconsistencies in reported prevalence rates. Many of the commonly used assessment instruments were standardized for younger populations and are relatively low in sensitivity for older populations. Fortunately, new screening instruments are being developed (e.g., Blow et al., 1992).

Using a number of measures is invaluable for accurate assessment. Such measures might include collateral information from significant others, the use of blood alcohol tests and drug toxicology screens, examination of biochemical markers, the examination of earlier medical records, and assessment of accompanying medical conditions and psychosocial problems.

Comorbidity

Older substance abusers are more likely to have medical problems than younger ones (which is true of the general population as well). Age-related diseases coexisting with substance abuse may include anemia, arrhythmias, dementia, diabetes, hypertension, incontinence, and osteoporosis (Gambert, 1992), as well as liver disease and pancreatitis. A demonstration treatment project for older, medically ill alcoholics (Willenbring, Olson, Bielinski, & Lynch, 1995) showed good results, including significantly lower mortality a year later.

Older patients with comorbid psychiatric diagnoses or organic disorder are difficult to treat. Moos, Mertens, and Brenman (1993) demonstrated that dually diagnosed older people required more hospitalization and more outpatient treatment and experienced higher relapse rates.

Detoxification

Brower, Mudd, Blow, Young, and Hall (1994) recently demonstrated that older patients take significantly longer to withdraw than younger patients, in spite of similarly long drug histories in both groups. Older patients are more likely to manifest sleeplessness, cognitive impairment, weakness, and hypertension than younger patients; it is advisable to medically monitor withdrawal of older patients.

Issues Involved in Assessment and Treatment Planning

Early-onset versus late-onset substance abuse. In gathering the history of the patient's alcohol or drug problem, it is important to know whether the problem began early in life or later and whether it has been continuous or intermittent. Noted earlier are differences between early- and late-onset abusers. The early-onset group more often reports a positive family history for substance abuse, a diagnosis of antisocial personality, and generally a poorer prognosis.

Treatment planning and the need for specificity of treatment for older substance-abusing and substance-dependent people. There is a long-standing debate about whether older patients need elder-specific programs of treatment. Earlier work was negative, but recent work (Atkinson, Tolson, & Turner, 1993; Krashner, Rodell, Ogden, Guggenheim, & Karsen, 1992) indicates that patients in an elder-specific program are more likely to complete the course of treatment and to be abstinent on follow-up.

Treatment Modalities

Chemotherapy. Medications (i.e., antabuse and naltrexone) are generally accepted in substance abuse treatment, but there is little available information about their effectiveness with older patients. Antabuse may be helpful with some middle-aged patients, but it is contraindicated with medically ill older patients. Zimberg (1995) indicated the usefulness of antidepressants in the treatment of depressed older substance abusers.

Psychosocial treatment. Although the role of stressors in the etiology of substance abuse among older people is controversial and the evidence is conflicting, there is support for the importance of such events (e.g., loss, retirement, and ill health) in the onset of late-onset or recent-onset substance abuse. Brennan and Moos (1995) differentiated problem drinkers and nonproblem drinkers in an older sample from medical facilities: Problem drinkers reported more negative life events and chronic stressors, fewer material resources, and less social support. Where stressors are an issue, they should be discussed in any treatment program (Gurnack, 1996).

Behavioral treatment. The Gerontology Alcohol Project in Florida (Dupree, Broskowski, & Schonfeld, 1984) was a day-treatment program for late-onset alcoholics, involving a self-management approach, skills acquisition, and reestablishment of social support. Held in a senior center, the group followed a manual, which included alcohol education, descriptions of antecedents and consequences of heavy drinking, and self-management of risk situations. There was significant improvement in most patients, and the program was quite successful. Glantz (1995) has recently described a cognitive therapy approach specifically for older alcoholics.

Group therapy. Group work, particularly supportive group therapies, seems very effective with older patients. Advantages include the counteracting of loneliness, support by age peers, and the opportunity to draw on others' life experiences. In a survey of recovering older people, respondents indicated a preference for elder-specific groups, the use of large print in written materials, and a relatively slow pace (Johnson, 1989).

Family therapy. There has been little work in the evaluation of different models of family treatment, and little is available about the effectiveness of marital or family therapy with substance abusers. The question of "enablers" within the family needs exploration, one study having suggested that the role of enablers was especially pertinent for older women substance abusers (Tabisz, Jacyk, Fuchs, & Grymonpre, 1993).

Community outreach. Graham et al. (1995) described their experience with a community-based project in Toronto, Ontario, Canada, providing individualized assistance to older people to maintain them in their homes, improve physical and emotional health, and reduce or eliminate substance dependence. Graham et al. noted that abuse of psychoactive prescription drugs, involving either side effects or alcohol and drug interaction, was high. The project did demonstrate improvement of about 40% in both reducing substance dependence and other areas, with an additional 35% showing improvement in only one area. Considering the base-rate prognosis for the group studied, the results are encouraging.

Self-help groups. Within Alcoholics Anonymous (AA), membership among those 50 years old and over has increased, and AA has developed some special groups for older alcoholics (Zimberg, 1995). As with group therapies in general, the social support aspect of AA is very important, and a preference for age peers in one's group has been expressed in the little evidence available.

To summarize, there are a number of items that the therapist would do well to consider (Nirenberg, Gomberg, & Cellucci, in press): (a) Recovery rates seem to be as good for older abusers as for younger substance abusers; (b) more patience is needed in working with older abusers, because timing of treatment effect is slowed; (c) the age differential between patient and therapist needs to be talked about, in part because self-disclosure to a much younger person may be painful for the patient; (d) therapists need to work with the families of older abusers; and (e) the dignity of the older person must be considered at all times.

Prevention

For early-onset alcoholics, it is late in the day to talk of prevention; perhaps the best that can be done is to improve early detection, so that treatment can be offered. Studies of health promotion or disease prevention programs from health areas other than substance use and abuse do suggest that such educational programs are well received and do produce improvements in health knowledge, lifestyle management, and quality of life. Interestingly enough, although older people are acutely health conscious, they appear to be the age group most lacking in current health information regarding such topics as smoking, exercise, and alcohol use. Health promotion and health education efforts can be one major area of prevention about alcohol and drug abuse.

Because there is a reported relationship, at least in a medical population, between negative life events and problem drinking, older persons who have suffered recent loss should be recruited for grief counseling and preventive work. Because there is evidence that the proportion of widows is high among older female alcohol abusers (Gomberg, 1995), it would seem wise to offer such programs to recently bereaved women. Some programs for individuals about to retire include information about alcohol and the interaction of alcohol and other drugs. Older persons are vulnerable to peer influences, and it has been noted that heavy drinking may be a potential problem in retirement communities (Alexander & Duff, 1988). Such communities may be a good place for alcohol information and prevention programs.

Hospitals are good sites for elderly health promotion, and many hospitals have such programs directed toward older patients. Hospitals not only make older people available as a target population but also may act as identifiers and interveners in their alcohol- or drug-related problems.

In addition, those who work with older people (e.g., senior community center personnel or Meals on Wheels volunteers) could be trained to be aware of early signs of difficulties with alcohol or drugs and to avoid immediately attributing such signs as confusion, falling, and the like to aging. Unfortunately, the fact remains that we know little about effective prevention in general and even less about the efficacy of prevention programs among older people.

References

Adams, W. L., Yuan, Z., Barboriak, J. J., & Rimm, A. A. (1993). Alcohol-related hospitalizations of elderly people. *Journal of the American Medical Association, 270,* 1222–1225.

Alexander, F., & Duff, R. W. (1988). Social interactions and alcohol use in retirement communities. *Gerontologist, 28,* 632–636.

American Psychiatric Association. (1994). *Diagnostic and statistical manual of mental disorders* (4th ed.). Washington, DC: Author.

Atkinson, R. M., Tolson, R. L., & Turner, J. A. (1990). Late versus early onset problem drinking in older men. *Alcoholism: Clinical and Experimental Research, 14,* 574–579.

Atkinson, R. N., Tolson, R. L., & Turner, J. A. (1993). Factors affecting outpatient treatment compliance of older male problem drinkers. *Journal of Studies on Alcohol, 54,* 479–487.

Balter, M. B., Levine, J., & Manheimer, D. I. (1974). Cross-national study of the extent of anti-anxiety/sedative drug use. *New England Journal of Medicine, 290,* 769–772.

Beresford, T. P., & Gomberg, E. S. L. (1995). *Alcohol and aging.* New York: Oxford University Press.

Blow, F. C., Brower, J., Schulenberg, J. E., Demo-Danenberg, L. M., Young, J. S., & Beresford, T. P. (1992). The Michigan Alcoholism Screening Test—Geriatric version (MAST–G): A new elderly specific screening instrument. *Alcoholism: Clinical and Experimental Research, 16,* 372.

Branch, L. G., & Jetter, A. M. (1984). Personal health practices and mortality among the elderly. *American Journal of Public Health, 74,* 1126–1130.

Brennan, P., & Moos, R. (1995). Life context, coping responses, and adaptive outcomes: A stress and coping perspective on late-life drinking problems. In T. P. Beresford & E. S. L. Gomberg (Eds.), *Alcohol and Aging* (pp. 230–248). New York: Oxford University Press.

Brower, K. J., Mudd, S. A., Blow, F. C., Young, J. P., & Hall, E. M. (1994). Severity and treatment of alcohol withdrawal in elderly vs. younger patients. *Alcoholism: Clinical and Experimental Research, 18,* 196–201.

Bucholz, K. K., Sheline, Y., & Helzer, J. E. (1995). The epidemiology of alcohol use, problems and dependence in elders: A review. In T. P. Beresford & E. S. L. Gomberg (Eds.), *Alcohol and aging* (pp. 19–41). New York: Oxford University Press.

Centers for Disease Control, National Center for Health Statistics. (1988). *Health, United States.* Washington, DC: U.S. Government Printing Office.

DeHart, S. S., & Hoffman, N. G. (1996). Screening and diagnosis: Alcohol use disorders in older adults. In A. M. Gurnack (Ed.), *Drugs and the elderly: Use and misuse of drugs, medicines, alcohol and tobacco* (pp. 25–53). New York: Springer.

DesJarlais, D. C., Joseph, H., & Courtwright, D. F. (1985). Old age and addiction: A study of elderly patients in methadone maintenance treatment. In E. Gottheil, K. A. Druly, T. E. Skoloda, & H. M. Waxman (Eds.), *The combined problems of alcoholism, drug addiction and aging* (201–209). Springfield, IL: Thomas.

Dufour, M. C., Archer, L., & Gordis, E. (1992). Alcohol and the elderly. *Clinics in Geriatric Medicine, 8,* 127–141.

Dupree, L. W., Broskowski, H., & Schonfeld, L. (1984). The Gerontology Alcohol Project: A behavioral program for elderly alcohol abusers. *Gerontologist, 24,* 510–516.

Fertig, J., & Allen, J. P. (1995). *Alcohol and tobacco: From basic science to clinical practice.* (NIAAA Research Monograph No. 30, NIH Publication No. 95-3931). Washington, DC: U.S. Government Printing Office.

Gambert, S. R. (1992). Substance abuse in the elderly. In J. H. Lowinson, P. Ruiz, & R. B. Millman (Eds.), *Substance abuse: A comprehensive textbook* (2nd ed., pp. 843–851). Baltimore: Williams & Wilkins.

Glantz, M. D. (1995). Cognitive therapy with elderly alcoholics. In T. P. Beresford & E. S. L. Gomberg (Eds.). *Alcohol and aging* (pp. 211–229). New York: Oxford University Press.

Glantz, M. D., & Backenheimer, M. S. (1988). Substance abuse among elderly women. *Clinical Gerontology, 8,* 3–24.

Gomberg, E. S. L. (1982). Alcohol use and alcohol problems among the elderly (Alcohol and Health Monograph 4). In *Special population issues* National Institute of Alcohol Abuse and Alcoholism, (DHHS Publication No. ADM 82-1193, pp. 263–290). Washington, DC: U.S. Government Printing Office.

Gomberg, E. S. L. (1990). Drugs, alcohol and aging. In L. K. Kozlowski (Ed.), *Research advances in alcohol and drug problems* (Vol. 19, pp. 171–213). New York: Plenum.

Gomberg, E. S. L. (1995). Older women and alcohol: Use and abuse. In M. Galanter (Ed.), *Recent developments in alcoholism: Vol. 12. Alcoholism and women* (pp. 61–79). New York: Plenum.

Gomberg, E. S. L., Hegedus, A. M., & Zucker, R. A. (Eds.). (in press). *Alcohol problems and aging* (NIAAA Research Monograph). Rockville, MD: National Institute on Alcohol Abuse and Alcoholism.

Gomberg, E. S. L., & Nelson, B. W. (1995). Black and White older men: Alcohol use and abuse. In T. P. Beresford & E. S. L. Gomberg (Eds.), *Alcohol and aging* (pp. 307–323). New York: Oxford University Press.

Gomberg, E. S. L., Walton, M. A., Bandekar, R., Coyne, J. M., & Blow, F. C. (July, 1997). *Alcohol and elderly health: Gender differences in lifetime abstainers versus former drinkers* [Abstract]. Poster session presented at the meeting of the Research Society on Alcoholism, San Francisco.

Gordon, T., & Kannel, W. B. (1983). Drinking and its relation to smoking, BP, blood lipids and uric acid. *Archives of Internal Medicine, 143,* 1366–1374.

Graham, K., Saunders, S. J., Flower, M. C., Timney, C. B., White-Campbell, M., & Pietropaolo, A. Z. (1995). *Addictions treatment for older adults: Evaluation of an innovative client-centered approach.* New York: Haworth.

Gurnack, A. M. (1996). *Drugs and the elderly: Use and misuse of drugs, medicines, alcohol and tobacco.* New York: Springer.

Hale, W. E., May, F. E., Marks, R. G., & Steward, R. B. (1987). Drug use in an ambulatory elderly population: Five year update. *Drugs, Intelligence, and Clinical Pharmacy, 21,* 530–535.

Hansen, E. H. (1989). Sex differences in the use of psychotropic drugs: An annotated review of Danish studies. In E. Haavio-Mannila (Ed.), *Women, alcohol, and drugs in the Nordic countries* (pp. 97–132). Helsinki, Finland: Nordic Council for Alcohol and Drug Research.

Harris, A. M., Anderson, P., & Lehto, J. (1995). *Alcohol in Europe—A health perspective.* Toronto, Ontario, Canada: Addiction Research Foundation.

Health Care Financing Administration, Office of National Cost Estimates (1990). National health expenditures, 1988. *Health Care Financing Review, 11,* 1–41.

Helzer, J. E., Bucholz, K., & Robins, L. N. (1995). Five communities in the United States: Results of an Epidemiologic Catchment Area survey. In J. E. Helzer & G. J. Canino (Eds.), *Alcoholism in North America, Europe, and Asia* (pp. 71–95). New York: Oxford University Press.

International Beverage Consumption and Production Trends. (1996). *World drink trends 1996.* Amsterdam: Produktschap Voor Gedistilleerde Dranken & NTC Publication.

International Profile: Alcohol and Other Drugs. (1994). Toronto, Ontario, Canada: Addiction Research Foundation in collaboration with the Program on Substance Abuse of the World Health Organization.

Johnson, L. K. (1989). How to diagnose and treat chemical dependency in the elderly. *Journal of Gerontological Nursing, 15,* 22–26.

Kleber, H. D. (1990). The nosology of abuse and dependence. *Journal of Psychiatric Research, 24*(Suppl. 2), 57–64.

Korrapati, M. R., & Vestal, R. F. (1995). Alcohol and medications in the elderly: Complex interactions. In T. P. Beresford & E. S. L. Gomberg (Eds.), *Alcohol and aging* (pp. 42–55). New York: Oxford University Press.

Krashner, T. M., Rodell, D. E., Ogden, S. R., Guggenheim, F. G., & Karson, C. N. (1992). Outcome and costs of two VA outpatient treatment programs for older alcoholic patients. *Hospital and Community Psychiatry, 43,* 985–989.

Kurtz, N. R., & Regier, M. (1975). The Uniform Alcoholism and Intoxication Treatment Act: The compromising process of social policy formation. *Journal of Studies on Alcohol, 36,* 1421–1441.

LaRue, A., Dessonville, C., & Jarvik, L. F. (1985). Aging and mental disorders. In J. E. Birren & K. W. Schaie (Eds.), *Handbook of the psychology of aging* (pp. 664–702). New York: Van Nostrand Reinhold.

Liberto, J. G., & Oslin, D. W. (1996). Early versus late onset of alcoholism in the elderly. In A. M. Gurnack (Ed.), *Drugs and the elderly: Use and abuse of drugs, medicines, alcohol and tobacco* (pp. 94–112). New York: Springer.

Maddox, G., Robins, L. N., & Rosenberg, N. (Eds.). (1984). *Nature and extent of alcohol problems among the elderly* (NIAAA Research Monograph No. 14, DHHS Publication No. ADM 84-1321). Washington, DC: U.S. Government Printing Office.

Mayfield, D., McLeod, G., & Hall, P. (1974). More detailed interview screening. *American Journal of Psychiatry, 131*, 1121–1123.

McCormack, P., & O'Malley, K. (1986). Biological and medical aspects of drug treatment in the elderly. In R. E. Dunkle, G. J. Petot, & A. B. Ford (Eds.), *Food, drugs and aging* (pp. 19–28). New York: Springer.

McKim, W. A., & Mishara, B. L. (1987). *Drugs and aging.* Toronto, Ontario, Canada: Butterworth.

Michigan Department of Public Health. (1994). *Substance abuse services for older adults* (Publication No. OA 089/lOM/9-94/NOG). Lansing: Author.

Moos, R. H., Mertens, J. R., & Brenman, P. L. (1993). Patterns of diagnosis and treatment among late-middle-aged and older substance abuse patients. *Journal of Studies on Alcohol, 54*, 479–487.

National Center for Health Statistics. (1996). *Health, United States, 1995.* Hyattsville, MD: Public Health Service.

National Institute on Alcohol Abuse and Alcoholism, Department of Health and Human Services, Alcohol and Health. (1997). *Ninth special report to the United States Congress on alcohol and health.* (NIH Publication No. 97-4017). Washington, DC: U.S. Government Printing Office.

Nirenberg, T. D., Gomberg, E. S. L., & Cellucim, A. (in press). Substance abuse disorders. In M. Hersen & V. B. Van Hasselt (Eds.), *Handbook of clinical geropsychology.* New York: Plenum.

O'Malley, K., Judge, T. G., & Crooks, J. (1980). Geriatric clinical pharmacology and therapeutics. In G. Avery (Ed.), *Drug treatment* (2nd ed., pp. 158–181). New York: Ach Press.

Pascarelli, E. F. (1985). The elderly in methadone maintenance. In E. Gooheil, K. A. Druley, T. E. Skoloda, & H. M. Wasman (Eds.), *The combined programs of alcoholism, drug addiction and aging* (pp. 210–214). Springfield, IL: Charles C Thomas.

Prentice, R. (1979). Patterns of psychotherapeutic drug use among the elderly. In *The aging process and psychoactive drug use* (pp. 17–41). Washington, DC: U.S. Government Printing Office.

Rubington, E. (1995). Elderly homeless alcoholic careers. In T. P. Beresford & E. S. L. Gomberg (Eds.), *Alcohol and aging* (pp. 293–306). New York: Oxford University Press.

Schonfeld, L., & Dupree, L. W. (1991). Antecedents of drinking for early and late onset elderly alcohol abusers. *Journal of Studies on Alcohol, 52*, 587–592.

Selzer, M. L. (1971). The Michigan Alcoholism Screening Test: The quest for a new diagnostic instrument. *American Journal of Psychiatry, 127*, 1653–1658.

Simonson, W. (1984). *Medications and the elderly.* Rockville, MD: Aspens Systems Corporation.

Tabisz, E. M., Jacyk, W. R., Fuchs, D., & Grymonpre, R. (1993). Chemical dependency in the elderly: The enabling factors. *Canadian Journal of Aging, 17*, 78–88.

Tarter, R. E. (1995). Cognition, aging and alcohol. In T. E. Beresford & E. S. L. Gomberg (Eds.), *Alcohol and aging* (pp. 82–98). New York: Oxford University Press.

U.S. Department of Health and Human Services, Drug Abuse Warning Network. (1996). Statistical Series. [Annual emergency department data 1994] (Series 1, No. 14-A). Unpublished raw data. Washington, DC: U.S. Government Printing Office.

Vestal, R. E., & Dawson, G. W. (1985). Pharmacology and aging. In C. E. Finch & E. L. Schneider (Eds.), *Handbook of the biology of aging* (pp. 744–819). New York: Van Nostrand Reinhold.

Willenbring, M. L., Olson, D., Bielinski, J., & Lynch, J. (1995). Treatment of medically ill alcoholics in the primary-care setting. In T. P. Beresford & E. S. L. Gomberg (Eds.), *Alcohol and aging* (pp. 249–262). New York: Oxford University Press.

Zimberg, S. (1995). The elderly. In A. M. Washton (Eds.), *Psychotherapy and substance abuse* (pp. 413–427). New York: Guilford Press.

18

Anxiety in Old Age

Forrest R. Scogin

Anxiety as an experience is something with which we are all familiar. Worry, restlessness, muscle tension, and sleep disturbance are experienced universally. But the person evidencing an anxiety disorder, particularly the prototypic generalized anxiety disorder (GAD), experiences these symptoms chronically and en masse. Furthermore, these symptoms cause significant distress and impairment in functioning. Anxiety disorders are highly prevalent and pervasive across the life span, and older adults are no exception to the rule.

DSM and the Epidemiology of Anxiety Disorders in Older Adults

The Diagnostic and Statistical Manual of Mental Disorders (4th ed.; *DSM–IV*; American Psychiatric Association, 1994) defines GAD as excessive anxiety and worry of at least 6 month's duration, about a number of events or activities. The worry must be difficult to control and associated with at least three of six symptoms: restlessness, fatigability, concentration difficulties, irritability, muscle tension, and sleep disturbance. Finally, there must be clinically significant distress or impairment related to the anxiety and worry. Many have found it convenient to think of anxiety as composed of cognitive (worry, concentration difficulties), somatic (fatigability, muscle tension, sleep disturbance) and emotional (restlessness, irritability) components.

One of the more important epidemiological studies is the Epidemiological Catchment Area (ECA) project. Using *Diagnostic and Statistical Manual of Mental Disorders* (3rd ed.; *DSM–III*; American Psychiatric Association, 1980) criteria, Myers et al. (1984) found that 6-month prevalence rates for anxiety disorders (phobias, panic disorder, agoraphobia, and obsessive–compulsive disorder) were lowest for the 65 years of age and older cohort. Lower rates of virtually all forms of psychopathology for older adults were a consistent finding in the ECA study, a finding with many possible explanations. For example, do those with anxiety disorders have earlier mortality, that is, is this a survival-of-the-fittest phenomenon? Or is it the case that living into old age confers coping skills that tend to repel anxiety disorders, given the plethora of stressors that can accompany aging? Answers to these questions are not easy to come by, because they require time-consuming, expensive longitudinal research. Nonetheless, anxiety appeared to be the most prevalent form of psychopathology, across all age cohorts, including the older cohort. One implication of the

ECA data is that there will almost certainly be increasing numbers of anxious older adults as successive cohorts enter old age and bring with them a history of anxiety disorders (and other forms of psychopathology).

A difficulty in determining the prevalence of anxiety among older people is that anxiety is a frequent symptom but relatively uncommon diagnosis. That is, older adults may experience severity or quantity of symptoms that do not meet the threshold for a diagnosable disorder, or they may present atypical symptom patterns. This subsyndromal patterning has been observed with regularity in geriatric depression. In essence, there is good reason to believe that anxiety disorders are more prevalent than indicated in the ECA study, and there is likely to be an increase in the proportion of older adults experiencing anxiety disorders as successive birth cohorts reach old age.

Specific phobia (previously known as simple phobia) is the most common albeit least impairing of the anxiety disorders. The ECA indicates 6-month prevalence rates of approximately 3% for men and 6% for women. Comparable rates for social phobia were approximately 1% for men and women, whereas rates for agoraphobia were approximately 1.5% and 2.5%, respectively. Generalized anxiety disorder prevalence rates ranged from about 1% to 7% across the ECA sites. Panic disorder was exceedingly rare in this survey, with no older men and approximately 0.2% of older women receiving this diagnosis. Finally, obsessive–compulsive disorder was observed in approximately 1% of men and women.

More recent surveys have been in general agreement with the ECA data, with a couple of notable exceptions. Raj, Corvea, and Dagon (1993) found panic disorder in approximately 9% of older people presenting for treatment at a psychiatric clinic. This sample is quite different from the population-based sample of the ECA but nonetheless suggests that panic disorder may be more prevalent than heretofore believed. Acierno, Hersen, and Van Hasselt (1996), in an informative review of the literature, suggested that GAD may be as prevalent as the specific phobias. Finally, anxiety due to a general medical condition is a syndrome with clear relevance for older adults, given the many ailments that can produce anxiety symptoms (e.g., gastrointestinal disorders).

Two disorders that have received virtually no attention by researchers but would seem to be particularly relevant to older people are posttraumatic stress disorder (PTSD) and acute stress disorder. The latter is a new addition to the diagnostic nomenclature and is similar to PTSD except that the symptoms are experienced immediately after a traumatic event and for no more than 1 month, at which time PTSD could be considered. In my experience, several older patients who underwent serious health crises (e.g., extensive surgery or stroke) were traumatized by the experience and suffered PTSD-like sequelae. Research on the epidemiology, course, and treatment of these stress disorders would be very helpful to our understanding of geriatric anxiety.

Etiology and Course of General Anxiety Disorder

Generalized anxiety disorder will be used to illustrate issues in the etiology and course of geriatric anxiety. Blazer, George, and Hughes (1991) found that approximately half of the participants age 65 and older had experienced GAD symptoms for less than 5 years. This suggests that late-onset GAD may be much more common than, for example, major depression. Stressful events can trigger the onset of excessive worry, the hallmark of GAD, and late adulthood carries with it the potential for significant stressors, perhaps most notably health problems. Older adults have been found to report most frequent worries about health, whereas younger adults worry most about family and finances (Person & Borkovec, 1995). Beck, Stanley, and Zebb (1996) contrasted older GAD patients with onset before 15 years of age with those with onset after age 39 and found essentially no differences. These data suggest that worries may be present across the life span but change in content consistent with the phase of life (e.g., health for older people).

The link between medical illness and anxiety is clearly indicated in conditions such as chronic obstructive pulmonary disease, vertigo, and Parkinson's disease; diagnoses of anxiety disorders are elevated in persons experiencing these illnesses. Wise and Rieck (1993) provide a useful framework for assessing anxiety in persons experiencing medical illnesses: First, rule out other mental disorders such as depression and delirium that include anxiety symptoms, rule out a medication side effect as the cause of the anxiety symptom, determine the timing of the onset of the anxiety symptoms in relation to the medical illness, and, finally, consider the anxiety as an adjustment reaction to the stress of being medically ill.

Comorbid Mental Disorders

Anxiety and dementia appear to be relatively common comorbid conditions. The reduced abilities in thinking and coping can create for the dementia patient a world of confusing and threatening stimuli. In more advanced stages of dementia, anxiety must be inferred from observation, but it is quite probable that the agitation, restlessness, and fearfulness seen in these patients are the functional equivalent of anxiety.

Anxiety and depression have repeatedly been shown to be conditions that tend to co-occur. This pattern is true with all age cohorts; in fact, some believe these conditions are facets of a higher order construct, which has been termed by some *negative affect*. Beck and Stanley (1997) suggested in their review that anxiety and depression are practically indistinguishable in older adults. As these authors noted, specification of the unique features of these disorders may help in specifying treatment recommendations.

Almost nothing is known about the course of anxiety disorders in older adults. For example, it would be helpful to know if late-onset GAD were more treatment responsive given the less chronic nature of the worry. It is also unclear if late-onset anxiety disorders, particularly GAD, are likely to remit or conversely tend to become chronic. The course of most anxiety disorders is chronic when onset is in younger adulthood. Future research could profitably be directed to questions of this type.

What Is Done?

The majority of older adults experiencing mental disorders, including anxiety, do not receive assistance, and if they do, it is most often provided through primary care physicians (Lasoski, 1989). The treatment for geriatric anxiety most often provided is pharmacotherapy, more specifically, the benzodiazepines. Anxiolytics are more likely to be used with older adults than with younger adults experiencing anxiety (Beck & Stanley, 1997), despite cautions raised in a number of sources (e.g., Wengel, Burke, Ranno, & Roccaforte, 1993). These cautions include increased cognitive impairment, sedation, interaction with other medications, and physical dependence. A common treatment goal for mental health care professionals working with anxious older adults is the attenuation or elimination of anxiolytic dependence. In my clinical experience, withdrawal from benzodiazepines has been a particularly difficult task.

Several psychosocial adjuncts or alternatives to pharmacotherapy have been tested, although the literature is scant. In fact, the Clinical Geropsychology section of Division 12's (Clinical Psychology) Task Force on Empirically Supported Treatments, chaired by Margaret Gatz and myself, found that no treatments met the criteria as a well established or probably efficacious treatment for geriatric anxiety. Of those showing promise, I will mention two. Relaxation training has been found to reduce anxiety in community-dwelling, cognitively intact older adults (Scogin, Rickard, Keith, Wilson, and McElreath, 1992). We found that both traditional progressive muscle relaxation and imaginal relaxation were effective, with the latter a useful alternative for those unable to do the tension-release cycles associated with progressive relaxation. The second modality is cognitive–behavior therapy. In the only study of psychotherapy with diagnosed anxious older adults, Stanley, Beck, and Glassco (1997) found that both cognitive–behavioral therapy and supportive therapy led to decreases in worry and anxiety symptoms for GAD participants. The paucity of treatment research is inexplicable in that anxiety disorders are prevalent and several treatment approaches proven efficacious with general adult populations could serve as models for modification with older people. Nonetheless, these promising beginnings suggest that psychosocial interventions may become a more viable alternative for anxious older people in the future.

References

Acierno, R., Hersen, M., & Van Hasselt, V. B. (1996). Anxiety-based disorders. In M. Hersen & V. B. Van Hasselt (Eds.), *Psychological treatment of older adults: An introductory text* (pp. 149–180). New York: Plenum.

American Psychiatric Association. (1980). *Diagnostic and statistical manual of mental disorders* (3rd ed.). Washington, DC: Author.

American Psychiatric Association. (1994). *Diagnostic and statistical manual of mental disorders* (4th ed.). Washington, DC: Author.

Beck, J. G., & Stanley, M. A. (1997). Anxiety disorders in the elderly: The emerging role of behavior therapy. *Behavior Therapy, 28,* 83–100.

Beck, J. G., Stanley, M. A., & Zebb, B. J. (1995). Psychometric properties of the Penn State Worry Questionnaire in older adults. *Journal of Clinical Geropsychology, 1,* 33–42.

Blazer, D., George, L. K., & Hughes, D. (1991). The epidemiology of anxiety disorders: An age comparison. In C. Salzman & B. D. Liebowitz (Eds.), *Anxiety in the elderly: Treatment and research* (pp. 17–30). New York: Springer.

Lasoski, M. C. (1986). Reasons for low utilization of mental health services by the elderly. In T. L. Brink (Ed.), *Clinical gerontology: A guide to assessment and intervention* (pp. 1–18). New York: Haworth Press.

Myers, J. K., Weissman, M. M., Tischler, G. L., Holzer, C. E., Leaf, P. J., Orvaschel, H., Anthony, J. C., Boyd, J. H., Kramer, M., & Stoltzman, R. (1984). Six-month prevalence of psychiatric disorders in three communities, 1980 to 1982. *Archives of General Psychiatry, 41,* 959–967.

Person, D. C., & Borkovec, T. D. (1995, August). *Anxiety disorders among the elderly: Patterns and issues.* Paper presented at the 103rd Annual Convention of the American Psychological Association, New York.

Raj, B. A., Corvea, M. H., & Dagon, E. M. (1993). The clinical characteristics of panic disorder in the elderly: A retrospective study. *Journal of Clinical Psychiatry, 54,* 150–155.

Scogin, F., Rickard, H. C., Keith, S., Wilson, J., & McElreath, L. (1992). Progressive and imaginal relaxation training for elderly persons with subjective anxiety. *Psychology and Aging, 7,* 418–424.

Stanley, M. A., Beck, J. G., & Glassco, J. D. (1997). Generalized anxiety in older adults: Treatment with cognitive behavioral and supportive approaches. *Behavior Therapy, 27,* 565–581.

Wengel, S. P., Burke, W. J., Ranno, A. E., & Roccaforte, W. H. (1993). Use of the benzodiazepines in the elderly. *Psychiatric Annals, 23,* 325–331.

Wise, M. G., & Rieck, S. O. (1993). Diagnostic considerations and treatment approaches to underlying anxiety in the medically ill. *Journal of Clinical Psychiatry, 54* (Suppl. 2), 22–26.

19

Depression and Depressive Symptoms in Old Age

Julia E. Kasl-Godley, Margaret Gatz, and Amy Fiske

Older adults may become clinically depressed, just as individuals at other ages. Despite disruptive challenges and changes that characteristically accompany old age, most older adults adapt well and evidence good mental health. However, a small minority are diagnosed with depressive disorders, and a somewhat larger proportion experience some symptoms of depression. This chapter examines symptom presentation and diagnosis of depression in late life, its frequency, the contexts in which it occurs, prognostic factors, and issues to consider during assessment and treatment.

Diagnosis

Diagnostic criteria for depression are found in the *Diagnostic and Statistical Manual of Mental Disorders*, 4th edition (*DSM–IV*; American Psychiatric Association, 1994) and the *International Classification of Disease*, 10th edition (*ICD–10*; World Health Organization, 1994). Categories include major depressive disorder, dysthymic disorder, and mild depressive episode (*ICD–10*) or minor depression (*DSM–IV*). (Due to limitations of space and due to its low prevalence in older adults, bipolar disorder will not be discussed here.)

An accumulating body of research identifies differences in symptom presentation in late life (for a review, see Caine, Lyness, King, & Connors, 1994). These include lower prevalence of dysphoria; fewer ideational symptoms (e.g., guilt or suicidal ideation); and more prominent specific somatic symptoms. Some somatic symptoms, for example, fatigue and changes in appetite and sexual activity, may reflect comorbid physical disorders or normal age-related changes. However, other somatic symptoms, namely, loss of interest, lack of energy, and sleep disturbance, can be useful in distinguishing depressed from nondepressed older individuals. Some authors have suggested that the symptom profile commonly seen in older adults represents a distinct subtype of depression. In the past, variants have been referred to as *masked* depression or *somatic* depression. More currently, *depletion syndrome* and *nondysphoric* depression are favored and seem to capture the phenomenon more accurately.

Delusions may be more common in older than in younger depressed individuals, especially those with late-onset depressive disorders. A later age of first onset also has been associated with increased cognitive impairment.

Prevalence

Using *DSM–III* (American Psychiatric Association, 1980) or *DSM–III–R* (American Psychiatric Association, 1987) diagnostic criteria, in representative surveys in the United States and several European countries, 1% to 2% of older adults have been found to have major depressive disorder, a rate that is lower than in other age groups. In contrast, rates of clinically significant depressive symptoms are higher in older compared with younger adults. For example, across nine studies using the Center for Epidemiologic Studies Depression Scale (CES–D), an average of 16% of older adults scored above the clinical cutoff. (For a summary of prevalence data, see Fiske, Kasl-Godley, & Gatz, 1998.) Given that depressive symptom counts reflect symptoms attributable to minor depression, bereavement, substance use, or a medical condition, it is not surprising that the occurrence of clinically significant depressive symptoms would outpace the rate of diagnosable depression in this age group.

The association between depression and age is complicated by the finding that older individuals report a lower lifetime prevalence of depression compared with younger individuals. Because older adults have had more years in which to experience depressive episodes, they would be expected to report a higher lifetime prevalence than younger persons. Several explanations have been posited: (a) cohort effects, that is, earlier born generations show lower rates of depression than later born generations; (b) biased estimates, due to forgetting symptoms over time, exacerbated by cognitive impairment; and (c) selective mortality among depressed individuals. The latter two factors appear insufficient by themselves to account for the finding.

At all ages, prevalence of major depressive disorders has consistently been found to be higher in women than in men, with older women showing upward of three times the rate for older men. This difference diminishes and may even reverse in very old age.

The relationship between late-life depression and race, ethnicity, culture, and nationality is not fully understood. Racial and ethnic differences could reflect culture or language or could indicate variation in risk factors such as health status, income, or education. Similarly, different findings on the CES–D in different countries (e.g., those of Heikkinen, Berg, & Avlund, 1995) may indicate real cross-national differences in rates of depression or could reflect language or sample-selection differences.

Prognosis

Prognosis in elderly depressed individuals is comparable to that in mixed-age samples, once differences in study designs or sample characteristics are controlled. Combined findings from several investigations (Brodaty et al., 1993; Green, Copeland, Dewey, Sharma, & Davidson, 1994; Hinrichsen, 1992) yield estimates ranging from 40% to 60% of depressed older adults achieving sustained recovery, 15% to 20% recovering with subsequent relapse or recurrence, and 30% to 40% remaining unremitted or chronic. Bereavement, low levels of life satisfaction, dysfunctional family members, worsening health status, and poor premorbid personality are particularly predictive of poor outcome. Strength of these predictors varies according to how outcome is defined and which other factors are controlled for (e.g., type of treatment, duration of follow-up period, intervening events, age of sample, and first age of onset).

Depression is associated with increased risk for mortality both among institutionalized and inpatient samples and in community-residing samples. Risk factors for death appear to include being male, being 75 years of age or older, a diagnosis of major depression with both melancholic and psychotic features, substantial health and mobility problems, and cognitive impairment. Depressive symptoms insufficient to meet diagnostic criteria, especially nondysphoric symptoms, also predict both morbidity and mortality.

Etiologic and Correlated Factors

Physical health, cognitive dysfunction, interpersonal relations, stressful life events, and genetic makeup are factors that represent the most common contexts under which depression occurs in older adults. We use the terminology of *correlated factors* because the temporal and causal relationship to depression is often difficult to ascertain.

Physical Health

Prevalence of depressive disorders is higher among medical outpatients, medical inpatients, and residents of long-term care facilities than in the general population (see review by Koenig & Blazer, 1992). For example, some 12% of nursing home residents meet criteria for major depressive disorder.

Possible relationships between physical illness and depression are multifold and not mutually exclusive, underscoring the importance of assessment. First, depression can be caused by biological changes brought about by physical illness or its treatment. Second, depression can lead to physical illness by creating vulnerabilities, possibly neuroimmune, or by undermining self-care efforts such as medication compliance. Third, depression can be a reaction to the stressors engendered by decline and physical illness, such as pain, reduced activity, functional disability, and negative perceptions of one's health. Pain can be related to depression both as an independent predictor and through its association with activity restriction. Fourth, physical illness and depression can co-occur as independent conditions.

To a large extent, these associations suggest an interdependence among biological and psychological factors. In particular, they could reflect a general wearing-down process leading to both depression and physical disease. The latter explanation would be consistent with the increased risk for mortality observed among depressed older adults.

Cognitive Dysfunction

Both diagnosed depression and elevated depressive symptoms have been found to be associated with varying degrees of cognitive dysfunction. Average prevalence of diagnosed depression among dementia cases has been calculated at 11% (ranging from 0% to 32%) in a review of studies of this question (Hooijer, Trede, & van Tilberg, 1995).

As with physical health, there can be multiple, shared, or reciprocal causes. First, depression can cause cognitive dysfunction, most likely mild impairments in specific domains (e.g., select frontal lobe skills, visuospatial tasks, memory). Poor concentration and attention, frequent concomitants of depression, may explain mild performance deficits. More severe cognitive impairment also has been observed, referred to as *pseudodementia* or *depression-related cognitive dysfunction*. A hallmark of this association is that the impairments lessen or disappear when the depression has been treated. Second, cognitive dysfunction can cause depression, for example, through a reaction to the dementia due to awareness of deficits. Third, depression can co-occur with severe cognitive impairment. In this case, depression represents a prodromal symptom or a comorbid condition, possibly reflecting related physiological processes.

There is some suggestion that depression-related cognitive dysfunction is an artificial category and reflects the early stages of a dementing process. Nevertheless, cognitive impairment in demented individuals can be exacerbated by depression, the treatment of which allows for some cognitive improvement. Various characteristics have been suggested to distinguish patients whose cognitive symptoms are due to depression alone from patients who are becoming demented, especially motivational disturbances and vegetative symptoms. History may be even more helpful than current features. See Kaszniak and Christenson (1994) for a comprehensive discussion of differential diagnosis.

Interpersonal Relationships, Social Support, and Stressful Experiences

Both diagnosed depression and depressive symptoms are correlated with interpersonal difficulties (Hinrichsen & Zweig, 1994). This association may reflect various processes: (a) Depressed individuals act in ways that strain and disrupt interpersonal relationships; (b) depression may influence an individual's perception of social relationships; or (c) losses in support or demanding, nonreciprocal interpersonal interactions may precipitate depression. Whether depression is an outcome of interpersonal strain seems to be determined, in part, by other variables such as assertiveness, self-efficacy or personal control, degree of social embeddedness, and concurrent stressors.

Stressful experiences—including discrete, disruptive negative life events, chronic strains, and daily hassles—have been found to be associated with depression (see Murrell & Meeks, 1992, for review). Among the most common and stressful events are physical illness, death, financial strains, family conflict, caregiving, and the need for institutionalization. However, the association between life events and depressive symptoms appears to be small and transitory, with the impact of events better explained by other factors (i.e., prior sympto-

matology and negative events, overall stress level, strength of personal resources, coping styles, social support, gender, and ethnicity).

Genetic Risk

Genetic factors also help to explain which older adults become depressed, although apparently early-onset depression has greater genetic determination
than depression that has its first onset in old age.

Suicide

The suicide rate for older adults in most countries is higher than that of any
other age group, with older men at the highest risk. Although most depressed
older adults do not commit suicide, many older adults who do commit suicide
are depressed. Assessment of suicide risk in older adults is complicated by the
fact that suicide occurs with less warning in older compared with younger
adults: Older individuals are less likely to express suicidal ideation directly or
to make nonlethal suicide attempts or gestures. (For approaches to suicide risk
assessment in this population, see McIntosh, Santos, Hubbard, & Overholser,
1994.) The most promising approach in working with suicidal individuals with
depressive disorders is to follow aggressive depression with effective treatment
of the depression. A logical vehicle for such interventions is physicians, given
that older adults who commit suicide have frequently seen a physician within
a short interval before death.

Treatment

Often, depressed older adults do not receive treatment. This omission can occur
because (a) the older adult fails to seek treatment for symptoms of depression,
(b) the older adult seeks treatment for other conditions and does not mention
depressive symptoms to the treating professional, often a primary care physician, or (c) the physician who sees the older adult does not recognize depression,
often because of comorbidity with physical health problems. As a consequence,
depression may go untreated, may not be treated until it becomes severe, or
may be mistreated (e.g., with anxiolytics or with sleeping pills) until it becomes
severe and gives the false impression of intractability and hopelessness. This
situation may unfortunately lead to greater emphasis on somatic treatments,
that is, psychotropic medications and electroconvulsive therapy.

The array of psychological treatments provided to depressed older adults
largely parallels those used to treat depression in adults generally. Empirical
evidence suggests that efficacy of psychological treatments for older adults is
similar to efficacy for adults generally (see summary by Gatz et al., in press).

Conclusion

Depression in older adults may look different than in other age groups in terms of prevalence, symptom presentation, and suicide risk—differences that can influence identification and assessment. Depression is likely to be associated with worsened physical health, memory impairment, disrupted interpersonal relationships, and stressful events, yet not all older adults who experience one or more of these stressors will become depressed. Interpersonal and intrapersonal resources such as social support, coping styles, perceived control and efficacy, and cognitive appraisals play a role in protecting against depression. For older adults who are depressed, prognosis is comparable to other age groups, although many do not receive treatment.

References

American Psychiatric Association. (1980). *Diagnostic and statistical manual of mental disorders* (3rd ed.). Washington, DC: Author.

American Psychiatric Association. (1987). *Diagnostic and statistical manual of mental disorders* (3rd ed., rev). Washington, DC: Author.

American Psychiatric Association. (1994). *Diagnostic and statistical manual of mental disorders* (4th ed.). Washington, DC: Author.

Brodaty, H., Harris, L., Peters, K., Wilhelm, K., Hickie, I., Boyce, P., Mitchell, P., Parker, G., & Eyers, K. (1993). Prognosis of depression in the elderly: A comparison with younger patients. *British Journal of Psychiatry, 163*, 589–596.

Caine, E. D., Lyness, J. M., King, D. A., & Connors, B. A. (1994). Clinical and etiological heterogeneity of mood disorders in elderly patients. In L. S. Schneider, C. F. Reynolds, B. D. Lebowitz, & A. J. Friedhoff (Eds.), *Diagnosis and treatment of depression in late life: Results of the NIH Consensus Development Conference* (pp. 23–53). Washington, DC: American Psychiatric Press.

Fiske, A., Kasl-Godley, J. E., & Gatz, M. (1998). Mood disorders in late life. In A. S. Bellack & M. Hersen (Eds.), *Comprehensive clinical psychology* (Vol. 7, pp. 193–229). Oxford: Elsevier Science.

Gatz, M., Fiske, A., Fox, L. S., Kaskie, B., Kasl-Godley, J. E., McCallum, T. J., & Wetherell, J. L. (in press). Empirically-validated psychological treatments for older adults. *Journal of Aging and Mental Health.*

Green, B. H., Copeland, J. R. M., Dewey, M. E., Sharma, V., & Davidson, I. A. (1994). Factors associated with recovery and recurrence of depression in older people: A prospective study. *International Journal of Geriatric Psychiatry, 9*, 789–795.

Heikkinen, R.-L., Berg, S., & Avlund, K. (1995). Depressive symptoms in late life: Results from a study in three Nordic urban localities. *Journal of Cross-Cultural Gerontology, 10*, 315–330.

Hinrichsen, G. A. (1992). Recovery and relapse from major depressive disorder in the elderly. *American Journal of Psychiatry, 149*, 1575–1579.

Hinrichsen, G. A., & Zweig, R. (1994). Family issues in late-life depression. *Journal of Long-Term Home Health Care, 13*, 4–15.

Hooijer, C., Trede, K., & van Tilberg, W. (1995). Is depression frequent in dementia? A simple quantitative aid in reviewing heterogeneous studies. In M. Bergener & S. I. Finkel (Eds.), *Treating Alzheimer's and other dementias* (pp. 146–153). New York: Springer.

Kaszniak, A. W., & Christenson, G. D. (1994). Differential diagnosis of dementia and depression. In M. Storandt & G. R. VandenBos (Eds.), *Neuropsychological assessment of dementia and depression in older adults: A clinician's guide* (pp. 81–117). Washington, DC: American Psychological Association.

Koenig, H. G., & Blazer, D. G. (1992). Epidemiology of geriatric affective disorders. *Clinics in Geriatric Medicine, 8*, 235–251.

McIntosh, S. L., Santos, J. F., Hubbard, R. W., & Overholser, J. C. (1994). *Elder suicide: Research, theory and treatment*. Washington, DC: American Psychological Association.

Murrell, S. A., & Meeks, S. (1992). Depressive symptoms in older adults: Predispositions, resources, and life experiences. In K. W. Schaie & M. P. Lawton (Eds.), *Annual review of gerontology and geriatrics* (Vol. 11, pp. 261–275). New York: Springer.

World Health Organization. (1992–1993). *International statistical classification of diseases and related health problems* (10th rev.). Geneva: Author.

20

Schizophrenia and Psychosis in Elderly Populations

Bertram P. Karon and Gary R. VandenBos

Patients manifesting psychotic symptoms can be found in all segments of the age continuum. These patients represent a complex clinical challenge regardless of whether they are 24 or 74 years old. Such "out of touch" patients presenting significant thought disorder, unexpected affect, and bizarre ways of relating interpersonally, who also may be hallucinating or threatening violence, often make therapists feel uncomfortable and, as a consequence, make it even more difficult for therapists to be helpful to them.

Definitional Confusion

Although there are definitional differences between schizophrenia and psychotic symptoms, the clinical manifestations and challenges are almost functionally equivalent. In the United States, such severe symptomatology is referred to as late-onset schizophrenia, although in Europe it is more likely to be referred to as late paraphrenia or simply paraphrenia.

For a diagnosis of schizophrenia, *DSM-IV* (American Psychiatric Association, 1994) requires, during the significant portion of a 1-month period, the presence of at least two of the following symptoms: delusions, hallucinations, disorganized speech, grossly disorganized or catatonic behavior, and negative symptoms (such as affective flattening, alogia, or avolition). However, when the delusions are extremely bizarre or hallucinations involve hearing voices, only the presence of one item is needed for a diagnosis. Occupational social dysfunction must be present such that there is a marked decrease from a previous achievement level attained in work, interpersonal relations, or self-care prior to the onset of the severe symptoms. In addition, there must be continuous signs of disturbance for at least 6 months. *DMS-IV* no longer requires the onset before the age of 45 that was included in the *DSM-III-R* (American Psychiatric Association, 1987).

The term "late-onset schizophrenia" was coined by Manfred Bleuler (1943) to describe the concept of schizophrenia with an onset between the ages of 40 and 60. Late paraphrenia is a concept popularized in England, which includes most delusional disorders starting after age 60 (Riecher-Rössler, Förstl, & Melse, 1995). Conceptually, these are somewhat different, but, practically, most mental health professionals use them as equivalent or interchange them. Some would argue, however, that late paraphrenia might best be accommodated under paranoid schizophrenia or persistent delusional disorder (Quintal, Day-Cody, & Levy, 1991).

Prevalence and Incidence

Between 3.2% and 10% of elderly patients hospitalized in psychiatric facilities have been reported as schizophrenic. The higher end of this range has been reported by Kay and Roth (1961) for both Swedish and English hospitals. Mid-range reports for hospitals in England and Wales were reported by Post (1980).

Community studies, of course, present lower figures. On the basis of self-report by the interviewed participants from a 5-site epidemiologic catchment area (ECA) study in the United States, the 1-year prevalence rate for schizophrenia was 1.2% for 18- to 29-year-olds, 1.5% for those age 30 to 44, 0.6 for 45 to 65-year-olds, and 0.2% for those over age 64 (Keith, Regier, & Rae, 1991). Also in the United States, Lowenthal (1964) reported that 2% of elderly in the San Francisco sample exhibited paranoid delusions, and in a later study Christenson and Blazer (1984) reported about 4% of those over age 65 manifested persecutory delusions.

It has recently been maintained that when a restrictive and precise definition of the diagnosis and standardized assessment methods with large representative populations are used, the incidence rate for schizophrenia appears relatively stable across countries and cultures over time for at least the last 50 years (Castle & Murray, 1993; Hafner & anderHeiden, 1997). This is inconsistent with the clear evidence that schizophrenia is more common in the United States when there is low socioeconomic status of the family of origin (Cohen, 1993; Myers, Bean, Pepper, & Hollingshead, 1968), and is more common cross-culturally in more industrialized parts of developing countries (Torrey, 1989) and of Sweden (Lewis, Davis, Andreasson, & Allebeck, 1992), and in areas with severe social disruption (e.g, Croatia and China during dislocation and forced industrialization; Teixeira, 1997). Certainly subjectively perceived stress is a risk factor. Nonetheless, the most typical age of onset of schizophrenia is 18 to 29 years. In general, age of onset is before age 45 in 75% of the cases, and age of onset is before 60 years in 90% of the cases. Thus, late-onset schizophrenia is relatively uncommon.

Nature of Schizophrenia Found in Elderly Samples

If one is working with a general outpatient population of elderly individuals, those patients diagnosed with schizophrenia will be comprised of two subgroups: those with early onset psychotic symptoms whose symptoms continue, and those with late-onset symptoms. The latter group will be much smaller than the former.

As noted, the prevalence of schizophrenia among successively older cohorts decreases. This occurs for several reasons, including the long-term natural course of schizophrenia. One must first ask what happened to all of the patients with early-onset schizophrenia.

First, some of them died. Between the ages of 40 and 64, individuals diagnosed with schizophrenia die at a higher annual rate than their counterparts in the general population. In the Netherlands, Giel, Dijk, and Van Weerden-Dijkstra (1978) found that the mortality of people with schizophrenia was double that of the general population. In the United States, data from the Monroe County Register show that mortality among males with schizophrenia was 2.5 times higher than among the general population of males in the same age group. Female schizophrenic mortality was 2.9 times greater than that in their female age group. The higher mortality rates among people with schizophrenia does not imply higher suicide rates for this group. Although suicide is the leading single cause of death among those with schizophrenia in the 40 to 64 age range, the suicide rate for this group is actually lower (at 6.36) than the suicide rate for the overall population (7.39) and for individuals suffering from depression (10.08).

Second, some schizophrenic people get better. Contrary to the classic *dementia praecox* model of a chronic and continually declining condition, a good proportion of people with schizophrenia get better as they age. Every long-term study in any country reports this finding. This is relatively new information (unfortunately, not included in the *DSM-IV*), and it gives mental health professionals cause for renewed optimism about schizophrenia. The general findings are (a) 20% to 25% of young schizophrenics get better, and (b) another 35% to 40% experience significant reduction in symptoms—and this improved functioning allows them to live relatively normal lives outside of hospitals with only minor or mild continuing symptoms. Thus, 60% to 65% of people with schizophrenia, will, basically, recover.

Bleuler (1972, 1978) reported on a follow-up of 208 patients for over an average of 22 years in Zurich on the basis of Bleuler's personal clinical knowledge. He found that 20% of the patients experienced complete remission; 33% had mild end-states; 24% had intermediate end-states; and 24% suffered from chronic, severe end-states. Huber, Gross, and Schuttler (1979) reported on a sample of 502 patients in Bonn, Germany followed-up after an average of 21.4 years. They found 26% were cured, 31% continued to exhibit mild symptoms, 29% had intermediate end-states, and only 14% exhibited chronic and severe end-states. Others have reported earlier findings. Likewise, Ciompi and Muller (1976) found that 27% fully recovered, 22% continued to have only mild symptoms, 24% had intermediate end-states, and 18% had chronic and severe end-states. They also found that mortality among schizophrenic males was 73% higher than their same age peers in the general population and, among schizophrenic females, 85% higher than their same age peers.

Similar findings have been reported in the United States. Harding, Brooks, Ashikaga, Strauss, and Breier (1987a, 1987b) reported on the 269 most chronic patients in the Vermont project. Their rehabilitation effort started in the mid-1950s, and the chronic institutionalized patients in their project had been hospitalized an average of 16 years. Patients participated in a pioneering rehabilitation program and were released in a planned deinstitutionalization program with initial community support. The community support was ended abruptly for lack of funding, but the patients were followed. At last follow-up, over 60% of the sample was over age 60. The most striking finding was that only 3% of the sample was hospitalized, whereas, depending on definition and criteria, between 17% and 34% were "cured" and functioning in the community in a superior manner. The majority of patients were manifesting modest symptoms but were living in the community, supporting themselves, and engaging in normal interpersonal and social interactions. Surprisingly, in Harding's (1988) data, the patients who fully recovered were among the 50% who had stopped taking their medication.

Factors Surrounding Late-Onset Schizophrenia

In our experience, individuals who experience schizophrenic symptoms for the first time late in life have generally lived a very sheltered life in which all of the rigorous demands of adult living have not been placed on them. They are more likely to be female (Castle & Murray, 1993; Hafner & anderHeiden, 1997; Yassa, Dastoor, Nastase, & Camille, 1993), although the male to female ratio varies widely among studies (Harris & Jeste, 1988). It is not uncommon for such individuals to have had reasonably good academic histories and employment records, although often in relatively undemanding positions. However, the premorbid social functioning of such individuals is often marginal, and pessimism, sensitivity, suspiciousness, and a tendency to be somewhat reclusive is common. Patients with late-onset schizophrenia are more likely to be unmarried, have few or no children, and be socially isolated. Deafness is a risk factor, with partial deafness being more of a risk factor than total deafness (Erlenmeyer-Kimling & Miller, 1986). The precipitating event that triggered their deterioration and eventual manifestation of latent psychotic symptoms is often the death of their elder parents, or of their elder siblings who have provided basic support for the patient and served as the buffer against external threats and pressure.

Treatment of Elderly People With Schizophrenia

The psychotherapeutic treatment of elderly people with schizophrenia is not different from the psychotherapy of younger people with schizophrenia (Karon & VandenBos, 1981). For the late-onset individual, it is important to help them view their life in context—their long history of successful functioning, the nature and extent of recent changes in their life, and the terrifying (for them) implications of these recent changes. It is critical to help them understand the terror that they are experiencing, to put those frightening reactions into the context of their changing life, and to help them see that their life is not hopeless nor are they powerless.

The use of antipsychotic medication with elderly patients can be problematic. The elderly are particularly sensitive to the side effects of such medication (Hymas, Naguib, & Levy, 1989), which limits the use of certain drugs for the elderly and mitigates against the use of high dosages (Castle & Howard, 1992).

Late-onset psychosis has a 50% improvement rate with medication (Pearlson et al., 1989), but psychopharmacology experts continue to call for more specific medications with less serious side effects (Psychopharmacology Panel of the Canadian Alliance for Research on Schizophrenia, 1994).

As with schizophrenia in younger people, the treatment of choice is psychotherapy with a competent therapist who has relevant experience or training. If the patient, the therapist, and the setting can tolerate it, the psychotherapy is best conducted without medication. If the patient asks for it, or the therapist is uncomfortable talking with disorganized patients, or the setting requires it, medication can be used, but it should be withdrawn as rapidly as the patient can tolerate. Medication as an adjunct makes behavioral control easier to attain but slows down the rate of underlying change. This is because medications damp affective responses, which is helpful in relation to the patient's current emotional reactions because schizophrenia is basically a terror syndrome. Anger and humiliation are also problems, but affective responses during the psychotherapy session are a helpful part of the process of change.

It is up to the therapist to help the patient create a livable world. As in any therapy, forming a therapeutic alliance is essential, but with psychotic patients, it is more difficult and forms a more persistent part of the therapist's work. Much of the psychopathology of schizophrenia is nothing but transference to the world at large. The severity of the symptoms generally means there have been more bad things to transfer, and hence, the transference to the therapist will tend to be negative. Frequently, the patient does not communicate, even what he or she understands, because he or she does not trust the therapist. It is important to tolerate not understand the patient; the moment a therapist decides not to abandon the patient no matter how confused or uncomfortable the therapist is he or she is already conducting good therapy. When there is ambiguity (or sometimes even when there is not), the therapist may be perceived as hostile, dangerous, shaming, belittling, or conspiring against the patient. This makes the therapeutic alliance harder to create and maintain. The therapist should try to be unambiguously helpful; the blank screen will inevitably become a monster.

Patients cannot tolerate examining themselves except within the confines of a dependable relationship with a warm, strong therapist. By strong, we mean simply a therapist who will deal with anything and will not abandon the patient just because the therapist does not understand, the material is painful, or the patient is hostile.

As in any therapy, what changes the patient is the internalization of the therapist as well as the insights gained. The patient internalizes the therapist into the superego so that the patient treats himself or herself in the kind, rational way the therapist would instead of in the rigid, punitive way that most patients treat themselves (on the basis of their early identifications). The patient internalizes the therapist into the ego as a model for how a human being might be, discarding those quirks of the therapist that are not useful. The patient internalizes the therapy relationship as a model of what a human relationship might be. This process of internalization is central to effective therapy, particularly with psychotic patients, but it goes on without explicit attention as an automatic part of the patient—therapist interaction when a therapist does his or her best to be helpful.

Because paranoid features tend to be more central for late-onset patients, it is useful to review the four bases for paranoid delusions (Karon, 1989). The most important basis for delusions, and the most important to understand, is the patient's need to make sense out of his or her world and experiences. It is not a pathological process, but the normal and universal human process of trying to make sense out of one's life, except that the patient has bizarre subjective experiences to explain. The patient's symptoms are bizarre experiences, and patients frequently have strange and difficult real-life experiences. The paranoid system is the best the patient can do. The brighter patients generally develop a more adequate paranoid system that often obviates the need for more deteriorated symptoms. A nonhumiliating, nonterrified therapist, who can tolerate being confused, will ask for as much information as the patient is willing to share. Because the paranoid system is not realistic (and the therapist knows more about people, the world, and how the human mind operates), the therapist can tactfully point out inconsistencies from the patient's point of view, and suggest alternative explanations (e.g., probable external realities and interpretations).

The second basis for paranoia, transference to the world at large, should be the therapist's first guess at the meaning of paranoid symptoms because it is the most frequent basis for delusional content. For example, "the green-haired alien man and the silver alien woman who control this dimension" are obviously likely to be the patient's parents.

The third basis is defense against pseudohomosexual anxiety, as described by Freud (1958), using the defenses of projection, reaction formation, displacement, and so forth. It is important to remember that the problem is not homosexuality, but rather, that the patient wants to have a close relationship with persons of the same sex, and *thinks* that that means he or she is homosexual. This engenders the defensive paranoid struggle. What must be interpreted is the loneliness, the normality of wanting to be close to someone of the same sex, and how we all need friends of both sexes.

The fourth basis is the teaching by a particular family of peculiar concepts or meanings to words, which the patient then erroneously believes the rest of the world shares. If one listens carefully, it is possible to discover the family-specific meanings that are often difficult to perceive (and, hence, correct) because the patient uses ordinary words with unusual, idiosyncratic meanings. The patient needs to be informed of the difference between their meaning and most other people's meanings.

Hallucinations should be listened to and used in the same way one uses dreams; that is, get the patient's associations and interpret them (as described by Freud, 1916, 1933; and Karon & VandenBos, 1981), insofar as the patient permits. Catatonic stupor is a terror state in which the patient is fully aware of what is going on but consciously feels that he (or she) will die if he moves. The therapist should talk meaningfully and communicate to the patient that he is safe. This should be continued until the patient is able to talk to the therapist.

The therapist must repeatedly distinguish between thoughts and feelings versus actions. Only actions have consequences. All thoughts and feelings are permissible; and actions can best be controlled if the patient dares to allow himself or herself freedom of feeling and of thought.

The role of insight is the same as in any psychoanalytic therapy: making the unconscious conscious, changing the defenses in part by awareness, making the connection between the past and the present. Understanding the transference is central. The more severely disturbed the patient, the more obvious the transference reactions. People with schizophrenia are constantly trying to solve their problems, but they are too frightened to deal with the real problems directly; they deal with symbols. Only when the symbolic act (or symptom) and the original traumatic experience are reconnected in consciousness can the person overcome it.

Peculiar to the late-onset patient is that the therapist may be intimidated by the age of the patient and treat the patient like the therapist's parent. The patient, too, may initially and from time to time relate to the therapist as if the therapist were one of his or her children. However, this is transitory and superficial. Predominantly, even the elderly patient with a much younger therapist will still develop transference reactions on the basis of his or her own mother and father, and the therapist must hear and interpret them when they are useful to the patient.

Most important of all is to remember that the later a patient breaks down, the more psychological strength he or she has; the patient was able to live for 55 or 65 years without breaking down. People have a mistaken stereotype that older patients have a poorer prognosis, which is based on general pessimistic fantasies about old age and on the fact that the longer a symptom has endured without changing, the poorer the prognosis is. In fact, if therapists are not intimidated and offer real psychotherapy to the late-onset patient, the results are apt to be very good.

References

American Psychiatric Association. (1994). *Diagnostic and statistical manual of mental disorders* (4th ed.; *DSM-IV*). Washington, DC: Author.

American Psychiatric Association (1987). *Diagnostic and statistical manual of mental disorders* (3rd ed. rev.; *DSM-III-R*). Washington, DC: Author.

Bleuler, M. (1943). Die spätschizophrenen Krankheitsbilder [The clinical picture in late schizophrenia]. *Fortschritte der Neurologie-Psychiatrie, 15,* 259–290.

Bleuler, M. (1972). Late schizophrenic clinical pictures. *Forschritte der Nerologie-Psychiatrie, 15,* 259–290. (Original work published in German, 1943)

Bleuler, M. (1978). *The schizophrenic disorders: Long-term patient and family studies.* New Haven: Yale University Press.

Castle, D. J., & Howard, R. (1992). What do we know about the aetiology of late-onset schizophrenia? *Eur Psychiatry, 7,* 99–108.

Castle, D. J., & Murray, R. M. (1993). The epidemiology of late-onset schizophrenia. *Schizophrenia Bulletin, 19,* 691–700.

Christenson, R., & Blazer, D. (1984). Epidemiology of persecutory ideation in an elderly population in the community. *American Journal of Psychiatry, 141,* 59–67.

Ciompi, L., & Muller, C. (1976). Life course and age of schizophrenics: Long term follow-up study through old age (in German). *Monographien aus dem Gesamtgebiete der Psychiatrie.* Psychiatry Series. Mono 12.

Cohen, C. I. (1993). Poverty and the course of schizophrenia: Implications for research and policy. Special section: Policy issues in mental health. *Hospital and Community Psychiatry, 44*, 951–958.

Erlenmeyer-Kimling, L., & Miller, N. E. (Eds.). (1986). Life-span research on the prediction of psychopathology. Hillsdale, NJ: Erlbaum.

Freud, S. (1916). Introductory lectures on psychoanalysis Part II. In J. Strachey (Ed. and Trans.), *The standard edition of the complete psychological works of Sigmund Freud* (Vol. 15, pp. 81–240). London: Hogarth.

Freud, S. (1933). New introductory lectures, lecture 29. In J. Strachey (Ed. and Trans.), *The standard edition of the complete psychological works of Sigmund Freud* (Vol. 22, pp. 7–30). London: Hogarth.

Freud, S. (1958). Psycho-analytic notes on an autobiographical account of a case of paranoia (dementia paranoides). In J. Strachey (Ed. and Trans.), *The standard edition of the complete psychological works of Sigmund Freud* (Vol. 12, pp. 3–82. London: Hogarth. (Original work published in 1911)

Giel, R., Dijk, S., & Van Weerden-Dijkstra, J. R. (1978). Mortality in the long-stay population of all Dutch mental hospitals. *Acta Psychiatrica Scandinavica, 57*, 361–368.

Hafner, H., & anderHeiden, W. (1997, March). Epidemiology of schizophrenia. *Canadian Journal of Psychiatry, 42*, 139–151.

Harding, C. M. (1988, July). *Chronicity in schizophrenia*. Paper delivered at the International Association of Psychosocial Rehabilitation Services conference, Philadelphia.

Harding, C. M., Brooks, G. W., Ashikaga, T., Strauss, J. S., & Breier, A. (1987a). The Vermont longitudinal study of persons with severe mental illness: I. Methodology, study sample, and overall status 32 years later. *American Journal of Psychiatry, 144*, 718–726.

Harding, C. M., Brooks, G. W., Ashikaga, T., Strauss, J. S., & Breier, A. (1987b). The Vermont longitudinal study of persons with severe mental illness: II. Long-term outcome of subjects who retrospectively met DSM-III criteria for schizophrenia. *American Journal of Psychiatry, 144*, 727–735.

Harris, M. J., & Jeste, D. V. (1988). Late-onset schizophrenia: An overview. *Schizophrenia Bulletin, 14*, 39–55.

Huber, G., Gross, G., & Schuttler, R. (1979). Schizophrenia: Developmental and social psychiatric long-term studies on schizophrenic patients hospitalized in Bonn from 1945 to 1959 (in German). *Monographien aus dem Gesamtgebiete der Psychiatrie, 21*.

Hymas, N., Naguib, M., & Levy, R. (1989). Late paraphrenia: A follow-up study. *International Journal of Geriatric Psychiatry, 4*, 23–29.

Karon, B. P. (1989). On the formation of delusions. *Psychoanalytic Psychology, 6*, 169–185.

Karon, B. P., & VandenBos, G. R. (1981). *Psychotherapy of schizophrenia: The treatment of choice.* New York: Aronson.

Kay, D. W. K., & Roth, M. (1961). Environmental and hereditary factors in the schizophrenia of old age ("late paraphrenia") and their bearing on the general problem of causation in schizophrenia. *Journal of Mental Science, 107*, 649–686.

Keith, S. J., Regier, D. A., & Rae, D. S. (1991). Schizophrenic disorders. In L.N. Robins & D.A. Regier (Eds.), *Psychiatric disorders in America* (pp. 33–52). New York: Free Press.

Lewis, G., Davis, A., Andreasson, S., & Allebeck, P. (1992). Schizophrenia and city life. *Lancet, 340*, 137–140.

Lowenthal, M. F. (1964). Lives in distress: The paths of the elderly to the psychiatric ward. New York: Basic Books.

Myers, J. K., Bean, L. L., Pepper, M. P., & Hollingshead, A. (1968). *A decade later: A follow-up of social class and mental illness.* New York: Wiley.

Pearlson, G. D., Kreger, L., Rabins, P. V., Chase, G. A., Cohen, B., Wirth, J. B., Schlaepfer, T. B., & Tune, L. E. (1989). A chart review study of late-onset and early-onset schizophrenia. *American Journal of Psychiatry, 146*, 1568–1574.

Post, F. (1980). Paranoid, Schizophrenia-like and schizophrenic states in the aged. In J. E. Birren & R. B. Sloane (Eds.), *Handbook of mental health and aging* (pp. 591–615). Englewood Cliffs, NJ: Prentice-Hall.

Psychopharmacology Panel of the Canadian Alliance for Research on Schizophrenia. (1994). Panel: Psychopharmacology. *Journal of Psychiatry & Neuroscience, 19*(Suppl. 1), 29–33.

Quintal, M., Day-Cody, D., & Levy, R. (1991). Late paraphrenia and ICD-10. *International Journal of Geriatric Psychiatry, 6,* 111–116.

Riecher-Rössler, W., Förstl, H., & Melse, U. (1995). Late-onset schizophrenia and late paraphrenia. *Schizophrenia Bulletin, 21,* 345–354.

Teixeira, M. A. (1997, October). *Problematics of specificity and assessment of psychosocial risk factors in the pathogenesis, course, and treatment of schizophrenia (and affective disorders).* Paper presented at the meeting of The International Society for the Psychological Treatment of the Schizophrenias and Other Psychoses, Westminster, London.

Torrey, E. F. (1989). Schizophrenia: Fixed incidence or fixed thinking? *Psychological Medicine, 19,* 285–287.

Yassa, R., Dastoor, D., Nastase, C., & Camille, Y. (1993). The prevalence of late-onset schizophrenia in a psychogeriatric population. *Journal of Geriatric Psychiatry & Neurology, 6,* 120–125.

Part III

Assessment and Intervention

21

Psychological Testing of Older People

Daniel L. Segal, Frederick L. Coolidge,
and Michel Hersen

With the expected rise in the number of older persons in general and the number of older persons seeking psychological services, psychological testing of older people quite likely will increase as well. Geropsychology is a rapidly growing specialty area in psychological practice and research, and as a consequence, several specialized testing instruments for older people have been created. Despite these advances, many popular instruments that were initially developed for use with young and middle-aged adults have not been adequately normed or evaluated with older adults, although there also is a strong beginning in this area.

In general, the purpose of testing, or clinical assessment, is to find out what types of problems the person is experiencing and what may have caused the problem, to assist in clarification of personality features, to identify and diagnose mental disorders, to develop initial case conceptualization and intervention plans, and to evaluate effects of treatment. However, traditional testing strategies require some modification for older persons, given their often complex problems, unique socialization and life circumstances, and frequent comorbid health problems and physical limitations. The purpose of this chapter is to discuss the major issues concerning testing of older adults and to describe measurement tools and testing strategies to assist clinicians in their assessment of older adults.

Psychometric Considerations Regarding Psychological Tests

The primary diagnostic guide is the *Diagnostic and Statistical Manual of Mental Disorders*, 4th edition (*DSM–IV*; American Psychiatric Association, 1994), which has specified criteria for several hundred mental disorders and encourages a full multiaxial diagnosis, including information on clinical disorders, personality disorders, medical conditions, psychosocial and environmental stressors, and a global assessment of functioning. Although the *DSM–IV* has separate sections for childhood and adult disorders, there is no specific section on or criteria for mental disorders in later life, although the course over the life span for some disorders is described. Generally, though, limited information on age-related manifestations of disorders is provided in the *DSM–IV*. Indeed, several researchers have suggested that some criteria for some mental disorders are inadequate when applied to older people, particularly for personality disorders (Falk & Segal, in press; Rosowsky & Gurian, 1991; Sadavoy, 1996; Segal & Coolidge, in press; Segal, Hersen, Van Hasselt, Silberman, & Roth, 1996) and substance abuse (King, Van Hasselt, Segal, & Hersen, 1994; Segal, Van Hasselt, Hersen, & King, 1996). Cultural, social, physical, and cognitive factors may affect classic symptom presentation for many psychiatric disorders in older people.

The output of the testing strategy we recommend is a thorough testing report concluding with a full multiaxial diagnosis according to *DSM–IV* convention. Although specific technical information about how to write psychological reports is beyond the scope of this chapter, several resources are available for the interested reader (e.g., Segal, 1998; Zuckerman, 1995). The primary psychometric issues regarding psychological testing of older adults concern the related topics of reliability, validity, and norms; and these are discussed next.

Reliability

Reliability of test scores refers to consistency or stability of measurement. A reliable test yields consistent scores when the person takes the test again after an interval. The estimates of reliability most relevant to psychological tests are internal consistency and test–retest reliability. *Internal consistency* is a measure of the extent to which items in a test are intercorrelated with each other. *Test–retest reliability* refers to the extent to which test scores are consistent from one administration to the next. Reliability is the first requirement for good measurement; thus, tests that are used with older people should show ample evidence of reliability.

Validity

Validity refers to the extent to which a test measures what it is intended to measure and the extent to which the test can be used to make accurate predictions. Reliability and validity are closely intertwined, as reliability is a necessary, but not sufficient, condition for validity. An unreliable test cannot possibly be valid, although it is possible for a test to have good reliability but poor validity if the test does not measure anything meaningful. The primary types of validity of tests are *content, construct, predictive,* and *concurrent.* Again, check to make sure tests you are using have been well validated in an older sample that is similar to the sample from which your client comes. Be cautious in interpreting tests without proven validity in older people.

Norms

Scores on most psychological tests rarely provide absolute measures of the construct being assessed (e.g., intelligence, depression, or paranoia). Rather, tests frequently indicate the relative performance of the respondent when compared with others. Thus, most popular psychological tests are standardized, which means that the same test has been given to many different people so that statistical *norms* can be established for the test. Norms provide standards for interpreting test scores, so that one's responses can be compared with a reference group. Without standardization and norms, it is difficult to determine if an older adult's score is typical, above average, or below average compared with a peer's.

Tests developed specifically for older people (described in the next section) have excellent norms. Likewise, standard intelligence tests have superb age norms. Other tests that were designed for young and middle-aged persons did not initially furnish norms for older adults, but researchers have since provided them. For example, normative data for the Wolpe–Lazarus Assertiveness Scale have been described in community-dwelling (Kogan, Hersen, Kabacoff, & Van Hasselt, 1995) and visually impaired (Hersen, Kabacoff, Ryan, et al., 1995) older people. Likewise the Brief Symptom Inventory has been studied in a large, older sample (Hale, Cochran, & Hedgepeth, 1984). Unfortunately, research has lagged behind on other tests with missing or inadequate norms for older people. Sometimes norms for an age group can change over time, as age groups are composed of different people with different life experiences. Watch out for outdated or irrelevant norms. Clinicians and researchers are encouraged to carefully review the technical manual for tests they use to determine if evidence for reliability and validity and relevant norms for older people are available. If not, be cautious in interpreting scores and work to develop psychometric data for the test.

Age-Related Physical Changes and Medication Issues

Evidence suggests that the majority of older people with psychological problems do not seek or receive adequate mental health services. Lazarus, Sadavoy, and Langsley (1991) aptly described the many barriers to psychological assessment and treatment facing many older people in the current cohort: their belief that some illnesses like depression and anxiety are expected concomitants of old age, their attribution of psychiatric symptoms to physical rather than psychiatric causes, emphasis on medical treatment, stigmatization and shame associated with psychiatric care, and negative family and physician attitudes about geriatric mental health. Unfamiliarity with current mental health treatment and a desire to remain independent also preclude intervention in some cases. Last, practical deterrents such as cost, inadequate insurance, transportation, and physical disabilities can prevent timely mental health evaluation (Lazarus et al., 1991).

Once older adults overcome these diverse barriers and present for evaluation, there are other problems that affect assessment, notably sensory and physical declines and medication effects. Next, we discuss these physical and medical issues that can make traditional assessment more difficult and can affect test performance in older adults.

Vision

Vision problems plague many older adults. In fact, each one of us will experience some form of visual impairment if we live long enough (Cavanaugh, 1997). Over time, visual acuity typically declines so that over 95% of persons over age 65 need glasses at some time and more light to see well. Severe vision problems are known to have negative psychological consequences because they are related to decreased self-esteem, mobility and autonomy; poorer social functioning; and depression in some older people (Hersen, Kabacoff, Van Hasselt, et al., 1995; Hersen, Van Hasselt, & Segal, 1995).

Hearing

The decline in hearing is a well-known age-related change, and serious hearing loss is widespread in older people. After about age 50, almost all adults lose some auditory acuity. Rate of serious impairment is higher for hearing than for vision, in that nearly 50% of normal older people have a significant impairment (Cavanaugh, 1997). Like vision loss, hearing impairment can have adverse psychological effects, such as impaired social functioning, isolation, loss of independence, paranoia, and depression.

Stamina and Information Processing

With increasing age, stamina or endurance typically declines due to changes in heart functioning, circulation, lungs, and muscle tissue. Similarly, rate of information processing and reaction time also slow with age. Most older adults are able to compensate for these changes and can still function effectively on the job or in play provided ample time is available to complete the task. As such, speeded psychological tests may not give a fair estimate of the older person's eventual functioning if age-graded norms are not available. When testing a skill or ability in which speed or time is a relevant performance criteria, performance within the time limit and eventual performance without the time limit should be noted. Marathon testing sessions may be tolerated by younger people, but older adults may fatigue and perform more poorly than they are capable, given appropriate rest and pacing of testing.

Medical Illnesses and Medication Use

Due to age-related increases in the frequency of chronic medical conditions (e.g., arthritis, poor circulation, or osteoporosis), older adults consume a disproportionate amount of prescribed and over-the-counter (OTC) medications. The most frequently prescribed medications for older adults include sedatives, minor tranquilizers, and cardiovascular agents, whereas widely used OTC medications are analgesics, antacids, and laxatives (Schilit & Gomberg, 1991). With increased drug use, older people are at increased risk for adverse drug effects because of harmful drug interactions and because they metabolize drugs at a slower rate than when they were younger.

We recommend that clinicians get detailed information about current medical conditions and medications. Information about medical illnesses is important because some conditions (e.g., thyroid dysfunction, mitral valve prolapse, epilepsy, multiple sclerosis, hypoglycemia, and brain tumors) can mimic signs of psychiatric conditions (American Psychiatric Association, 1994). Likewise, certain medications are known to cause psychological symptoms, for example, some antihypertensive drugs and steroids can induce depressive symptoms; some stimulants and steroids can cause maniclike symptoms; and some analgesics, bronchodilators, and anticonvulsants can cause anxiety symptoms (American Psychiatric Association, 1994). Moreover, diverse drug interactions can cause memory problems that mimic a dementing illness, such as Alzheimer's disease. In any case, careful attention paid to drugs and medical conditions can assist the clinician in understanding the client's current problems.

Clinical Conditions and Assessment Tools

Depression

Depression is a common and often serious psychological disorder in older people. In fact, current estimates suggest that between 1% and 4% of community-dwelling older adults suffer from diagnosable major depression (Blazer, Hughes, & George, 1987), whereas an additional 9%–30% suffer from subclinical but still significant levels of depression (Blazer, 1993). Depression is frequently a presenting problem for older adults seeking psychiatric services, and because treatment of it for them is largely efficacious (Spar & LaRue, 1990), accurate detection is imperative.

Several popular self-report depression inventories are readily available for clinical use. The Beck Depression Inventory (BDI; Beck, Ward, Mendelson, Mock, & Erbaugh, 1961) is widely used in clinical research and practice as a depression-screening device. The BDI is a 21-item self-report questionnaire. Each item describes a specific manifestation of depression; the respondent reads four evaluative statements and indicates his or her current severity level of depression. Thirteen items assess psychological symptoms of depression, whereas eight items assess somatic symptoms. Potential scores range from 0 to 63, with higher scores corresponding to higher levels of depression. The main criticisms of the BDI are that it has many somatic items, which may not be reflective of depression in some older people, and that the response format is not as simple as other self-reports, described next.

The Center for Epidemiologic Studies Depression Scale (CES–D; Radloff, 1977) is another option for the assessment of depression in older people. The CES–D was developed primarily as a research instrument and has been widely used in community studies with adolescents and adults, although fewer data are available with older adults (Radloff & Teri, 1986). It has 20 self-report items that tap depressive symptoms experienced over the past week. An advantage of the CES–D is that it is not heavily weighted with somatic items, which can show falsely elevated levels of depression in physically ill (but nondepressed) older adults. Murrell, Himmelfarb, and Wright (1983) reported an impressive hit rate (percentage of respondents correctly classified) of 82% in a large, older sample within a community. More recently, the CES–D was shown to have excellent internal consistency (α = .82), good test–retest reliability (.52), and strong evidence for validity when compared with clinical diagnosis (sensitivity = 76%, specificity = 77%, hit rate = 77%) in a sample of 1,005 community-residing older adults (Lewinsohn, Seeley, Roberts, & Allen, 1997).

By far, the most popular and appropriate self-report inventory for depression in older people is the Geriatric Depression Scale (GDS; Yesavage et al., 1983). This easily administered scale was developed as a basic screening measure for depression in older adults, and it has been widely used in studies of depression in later adulthood. The GDS consists of 30 items, presented in a simple yes/no format. Items focus on cognitive and behavioral aspects of depression, and somatic items are excluded. In 20 of the 30 items, the answer yes indicates depression; in the remaining 10, the answer no indicates depression. The person's total GDS score consists of the sum of all items. A score of 0–10 indicates no depression, 11–20 indicates mild depression, and 21–30 indicates moderate-to-severe depression. Strengths of the GDS include the simple yes/no response format and the absence of somatically oriented items. The original scale is in the public domain, due to it being partly the result of federal support. The full GDS, scoring key, and primary references are available on the Internet website for the GDS at http://www-leland.stanford.edu/~yesavage/GDS.html.

The GDS has exceptional psychometric properties with older adults. Internal consistency and split-half reliability coefficients are both quite high at .94 (Yesavage et al., 1983). Test–retest reliability coefficients are also satisfactory over a span of 1 week (.85) and after a 5-min delay (.86; Brink et al., 1985). Regarding validity, Yesavage et al. found that GDS scores of nondepressed, mildly depressed, and severely depressed older participants were significantly different. Evidence for concurrent validity for the GDS has been provided by Yesavage et al., who correlated GDS scores with the Zung Self-Rating Depression Scale (r = .83) and Hamilton Rating Scale for Depression (r = .84). The GDS has shown high concurrent validity with the BDI in two studies (r = .73; Hyer & Blount, 1984; r = .91; Olin, Schneider, Eaton, Zemansky, & Pollock, 1992) and with the Hamilton Depression Rating Scale (r = .83; Hyer & Blount, 1984). Sheikh et al. (1991) reported that the GDS has good factorial validity. In a recent validity study with 59 older psychiatric outpatients, maximum discrimination of a current major depressive episode (based on structured interview) resulted with cutoff scores of 22 for the BDI and 16 for the GDS (Kogan, Kabacoff, Hersen, & Van Hasselt, 1994). Specifically, the validity scores for the BDI were as follows: sensitivity = 64%, specificity = 73%, positive predictive power = 75%, negative predictive power = 61%, and hit rate = 68%. Validity scores for the GDS were as follows: sensitivity = 79%, specificity = 69%, positive predictive power = 77%, negative predictive power = 72%, and hit rate = 75%. Overall, BDI values were typically slightly lower than GDS values but still in the moderate to excellent range. Combined BDI and GDS scores did not result in improved prediction of a current major depressive episode as compared with the GDS alone. This study suggests that both measures are valid quick screening instruments in discriminating major depression in older outpatients, although the GDS has slightly better validity scores.

Despite popularity of the self-report devices described previously, a definitive diagnosis of depression (or any psychological disorder for that matter) should never be made on the basis of self-report inventories alone, which can be subject to response biases (e.g., social desirability) and generally can be easily faked. Like others (e.g., Lewinsohn et al., 1997), we recommend a two-step process whereby elevated self-reported scores on the screening instrument are followed up by a clinical or structured interview to confirm presence or absence of the disorder. Several available multidisorder structured interviews are discussed later.

Suicide

A common referral question for a psychological assessment battery on an older person has to do with an evaluation of the person's potential for self-harm. Indeed, a full evaluation of suicidal risk should be a part of any standard testing battery. The reason for this is twofold: (a) to protect the client during a crisis point when the person may be irrational, psychotic, or severely depressed, and may want to escape from emotional turmoil by ending her or his life and (b) to protect the clinician, who can be held legally liable if a thorough suicidal assessment was not performed or if the clinician failed to take proper steps to prevent the client from self-harm and the client committed suicide.

Suicide is a significant clinical problem for younger and older clients alike. However, suicide rates generally increase with age, with the highest rates among persons over age 65 (Moscicki, 1995), although there is variability across countries and between male and female populations. In addition to age, other risk factors to consider include male gender, depression, hopelessness, substance abuse, previous suicide attempt, widowhood, and physical illness. General queries about suicidal ideation should be followed up with probes about specific plans and intent. Formal assessment measures include the Scale for Suicidal Ideation (Beck, Kovacs, & Weissman, 1979), which is a 19-item scale that is completed by a clinician after a semistructured interview, and the Geriatric Hopelessness Scale (GHS; Fry, 1986). The GHS is a 30-item yes/no self-report scale designed to assess pessimism and cognitions of hopelessness in older adults, which are theoretically related to suicidal behavior in Beck's model of depression. Items refer to the affective, motivational, and cognitive components of hopelessness in the respondent. According to Fry (1984), internal consistency of the scale is .69, and split-half reliability is .73. The GHS has been shown to be a valid measure based on high correlations with numerous other measures of theoretically related constructs (Fry, 1984). If the assessment reveals that the client is currently at risk for self-harm, the clinician must act to protect the client. If the client is in immediate and imminent danger of suicide and less restrictive treatments are not sufficient, the clinician is required to hospitalize the client.

Anxiety

Epidemiological studies suggest that anxiety symptoms are highly prevalent in older people (see Hersen, Van Hasselt, & Goreczny, 1993). Until recently, however, most assessment measures, normed and validated with younger populations, were indiscriminately applied to older people without having been evaluated psychometrically with this group, in terms of norms, internal consistency, reliability, factorial structure, and validity. Unlike the GDS for depression, there is no parallel specific measure of anxiety in older people. The assessment of anxiety in this group is inherently difficult because many anxiety symptoms by definition are physical symptoms (e.g., nausea, headaches, trembling, and heart pounding). As such, underlying medical conditions and medications, rather than psychological factors, could account for some symptoms.

Besides the Minnesota Multiphasic Personality Inventory (MMPI) and structured interviews (described later), two of the most commonly used self-report measures of anxiety are the Beck Anxiety Inventory (BAI; Beck & Steer, 1990) and the State–Trait Anxiety Inventory (STAI; Spielberger, 1983). The STAI is a theoretically derived 40-item Likert scale, which assesses separate dimensions of state anxiety (Items 1–20) and trait anxiety (Items 21–40). Each item is rated on a 4-point intensity scale. The BAI is a 21-item self-rating scale, which measures severity of anxiety and discriminates anxiety from depression. Each symptom is rated on a 4-point scale ranging from 0 (*not at all*) to 3 (*severely, I could barely stand it*), and the total scores can range from 0 to 63, with higher scores indicating higher levels of anxiety. Thirteen items assess physiological symptoms, five describe cognitive aspects, and three represent both somatic and cognitive symptoms. Both measures are well validated in diverse younger populations.

Recently, psychometric properties and clinical utility of these two measures were examined in a large sample of older outpatients ($N = 217$) with diverse psychiatric disorders (Kabacoff, Segal, Hersen, & Van Hasselt, 1997). Results indicated that both scales demonstrated high internal reliabilities. The BAI demonstrated good factorial validity (with Somatic Anxiety and Subjective Anxiety subscales emerging), but the STAI did not show factorial validity, because separate State and Trait factors were not found. Both the BAI and the Trait subscale of the STAI discriminated anxiety-disordered clients from those without an anxiety disorder, but the State subscale did not discriminate between groups. When used to predict presence of an anxiety disorder, no single cutoff score for either the BAI or STAI was optimal due to relative trade-offs regarding sensitivity and specificity. Moreover, combined BAI and STAI scores did not result in improved prediction of a current anxiety disorder, as compared with the BAI alone. These results suggest that the BAI is somewhat useful as a quick screening instrument in detecting an anxiety disorder in older psychiatric outpatients, although results were not as strong as previous findings regarding predictive accuracy of the GDS in detecting depression in older people. In conclusion, although clinical and research interest in anxiety disorders in older people has lagged somewhat behind that in mood and cognitive disorders, increased attention of late will quite likely increase our ability to better measure anxiety in this group.

Substance Abuse and Dependence

Substance abuse can be a problem with older people, as with any other age group. Estimates of problem drinking or alcoholism in older adults range between 2% and 10% (King et al., 1994). Use of illicit drugs (e.g., cocaine, hallucinogens, and marijuana) among older people is relatively uncommon, with the exception that some heroin users survive into old age (Schilit & Gomberg, 1991). However, illicit drug use is expected to increase substantially as younger cohorts of heavy drug users age. Older people are also at great risk for unintentionally abusing OTC and prescription medications owing to their high use rates. Moreover, some researchers suggest that substance abuse sometimes is underdiagnosed and underreported in older people (Dupree, 1989; King et al., 1994). Many so-called "hidden" alcoholics remain undetected, partially because of inadequate case-finding strategies (Dupree, 1989), limited relevance of some *DSM* criteria for substance abuse, and inadequate screening devices (King et al., 1994). Unfortunately, lack of accurate diagnosis is a major barrier to adequate intervention (for review of treatment issues, see Segal, Van Hasselt, et al., 1996).

Recently, however, there has been an attempt to adapt existing instruments, such as the CAGE, for use in geriatric populations and to develop and validate an elder-specific assessment measure. The CAGE (Mayfield, McLeod, & Hall, 1974) is a short, four-item, self-report questionnaire designed to detect alcohol abuse. Limited data suggest that the CAGE is useful as a gross screening device for alcohol abuse in older people, although large definitive studies are lacking. To address the need for quality assessment tools for use with the older people, the Michigan Alcoholism Screening Test (MAST) has recently been modified into an elder-specific measure, the MAST—Geriatric Version (MAST–G; Blow et al., 1992). Notably, the MAST–G is becoming widely and successfully used in clinical practice. It contains 24 simple yes/no items unique to older problem drinkers. In all cases, yes is the pathological response, and a cutoff of 5 positive responses indicates an alcohol problem (Blow et al., 1992). The MAST–G has excellent psychometric properties. Using the *Diagnostic and Statistical Manual of Mental Disorders* (3rd ed. rev.; *DSM–III–R*; American Psychiatric Association, 1987) diagnosis of alcohol dependence as the validation criteria, the MAST–G was found to have a sensitivity of 93.9% and specificity of 78.1%. Factor analysis revealed five dimensions: Loss and Loneliness, Relaxation, Dependence, Loss of Control With Drinking, and Rule Making. In any case, a thorough evaluation of substance abuse should be a part of any standard battery, because the disorder not only can be severe and debilitating in its own right but also can make other comorbid conditions, such as anxiety and depression, worse. In addition, substance abuse is linked to increased rates of suicide.

Cognitive Impairment

Assessment of cognitive functioning is an important part of any thorough geriatric assessment, because cognitive impairment is a major problem facing older people. Accurate assessment of cognition is important because other test results may not be valid if the sufferer's judgment is significantly impaired. Also, early detection of cognitive disorders is crucial because many symptoms are reversible, especially for delirium.

The primary *DSM–IV* cognitive disorders are dementia and delirium. *Delirium* refers to a clouding of consciousness with accompanying impaired concentration, disorientation, and perceptual disturbances that develop over a short period of time (hours to days). Because delirium is often obvious and acute, there are no specific tests for it. However, if delirium is suspected in older people, they should be quickly referred for medical treatment, because delirium is typically reversible but can be deadly if the underlying cause (e.g., infections, drug intoxication or withdrawal states, or malnutrition) is not corrected.

Dementia is a syndrome of multiple cognitive deficits, including impairment in memory but excluding impairment in consciousness. Dementia is often described as a gradual deterioration of intellectual abilities (usually over several years) to the point that the person is unable to identify close family members, perform basic self-care skills, or even speak in the end stage. Community studies suggest that 3%–8% of persons over age 65 experience severe dementia whereas 10%–18% have mild cognitive deficits (Cummings & Benson, 1992; Spar & LaRue, 1990). Prevalence rates clearly increase with age, so that 20%–30% of persons over age 85 are diagnosable with dementia (American Psychiatric Association, 1994; Skoog, Nilsson, Palmertz, Andreasson, & Svanborg, 1993). Note, however, that prevalence rates vary from country to country, also depending on how the disorder is technically defined. The most common type in American and most European older people is dementia of the Alzheimer's type, which accounts for 50%–70% of dementias.

We suggest that at a minimum, clinicians screen for cognitive impairment in all older clients during the testing session. Even a brief mental status examination (tapping such broad areas as mood, hallucinations, delusions, judgment, insight, and gross cognitive functioning) will greatly facilitate diagnosis and treatment planning and can serve as a baseline measurement. If cognitive impairment is evident, always get a full history, including onset and course of cognitive decline. The family may be the best source of this information if the client is in fact cognitively impaired.

There are several brief, standardized, easily administered screening exams for mental status and cognitive impairment that can assist clinicians in this endeavor. One of the most popular tools is the Folstein Mini Mental State Exam (Folstein, Folstein, & McHugh, 1975). This brief cognitive screening device for dementia takes 5–10 min to administer and is well validated. Items tap orientation, concentration, memory, language, and gross motor skills. Scores range from 0 to 30, with scores under 25 indicating a need for further testing and evaluation and scores below 20 indicating definite cognitive impairment. Other popular screening tools include the Short Portable Mental Status Questionnaire (Pfeiffer, 1975) and the Blessed Dementia Index (Blessed, Tomlinson, & Roth, 1968). A final helpful instrument is the Dementia Rating Scale (Mattis, 1988), which is a psychometrically sound, interviewer-administered neuropsychological instrument designed specifically for dementia evaluation in older people. The Dementia Rating Scale consists of 36 tasks and takes about 30 min to complete. Note that one cannot diagnose dementia with any brief screening device. Laboratory tests (e.g., complete blood count [CBC], electrolyte panel, or urinalysis), high-tech brain-imaging procedures (e.g., computerized tomography, or magnetic resonance imaging), and neuropsychological testing are used to follow up positive cases from the screening. Finally, a thorough evaluation is needed to rule out depression because some depressed older people complain about memory and concentration deficits and can look demented even though no dementing illness is actually present.

Personality Disorders

It is vitally important when testing older adults to pay attention to possible underlying personality disorders. Indeed, personality dysfunction can cloud the diagnostic picture and negatively impact treatment efficacy of *DSM–IV* Axis I disorders in older people (Falk & Segal, in press; Segal et al., in press; Segal, Hersen, et al., 1996). Some researchers suggest that personality disorders are sometimes unrecognized in older people due to inadequate criteria for some disorders and the florid, more easily recognizable presentation of Axis I conditions (Rosowsky & Gurian, 1991; Sadavoy, 1996; Segal & Coolidge, in press; Segal et al., 1996). To aid the clinician, many self-report and structured interviews have been designed to evaluate a wide range of *DSM–IV* personality disorders. Popular and psychometrically sound self-report devices include the Millon Clinical Multiaxial Inventory–III (Millon, 1994), the Personality Diagnostic Questionnaire–4 (Hyler, 1994), and the Coolidge Axis II Inventory (CATI; Coolidge & Merwin, 1992). All have been applied to older people at least minimally and will help clinicians detect personality pathology. Positive cases should be further examined with structured interviews (discussed below) for definitive diagnosis because self-report devices tend to overpathologize.

Although the CATI (Coolidge & Merwin, 1992) stands as one of the newer personality inventories, it has been normed and used extensively in older populations. The CATI contains 225 items answered on a 4-point Likert scale ranging from *strongly disagree* to *strongly agree*. The CATI was originally designed to measure Axis II personality disorders, as described in the *DSM–III–R*, and was revised for the *DSM–IV*. The CATI also was specifically designed to assess neuropsychological symptoms through three subscales assessing memory and concentration difficulties, somatic symptoms related to brain dysfunction, and language and comprehension problems. It also has Axis I measures of depression, anxiety, schizophrenia, and psychotic thinking. In addition, the CATI possesses a validated significant-other evaluation form (Coolidge, Burns, & Mooney, 1995) as well as large-print forms for older or sight-impaired individuals. Because 16% of the original normative sample ($N = 1,223$) ranged in age from 60 to 92 years ($n = 200$), separate studies comparing the nonpsychiatric elderly with the original normative sample were not necessarily required.

In 1992, Coolidge, Burns, Nathan, and Mull investigated whether personality disorders diminish or become less prominent in older as compared with younger people. In a preliminary study of only 36 healthy, older, community-dwelling people (mean age 69, range = 61 to 78 years) compared with 573 younger people (mean age = 24, range = 16 to 58 years), they found that the older group was significantly more elevated than the younger group on the Obsessive–Compulsive and Schizoid personality disorder scales and significantly less elevated on the Antisocial, Borderline, Histrionic, Narcissistic, Paranoid, Passive–Aggressive, Sadistic, and Self-Defeating scales. Mean elevations on the Obsessive–Compulsive and Schizoid scales for the older group were both greater than 2 standard deviations above the normative group means. Specific-item analyses on the Obsessive–Compulsive scale revealed that that the older group scored significantly higher than the younger group on the items relating to restricted affectivity and insensitivity to criticism. Neural substrate changes were proposed as a causal mechanism.

Coolidge, Janitell, and Griego (1994) examined the comorbidity of depression, anxiety, and personality disorders in a sample of 83 healthy, community-dwelling older people (mean age = 70 years). They found a surprisingly high rate of personality disorders (18% of the sample) and significant set correlations between depression, anxiety, and personality disorders. The Schizoid personality disorder scale was the most frequently elevated in the sample. It also appeared that high states of anxiety were better predictors of personality disorders than was depression. The overall results supported the hypothesis that personality disorders appear to be more common when anxiety and depression are present in older people. Because mental health professionals are more likely to evaluate older persons for depression and anxiety than for personality disorders and because personality disorders appear to be comorbid with anxiety and depression, it would behoove clinicians to be aware of these findings when treating older people with anxiety and depression, because therapeutic intervention and treatment outcome might be affected.

Coolidge et al., (in press) also examined the CATI profiles in two psychiatric samples, one of chronically psychiatric older people (n = 30; mean age = 63, range = 56 to 83 years; a majority were diagnosed with schizophrenia) and the other of younger schizophrenic inpatients (n = 30; mean age = 39, range = 22 to 54 years). The prevalence rate of personality disorders was high for both groups (about 62% of the entire sample) and slightly higher in the younger group, but there was no significant difference between the two groups on the prevalence rate of the Obsessive–Compulsive personality disorder. There were also no significant differences between the two groups on the percentage of each sample with a clinically elevated Depression or Anxiety scale on the CATI.

Structured Interviews for Clinical and Personality Disorders

Many structured interviews are available to help clinicians and researchers evaluate most major *DSM–IV* Axis I (clinical) syndromes and all standard Axis II (personality) disorders. Structured interviews have many beneficial features, including comprehensive, systematic, and objective coverage of disorders of interest and improved reliability and validity, compared with unstructured interviews (for full description of major issues and instruments, see Segal, 1997; Segal & Falk, 1998). Likewise, self-report screening tools described earlier (e.g., for anxiety and depression) should routinely be followed by a more thorough structured interview to clarify the diagnostic picture. Well-validated interviews for Axis I disorders include the Structured Clinical Interview for *DSM–IV* Axis I (SCID–I; First, Spitzer, Gibbon, & Williams, 1995), the Diagnostic Interview Schedule—IV, and the Schedule for Affective Disorders and Schizophrenia (Endicott & Spitzer, 1978). Popular and psychometrically sound interviews for personality disorders include the Structured Clinical Interview for DSM–IV Axis II Personality Disorders (SCID–II; First, Gibbon, Spitzer, Williams, & Benjamin, 1997), Structured Interview for *DSM–IV* Personality (Pfohl, Blum, & Zimmerman, 1995), and the International Personality Disorder Examination (World Health Organization, 1995). Although all of these instruments have been applied with various geriatric populations, published reliability and validity data are limited, especially for the Axis II interviews (Segal, Hersen, et al., 1996).

In an earlier review (Segal, Hersen, & Van Hasselt, 1994), we called for increased evaluations of the reliability of the structured interviews in minority populations, including older adults. Our research group has conducted two such reliability studies of the SCID–I with older people. In the first study (Segal, Hersen, Van Hasselt, Kabacoff, & Roth, 1993), 33 older psychiatric inpatients and outpatients were evaluated (mean age = 67.3 years). SCID–I interviews were administered by master's level clinicians and were audiotaped for retrospective review by an independent rater. Reliability estimates (kappa) were calculated for current major depression (47% base rate, κ = .70) and the broad diagnostic categories of anxiety disorder (15% base rate, κ = .77) and somatoform disorder (12% base rate, κ = 1.0). The second investigation (Segal, Kabacoff, Hersen, Van Hasselt, & Ryan, 1995) targeted older outpatients exclusively (N = 40; mean age = 67.1 years) and evaluated a larger number of diagnoses. Diagnostic concordance was determined for the general groupings of mood disorder (60% base rate), anxiety disorder (25% base rate), somatoform disorder (9% base rate), and substance use disorder (9% base rate). Agreement for the broad diagnostic group of somatoform disorder (κ = .84) was almost perfect, whereas concordance was slightly lower, but still substantial, for mood disorder (κ = .79) and anxiety disorder (κ = .73). Data for substance use disorder (κ = .23) reflected poor agreement. For specific illnesses, kappas were high for major depression (58% base rate, κ = .90) and panic disorder (15% base rate, κ = .80), and moderate for dysthymia (9% base rate, κ = .53). Taken together, these two studies suggest that reliability of the SCID–I administered to older adults appears very promising. In conclusion, it has been our experience that older people respond particularly well to structured interviews because they like the comprehensive nature of the assessment and extended time with the interviewer. However, adequate rapport should be established, and the interview procedure carefully explained before beginning the interview.

Personality Assessment

The accurate personality assessment of older people presents all of the issues associated with the assessment of younger persons, such as the reliability and validity of the assessment techniques, but also adds some complex and difficult problems associated with general developmental personality theory. Among these problems are the important theoretical issue of whether personality changes across the life span and the related issue of how psychological tests standardized on younger persons may be applied to older populations.

Minnesota Multiphasic Personality Inventory–II

Probably no single personality measurement has been used more with older people than the MMPI, despite the fact that separate norms for them are not readily available. The MMPI was developed by Hathaway and McKinley at the University of Minnesota in the early 1940s (Groth-Marnat, 1990). The current version, the MMPI–II (Butcher, Dahlstrom, Graham, Tellegen, & Kaemmer, 1989) contains 567 items, but the traditional 10 clinical scales and 3 Validity Scales can be obtained with administration of the first 370 items. One advantage of the MMPI–II over its predecessor has been the addition of Content scales, which were designed to assess additional personality dimensions such as anxiety, depression, low self-esteem, and health concerns.

It has been frequently noted, however, that the length of time of administration (from 1 to over 2 hr) for either the MMPI or the MMPI–II may be particularly difficult for older people especially for older clinical patients. Short forms of the MMPI have been used as a result (see Newmark, Newmark, & Faschingbauer, 1974), but there are few studies assessing short forms of the MMPI–II with geriatric populations.

Age differences on the standard MMPI–II have been addressed in few investigations. In a cross-sectional study, Butcher et al. (1991) contrasted 1,459 men from a normative aging study (mean age = 61 years) versus 1,138 men from the MMPI restandardization study (mean age = 42 years). They found that the older sample scored significantly higher on the Depression scale of the MMPI and significantly lower on the Psychopathic Deviance and Mania scales. Although the researchers used nearly exclusively White, middle-class men in a cross-sectional study, they argued that the results suggested that older men did not require separate norms on the MMPI–II.

The latter finding of higher Depression scale scores in older people on the MMPI and MMPI–II has been frequently supported, although it has been argued that geographic, societal, and population factors may actually account for differences between younger and older respondents on the test more so than age-related differences (Koeppl, Bolla-Wilson, & Bleecker, 1989). It has also been suggested (e.g., Harmatz & Shader, 1975) that these higher depression scores are more likely an artifact of the somatic and physical stamina bias of the items on the MMPI Depression scale. Furthermore, the MMPI Depression scale contained the item "I believe in the second coming of Christ." Although a "false" response may have been a sign of depression in the original sample, consisting largely of Christian Minnesota farmers, it does not appear to be a valid indicator of depression for people of numerous other religious persuasions. When only the items directly relevant to mood are isolated as a separate depression scale on the MMPI, then the average older person does not appear more depressed than younger people. However, the average clinician may not have the time nor expertise to indulge in such lengthy perturbations so as to tailor the MMPI Depression scale for older people.

With respect to gender differences in older people on the MMPI–II, Strassberg, Clutton, and Korboot (1991) tested 110 nonpsychiatric, Australian residents (mean age = 71, age range = 60 to 96 years, N = 60 women and 50 men). There were no statistically significant gender differences, although there were some trends for men to be higher than women on the Depression scale (male mean T score = 59, female mean T score = 54) and for both groups to be lower (mean T score < 45) on the Psychopathic Deviance, Paranoia, and Mania scales. Both groups' peak scores appeared on the Hypochondriasis scales, perhaps reflecting greater concerns of older people with regard to their health.

Overall, it may be surmised that despite the MMPI–II's frequent use, its validity with older populations—in particular, psychiatric older people—has not yet been well established. Preliminarily, it does appear that higher scale scores for nonpsychiatric older people on the Depression and Hypochondriasis scales may be related to the high number of items on the scales testing common physical symptoms rather than depressive mood or fears of dying from a single fatal disease.

Rorschach and Thematic Apperception Test

The Rorschach is a time-honored projective personality test originally designed by Hermann Rorschach and published in 1921 (Groth-Marnat, 1990). It consisted of 10 bilaterally symmetrical inkblots chosen for their prior, specific abilities to elicit certain classes of responses from normal people (e.g., mother responses, authority figure responses, flying objects, and sexual content). Rorschach died shortly after his eponymous test's publication, but at least five different major scoring systems were popularized and in widespread use until the late 1960s. In 1969, Exner began devising his revolutionary scoring system, which now enjoys virtually unrivaled popularity. Exner's scoring system uses only empirically derived interpretations as well as standardized administration and scoring instructions. Exner's adherence to strict empirical validation has led to a veritable renaissance in the teaching and use of the original Rorschach test.

A classic text regarding interpretations of the Rorschach test with respect to older people was published in 1973 by Ames, Metraux, Rodell, and Walker and was titled *Rorschach Responses in Old Age*. However, Ames et al.'s, findings were not pleasant: Aging appeared to produce responses that were more restricted, empty, labile, and less in contact with reality than those of younger people. However, subsequent empirical studies did not fully support their contentions. The major criticisms centered on the nature of the Ames et al. sample (a greater preponderance of institutionalized patients and a lack of age stratification; e.g., Reichlin, 1984). More recent research, by Gross, Newton, and Brooks (1990), claimed that age and even intellectual level have minimal impact on Rorschach responses. Peterson (1991) argued that his experience, particularly with healthy older people, revealed Rorschach responses far richer and fecund than Ames and his colleagues had suggested. As Grotjahn (1951) noted, older people cannot typically look to the distant future for meaning in their lives. They must look into their past for understanding and satisfaction. Therefore, Peterson (1991) proposed tailoring Rorschach administration to the older adult by asking him or her "to reminisce in response to the earlier precept" (p. 534). Although Peterson (1991) acknowledged that this might spuriously increase the Rorschach responses, he felt that the original test biases of Ames et al. just as equally led to an artificial coarctation of the responses of older people, resulting in their claims of a barrenness of the older adult's inner world.

The Thematic Apperception Test (TAT; Murray, 1943) is another widely used projective test. The TAT consists of 31 black-and-white pictures, which pull for certain themes, such as sexuality, achievement, interpersonal relationships, and parental relationships. Some cards are well structured and clear, some are somewhat ambiguous, and still others are bizarre. Many of the pictures involve depictions of single individuals or dyads, although middle-aged or older adults are clearly depicted in only 5 of the 31 cards. Typically 10–20 cards are selected by the clinician and administered, and the respondent is asked to tell a story explaining what is happening in the picture currently, what led up to the picture, what is going to happen, and what the characters are feeling.

Because respondents typically identify with one character in the picture, the utility with older adults may be somewhat compromised. To address this issue, the Senior Apperception Test, which has many elderly-relevant pictures and themes, has been devised. It is our clinical impression that the standard TAT can be used with older clients but that the specialized version is preferable.

A final projective test that may be useful is the Geriatric Sentence Completion Form (LeBray, 1992), which consists of 30 fragmentary sentence stems, which the older client is asked to complete. This elder-specific version is designed to measure attitudes and personal characteristics of persons age 60 and over and taps many age-related themes, such as attitude toward death and growing old. As with the Senior Apperception Test, we recommend that the elder version of incomplete sentences is used rather than the standard adult version.

The NEO Personality Inventory and Five-Factor Model of Personality

Costa and McCrae proposed a five-factor model of both the normal and abnormal personality structure (Costa & McCrae, 1996) and promoted their operationalization of the model in the revised NEO Personality Inventory (NEO–PI; Costa & McCrae, 1988; see chapter 3, this volume). Their five-factor model is based on earlier work by Norman (1963). The five factors are as follows: Neuroticism, Extraversion, Openness to Experience, Agreeableness, and Conscientiousness. The revised NEO–PI form (can be completed in 30–40 minutes and is answered on a 5-point Likert scale anchored by *strongly disagree* and *strongly agree*. Costa and McCrae claimed that the five-factor model could explain the normal personality as well as abnormal personality dimensions, although these claims appear arguable (see Ben-Porath & Waller, 1992; Coolidge et al., 1994).

Costa and McCrae (1996) argued that one's personality structure changes little after the age of 30, at least according to research with the NEO–PI. Changes do occur between ages 20 to 30, such as a lowering of overall Neuroticism scores and Extraversion coupled with increased levels of Agreeableness and Conscientiousness. However, they argue that with few exceptions, people's personalities remain constant after the age of 30 only until dementing disorders may become prominent. Costa and McCrae and others (e.g., Malatesta & Kalnok, 1984) propose, particularly in regard to depression and overall affect, that "older adults are simply adults who happen to be older" (Costa & McCrae, 1996, p. 378).

In summary, this brief sampling of some common or recent research of psychological assessment of older people reveals a complete gamut of opinions, from the increasing barrenness of the older adult's inner world to the simplicity of older adults as adults who happen to be older. It does appear, and perhaps not surprisingly, that the determination of their psychological state will be strongly determined by measurement device, specific characteristics of the person being tested (e.g., age, gender, ethnicity, cohort, socioeconomic class, and religion), administration techniques and instructions (e.g., large-print form availability and time-limited format), and conscious or unconscious researcher biases. Nevertheless, there seems to be some evidence for some kind of diminishment of responding in older people but the reasons for the diminution are far from clear. There also appears to be some arguments for the constancy of the adult personality; however, their nature and supporting neural substrate mechanisms certainly require further elucidation.

Intelligence (IQ) Assessment

There is no area in psychology richer in controversy than the assessment of intelligence. The difficulty of intellectual assessment is exacerbated by its own abstract nature. It can only be inferred from observable behavior, yet the illusory label, *intelligence*, no doubt refers to a complex group of mental processes.

The modern history of intelligence assessment can be traced to Binet, a French psychologist, and his colleague, Simon, who, beginning in 1904, attempted to distinguish, with a series of questions, between slow and normal learners in the French school system. In 1916, Terman, a Stanford University professor, translated, standardized, and improved on Binet and Simon's test by developing the intelligence quotient (IQ). His formula for obtaining IQ was to divide a child's mental age by chronological age and multiply the result by 100. The new, improved version of Binet and Simon's test became known as the Stanford–Binet Intelligence test and was used widely, almost without rival, until the 1950s (Matarazzo, 1972). Wechsler, an American psychologist, became dissatisfied with the Stanford–Binet test primarily because he found it more suitable for children than adults. Wechsler began developing a broader and what he called "functional" definition of intelligence. He argued that the then current concept of intelligence was too narrowly defined and that the

Stanford–Binet test was not suitable for adults. His work culminated in the Wechsler–Bellevue Scale (1939), and it was revised to form the Wechsler Adult Intelligence Scale (WAIS; Wechsler, 1955). The revised WAIS, known as the WAIS–R (1981), is now currently the most popular intelligence test in the entire world.

The WAIS–R consists of 11 separate subtests, six verbal and five performance. Raw scores for each scale are converted into scaled scores ($M = 10$, $SD = 3$). The scaled scores are added together separately for the verbal and performance subtests. Based on groupings of the participant's age, scaled score sums are converted into a verbal intelligence quotient (VIQ), performance intelligence quotient (PIQ), and a full scale intelligence quotient (FIQ). Furthermore, scaled score equivalents of raw scores by age groups may be obtained through the WAIS–R manual. Although these scaled score equivalents are not to be used in the computation of equivalent IQs, they may be used for overall scale pattern analysis. In this latter regard, Wechsler's test is original and unique in the assessment field by its offering of test scores based on large groups of age-stratified people and also test score equivalents specifically based on age group norms through age 70–74 years. The WAIS–R was also standardized on 1,880 people, age 16 to 75 years, according to nine different age groupings with an equal number of males and females in each age group. Census data were used to apportion the sample into race and geographic regions.

Aging and intelligence have long been a topic of debate (Kirkpatrick, 1903). A classic series of studies by Schaie (e.g., 1958, 1983) and his colleagues has helped to establish what now have become almost unchallenged facts in psychological assessment: (a) Declines in intelligence come much later than previously believed, (b) they vary widely from person to person, (c) the nature of the decline itself varies across abilities, and (d) educational level is negatively correlated with intellectual decline.

Many studies of cognitive aging have been conducted on the Wechsler and other intelligence scales, researchers (e.g., Flynn, 1987; Parker, 1986) have analyzed the peak performance across a number of IQ tests and found that peak performance appears to occur later with every succeeding generation at a rate of about 3 IQ points per decade. In addition, in 1916, the peak global performance age was 16 years; in 1926, it was 20; in 1931, it was 18.5; in 1937, it was 22; in 1953, it was 27; and in 1978, it was 30 years of age. It is thought that increases in years of education account for the largest share of the causal variance. Data from Kaufman, Reynolds, and McLean (1989) suggest that education alone accounts for over 45% of the variance in VIQ, whereas age accounts for only 3%. In PIQ, education accounts for 33% of the variance, whereas age alone accounts for 28%. And in FIQ, education accounts for 46% of the variance, whereas age alone accounts for 13%.

Interestingly, if peak performance in verbal intelligence is determined after controlling for education level, the peak VIQ is obtained for age 55 to 64 years, and even more amazing is that peak VIQ at age 70 to 74 is even greater than at age 20 to 24. The picture for PIQ is not so sanguine. PIQ drops steadily after the age of 20 to 24, although the decline at age 70 to 74 represents about a 25% decrement from peak ability.

Peak performance data support Cattell's (1963) theory of *crystallized* versus *fluid* intelligence. The theory, elaborated by Horn (1985), states that crystallized intelligence depends to the largest extent on accumulated knowledge from one's culture. Thus, crystallized intelligence should increase (or at the very least remain stable) across the life span. Fluid intelligence is thought to depend on physiological integrity and functioning and, thus, should decline with increasing age. Thus, the WAIS–R data largely support the Cattell–Horn theory. Horn (1985) estimated that the performance rate of decline is approximately 5 IQ points per decade.

An alternate hypothesis to fluid intelligence decline is the fact that older people are simply slower than younger people, and all of the performance subtests of the WAIS–R have time limits and bonus points for speedy solutions. Although slowness associated with aging is an incontestable fact, evidence is fairly strong that slowness alone cannot account for the decline in PIQ. Even when time limits are ignored, older people will still score lower than younger people on nearly all of the WAIS–R performance subtests. Salthouse (1984) suggested that the age-related decline must be attributed to a basic maturational alteration of the central nervous system, resulting in a slowing of the processing of almost all types of information. Research also firmly supports the hypothesis that despite the decline in PIQ with increasing age, PIQ still remains a good predictor of the g factor, or general intelligence, in older adults (see Kaufman, 1990, for a review of this evidence).

When the individual subtests are rank ordered by the greatest decline according to age from the WAIS–R standardization sample ($N = 1,880$), the following pattern appears (the denotation V indicates that the subtest is a measure of VIQ, and P indicates a measure of PIQ): 1. Digit Symbol (P), 2. Picture Arrangement (P), 3. Block Design (P), 4. Object Assembly (P), 5. Picture Completion (P), 6. Similarities (V), 7. Digit Span (P), 8. Arithmetic (P), 9. Comprehension (V), 10. Information (V), 11. Vocabulary (V).

The preponderance of performance subtests as the most sensitive to aging is not surprising given the previous discussion. The information, however, is useful in a variety of ways. Although individual patterns may vary, clinicians may use the previous table to document what may represent potentially abnormal aging patterns. For example, if an older person obtained their lowest scores on the Vocabulary or Information subtests, the clinician would certainly be well advised to investigate further. Coolidge, Peters, Brown, Harsch, and Crookes (1985) found that in an older sample of patients suffering from dementia ($N = 50$), the Vocabulary subtest stayed intact throughout the milder stages of dementia. They also found when the Block Design scaled score fell below half of that of the Vocabulary scaled score, an indication that dementia was likely.

Clinicians should be advised, however, that a statistical abnormality may not translate into a clinical or pathological abnormality. Thus, pattern comparisons may be useful to form hypotheses and for performance comparison purposes, but caution is always wise in any statistical pattern analysis. The clinical relevance of any pattern analysis finding should always be thoroughly investigated.

In conclusion, the WAIS–R remains an excellent test of intelligence for all adults. Because of the careful age, gender, race, and geographic stratification in its standardization, the use of the WAIS–R is continually substantiated at least on a psychometric basis. There are, however, potentially as many uses as abuses with the WAIS–R. Although Wechsler (1981) thought that it might measure motivation (the trait) to some degree, it is clear that it largely does not measure motivation, nor does it measure the worth of a person. Thus, clinicians should again be urged to use caution and to use their own intuition when evaluating any adult, but particularly older adults. As a measure of intellectual performance or decline, the WAIS–R is probably peerless. But as a measure of creativity, emotional stability, conscientiousness, leadership, a person's value to most organizations or systems, or a plethora of other referral questions, the WAIS–R may be inappropriate. Notably, the WAIS–III (Wechsler, 1997) has recently been published and likely will continue to set the standard for intelligence testing in older people.

Guidelines for Testing Older Adults

As highlighted throughout this chapter, psychological testing of older adults is different in many ways than the typical assessment of younger persons. We hope the following guidelines and tips will assist clinicians in their assessment of older adults. In general, a recurring theme will be that the clinician needs to be more flexible when engaging older clients.

1. Adjust the environment to reduce the impact of sensory and physical declines. For example, the testing room should be brightly lit and quiet. It can be helpful to sit closer to the respondent and to speak slowly, loudly, and concretely, without psychological jargon. Make sure respondent is using her or his hearing aids or glasses. Some test print is too small for anyone with a visual impairment. Big-print versions of some tests are available and should routinely be used even with healthy older people. Other tests can be retyped in larger fonts. If visual impairment is severe, oral administration of some self-reports may be necessary. Finally, testing the older person at home can be a useful alternative if transportation is problematic or a functional assessment is required.

2. Adjust traditional time constraints. Allow sufficient time for the older person to complete self-report tests and to respond to interview questions. It is important not to rush the person because many older adults rate their health care based on how much time they spend with the professional, and rapport will deteriorate if the client is not given ample time. Long, detailed interviews and testing batteries are not tolerated well by many older people. Many older adults need more frequent breaks during testing, and it is often necessary and helpful to divide testing sessions, because of fatigue. Be sensitive here, because the person's score will not be an accurate reflection of the measurement construct if he or she is fatigued. Finally, conduct the testing in the morning because fatigue may impair performance later in the day.

3. Explain clearly the purpose and procedures of the assessment process

and the client's role. Address any concerns or fears the older person has about the evaluation. The current cohort of older people was raised in an era when psychiatric services were reserved mainly for the severely mentally ill and psychiatric care was associated with tremendous shame and stigmatization. Some people may erroneously believe that the purpose of the testing is to "find out if they are crazy," and they need reassurances and education about the clinician's more benign intentions. Expressions of empathy and compassion help build rapport between clinician and client.

4. Be open to discussing the client's concerns about the clinician's age. Older clients may see younger therapists as similar to their children or the child they never had. It is helpful to acknowledge existing age differences and to ask the client to express their concerns, so the issue is addressed up front.

5. Generally address the person by her or his proper name, to denote respect. Follow the client's lead if he or she wants to be more familiar and on a first name basis.

6. The older client is usually interviewed first and alone. This denotes respect for the person and may elicit information not otherwise obtainable when family members are present (Lazarus et al., 1991).

7. Make greater use of ancillary sources of information. This is a basic tenet in geriatric assessment. Whenever possible, close family members and caregivers are interviewed for corroborative information and to obtain information not available from the client (i.e., when there is cognitive impairment or in conditions where the person may lack insight, such as substance abuse and psychotic disorders). Involving family members in the assessment process also can help secure their cooperation with the intervention plan. A close evaluation of the family and relationship patterns can also suggest the need for family therapy.

8. Maintain an active therapeutic stance when evaluating the client and working through patient and family resistances to assessment and therapy (Lazarus et al., 1991). Also, encourage active collaboration and participation on the part of the older client who is used to the more passive medical model of evaluation and treatment.

9. Provide overt expressions of concern for the older client (Lazarus et al., 1991). Many older adults respond especially well to gentle physical touching (e.g., hold hand during an interview or pat on shoulder). Likewise, symbolic giving such as offering a cup of water or tea is typically greatly appreciated and helps the older person feel more comfortable.

10. Fully assess concomitant medical conditions and medication use. It is crucial to take a thorough medical history from the client, including an assessment of prescribed and OTC medications. As noted previously, this is important to consider because many older people have at least one chronic medical condition and many medical illnesses and the medications used to treat them can cause psychiatric conditions (e.g., delirium, depression, anxiety, and psychosis). Have older clients

bring all medications to the testing session. Finally, referral for a thorough medical workup is always indicated if the client has not recently been medically evaluated. Medical causes must first be ruled out before psychiatric diagnoses can be assigned.

11. Use elder-specific assessment measures when available, including the GDS, GHS, Geriatric Sentence Completion Form, and Senior Apperception Test. If elder-specific measures are not available, thoroughly investigate the psychometric properties of the instrument with older populations and be aware of the normative sample used in scoring. If data on operating characteristics and clinical utility of the instrument with older people are not available or are limited, be cautious in interpreting the results.

12. Make realistic treatment goals that consider the patient's limitations, to avoid frustration and a sense of failure. For example, improvement in functioning is not an appropriate goal for patients with dementia, whereas treatment for depression often results in a full recovery.

13. Provide greater assistance in coordinating services with other health professionals that may help with the client's care, such as social services, housing, financial aid, and psychiatric evaluation. Older people typically are less skilled in getting appropriate services from bureaucratic agencies than younger adults. And because your testing recommendations will frequently include referrals to other agencies, your client will require help in managing this task.

14. Instill hope. Remember that one purpose of assessment is to develop treatment options. Be appropriately optimistic with the older clients if interventions are likely to assist the clients in tackling their problems. Indeed, the instillation of hope may even be therapeutic in its own right and is especially important for older people who often are unaware of the benefits of psychological interventions.

Conclusion

In this chapter, we reviewed many general issues regarding the psychological testing of older adults, including psychometric concerns about assessment tools and health-related deficits that can impact testing. We also reviewed the most common clinical disorders and conditions, provided information on assessment instruments that clinicians may use, and offered guidelines for conducting a testing battery on older adults. Clinicians and researchers also should be aware of two useful reference tools regarding the assessment of older adults. The first is the *Geropsychology Assessment Resource Guide* (Bialk & Vosburg, 1993), which was developed by Department of Veterans Affairs psychologists. This guide provides general (one-page) descriptions of 116 assessment instruments, including information on advantages and disadvantages, primary source references, and vendors. The second helpful resource is the *Psychological Assessment of Older Adults: A Graduate Education Teaching Module* (Qualls, Wacker, & Bloodworth, 1997) which was designed to help teachers of graduate psychological testing courses include specialized information on testing of older adults.

We hope this chapter helps clinicians and researchers in their testing of older persons, with the outcome of a deeper understanding of the older persons' concerns and problems and more effective intervention strategies.

References

American Psychiatric Association. (1987). *Diagnostic and statistical manual of mental disorders* (3rd ed., rev.). Washington, DC: Author.

American Psychiatric Association. (1994). *Diagnostic and statistical manual of mental disorders* (4th ed.). Washington, DC: Author.

Ames, L. B., Metraux, R. W., Rodell, J. L., & Walker, R. N. (1973). *Rorschach responses in old age* (2nd ed.). New York: Brunner/Mazel.

Beck, A. T., Kovacs, M., & Weissman, A. (1979). Assessment of suicidal ideation: The Scale for Suicidal Ideation. *Journal of Consulting and Clinical Psychology, 47,* 343–352.

Beck, A. T., & Steer, R. A. (1990). *Manual for the Beck Anxiety Inventory.* San Antonio, TX: Psychological Corporation.

Beck, A. T., Ward, C. H., Mendelson, M., Mock, J., & Erbaugh, J. (1961). An inventory for measuring depression. *Archives of General Psychiatry, 4,* 53–63.

Ben-Porath, Y. S., & Waller, N. G. (1992). Five big issues in clinical personality assessment: A rejoinder to Costa and McCrae. *Psychological Assessment, 4,* 23–25.

Bialk, B. S. & Vosburg, F. L. (Eds.). (1993). *Geropsychology assessment resource guide.* Milwaukee, WI. Department of Veterans Affairs, National Center for Cost Containment. (NTIS No. PB 93-213 684)

Blazer, D. G. (1993). *Depression in late life* (2nd ed.). St. Louis, MO: Mosby.

Blazer, D. G., Hughes, D. C., & George, L. K. (1987). The epidemiology of depression in an elderly community population. *Gerontologist, 27,* 281–287.

Blessed, G., Tomlinson, B., & Roth, M. (1968). The association between quantitative measures of dementia and of senile changes in the cerebral grey matter of elderly subjects. *British Journal of Psychiatry, 114,* 797–811.

Blow, F. C., Brower, K. J., Schulenberg, J. E., Demo-Dananberg, L. M., Young, J. P., & Beresford, T. P. (1992). The Michigan Alcoholism Screening Test—Geriatric version (MAST–G): A new elderly-specific screening instrument. *Alcoholism, 16,* 372.

Brink, T. L., Curran, P., Dorr, M. L., Janson, E., McNulty, U., & Messina, M. (1985). Geriatric Depression Scale reliability: Order, examiner and reminiscence effects. *Clinical Gerontology, 3,* 57–59.

Butcher, J. N., Aldwin, C. M., Levenson, M. R., Ben-Porath, Y. S., Spiro, A., & Bosse, R. (1991). Personality and aging: A study of the MMPI–2 among older men. *Psychology and Aging, 6,* 361–370.

Butcher, J. N., Dahlstrom, W. G., Graham, J. R., Tellegen, A., & Kaemmer, B. (1989). *MMPI–2: Manual for administration and scoring.* Minneapolis: University of Minnesota Press.

Cattell, R. B. (1963). Theory of fluid and crystallized intelligence: A critical experiment. *Journal of Educational Psychology, 54,* 1–22.

Cavanaugh, J. C. (1997). *Adult development and aging* (3rd. ed.). Pacific Grove, CA: Brooks/Cole.

Coolidge, F. L., Burns, E. G., & Mooney, J. A. (1995). Reliability of observer ratings in the assessment of personality disorders: A preliminary study. *Journal of Clinical Psychology, 59,* 223–238.

Coolidge, F. L., Burns, E. G., Nathan, J. H., & Mull, C. E. (1992). Personality disorders in the elderly. *Clinical Gerontologist, 12,* 41–55.

Coolidge, F. L., Janitell, P. M., & Griego, J. A. (1994). Personality disorders, depression and anxiety in the elderly. *Clinical Gerontologist, 15,* 80–83.

Coolidge, F. L., & Merwin, M. M. (1992). Reliability and validity of the Coolidge Axis II Inventory: A new inventory for the assessment of personality disorders. *Journal of Personality Assessment, 59,* 223–238.

Coolidge, F. L., Peters, B. M., Brown, R. E., Harsch, T. L., & Crookes, T. G. (1985). Validation of a WAIS algorithm for the early onset of dementia. *Psychological Reports, 57,* 1299–1302.

Coolidge, F. L., Segal, D. L., Pointer, J. C., Knaus, E. G., Yamazaki, T. G., & Silberman, C. S. (in press). Personality disorders in elderly inpatients with chronic mental illness. *Journal of Clinical Geropsychology*.

Costa, P. T., Jr., & McCrae, R. R. (1992). *Revised NEO Personality Inventory (NEO-PI-R) and NEO Five-Factor Inventory (NEO-FFI) professional manual*. Odessa, FL: Psychological Assessment Resources.

Costa, P. T., Jr., & McCrae, R. R. (1996). Mood and personality in adulthood. In C. Magai & S. H. McFadden (Eds.), *Handbook of emotion, adult development, and aging* (pp. 369–383). New York: Academic Press.

Cummings, J. L., & Benson, D. F. (1992). *Dementia: A clinical approach* (2nd ed.). Boston: Butterworth-Heinemann.

Dupree, L. W. (1989). Comparison of three case-finding strategies relative to elderly alcohol abusers. *Journal of Applied Gerontology, 8*, 502–511.

Endicott, J., & Spitzer, R. L. (1978). A diagnostic interview: The Schedule for Affective Disorders and Schizophrenia. *Archives of General Psychiatry, 35*, 837–844.

Exner, J. E. (1969). *The Rorschach systems*. New York: Grune & Stratton.

Falk, S. B., & Segal, D. L. (in press). Personality disorders. In M. Hersen & V. B. Van Hasselt (Eds.), *Handbook of clinical geropsychology*. New York: Plenum.

First, M. B., Gibbon, M., Spitzer, R. L., Williams, J. B. W., & Benjamin, L. S. (1997). *Structured Clinical Interview for DSM–IV Axis II Personality Disorders (SCID–II)*. Washington, DC: American Psychiatric Press.

First, M. B., Spitzer, R. L., Gibbon, M., & Williams, J. B. W. (1995). *Structured Clinical Interview for Axis I DSM–IV Disorders—Patient edition (SCID–I/P, Version 2.0)*. New York: New York State Psychiatric Institute, Biometrics Research Department.

Flynn, (1987). Massive gains in 14 nations: What IQ tests really measure. *Psychological Bulletin, 101*, 171–191.

Folstein, M. F., Folstein, S. E., & McHugh, P. R. (1975). Mini Mental State: A practical method for grading the cognitive state of patients for the clinician. *Journal of Psychiatric Research, 12*, 189–198.

Fry, P. S. (1984). Development of a Geriatric Scale of Hopelessness: Implications for counseling and intervention with the depressed elderly. *Journal of Counseling Psychology, 31*, 322–331.

Fry, P. S. (1986). Assessment of pessimism and despair in the elderly: A Geriatric Scale of Hopelessness. *Clinical Gerontologist, 5*, 193–201.

Gross, A., Newton, R. R., & Brooks, R. B. (1990). Rorschach responses in healthy, community dwelling older adults. *Journal of Personality Assessment, 55*, 335–343.

Groth-Marnat, G. (1990). *Handbook of psychological assessment*. New York: Wiley.

Grotjahn, M. (1951). Some analytic observations about the process of growing old. In G. Roheim (Ed.), *Psychoanalysis and the social sciences* (Vol. 3, pp. 301–312). New York: International Universities Press.

Hale, W. D., Cochran, C. D., & Hedgepeth, B. E. (1984). Norms for the elderly on the Brief Symptom Inventory. *Journal of Consulting and Clinical Psychology, 52*, 321–322.

Hamilton, M. (1960). A rating scale for depression. *Journal of Neurology and Neurosurgery, 23*, 56–61.

Harmatz, J. S., & Shader, R. E. G. (1975). Psychopharmacological investigations in healthy elderly volunteers: MMPI Depression scale. *Journal of the American Geriatrics Society, 23*, 350–354.

Hersen, M., Kabacoff, R. I., Ryan, C. F., Null, J. A., Melton, M. A., Pagan, V., Segal, D. L., & Van Hasselt, V. B. (1995). Psychometric properties of the Wolpe–Lazarus Assertiveness Scale for older visually impaired adults. *International Journal of Rehabilitation and Health, 1*, 179–187.

Hersen, M., Kabacoff, R. I., Van Hasselt, V. B., Null, J. A., Ryan, C. F., Melton, M. A., & Segal, D. L. (1995). Assertiveness, depression, and social support in older visually impaired adults. *Journal of Visual Impairment and Blindness, 7*, 524–530.

Hersen, M., Van Hasselt, V. B., & Goreczny, A. J. (1993). Behavioral assessment of anxiety in older adults: Some comments. *Behavior Modification, 17*, 99–112.

Hersen, M., Van Hasselt, V. B., & Segal, D. L. (1995). Social adaptation in older visually impaired adults: Some comments. *International Journal of Rehabilitation and Health, 1*, 49–60.

Horn, J. L. (1985). Remodeling old models of intelligence. In B. B. Wolman (Ed.), *Handbook of intelligence* (pp. 267–300). New York: Wiley.

Hyler, S. E. (1994). *Personality Diagnostic Questionnaire, 4th edition (PDQ-4)*. New York: New York State Psychiatric Institute.

Hyer, L., & Blount, J. (1984). Concurrent and discriminant validities of the Geriatric Depression Scale with older psychiatric inpatients. *Psychological Reports, 54*, 611–616.

Kabacoff, R. I., Segal, D. L., Hersen, M., & Van Hasselt, V. B. (1997). Psychometric properties and diagnostic utility of the Beck Anxiety Inventory and the State–Trait Anxiety Inventory with older adult psychiatric outpatients. *Journal of Anxiety Disorders, 11*, 33–47.

Kaufman, A. S. (1990). *Assessing adolescent and adult intelligence*. Needham Heights, MA: Allyn & Bacon.

Kaufman, A. S., Reynolds, C. R., & McLean, J. E. (1989). Age and WAIS-R intelligence in a national sample of adults in the 20- to 74-year age range: A cross-sectional analysis with educational level controlled. *Intelligence, 13*, 235–253.

King, C., Van Hasselt, V. B., Segal, D. L., & Hersen, M. (1994). Diagnosis and assessment of substance abuse in older adults: Current strategies and issues. *Addictive Behaviors, 19*, 41–55.

Kirkpatrick, E. G. (1903). *Fundamentals of child study: A discussion of instincts and other factors in human development with practical applications*. New York: Macmillan.

Koeppl, P. M., Bolla-Wilson, K., & Bleecker, M. L. (1989). The MMPI: Regional difference or normal aging? *Journal of Gerontology, 44*, 95–99.

Kogan, E. S., Hersen, M., Kabacoff, R. I., & Van Hasselt, V. B. (1995). Psychometric properties of the Wolpe–Lazarus Assertiveness Scale with community-dwelling older adults. *Journal of Psychopathology and Behavioral Assessment, 17*, 97–109.

Kogan, E. S., Kabacoff, R. I., Hersen, M., & Van Hasselt, V. B (1994). Clinical cutoffs for the Beck Depression Inventory and Geriatric Depression Scale with older adult psychiatric outpatients. *Journal of Psychopathology and Behavioral Assessment, 16*, 233–242.

Lazarus, L. W., Sadavoy, J., & Langsley, P. R. (1991). Individual psychotherapy. In J. Sadavoy, L. W. Lazarus, & L. F. Jarvik (Eds.), *Comprehensive review of geriatric psychiatry* (pp. 487–512). Washington, DC: American Psychiatric Press.

LeBray, P. R. (1992). *Geriatric Sentence Completion Form*. Odessa, FL: Psychological Assessment Resources.

Lewinsohn, P. M., Seeley, J. R., Roberts, R. E., & Allen, N. B. (1997). Center for Epidemiologic Studies Depression Scale (CES–D) as a screening instrument for depression among community-residing older adults. *Psychology and Aging, 12*, 277–287.

Malatesta, C. Z., & Kalnok, M. (1984). Emotional experience in younger and older adults. *Journal of Gerontology, 39*, 301–308.

Matarazzo, J. D. (1972). *Wechsler's measurement and appraisal of adult intelligence*. Baltimore: Williams & Wilkins.

Mattis, S. (1988). *Dementia Rating Scale*. Odessa, FL: Psychological Assessment Resources.

Mayfield, D., McLeod, G., & Hall, P. (1974). The CAGE questionnaire: Validation of a new alcoholism screening instrument. *American Journal of Psychiatry, 131*, 1121–1123.

Millon, T. (1994). *Millon Clinical Multiaxial Inventory III (MCMI III) manual*. Minneapolis, MN: National Computer Systems.

Moscicki, E. K. (1995). Epidemiology of suicide. *International Psychogeriatrics, 7*, 137–148.

Murray, H. A. (1943). *Thematic Apperception Test*. Cambridge, MA: Harvard University Press.

Murrell, S. A., Himmelfarb, S., & Wright, K. (1983). Prevalence of depression and its correlates in older adults. *American Journal of Epidemiology, 117*, 173–185.

Newmark, C. S., Newmark, L., & Faschingbauer, T. R. (1974). Utility of three abbreviated MMPIs with psychiatric outpatients. *Journal of Nervous and Mental Disease, 159*, 438–443.

Olin, J. Y., Schneider, L. S., Eaton, E. M., Zemansky, M. F., & Pollock, V. E. (1992). The Geriatric Depression Scale and the Beck Depression Inventory as screening instruments in an older adult psychiatric outpatient population. *Psychological Assessment, 4*, 190–192.

Parker, K. C. H. (1986). Changes with age, year-of-birth cohort, age by year-of-birth interaction, and standardization of the Wechsler adult intelligence tests. *Human Development, 29*, 209–222.

Peterson, C. A. (1991). Reminiscence, retirement, and Rorschach responses in old age. *Journal of Personality Assessment, 57*, 531–536.

Pfeiffer, E. (1975). A short portable mental status questionnaire for the assessment of organic brain deficit in elderly patients. *Journal of the American Geriatrics Society, 23*, 433.

Pfohl, B., Blum, N., & Zimmerman, M. (1995). *Structured Interview for DSM–IV Personality (SIDP–IV)*. Iowa City: University of Iowa.

Qualls, S. H., Wacker, H., & Bloodworth, M. (1997). *Psychological assessment of older adults: A graduate education teaching module*. University of Colorado at Colorado Springs and University of Colorado Health Sciences Center.

Radloff, L. S. (1977). The CES–D Scale: A self-report depression scale for research in the general population. *Applied Psychological Measurement, 1*, 385–401.

Radloff, L. S., & Teri, L. (1986). Use of the Center for Epidemiologic Studies Depression Scale with older adults. *Clinical Gerontologist, 5*, 119–136.

Reichlin, R. E. (1984). Current perspectives on Rorschach performance among older adults. *Journal of Personality Assessment, 48*, 71–81.

Rosowsky, E., & Gurian, B. (1991). Borderline personality disorder in late life. *International Psychogeriatrics, 3*, 39–52.

Sadavoy, J. (1996). Personality disorder in old age: Symptom expression. *Clinical Gerontologist, 16*, 19–36.

Salthouse, T. A. (1984, August). *Speculations on the what, when, and why of mental aging*. Paper presented at the 92nd Annual Convention of the American Psychological Association, Toronto, Ontario, Canada.

Schaie, K. W. (1958). Rigidity–flexibility and intelligence: A cross-sectional study of the adult life-span from 20 to 70. *Psychological Monographs, 72* (9, Whole No. 462).

Schaie, K. W. (1983). *Longitudinal studies of adult psychological development*. New York: Guilford Press.

Schilit, R. & Gomberg, E. S. L. (1991). *Drugs and behavior*. Newbury Park, CA: Sage.

Segal, D. L. (1997). Structured interviewing and *DSM* classification. In S. M. Turner & M. Hersen (Eds.), *Adult psychopathology and diagnosis* (3rd. ed., pp. 25–57). New York: Wiley.

Segal, D. L. (1998). Writing up the intake interview. In M. Hersen & V. B. Van Hasselt (Eds.), *Basic interviewing: A practical guide for counselors and clinicians* (pp. 129–149). Hillsdale, NJ: Erlbaum.

Segal, D. L., & Coolidge, F. L. (in press). Personality disorders. In A. S. Bellack & M. Hersen (Eds.), *Comprehensive clinical psychology: Vol. 7. Clinical geropsychology*. New York: Elsevier Science.

Segal, D. L., & Falk, S. B. (1998). Structured diagnostic interviews and rating scales. In M. Hersen & A. S. Bellack (Eds.), *Behavioral assessment: A practical handbook* (4th ed., pp. 158–178). New York: Allyn & Bacon.

Segal, D. L., Hersen, M., Kabacoff, R. I., Falk, S. B., Van Hasselt, V. B., & Dorfman, K. (in press). Personality disorders and depression in the elderly. *Journal of Mental Health and Aging*.

Segal, D. L., Hersen, M., & Van Hasselt, V. B. (1994). Reliability of the Structured Clinical Interview for DSM–III–R: An evaluative review. *Comprehensive Psychiatry, 35*, 316–327.

Segal, D. L., Hersen, M., Van Hasselt, V. B., Kabacoff, R. I., & Roth, L. (1993). Reliability of diagnoses in older psychiatric patients using the Structured Clinical Interview for DSM–III–R. *Journal of Psychopathology and Behavioral Assessment, 15*, 347–356.

Segal, D. L., Hersen, M., Van Hasselt, V. B., Silberman, C. S., & Roth, L. (1996). Diagnosis and assessment of personality disorders in older adults: A critical review. *Journal of Personality Disorders, 10*, 384–399.

Segal, D. L., Kabacoff, R. I., Hersen, M., Van Hasselt, V. B., & Ryan, C. F. (1995). Update on the reliability of diagnosis in older psychiatric outpatients using the Structured Clinical Interview for DSM–III–R. *Journal of Clinical Geropsychology, 1*, 313–321.

Segal, D. L., Van Hasselt, V. B., Hersen, M., & King, C. (1996). Treatment of substance abuse in older adults. In J. R. Cautela & W. Ishaq (Eds.), *Contemporary issues in behavior therapy: Improving the human condition* (pp. 69–85). New York: Plenum.

Sheikh, J. I., Yesavage, J. A., Brooks, J. O., Friedman, L. F., Gratzinger, P., Hill, R. D., Zadeik, A., & Crook, T. (1991). Proposed factor structure of the Geriatric Depression Scale. *International Psychogeriatrics, 3*, 23–28.

Silberman, C. S., Roth, L., Segal, D. L., & Burns, W. (1997). Relationship between the Millon Clinical Multiaxial Inventory–II and Coolidge Axis II Inventory in chronically mentally ill older adults: A pilot study. *Journal of Clinical Psychology, 53*, 559–566.

Skoog, I., Nilsson, L., Palmertz, B., Andreasson, L., & Svanborg, A. (1993). A population-based study of dementia in 85-year-olds. *New England Journal of Medicine, 328*, 153–158.

Spar, J. E., & LaRue, A. (1990). *Concise guide to geriatric psychiatry*. Washington, DC: American Psychiatric Press.

Spielberger, C. D. (1983). *Manual for the State–Trait Anxiety Inventory*. Palo Alto, CA: Consulting Psychologists Press.

Strassberg, D. S., Clutton, S., & Korboot, P. (1991). A descriptive and validity study of the Minnesota Multiphasic Personality Inventory—2 (MMPI–2) in an elderly Australian sample. *Journal of Psychopathology and Behavioral Assessment, 3*, 301–311.

Wechsler, D. (1939). *The measurement of adult intelligence*. Baltimore: Williams & Wilkins.

Wechsler, D. (1955). *Manual for the Wechsler Adult Intelligence Scale*. New York: Psychological Corporation.

Wechsler, D. (1981). *Manual for the Wechsler Adult Intelligence Scale—Revised*. San Antonio, TX: Psychological Corporation.

Wechsler, D. (1997). *Wechsler Adult Intelligence Scale, 3rd edition (WAIS-III)*. San Antonio: Psychological Corporation.

World Health Organization. (1995). *The International Personality Disorder Examination (IPDE) DSM–IV Module*. Washington, DC: American Psychiatric Press.

Yesavage, J. A., Brink, T. L., Rose, T. L., Lum, O., Huang, V., Adey, M. B., & Leirer, V. O. (1983). Development and validation of a geriatric depression screening scale: A preliminary report. *Journal of Psychiatric Research, 17*, 37–49.

Zuckerman, E. L. (1995). *Clinicians thesaurus: The guide for writing psychological reports* (4th ed.). New York: Guilford Press.

22

Neuropsychological Assessment in Old Age

Knut Hestad, Bjørn Ellertsen, and Hallgrim Kløve

A basic assumption in clinical neuropsychology is that systematic measurement of intellectual, motor, and sensory functions, with an appropriate and standardized battery of tests, provides a basis from which inferences may be made regarding the organic integrity of the brain. A considerable body of scientific knowledge, including neuroimaging and functional neuroimaging techniques, is presently available to support this approach. In addition, it has become customary to include personality assessment both for the purpose of differential diagnosis as well as for an evaluation of emotional status. Psychophysiological measurements of arousal and central nervous system (CNS) activation are also often a part of the neuropsychological evaluation (Kløve, 1995).

Neuropsychological assessment is aimed at establishing associations between CNS damage or CNS function and behavior, so called *brain–behavior relationships*. This usually is accomplished by evaluating the patient with a battery of tests that has been validated both on healthy people and individuals with different kinds of CNS disorders. Different procedures are adhered to by different neuropsychologists when doing a general neuropsychological evaluation, depending on methodological orientation and assessment procedures. The most common and different approaches used in the United States are described and discussed in Grant and Adams (1996). The United States approaches vary a great deal with regard to how extensive the neuropsychological battery is and which tests are used. Whereas some neuropsychologists insist on using a standardized battery of tests, others prefer to select tests on the basis of the presented clinical problem. These traditions are, for the most part, psychometrical. In contrast is Luria's (1966) qualitative neuropsychological approach used by many clinicians in different countries. In the former Soviet Union, all tests that resembled intelligence tests were prohibited in the 1930s and any researcher or clinician who employed such methods risked prison or worse punishment (Danielsen, 1996). The development of Luria's neuropsychological approach, which is without any standardized psychometric tests, must be seen in light of this fact. This qualitative approach resembles an expanded clinical neurological examination in many ways, and the evaluation is based on clinical interpretation of findings and not on normative data for the procedures in question.

When doing a neuropsychological assessment of older individuals, it is necessary to know how normal individuals without brain disorders perform. In general, the neuropsychological tests chosen for the evaluation of older adults have to adhere to basic psychometrical criteria and yield as few false positive results as possible. To obtain these goals, validation studies are important. Epidemiological studies of psychological or mental disturbances in older people show that there is a similar prevalence of such difficulties in older adults as there is in the general population, except for cognitive functions, which show a higher prevalence of impairment in people in older age-classes (Bland, Newman, & Orn, 1988). We recommend that neuropsychological assessment of older patients be performed using methods that are selected on the basis of scientific knowledge about performance of both the normally and the abnormally functioning older adult. The same basic selection criteria regarding contents of tests must be adhered to when doing neuropsychological assessment of younger patients. Ideally, an evaluation should cover the following areas:

1. Measures of intellectual performance, ideally yielding a function profile and, if possible, establishing the patient's premorbid intellectual level.
2. Measures of different kinds of memory functions.
3. Measures that make it possible to make inferences with regard to the integrity of the right versus left hemisphere of the brain.
4. Measures that make it possible to make inferences about the relative integrity of anterior versus posterior brain areas.
5. Measures of the CNS arousal and activation.
6. Measures that allow the investigation to be relatively short in duration, without sacrificing general reliability and validity.

An extensive neuropsychological battery of tests for elderly people may consist of the Wechsler Adult Intelligence Scale (WAIS; Wechsler, 1955, 1981), the revised Wechsler Memory Scale (WMS-R; Wechsler, 1987), the expanded Halstead-Reitan Test battery (Heaton, Grant, & Matthews, 1991), The Minnesota Multiphasic Personality Inventory (MMPI; Dahlstrom, Welsh, & Dahlstrom, 1975), and appropriate psychophysiological methodology for the measurement of tonus and reactivity in the autonomic nervous system.

However, one should always take into consideration the physical and mental condition of the patient. The assessment battery just described is far too extensive and demanding for a large proportion of older patients seen by clinical neuropsychologists. Our experience with the oldest old who are healthy is that examiners have to use much more time than when younger patients are assessed with the same methods and that rest breaks are important. Neuropsychological assessment of the oldest old may also be complicated by impairment of vision, hearing, and motor performance. In one of our studies (unpublished), after examining 65 participant's who were between 64 and 105 years old, 4 of the oldest individuals had to be excluded because of poor vision and hearing. It is often obvious that a patient is demented. In these cases many of the tests of higher cognitive functions will not yield any more information about the patient's functioning than a shorter battery of tests. It is also our experience that both the WAIS and the WMS-R can be very disagreeable for older patients. When this is the case, we usually select subtests from the WAIS and use other memory measures for our examination. If the presenting problem or test results indicate apraxia or language problems, it may become necessary to expand the evaluation accordingly by including appropriate and more extensive tests of such functions.

Brain Change With Age

As individuals grow older the brain changes. It becomes smaller, and it functions less well than when the person was younger. Thus, the brain is impaired, although it is a question of choice whether to label this brain damage or not. It is mandatory for all neuropsychologists working with older patients to have detailed knowledge about this aging process. If not, the assessment may easily become an uncritical administration of tests that yield little understanding of the brain–behavior relationships in the older adults.

The best documented brain change in normal aging is an overall decrease in brain weight and volume (Berg, 1988; Dekaban & Sadowsky 1978; Kemper, 1984). Adams and Victor (1989) stated that the average male brain declines from 1394g to 1161g from the third decade of life to the beginning of the tenth decade. The weight loss is a result of degeneration of neurons and their replacement with Glial cells. Other gross changes in brain morphology in older adults that have been observed at autopsy include gyral atrophy and ventricular dilations (Berg, 1988).

The ratio of gray to white matter in the cerebral hemispheres increases with age, suggesting an age-related loss of myelin (Miller, Alston, & Corsellig, 1980). This loss is greatest in regions where myelinization is completed relatively late in the developmental cycle, that is, in association and limbic cortexes, as opposed to motor, somesthetic, visual, and auditory regions (Kemper, 1984). Neuroimaging data have confirmed the earlier neuropathological findings and also have extended the knowledge in this area. Pfefferbaum, Zatz, and Jernigan (1986), using a computer interactive method for quantifying cerebral fluid and tissue in brain computer tomography (CT) scans, showed that when data were statistically transformed to produce more normal distributions, the correlation between brain volume and old age increased. The data indicated diffuse loss of brain tissue over the entire adult range, with an accelerated loss after the age of 60.

Boone et al. (1992) studied 100 healthy, older individuals with Magnetic Resonance Imaging (MRI). Approximately 50% showed no white matter lesions, 25% showed minimal or moderate lesions, and 6% showed large areas of MRI hyperintensities greater than $10cm^2$. Even if there are no overt clinical signs of brain disorder, such changes are bound to show up as impairment on appropriate neuropsychological tests. The structural data are supported by functional studies. Martin, Friston, Colebatch, and Frackowiak (1991), using Positron Emission Tomography (PET) in 30 normal volunteers aged 30 to 85 years, demonstrated age-related decreases in resting regional cerebral bloodflow in limbic structures and association cortex. These authors suggested that the decreases constitute the cerebral substrate of normal age-related cognitive change.

Earnest, Heaton, Wilkionson, and Manke (1979) found significant correlations between scores on the Digit Symbol Test and both linear and planimetrical measures of lateral ventricular parameters in both normal older adults and older adults with dementia. Albert and Stafford (1986) found that fluid volume measures of the ventricles and the sulci correlated highly with memory test scores, confrontation naming, visuo-spatial abilities, and abstract reasoning, with maximal correlations found on the CT slice containing primarily temporal and frontal lobes.

Questions Related to Premorbid Abilities, Age, and Education

Babcock introduced, around 1930, the idea of comparing performance on tests that are relatively resistant to the effects of cerebral impairment with tests that involve new learning or motor speed (Walsh, 1978). Tests that "held up" against cerebral damage were considered useful for the evaluation of premorbid levels of functioning and could thus serve as a basis for comparison of performance on other tests. This notion served as the basis for the Wechsler's Deterioration Index (Wechsler, 1958), which expresses the relative performance on WAIS subtests that are minimally affected by brain impairment (*hold* tests) as compared with subtests that are maximally affected (*don't hold* tests). The index became quite popular, but later studies have failed to demonstrate the clinical usefulness with regard to diagnosis of brain impairment. For example, among the WAIS subtests, the digit symbol subtest, a supposed don't hold test, is the one that most often is impaired in patients with CNS disorders (Lezak, 1983).

There is undoubtedly an age-related reduction in both intellectual capacity and neuropsychological performance. This impairment can easily be mistaken as a sign of CNS damage if the investigator evaluates the performance of a 90-year-old and a 30-year-old person according to the same rules of interpretation. The Grooved Pegboard Test may serve as an example. Using 150 seconds to complete the Grooved Pegboard Test with the dominant hand is normal in a 85-year-old healthy older woman, but is a highly impaired performance in a 30-year-old woman.

There are also undoubtedly many older adults who have brain disorders related to the aging process that are undiagnosed because they function well clinically. Heaton, Grant, and Matthews (1986) developed comprehensive age and education corrected norms for the expanded Halstead-Reitan test battery. This work was done to make it possible to control for factors that may influence the test performance of the individual. However, Reitan and Wolfson (1995) argued that the effects of age and education are minimal in brain-damaged individuals, as opposed to those without brain damage. Their results suggest that adjusting raw scores according to age and education may not be a clinically valid procedure for brain-damaged patients, and only tends to invalidate the raw scores of neuropsychological tests (Reitan & Wolfson, 1995). There is undoubtedly an association between the WAIS and the Halstead-Reitan test scores on one hand and normal aging effects on the other. However, this is not seen on the Halstead-Reitan battery of neuropsychological tests and is only seen to some extent on the WAIS in brain-damaged persons. The age and education factors seem to have been "washed out" by the cerebral damage, thus rendering age and education correction of test scores not only unnecessary but also inadvisable. Despite these conclusions, we still find it advisable to use participants of the same age, without brain damage or disorders, as controls in clinical neuropsychological research on older people as well as on younger people.

When looking at the history of the psychology of aging, Edward L. Thorndike (1928) claimed that the ability to learn steadily improves until 20 to 25 years of age and stays stable until the middle 40s. Thorndike did, however, underscore that there are large individual differences in this respect. In 1958, David Wechsler stated that every human capacity will, after a starting growth, reach its maximum and then start to decline. This decline is initially very slow, but will eventually accelerate considerably. At what age maximum is reached varies from ability to ability, but in most cases it is in the middle 20s. He stated that "nearly all studies dealing with the age factor in adult performance have shown that most human abilities, in so far as they are measurable, decline progressively after reaching a peak somewhere between ages 18 and 25" (Wechsler, 1958, p. 135). As soon as decline and decrement has started, the process continues uninterrupted. Accordingly, both IQ values and scaled subtest scores are increasingly adjusted for age after the age of 40.

By the middle 1970s, the notion of inevitable and pervasive age-related decline was greatly weakened. Baltes and Schaie (1974) emphasized the diversity of aging-cognition relations, plasticity in old-age abilities, and the marked individual differences that exist between older people. Theoretically and testwise, intellectual abilities have been divided into two broad categories, (a) *crystallized intelligence*, which refers to overlearned knowledge and skills that are based on formal and informal education, and (b) *fluid intelligence*, which represents abilities having to do with problem solving and reasoning (Cattell, 1963; Horn, 1970, 1982). Normal aging is characterized by a widening gap between fluid and crystallized intelligence or abilities. An example of a test with crystallized content is the WAIS information subtest, which is a test of academic knowledge. An example of a test with fluid content is the WAIS block design subtest. In this subtest the individual uses colored cubes to reproduce two-dimensional geometric designs.

Theoretically, fluid intelligence is more dependent on the current integrity of the CNS than crystallized intelligence, thus rendering fluid abilities more susceptible to age related decline and CNS damage. In normal aging, crystallized abilities may be expected to improve or remain stable with the passage of time, whereas fluid abilities may be predicted to decline because of decremental changes in the central and peripheral nervous system. This has to be taken into consideration when doing neuropsychological examination of older people. The decline in performance on the performance subtests with advancing age, and the comparative stability in performance on the verbal subtests, have been demonstrated in a number of cross-sectional (Botwinick, 1977) and longitudinal (Botwinick, 1977; Jarvik & Bank, 1983; Salthouse, 1991; Sands, Terry, & Meredith, 1989; Schaie, 1983; Wechsler, 1981) studies. Age-related decline has also been seen on most of the tests in the Halstead-Reitan neuropsychological test battery (Heaton, Grant, & Matthews, 1986). However, an interesting fact from a study by Schludermann and Schludermann (1983) is that some tests that are sensitive to brain damage, such as the Seashore Rhythm Test, are quite age resistant. The pattern of age-related cognitive decline has been referred to as the "classic aging pattern" by Albert and Kaplan (1980, p. 403).

It has been demonstrated that adult age differences on tests of reasoning are significantly attenuated by statistically controlling for simple processing speed (Salthouse, 1991; Schaie, 1989). For example, Salthouse (1991) found that age alone accounted for 17% to 19% of the variance in measures of fluid abilities among healthy 20- to 84-year-old adults using hierarchical multiple regression. After controlling for variance associated with simple comparison speed, the effect of age on reasoning tasks was reduced to less than 5% of the explained variance. Therefore older individuals will perform much more poorly on most timed tests than will younger individuals.

Functions that appear to be stable during aging include simple attention, primary and tertiary memory (immediate recall and long-time knowledge), and everyday communication through language. Crystallized verbal intelligence continues to improve throughout adulthood, and the ability to deal with practical problems of daily activities seems to increase with experience into old age if the individual stays healthy (La Rue, 1992). This latter point should not be confused with decrement in abstract problem solving.

To evaluate the above conclusions regarding the neuropsychological performance of older individuals it is necessary to know what kind of scientific methods were chosen in the studies cited. By and large, cross-sectional studies have demonstrated more pronounced impairment than longitudinal studies have in older individuals. Longitudinal studies have also shown that the impairment of cognitive functions starts later than what is typically concluded from cross-sectional studies. The only longitudinal study from Norway in this area has been performed by Sol Seim. She followed a group of people from age 13 to 70 (Seim, 1997). Evaluation of the data from the examination at age 70 have recently been presented. Among those who returned for retesting at age 70, there was a relatively stable within group rank, as measured by the Mønnesland IQ test (1936) and Raven's Progressive Matrix (1938). In Seim's study, the group mean IQ on Mønnesland was 117 at both 30 and 60 years of age. Although 37 participants obtained a lower score in 1984 than in 1956, 6 participants obtained the same score and 15 participants had a better score at age 60 than they did at age 30. Thus, the last subgroup showed an incremental development in cognitive performance. Seim concluded that there was no obvious or typical trend of decrement in intelligence at the age of 60. Some people show decrement at this age or before, whereas others are stable and still others show improved IQ score. Furthermore, she found that most of the participants who did not return for retesting had poor scores on their initial examination (Seim, 1988).

Anastasi proposed in 1954 that although the intelligent individual shows a positive acceleration in development at a higher age, the less intelligent person may show a deceleration. Thus, individuals who may show a decline in test scores may be more prone to drop out of such longitudinal studies. This may be at least part of the reason why longitudinal studies show later decline in test scores than cross-sectional studies.

Seim's conclusions for the participants at age 70 were largely the same as for those at age 60. In addition, she found an association between medical illness and decline in neuropsychological performance. This is in agreement with a large study from Gothenborg, "Intellektet väl bibehåldet" (the intellectual abilities well preserved), cited by William-Olsson and Svaneborg (1984). The population-based studies from Gothenborg also showed that the 70- to 75-year-olds of the 1980s were better functioning than a same age cohort studied 5 years earlier (William-Olsson & Svanborg). Furthermore, nine out of ten 79-year-old individuals were healthy and strong enough to live outside hospitals or nursing homes. The study showed, however, that one out of four 75-year-olds needed a hearing aid. They concluded that impaired memory is not an inevitable consequence of old age (William-Olsson & Svanborg). This study, as well as others, underscores that the variation is large with regard to cognitive abilities in the elderly, and that variation is large both across individuals and across cognitive domains within the individual.

The Seattle Longitudinal Aging Study (Schaie, 1983), showed that intellectual change across specific age intervals varies for different birth cohorts. For example, one comparison showed that individuals born in 1917 tended to decline in intellectual performance between the ages of 39 and 46 years, whereas those born in 1924 improved in performance across the same age span. When looking at the age span between 67 and 74 years, decline in test scores was much greater for individuals born in 1889 than for those born in 1896 (Schaie & Labovie-Vief, 1974; Confirmed by Hertzog & Schaie, 1986, 1988). On the basis of this study, decline seems to begin at some point between the ages of 55 and 70, with large individual differences in age of onset.

On the basis of the above research it is obviously necessary to have appropriate test material and reference data to evaluate the results from older patients who have been referred to neuropsychological evaluations with suspected CNS disorders. There are large individual variations in decrement of neuropsychological functions in healthy older people. This variation in neuropsychological performance among and within individuals makes neuropsychological assessment in older patients particularly challenging. This is, of course, of vital concern for neuropsychological test norm development for older human beings. A major concern in this respect is the age cohort differences. It may, for instance, not be appropriate to use 30-year-old scoring criteria or norms on the older person living today, but this is nevertheless done by many clinicians. Age-related neuropsychological decline, which presumably reflects normal cerebral changes, may, however, be quite different from neuropsychological impairment because of acquired brain pathology, as discussed previously.

Pathological Aging and Neuropsychology

As for younger people, there are many conditions that may elicit neuropsychological evaluation of older people. Questions related to different types of dementia and stroke are the most common, including differential diagnostic evaluation of depression versus CNS pathology. In such cases the tentative diagnosis may be dementia, and there may be a need to find out which type of dementia the patient has and whether depression is primary or secondary in the clinical picture. Such differential diagnostic assessment has important consequences for the choice of therapeutic and treatment procedure. However, the reason for referral to neuropsychological examination need not be a question about any specific diagnosis. It is becoming more usual than not to refer older people to evaluate specific behavioral problems or abilities related to such questions as keeping a driver's license. Questions regarding minor cognitive deficits, such as memory impairment, are also common.

The Clinical Interview

A thorough clinical interview is always an important part of the neuropsychological evaluation. It is important to interview both the patient and one or more individuals who know the patient well, usually a family member. This point is obvious if the patient has lost insight regarding his or her situation, but in our opinion it should serve as a general rule.

There are different opinions with regard to the order of testing and interviewing. Ralph Reitan (personal communication, December 1997) recommended that the interview be done when the patient's test results are available. He uses the expanded Halstead-Reitan test battery for all patients and his approach is to evaluate the test results blindly, without having any clinical information about the patient available to him at that time. In this way the clinical data do not bias the evaluation of the test performance. Other clinicians, such as Arthur Benton regard the neuropsychological examination as a clinical examination (Tranel, 1996), and not as a laboratory procedure. Accordingly, assessment procedures and tests are chosen on the basis of information about the patient. Thus, the neuropsychological test approach becomes a consequence of the clinical interview.

We usually interview both before and after testing. When testing older patients it is important for clinicians to get a clinical impression of the patients' mental and somatic health, which varies largely among individuals, before testing is performed. If this clinical interview reveals significant cognitive deficits, with impairment of higher intellectual abilities, language, or both, it is not appropriate for investigators to let the patient go through a long and demanding testing procedure. Expected test performance must, in other words, be evaluated to arrive at an appropriate degree of test intervention. When talking to the patient after testing it is important to discuss the test results and, if necessary, expand the neuropsychological examination. It is very important to observe the patient, to get the patient's impression of his situation and possible impairment, and to get extensive background information to be able to evaluate the test performance.

Stroke

The majority of strokes are cerebral infarctions, which account for about 80% of the cases. Cerebral hemorrhage account for about 10% to15% of stroke cases (Bowler & Hachinski, 1996). Stroke is the third leading cause of death after heart disease and cancer (Bonita, 1992). The incidence of stroke increases with increasing age, with higher number of strokes occurring in men than in women.

How the stroke will affect neuropsychological performance is a matter of where in the brain the infarction or hemorrhage is located, what kind of damage is caused, and the size of the lesion. Luria (1966) emphasized that brain damage causes syndromes of cognitive impairment and not just impairment of a few abilities. There are typical localizing signs, such as hemiplegia, which is caused by infarction in the motor area of the contralateral frontal lobe, or sensory difficulties related to damage of the parietal or occipital lobes. However, such major impairments are usually part of impairment of larger cognitive domains, particularly when the association cortex is involved. Most neuropsychological tests used assess several components of different cognitive skills, and each component may itself be subserved by different brain regions. A typical example of such a test is the Tactual Performance Test (Reitan & Davison, 1974), which among other components evaluates motor performance, tactile perception, visual imagination, executive functions, and visuo-spatial abilities.

We have repeatedly underscored that it is important to take into consideration the patient's ability to perform when doing the neuropsychological assessment. This can be well exemplified in stroke patients. Patients with pronounced language difficulties due to insults in the left cerebral hemisphere are much more difficult to assess with an extensive standardized battery like the Halsted-Reitan tests than are patients with right hemisphere involvement and no language difficulties. Patients with left cerebral hemisphere damage very often also show apraxia in the limbs, mouth, or both (Luria, 1966; Rothi, & Heilman, 1996).

Stroke patients often tire more easily than they are used to. In addition, emotional problems are quite usual. Both depression and anxiety are common parts of this clinical picture. The behavioral manifestations of emotional changes can often be seen as short episodes of crying, but laughter may also be easily elicited. Many of the patients who are referred to neuropsychological assessment have had several incidences of stroke, and there may also be a combination of cerebral infarctions and hemorrhages.

A typical example is presented in the following case of a 74-year-old right-handed patient with 18 years of education. He had an intracerebral hemorrhage about 9 months before the assessment. A CT had shown a 3.5 centimeter large intracerebral haematoma in the parietal lobe in his right hemisphere. There was some compression of the right lateral ventricle and some dilatation of the left lateral ventricle. There was also a small hypodense area in the parietal lobe that could be an old infarction. In addition, there was sign of a small, probable old infarction laterally to the left frontal horn. Prior to the mentioned hemorrhage, it was reported that the patient had two episodes of Transient Ischemic Attacks, but these did not lead to any extensive clinical examination. One month after the first hemorrhage the patient experienced a new stroke. In addition to the earlier findings, his CT revealed a new 2 x 2½ centimeter intracerebral hemorrhage to the left of the midline and rostrally to the corpus collosum. There were also a number of ischemic parenchymal changes compared with the first CT. After the first incidence the patient had language difficulties characterized as expressive aphasia by the physician who examined him. This problem did, however, disappear over the next 6 months. After the

Table 1.   WAIS IQ and Scaled Scores in a 74-year-old Man with Stroke 10 Months Ago

WAIS Test results			
Age: 74 year			
Verbal IQ = 116			
Performance IQ = 82	Difference = 34		
Total IQ = 102			
		Scaled scores	Age corrected
Information	=	13	14
Comprehension	=	10	17
Arithmetic	=	5	7
Similarities	=	13	16
Digit Span	=	10	15
Vocabulary	=	13	15
Digit Symbol	=	3	9
Picture Completion	=	9	14
Block Design	=	2	4
Picture Arrangement	=	0	0
Object Assembly	=	2	5
Wechsler deterioration index = 0.24			

second incident, the patient experienced that his handwriting had changed to the worse and that he had difficulties writing.

During the interview the patient had no problems telling about the incidences, but he could not remember the episodes clearly. He explained that his language difficulties were experienced as a problem completing sentences. His speech was a little staccato during the interview, but he had no problems finding words or expressing himself. He started to cry a couple of times during the interview, and seemed to be emotionally labile. He also reported that he was slightly unsteady when walking but that this had been worse shortly after the strokes. Further, he told about memory difficulties and used a notebook to keep track of things. He also had some difficulties finding his way around. During testing, which was done over several days, he cried easily, but wiped away the tears and said that in a way he had lost control over them. This did not seem to bother him much and he was well motivated and easy to work with during the examination.

The patient was tested with the WAIS, the Hopkins Verbal Learning Test, both simple and more complex drawing tests, most of the Halstead-Reitan tests, and motor and sensory tests. The results from the WAIS can be seen in Table 1. There was a difference between his verbal and performance IQ of 34 points. His lowest age-corrected scaled score was on the picture arrangement subtest where he was unable to solve any task. He also showed low scores on the block design, object assembly, and arithmetic subtests. His best scores were on the similarities and vocabulary subtests. The Hopkins Verbal Learning Test (HVLT;

Figure to be copied:

Trial 1.

Trial 2.

Trial 3.

Figure 1a.   Copy abilities in a 74-year-old man with strokes.

Brandt, 1991) is composed of 12 words that the individual is asked to recall. Memory functions are tested by three immediate recalls, followed by a delayed recall (20 minutes), and at last a recognition test where the patient is presented words and asked whether they have been presented previously. Half of the words that are presented are new and half of these new words belong to the same semantic category as the words that were presented previously. This last part of the test is very similar to cued recall.

The performance of the patient on the three immediate recalls was 4, 5, and 5 words, which is slightly under average performance for his age group. There was no memory loss during the 20-minute delay. His recognition of words showed a discrimination score of 8, which did not add much information with regard to his memory performance. The patient was also assessed with visual performance tests. This assessment started with a presentation of the four simple figures seen on Figure 1a, which he first copied, followed by an immediate

Copy part:

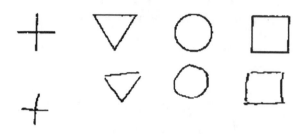

Immediate recall:
First trial:

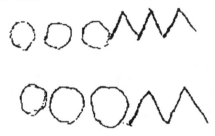

Second trial:

Third trial:

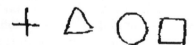

Delayed recall:

Figure 1b.   Figures that first should be copied and then recalled.

Figures to be copied:

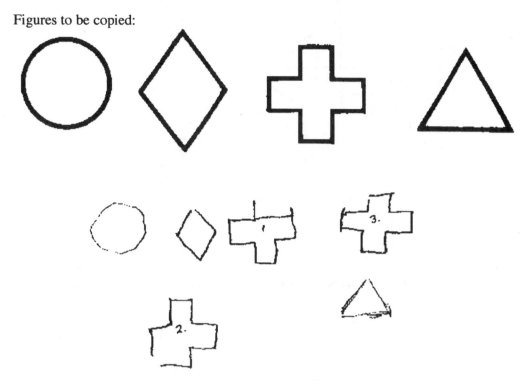

Figure 2.   Copy ability of simple figures in a 74-year-old man with strokes.

recall trial. This part of the memory testing revealed severe impairment, where parts of another drawing, which he did just before the memory part, were mixed into his recall. He was allowed to do the immediate recall three times with new exposures before each recall, and the results improved (see Figure 1b). On the delayed recall (20 minutes) the result was poor and he also made a perseverative error in that he drew a Greek cross that he had seen during another part of the examination. The visual memory tests were designed so that he had to draw the figures first, and he had great difficulties with his drawings. His drawings from the Aphasia Screening Test of the Halstead-Reitan test battery can be seen in Figure 2. The language content of the test was performed well. He had to use some time to figure out one of the naming questions and was a bit unsure about how to spell one of the words and asked if his spelling was correct. When he was asked to write words, he made two minor errors. Easy arithmetical tasks were completed correctly, but he used about 20 seconds to multiply 17 × 3.

The Rey Complex Figure Test (RCFT; Rey, 1941) was also administered, and he was allowed to work on the drawing until he thought it was satisfactory. He used 1½ hours to complete this task and the result can be seen in Figure 3. Usually this drawing is finished within 15 minutes in healthy older people. The delayed recall can be seen in the same figure. His difficulties are obvious. He performed poorly on most of the tests of higher cognitive functions, which can be seen in Table 2. He spent a long time on the Trail Making Test, but he managed to finish both parts A and B, in contrast to many patients with brain injuries. On

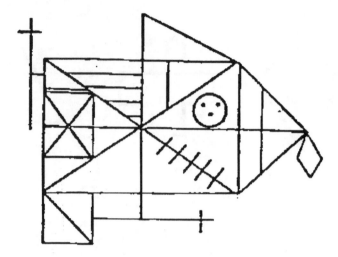

Copy part: The patient was allowed to use eraser (which clearly can be seen) to complete the figure as best as he could.

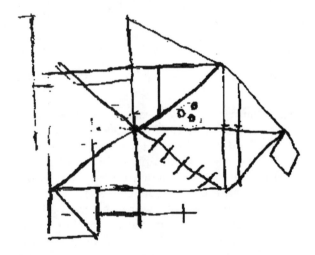

Delayed recall:

Figure 3. Copy ability of a complex figure in a 74-year-old man with strokes. Rey Complex Figure.

Table 2. Neuropsychological Test Results in a 74-Year-Old Man with Strokes

Male,   Age: 74 years,   Dominant hand: Right

Halstead-Reitan Tests

	Raw Scores	T Scores
Category Test	78	36
Tactual Performance Test Dominant Hand	Just 1 block	
Tactual Performance Test Non dominant Hand	Just 1 block	
Tactual Performance Both Hands	Just 3 blocks	
Tactual Performance Memory	3	19
Tactual Performance Location	0	31
Seashore Rhythm Test	19	27
Trail Making Test part A	154	0
Trail Making Test part B	350	0
Finger Tapping	35.6	42

Impairment index: 0.9

Knox Cube Test	8.5	25

MOTOR TESTS:

	T SCORES	
	Dominant	Nondominant
Finger Tapping Test	42	57
Foot Tapping	48	47
Dynamometer	52	53
Grooved Pegboard	0	0

SENSORY EXAMINATION: Raw Scores

	Dominant	Nondominant
Finger Agnosia	9	4
Sandpaper Test	67	66
Tactile forms	62 (1 error)	34
Fingertip write	8	7
Tactile Stimulation	0	
of Hands:	error bilaterally	
Auditory Stimulation	0	0

Visual field Stimulation	Right	Left
Upper	0	0
Lower	0	0

T SCORES

MOTOR STEADINESS TESTS:	Dominant	Nondominant
Maze Coordination Timer	23	41
Maze Coordination Counter	7	27
Vertical Groove Steadiness Timer	50	52
Vertical Groove Steadiness Counter	46	49
Horizontal Groove Steadiness Timer	49	52
Horizontal Groove Steadiness Counter	40	50
Resting Steadiness Timer	47	60
Resting Steadiness Counter	29	52

the Tactual Performance Test (TPT) he managed to place only one block with his right and then left hand and three blocks when both hands were tested. The three blocks were all remembered in the memory part of the test. Both the Seashore Rhythm Test and the Knox Cube Test yielded results more than two standard deviations below average for his age group. He performed very poorly on the Grooved Pegboard Test, which is a test of manual dexterity. Otherwise, he performed well on most motor tests. The motor steadiness test battery revealed minor impairment, indicating some tremor in the hands, with worse performance in the right relative to the left hand. On the sensory tests he performed worse with the right relative to the left hand on the tactile tests, but he had problems on both sides. He had no problems detecting auditory stimuli laterally or bilaterally and there was no indication of any visual field deficits.

In conclusion, the patient clearly showed moderate to severe neuropsychological impairment. Interpretation of his test performance clearly indicated that there were signs of bilateral CNS impairment, but the patterns of performance indicated that the right hemisphere was more involved than the left. His difficulties were particularly related to visuo-spatial functions, which can be seen clearly on the subtests from the WAIS, on the TPT, and in his drawing problems. This is probably because of his parietal lesions seen on the CT. There were pronounced memory problems and reduction of higher cortical functions as measured by the Trail Making Test, the TPT, and the Category test (the last one however, showed a slightly better result). There was also impairment of fine motor control. The patient probably functioned cognitively above average before the brain insults, which can be inferred from the many good scores on the verbal subtests of the WAIS. Thus the test results matched very well with the finding on CT. His language abilities were only mildly impaired, and only his writing created minor problems for him in his everyday life. The clinical interview revealed that the patient had emotional problems, which probably were related to his cerebral condition.

In treatment and rehabilitation work it is necessary to know as much as possible about which abilities are intact and which are not. This becomes particularly important when evaluating where it is important to obtain improvement. This patient was highly motivated for the neuropsychological evaluation and he exhibited a good ability to work hard over time. It was important for him to do as well as possible. It was also seen that when he worked to solve the tasks that were put in front of him, the results became much better by practice. It is crucial for this and other patients to gain insight into how the cerebral damage has altered their functions when trying to establish a new life after a stroke. This patient was moderate to severely impaired on the neuropsychological tests. However, he managed to complete most of them. Many stroke patients experience more language difficulties, apraxia, and perseveration, which makes it very difficult to complete a neuropsychological examination. However, the most important factors in restitution are motivation and planning abilities.

Dementia

Very often, when patients with dementia are asked if there is anything wrong with their memory, they will answer that nothing is wrong. If the patient does acknowledge memory decline, it is minimized or often attributed to circumstances, such as working excessively. Typical statements are "I have been working so much lately, so I need to have a rest," or "I am tired but there is nothing wrong with me."

One of the main difficulties, especially for Alzheimer's patients, is keeping track of time. The patient may, for instance, often have difficulties answering whether he or she was married before or after World War II, or how old their daughter or son is.

There are many different types of dementias. In the *Diagnostic and Statistical Manual of Mental Disorders*, 4th edition (*DSM-IV*, American Psychiatric Association, 1994), dementia is defined by the development of multiple cognitive deficits. There has to be memory impairment and at least one of the following: aphasia or language disturbance, apraxia, agnosia, or disturbances in executive dysfunctions. The observed deficits must be severe enough to cause significant impairment in social or occupational functioning. In the 60 to 64 year age range about 1% of the population has dementia; the prevalence at age 90 is about 30% of the population (Hofman et al., 1991).

There are some small gender differences in that there is a tendency for higher prevalence of dementia among young old men when compared with women (around 60 years), and somewhat higher prevalence of dementia in old old women compared with men. Perls (1995) calls this a crossover gender phenomenon. He speculates that because men die earlier from their dementia than women, older men, on the average, are more cognitively intact than women of similar age. Men are, however, at greater risk for vascular dementia than women (Gorelick, Mangone, & Bozzola, 1996).

Perls (1995) also questioned whether there is an increased risk of dementia as the individual grows older and concluded that this is true only to some extent. The incidence of dementia, and particularly of Alzheimer's disease, accelerates from the age of 60 through the 80s but then starts to decline (Perls, 1995). There is indeed evidence suggesting that some people may be particularly resistant to disorders that disable and kill most people before age 90, as exemplified by Jeanne Calmont, who died at 123 years of age, and other healthy centenarians.

The two most common types of dementia are Alzheimer's disease and Vascular Dementia. Because these two types of dementia represent the overwhelming majority of the dementing cases, data and examples presented in the following discussion will be of these two types. Alzheimer's disease accounts for 44% to 60% and Vascular Dementia accounts for about 10% to 45% of the cases (Adams & Victor, 1989; Bjertness, 1995; Gorelick, Mangone, & Bozzola, 1996). The relative proportions of these etiologies vary across studies. Earlier studies usually showed lower prevalence rates than more recent ones for vascular dementia. Also, a major proportion of the remaining progressive and irreversible dementias are found to have both Alzheimer's disease and vascular brain changes on autopsy. For one genotype, ApoE4, which is associated with Alzheimer's disease, there is an association with coronary and vascular disease (Kosunen et al., 1995). In many dementias there may be a comorbidity of depression. It has been observed that individuals who have both dementia and depression have a worse prognosis related to survival than those who have "just" dementia (Forsell, Jorm, & Winblad, 1994; O'Conner, Pollitt, & Roth, 1990).

Alzheimer's type of dementia is characterized by a gradual onset and continuing cognitive decline (American Psychiatric Association, 1994). There are at least two types of the disease. The first type has an early onset, 65 years old or younger, and the second has a late onset, 65 years old and older. However, the clinical symptoms are often very similar. Nonetheless, earlier onset of the disease has been associated with larger neuropsychological impairment when the duration of illness has been considered (Brandt et al., 1989).

The *DSM-IV* criteria regarding vascular dementia are quite similar to Alzheimer's disease, but neurological signs and symptoms that may be present in this disorder are also included. Cerebral infarctions are the most common cause of vascular dementia (Gorelick, Mangone, & Bozzola, 1996).

Alzheimer's disease may create damage in different parts of the brain, thus creating different kinds of behavioral disorders. In the cases of Alzheimer's disease, the anatomical changes in the brain are mostly seen in cortical areas, but also are seen in subcortical areas such as the hippocampus, gyrus cingulum, amygdala, nucleus basalis meynert, dorsal raphe nucleus, substantia nigra, and locus coeruleus. The hippocampus is always damaged bilaterally. The pathological hallmark of Alzheimer's disease is the development of neurofibrillary tangles and plaques in the mentioned areas. On autopsies, the number of tangles that can accumulate before clinical signs of Alzheimer's disease emerge varies greatly among individuals.

There have been a number of studies of cognitive performance and neurodegenerative markers. The best known is probably the study by Tomlinson, Blessed, and Roth (1968), who examined brains of patients with dementia and normal controls. They found a significant correlation between plaque counts and mental status. However, a study by Katzman et al. (1988) illustrated that some individuals have normal cognitive function despite increased plaque counts. That is, of the 29 cognitively normal individuals examined, 10 showed brain findings that were consistent with Alzheimer's disease. Brains in this group were on the average heavier than those of the other individuals, and they also contained more large neurons in several brain regions. The investigators speculated that these individuals may have had "incipient Alzheimer's disease" but did not show it behaviorally because of "greater brain reserve"(p. 138). Perhaps this is due to a slow build up of tangles, which the brain can adapt to. It is also possible that the higher number of neurons and synapses can compensate for the damaged brain cells. This may be illustrated by the epidemiological finding that individuals with higher education are less prone to develop dementia of Alzheimer's type, or at least show a later starting point for the disease, than are individuals with less education (Katzman, 1993; Ott et al., 1995).

A second important finding from the same study was that brains of dementia and nondementia patients in the very-old group, with a mean age of 85 years, did not differ as much as younger patient groups of dementia and nondementia patients. A final finding was that there was no autopsy evidence of Alzheimer-type pathology or other cerebral pathology that might have been the cause of poor performance for 11% of the patients with clinical dementia. The etiology of dementia in these cases was not determined. Morris, Storandt, Rubin, Mckeel, and Grand (1995), presented data from 21 older people with "normal" cognitive functioning. However, 7 of them were clinically rated as "questionably" suffering from dementia. On the basis of autopsy findings, participants were divided into those functioning normally and those with Alzheimer's disease for comparisons. Simple mental status examinations were not useful in differentiating between these groups although there were significant group differences in senile plaque densities. Furthermore, Morris et al. (1995) suggested that increasing age is associated with increased numbers of tangles in the hippocampus and that semantic memory and visuo-spatial tests may be more sensitive to Alzheimer's changes than simple mental status testing.

Accordingly, we emphasize that it is important to apply a battery of tests that tells something about intact abilities and the quality and quantity of impairment across a wide range of cognitive abilities. It is highly inadvisable to base a description of the cognitive impairment of the patient on only one or two neuropsychological tests. The Mini Mental Status Examination (MMSE; Folstein, Folstein, & McHugh, 1975) has become some kind of gold standard regarding diagnosis of dementia, evaluation of mental status, and assessment of the seriousness of the dementia. The MMSE has, however, been criticized because it says little about the quality of the behavior that is intact or impaired. It has also been criticized for being biased with a high verbal language content (Tombaugh & McIntyre, 1992). This means that individuals who have great language difficulties will perform very poorly on this mental examination but will still be fully oriented about time and place and will have a good memory. Their language problems may create difficulties for them. The MMSE also often fails to diagnose people with a high IQ who have a beginning dementia. Such individuals often perform in the normal range. Conversely patients with a low IQ may perform in the area of a mild dementia without having dementia.

When looking at the *DSM-IV* criteria for Alzheimer's disease, it is our clinical impression that impairment of memory functions, language, and visuo-spatial abilities are more usual than agnosias and apraxias, at least in the beginning of a dementing development of the Alzheimer's type. The same is usually the case in the vascular dementias if the dementing process starts with small infarctions in the subcortical areas of the brain. If the dementing process starts after a significant stroke, it is more usual to see motor impairment or localized neurological signs as sensory difficulties, apraxia (often in connection with language difficulties), and perseveration.

The memory difficulties of Alzheimer's disease are exemplified in Figure 4. In one of our studies (Hestad, Dybing, & Kløve, 1997), the Hopkins Verbal Learning Test was applied in an evaluation of memory difficulties in normal healthy older volunteers and patients who were referred to an outpatient geriatric clinic. The demographic data of the study population can be seen in Table 3. The patients were divided into three subgroups on the basis of clinical diagnosis: probable Alzheimer's disease, patients with different kind of cerebral injuries and diseases, and a group of patients where no cerebral injury was diagnosed. The Alzheimer patients performed worse than the other participants on most of the subtests on the HVLT. The two other patient groups performed similarly to the healthy volunteers on the first immediate verbal recall. How-

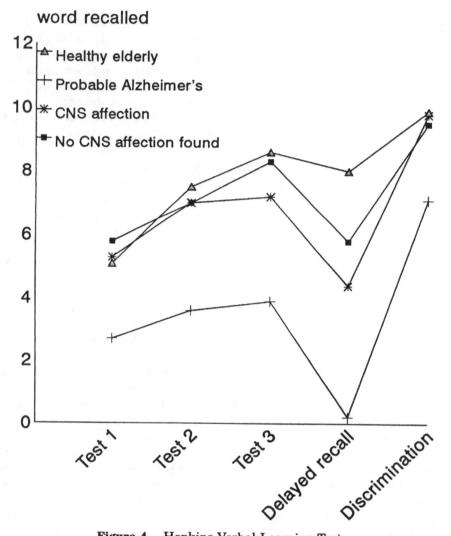

Figure 4. Hopkins Verbal Learning Test.

ever, their performance declined across trials as compared with the healthy volunteers. The trend was that the patient groups performed worse than the healthy group across immediate recall two and three. The performance on delayed recall was significantly below the healthy volunteers for all three patient groups, with the Alzheimer patients performing the worst. Most of the Alzheimer patients did not remember a single word; one of them remembered one word. The most typical clinical hallmark of Alzheimer's disease is the loss of the capacity to perform on explicit memory tests after a delay of some minutes. On the delayed recall, all patient groups scored significantly below the performance of the healthy group. The age of the two patient groups with best performance on the first immediate recall was significantly lower than the healthy comparison group, which probably explains the initial good performance.

An interesting and important point is that Alzheimer patients tend to ob-

Table 3. Boston Naming Test, Mean, (SD), Range, and p-Values Based on Nonparametric Statistics

Test item	Healthy elderly $N = 22$	Alzheimer's patients $N = 28$	Vascular and alcohol determined dementia $N = 7$	Chi-square p-values
The Boston Naming Test Spontaneous	43.36 (8.6) 22–58	26.92 (12.2) 5–48	27.28 (11.5) 14–45	29.56 <.0001
The Boston Naming Test After stimulus cues	51.09 (7.4) 28–60	28.25 (12.3) 5–48	27.71 (11.7) 14–46	32.69 <.0001
The Boston Naming Test After phonetic cues	54.90 (5.4) 34–60	30.53 (12.5) 5–50	27.71 (11.7) 14–46	37.05 <.0001
MMSE	28.8 (1.2) 25–30	17.2 (5.4) 6–26	21.0 (4.5) 15–27	40.30 <.0001

Note. The participants were not significantly different on age and education. MMSE = Mini Mental Status Examination.

tain relatively good scores on the recognition part of the test, as can be seen on the discrimination score in Figure 4. This is important because it probably means that there are traces of memory that can be used in reminiscence training of the patient to keep as much as possible intact in the patient's daily conversation and awareness. This tendency to make use of cues can also be seen in language tests with Alzheimer patients. Hestad, Dybing, Haugen, and Kløve (in press) applied The Boston Naming Test (Kaplan, Goodglass, & Weintraub, 1976) in an evaluation of anomic difficulties in normal healthy elderly volunteers and patients with dementia who were referred to an outpatient geriatric clinic. The Boston Naming Test is a well-known language test where the patient is asked to name pencil drawn objects. The patient's spontaneous answers are recorded. If the patient is unable to name the object, cues are given to help him or her. First stimulus cue in relation to naming a drawing of a bed is "a furniture." If the patient still does not manage to name the object he gets the phonetic cue "the word starts with *b*."

The different scores from the test are added, yielding a possible maximum score of 60. The patients were divided into two subgroups on the basis of clinical diagnosis and laboratory findings such as CT and PET: probable Alzheimer's disease and patients with dementia of vascular or substance abuse etiology. The patients with dementia performed much worse than the healthy volunteers on the Boston Naming Test, regardless of diagnosis. The difference between healthy participants and participants with dementia increased with both stimulus and phonemic cues. However, the Alzheimer's group improved their performance to some degree when the stimulus and phonemic cues were given. This was not the case for the vascular, substance-abuse group, as shown in Figure 5. Otherwise, it was not easy to discriminate between patients with

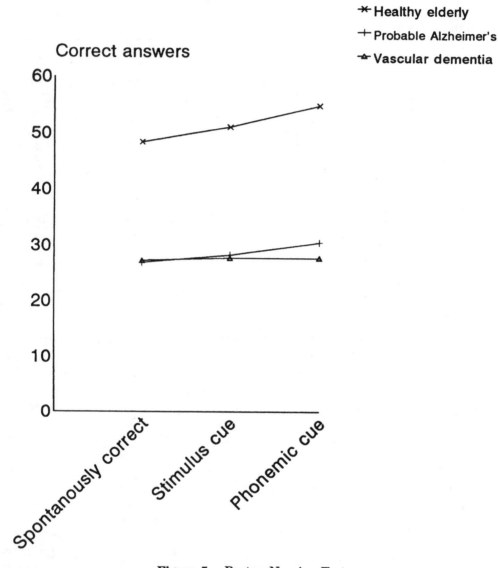

Figure 5.   Boston Naming Test.

Alzheimer's disease and vascular dementia on the basis of data from the Boston Naming Test, although the tendency was that individuals with Alzheimer's disease made use of cues in the naming procedure.

Besides the devastating memory and language difficulties found in individuals with Alzheimer's disease, there also can be visuo-spatial difficulties that can be seen on tasks of figure drawing. Very often, visuo-spatial difficulties cause patients to have problems finding their way around. Typical examples of figure copying from healthy individuals and patients with Alzheimer's disease and vascular dementia are presented in Figure 6, using the RCFT. There are both quantitative and qualitative scoring criteria for the RCFT (Bylsma, Bob-

A) A healthy 82-year-old man.

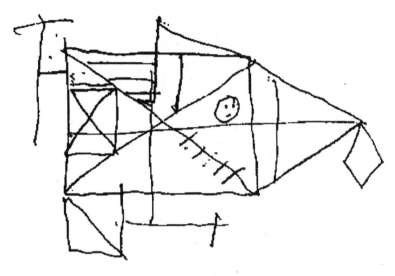

B) A 62-year-old woman with an mild early onset of probable Alzheimer's disease. She used more than 30 minutes to complete the drawing.

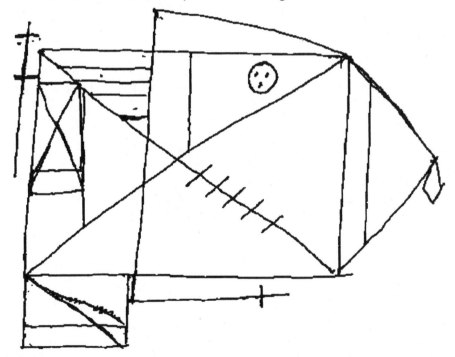

Figure 6.   Copies of Rey Complex Figure from one healthy older participant and three patients. The drawings are a little smaller than the originals to fit the pages (*figure continues next page*).

C) A 60-year-old patient with cognitive decline, possibly early Alzheimer's type.

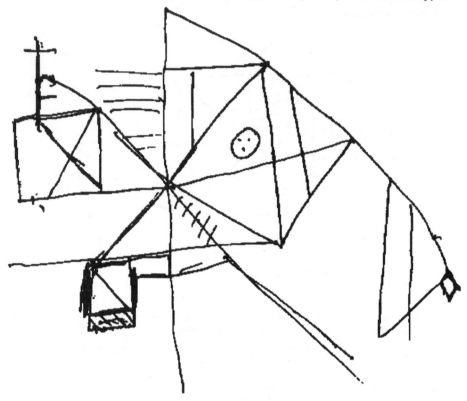

D) A 56-year-old man who developed delusions. His MMSE was 16. It was concluded that his delusions probably were related to dementia.

Figure 6. (*Continued*)

E) Six months later he was again referred to neuropsychological evaluation. His MMSE was now 24 and his Full Scale IQ was 88. The lowest WAIS age-scaled score was 5 (block design and arithmetic). After 8 to 9 months, he totally deteriorated. It was concluded that the patient was suffering from vascular dementia with delusions and plateau development.

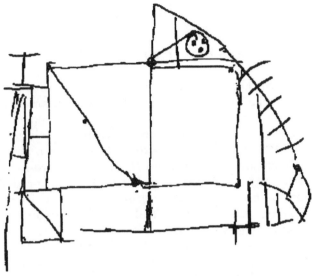

F) A 82-year-old male patient who suffered from severe depression.

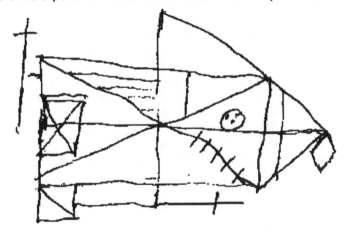

Figure 6.

holz, Schretlen, & Correa, 1995; Bylsma, Carlson, Schretlen, Zonderman, & Resnick, 1997; Lezak, 1983), which can facilitate the evaluation of the performance of the drawing part of the test.

As mentioned previously, differential diagnostic evaluation of dementia versus depression is a common cause of referral for neuropsychological evaluation. It is our experience that depressed persons may perform worse than healthy individuals on neuropsychological tests, but their performance is not even as similarly reduced as that found in beginning or moderate dementia. This can be exemplified by the RCFT of a 82-year-old man with severe depression. His performance is much more similar to healthy individuals than brain impaired patients (see Figure 6).

Terminal Drop or Decline

Occasionally, older individuals with minor symptoms of memory difficulties or revitalization are referred for neuropsychological assessment. Data from several longitudinal aging studies suggest that minor neuropsychological impairment may suggest dementia 2 to 4 years prior to the diagnosis or mortality (Johansson & Zarit, 1997). Individuals who show decline across successive testings are empirically closer to death than those with more stable performance, a phenomenon sometimes referred to as *terminal drop* or decline (Riegel & Riegel, 1972). Jarvik and Blum (1971) studied survival in twins. At each of several retest occasions, individuals who showed decline on certain *critical loss* tests (vocabulary, similarities, and digit symbol of the WAIS) were significantly more likely to die within 5 years after testing than those without such cognitive losses. Even stronger evidence was obtained when monozygotic twin pairs were studied: In 10 out of 11 pairs, the partner with a critical loss or decline in test score died first. None of the participants were actually ill at the time of assessment. However, many had chronic medical conditions, such as arteriosclerotic disease.

In these individuals, mild cognitive losses noted years prior to death may have been mirroring subclinical cerebral dysfunction caused by a medical disease. Likewise, these cognitive changes may correspond to cerebral blood flow declines found in people with hypertension, heart disease, or diabetes. Nonetheless, this kind of cognitive drop has also been seen in younger study participants. In studying HIV-1 infected drug users in a 3½ year follow-up study, Hestad, Aukrust, Ellertsen, and Kløve (1996) observed a decline in performance particularly on part B of the Trail Making Test for those participants who died during the study. They did not necessarily have AIDS at the time of death.

Conclusion

In general, the neuropsychological tests chosen for the evaluation of older adults have to adhere to basic psychometrical criteria and ideally yield as few false positives results as possible. It is recommended that the tests include measures of language and memory functions as well as nonverbal extra visuospatial tests of problem solving and tests of motor and sensory-perceptual abilities. The test battery should be as sensitive and specific as possible with regard to typical impairment in pathological aging, and they should discriminate maximally between normal aging and CNS disorders such as the different dementias. Ideally, the test battery should make it possible to differentiate among the most common types of dementia and between dementia and affective disorders.

It should, however, be kept in mind that depression quite often is a comorbidity of dementia and not a differential diagnosis.

References

Adams, R. D., & Victor, M. (1989). *Principles of neurology* (4th ed.). New York: McGraw-Hill.

Albert, M. S., & Stafford, J. L. (1986). Computed tomography studies. In M. S. Albert & M. B. Moss (Eds.), *Geriatric neuropsychology* (pp. 211–227). New York: Guilford Press.

Albert, M. S., & Kaplan, E. (1980). Organic implication of neuropsychological deficits in the elderly. In L. W. Poon, J. L. Fozard, L. S. Cermak, D. Arenberg, & L. W. Thompson (Eds.) *New directions in memory and aging: Proceedings of the George A. Talland Memorial Conference.* Hillsdale, NJ: Erlbaum.

American Psychiatric Association. (1994). *Diagnostic and statistical manual of mental disorders, (4th ed),* Washington, DC: Author.

Anastasi, A. (1954). *Psychological testing.* New York: Macmillan.

Baltes, P. B., & Schaie, K. W. (1974). Aging and IQ: The myth of the twilight years. *Psychology Today, 7,* 35–40.

Berg, L. (1988). The aging brain. In R. Strong, W. G. Wood, & W. J. Burke (Eds.), *Central Peruvians disorders of aging: Clinical inter-venation and research* (pp. 1–16). New York: Raven Press.

Bjertness, E. (1995). Forekomst av demens—hvilke tall kan man stole på [Prevalence of dementia—which numbers are to be trusted]. In Å-M. Nygård, A. Eek, K. Engedal, & Ø. Kirkevold (Eds.), *Ja, tænke det, ønske det, ville det . . .* [Yes, thinking it, wishing it wanting it . . .] (pp. 31–45). Oslo: INFO-banken.

Bland, R. C., Newman, S. C., & Orn, O. (1988). Prevalence of psychiatric disorders in the eldrely. *Acta Psychiatrica Scandinavica, 77,* 57–63.

Bonita, R. (1992). Epidemiology of stroke. *Lancet, 339,* 342–344.

Boone, K. B., Miller, B. L., Lesser, I. M., Mehringer, C. M., Itill-Gutiewez, E., Goldberg, M. A., & Bermah, N. G. (1992). Neuropsychological correlates of white-matter lesions in healthy elderly subjects. *Archives of Neurology, 49,* 549–554.

Botwinick, J. (1977). Intellectual abilities. In J. E. Birren & K. W. Schaie (Eds.), *Handbook of psychology of aging* (pp. 580–605). New York: Reinhold.

Bowler, J. V., & Hachinski, V. (1996). Epidemiologi of cerebral infarction. In P. B. Gorelick, (Ed.), *Atlas of cerebrovascular disease* (pp. 1.3–1.18). Chicago: Churchill-Livingstone.

Brandt, J. (1991). The Hopkins Verbal Learning Test: Development of New Memory Test with six equivalent forms. *The Clinical Neuropsychologist, 5,* 125–142.

Brandt, J., Mellits, D. E., Rovner, B., Gordon, B., Selnes, O. A., & Folstein, M. (1989). Relation of age at onset and duration of illness to cognitive functioning in Alzheimer's disease. *Neuropsychiatry, Neuropsychology, and Behavior Neurology, 2,* 93–101.

Bylsma, F. W., Bobholz, J. H., Schretlen, D., & Correa, D. D. (1995). A brief, reliable approach to coding how subjects copy the Rey-Osterrieth Complex Figure (CFT). *Journal of the International Neuropsychological Society, 1,* 148.

Bylsma, F. W., Carlson, M. C., Schretlen, D., Zonderman, A., & Resnick, S. (1997). Rey-Osterrieth Complex Figure Test (CFT) Q-Score performance in 328 healthy adults aged 20 to 94. *Journal of the International Neuropsychological Society, 3,* 70.

Cattell, R. B. (1963). Theory of fluid and crystallized intelligence: A cortical experiment. *Journal of Educational Psychology, 54,* 1–22.

Dahlstrom, W. G., Welsh, G. S., & Dahlstrom, L. E. (1975). *An MMPI handbook. Vol. 1. Clinical interpretation* (Rev. ed.). Minneapolis: University of Minnesota Press.

Danielsen, E. (1996). *Vygotsky. Psykologiens Mozart. Introduksjon til L. S. Vygotsky og den kulturhistoriske skole* [Vygotsky. The Mozart of psychology. An introduction to L. S. Vygotsky and the culture-historical school]. Copenhagen: Dansk Psykologisk Forlag.

Dekaban, A. S., & Sadowsky, D. (1978). Changes in brain weights during the span of human life: Relation of brain weights to body heights and body weights. *Annals of Neurology, 4,* 345–356.

Earnest, M. P., Heaton, R. K., Wilkinson, W. E., & Manke, W. F. (1979). Cortical atrophy, ventricular enlargement and intellectual impairment in the aged. *Neurology, 28,* 1138–1143.

Folstein, M. F., Folstein, S. E., & McHugh, P. R. (1975). "Mini-Mental State": A practical method for grading the cognitive state of patients for the clinician. *Journal of Psychiatry Research, 12,* 189–198.

Forsell, Y., Jorm, A. F., & Winblad, B. (1994). Outcome of depression in demented and nondemented elderly: Observations from a three-year follow-up in a community-based study. *International Journal of Geriatric Psychiatry, 9,* 5–10.

Grant, I., & Adams K. M. (Eds.). (1996). *Neuropsychological assessment of neuropsychiatric disorders* (pp. 81–101). New York: Oxford University Press.

Gorelick, P. B., Mangone, C., & Bozzola, F. (1996). Epidemiology of vascular dementia. In P. B. Gorelick (Ed.). *Atlas of cerebrovascular disease* (pp. 3.0–3.8). Chicago: Churchill-Livingstone.

Heaton, R. K., Grant, I., & Matthews, C. G. (1986). Differences in neuropsychological test performance associated with age, education, and sex. In I. Grant & K. M. Adams (Eds.), *Neuropsychological assessment of neuropsychiatric disorders* (pp. 100–120). New York: Oxford University Press.

Heaton, R. K., Grant, I., & Matthews, C. G. (1991). *Comprehensive norms for an expanded Halstead-Reitan Battery: Demographic corrections, research findings, and clinical applications.* Odessa, FL: Psychological Assessment Resources.

Hertzog, C. (1989). Influences of cognitive slowing on age differences in intelligence. *Developmental Psychology, 25,* 636–651.

Hertzog, C., & Schaie, K. W. (1988). Stability and change in adult intelligence: 2. Simultaneous analysis of longitudinal means and covariance structures. *Psychology and aging, 3,* 122–130.

Hertzog, C., & Schaie, K. W. (1986). Stability and change in adult intelligence: 1. Analysis of longitudinal covariance structures. *Psychology and Aging, 1,* 159–171.

Hestad, K., Aukrust, P., Ellertsen, B., & Kløve, H. (1996). Neuropsychological deficits in HIV-1 seropositive and seronegative intravenous drug users (IVDUs): A follow-up study. *Journal of the International Neuropsychological Society, 1,* 126–133.

Hestad, K., Dybing, E., & Kløve, H. (1997). Hukommelsestesing av eldre hvor det er mistanke om demens [Memory testing of elderly people with suspected dementia]. *Journal of the Norwegian Psychological Association, 34,* 483–488.

Hestad, K., Dybing, E., Haugen, P. K., & Kløve, H. (in press). Språkforstyrrelser hos demente pasienter undersøkt med Boston Naming Test [Language problems in demented patients as evaluated by the Boston Naming Test]. *Journal of the Norwegian Psychological Association.*

Hofman, A., Rocca, W. A., Brayne, C., Breteler, M. M. B., Clarke, M., Cooper, B., Copeland, J. R. M., Dartigues, J. F., Da Silva Droux, A., Hagnell, O., Heeren, T. J., Engedal, K., Jonker, C., Lindesay, J., Lobo, A., Mann, A. H., Molsa, P. K., Morgan, K., O'Connor, D. W., Sulkava, R., Kay, D. W. K., & Amaducci, L. (1991). The prevalence of dementia in Europe: A collaborative study of 1980–1990 findings. *International Journal of Epidemiology, 20,* 736–748.

Horn, J. L. (1970). Organization of data on life-span development of human abilities. In L. R. Goulet & P. B. Baltes (Eds.), *Life-span developmental psychology: Research and theory* (pp. 423–466). New York: Academic Press.

Horn, J. L. (1982). The aging of human abilities. In B. B. Wolman (Ed.), *Handbook of developmental psychology* (pp. 847–870). New York: Prentice-Hall.

Jarvik, L. F., & Blum, J. E. (1971). Cognitive declines as predictors of mortality in twin pairs: A twenty-year longitudinal study of aging. In E. Palmore & F. C. Jeffers (Eds.), *Prediction of life span* (pp. 199–211). Lexington, MA: Heath.

Jarvik, L. F., & Bank, L. (1983). Aging twins: Longitudinal psychometric data. In K. W. Schaie (Ed.), *Longitudinal studies of adult psychological development* (pp. 40–63). New York: Guilford Press.

Johansson, B., & Zarit, S. H. (1997). Early cognitive markers of the incidence of dementia and mortality: A longitudinal population-based study of the oldest old. *International Journal of Geriatric Psychiatry, 12,* 53–59.

Kaplan, E., Goodglass, H., & Weintraub, S. T. (1976). *Boston Naming Test,* (experimental ed.). Boston: Veterans Administrations Hospital.

Katzman, R., Terry, R., Deteresa, R., Brown, T., Davis, P., Fuld, P., Renbing, X., & Peck, A. (1988). Clinical, pathological and neurochemical changes in dementia: A subgroup with preserved mental status on numerous neocortical plaques. *Annals of Neurology, 23,* 138–144.

Kemper, T. (1984). Neuroanatomical and neuropathological changes in normal aging and in dementia. In M. L. Albert (Ed.), *Clinical neurology of aging* (pp. 9–52). New York: Oxford University Press.

Kløve, H. (1995). Klinisk nevropsychologi (Clinical neuropsychology). *The Journal of the Norwegian Medical Association, 115*, 1947–1951.

Kosunen, O., Talasniemi, S., Lehtovirta, M., Heinonen, O., Helisalmi, S., Mannermaa, A., Paljarvi, L., Ryynanen, M., Riekkinen, P. J., Sr., & Soininen, H. (1995). Relation of coronary atherosclerosis and apolipoprotein E genotypes in Alzheimer patients. *Stroke, 26*, 743–748.

La Rue, A. R. (1992). *Aging and neuropsychological assessment.* New York: Plenum Press.

Lezak, M. (1983). *Neurological assessment* (2nd ed.). New York: Oxford University Press.

Luria, A. R. (1980). *Higher cortical functions in man* (2nd ed.). New York: Plenum.

Martin, A. J., Friston, K. J., Colebatch, J. G., & Frackowiak, R. S. J. (1991). Decreases in regional cerebral blood flow with normal aging. *Journal of Cerebral Blood Flow and Metabolism, 11*, 684–689.

Miller, A. K. H., Alston, R. L., & Corsellig, J. A. N. (1980). Variation with age in the volumes of gray and white matter in the cerebral hemispheres of man: Measurements with an image analyzer. *Neuropathological and Applied Neurobiology, 6*, 119–132.

Mønnesland, K. L. (1936). *Gruppeprøver* [Group tests]. Oslo: Nordlis forlag.

Morris, J. C., Storandt, M., Rubin, E. H., Mckeel, D. W., Jr., & Grand, E. A. (1995). Clinical, psychometric, and pathological distinctions between very mild Alzheimer's disease and normal aging. *Journal of the International Neuropsychological Society, 1*, 351.

O'Conner, D. W., Pollitt, P. A., & Roth, M. (1990). Coexisting depression and dementia in a community survey of the elderly. *International Psychogeriatry, 2*, 45–53.

Ott, A., Breteler, M. B., van Harskamp, F., Claus, J. J., van der Cammen, T. J. M., Grobbee, D. E., & Hofman, A. (1995). Prevalence of Alzheimers's disease and vascular dementia: Association with education. The Rotterdam study. *The British Medical Journal, 310*, 970–973.

Perls, T. T. (1995). The oldest old. *Scientific American, 272*, 50–55.

Pfefferbaum, A., Lim, K. O., Rosenbloom, M., & Zipursky, R. B. (1990). Brain Magnetic Resonance Imaging: Approches for investigating schizophrenia. *Schizophrenia Bulletin, 16*, 453–476.

Pfefferbaum, A., Zatz, L. M., & Jernigan, T. L. (1986). Computer-interactive method for quantifying cerebrospinal fluid and tissue in brain CT scans: Effects of aging. *Journal of Computer Assistant Tomography, 10*, 571–578.

Raven, C. J. (1938). *Progressive matrices: Sets A, B, C, D and Testimonial.* London: H.K. Lewis.

Reitan, R. M., & Davison, L. A. (1974). *Clinical neuropsychology: Current status and applications.* New York: Hemisphere.

Reitan, R., & Wolfson, D. (1995). Influence of age and education on neuropsychological test. *The Clinical Neuropsychologist, 9*, 151–158.

Rey, A. (1941). L'examen psychologique dans les cas d'encephalopathie traumatique [Psychological examination of traumatic encephalopathy cases]. *Archives de Psychologie, 28*, 286–340.

Riegel, K. F., & Riegel, R. M. (1972). Development, drop, and death. *Developmental Psychology, 6*, 309–316.

Rothi, L. J. G., & Heilman, K. M. (1996). Liepman (1900 and 1905): A definition of apraxia and a model of praxis. In C. Code, C. W. Wallesch, Y. Joanette, & A. L. Lecours, (Eds.), *Classic cases in neuropsychology.* London: Psychology Press.

Salthouse, T. A. (1991). Mediation of adult age differences in cognition by reductions in working memory and speed of processing. *Psychological Science, 2*, 179–183.

Sands, L. P., Terry, H., & Meredith, W. (1989). Change and stability in adult intellectual functioning assessed by Wechsler item responses. *Psychology and Aging, 11*, 79–87.

Schaie, K. W. (1983). *Longitudinal studies of adult psychological development.* New York: Guilford Press.

Schaie, K. W. (1989). Perceptual speed in adult hood: Cross-sectional and longitudinal studies. *Psychological Aging, 4*, 443–453.

Schaie, K. W., & Labouvie-Vief, G. (1974). Generation versus ontogenetic components of change in adult cognitive behavior: A fourteen year cross-sequential study. *Developmental Psychology, 10*, 305–320.

Schludermann, E. H., & Schludermann, A. N. (1983). Halstead's studies in the neuropsychology of aging. *Archives of Gerontology and Geriatrics, 2*, 49–172.

Seim, S. (1988). *Tenåringen blir voksen og eldre. Intelligens og personlighet fra 13 til 30 til 60 år* [The teenager grows up and becomes older. Intelligence and personality from 13 to 30 to 60 years of age] (NGI rapport 8). Oslo: Norsk Genontologisk Institutt.

Seim, S. (1997). *Tenåringen blir pensjonist* [The teenager reaches retirement] (Rapport 23). Oslo: Norsk institutt for forskning om oppvekst, velferd og aldring.

Thorndike, E. L. (1928). *Adulate Leavening*. New York: MacMillan.

Tombaugh, T. N., & McIntyre, N. J. (1992). The Mini-Mental State Examination: A comprehensive review. *Journal of American Geriatrics Society, 40,* 922–935.

Tomlinson, B. E., Blessed, G., & Roth, M. (1968). Observations on the brains of nondemented old people. *Journal of Neurological Science, 7,* 331–356.

Walsh, K. W. (1978). *Neuropsychology. A clinical approach*. Edinburgh, Scotland: Churchill-Livingstone.

Wechsler, D. (1955). *Wechsler Adult Intelligence Scale*. New York: The Psychological Cooperation.

Wechsler, D. (1958): *The Measurement and Appraisal of Adult Intelligence* (4th ed.). Baltimore, MD: Williams and Wilkins.

Wechsler, D. (1981). *Wechsler Adult Intelligence Scale* (rev.). New York: Psychological Corporation.

Wechsler, D. (1987). *WMS-R. Wechsler Memory Scale—Revised. Manual*. San Antonio: The Psychological Corporation.

William-Olsson, M., & Svanborg, A. (1984). *Gammal eller ung på äldre dar* [Old or young in older days]. Malmø, Sweden: Utbildningsproduktion.

23

Psychotherapy With Older Adults

Inger Hilde Nordhus, Geir Høstmark Nielsen,
and Gerd Kvale

The general question addressed in this chapter is whether psychotherapy is a beneficial treatment modality for older adults. An obvious way of answering this question is to review relevant conceptual formulations and empirical studies describing effectiveness of various treatment approaches. Despite historical pessimism about the ability of older people to change and thus benefit from psychotherapy, recent empirical and clinical literature indicates that psychotherapeutic techniques can be effective in ameliorating psychological distress in older adults (Teri & Logsdon, 1992). Nevertheless, many psychologists avoid becoming involved in the provision of clinical services to the older segment of the population (Gallagher-Thompson & Thompson, 1995). Hence, the current challenge facing psychologists is to realize why late life is increasingly important for clinicians, implying competence development through clinical practice with older people.

In a recent volume on psychotherapy and aging, Zarit and Knight (1996) pointed to the need for clinicians to develop competence through their own ongoing education, emphasizing that the demand for treatment greatly exceeds the number of clinicians with formal training in geropsychology. Geropsychology has been slowly emerging as a specialty area within clinical and counseling psychology. Until now, few training programs have offered specialization in the field. The wide array of professional skills needed by geropsychologists is currently being defined, among which practicum and internship experiences are central elements.

During our implementation of a supervised clinical training program for psychology graduate students, a series of recurrent themes has been brought to our attention. Framed as questions from our students, these are, Do elderly people suffer from specific psychological distress and mental diseases? Do they have to deal with age-specific issues? Are there common problems that bring older adults into psychotherapy, and if so, what does this imply in terms of therapeutic strategies and modifications? Basically, these questions all relate to what extent chronological age is an informative variable for therapeutic work.

With these questions in mind, we first focus on central diagnostic and developmental issues critical in therapy planning, followed by a brief overview of recent empirical approaches to psychotherapy with older adults. The further discussion is largely based on our experience from implementing a training program applying individual psychotherapy with older adults in a university outpatient clinic. The theoretical and conceptual basis for the training program is presented, with case vignettes illustrating similarities and differences in therapeutic considerations as compared with younger age groups. To capture the complexity of the general question raised, we relate the discussion to the broader context of mental health needs of older adults as well as services offered.

Diagnostic Issues

Epidemiological information about the most common psychological or psychiatric disorders of late life, describing risk factors and prognostic data, presents a number of factors that combine to make mental health needs an issue of great importance. This information has demonstrated problems related to case identification, which eventually has formed the basis for age-specific hypotheses on mental disorders. Depending on assumptions about life expectancy, older adults 85+ years of age continue to increase, an increase indicating that not just individuals affected by dementia will increase. Because the baby boom cohort already has shown relatively high rates of depression, anxiety, and substance abuse, we can anticipate that these trends will accompany them into old age (Gatz & Finkel, 1994).

Deriving prevalence figures from various sources, Gatz and Smyer (1992) estimated the 1-year prevalence of all mental disorders among persons 65 and older at 20% to 22%. For most conditions other than the dementias, however, rates are lower in older adults than in younger age groups. Relying on data from the Epidemiologic Catchment Area (ECA) Survey, the most common psychological or psychiatric disorders of later life are specific anxiety disorders: phobic disorder (standardized 1-month prevalence of 4.8% for those 65+ years of age); dysthymic disorder (or chronic depression; 1.8%); and major depression (<1%; 0.4% in men and 1.4% in women). The rate of major depression was found to be about one fourth of that reported in adults age 18 to 44 (Regier et al., 1988).

The assumption that aging is associated with an increased risk of depression is a recurring theme in gerontological literature, and reported rates of depression vary greatly according to the scales and diagnostic criteria used. Although the prevalence of major depression is relatively low among older people, a substantial proportion report high levels of depressive symptomatology (Williamson & Schulz, 1992). Two interrelated explanations are given: The first is related to the prevalence of physical illness in old age. Somatic symptoms associated with depression include sleep and appetite disturbances; endorsement of these and related symptoms may reflect the development of physical conditions rather than depression. On the other hand, a factor repeatedly shown to be associated with affect disturbance, most commonly depressive symptoms, is physical illness or disability (Koenig & Blazer, 1992). The second explanation is that dysphoria and other more delimited forms of psychological distress seem to be more frequent in old age and as such may be indicative of specific age-related symptomatology (Newmann, 1989). The distinction between a clinical syndrome of depression and symptoms indicative of reduced life satisfaction is not always elaborated, however, whether it is an artifact or has substantial clinical value.

The question of diagnostic equivalence between younger and older adults also has been approached from a methodological perspective, considering older adults less likely to report or admit having psychological problems, because either they are less likely to admit having psychiatric symptoms, therefore preferring somatic presentations of their problems, or they perceive their problems in terms of a more general health decline (Tweed, Blazer, & Ciarlo, 1991). It has been argued that older adults are more likely to have depressive symptoms that do not fit into the currently available diagnostic categories (Tweed et al., 1991). But in the absence of consensus regarding definition and measurement of depression in old age, it may be difficult to appreciate the clinical significance of the milder symptom clusters. There is reason to believe that older adults with subclinical levels of depression or with somatic presentations of such symptoms are currently being treated for their somatic symptoms in the primary care setting and that they seldom are assessed in preparation for psychological treatment.

Data from the ECA survey showed that the combined prevalence of panic disorder, obsessive–compulsive disorder, and phobias ranged between 5.7% and 33% (Regier et al., 1988). Phobias were found to be the most common psychiatric disorder in older women and the second most common in older men. In a review and critique of the ECA data, Blazer, George, and Hughes (1991) indicated that the lower prevalence reported for all types of anxiety disorder among older adults (65+ years of age) may possibly be a consequence of underreporting in the older age group caused by a higher threshold for reporting these symptoms. They hypothesized that if and when that threshold was reached, the older people probably would seek assistance. According to Livingston and Hinchliffe (1993), it is likely that older people are able to prevent anxiety attacks by avoidance strategies, often at the cost of greater dependency or disability. Still, Blazer et al. documented that both 6-month and lifetime prevalence of all anxiety disorders declined somewhat from the middle-aged to the older group, although a combined prevalence of 19.7% for the 6-month period and approximately 34% for lifetime (all anxiety disorders) was found. They argued that these data suggest that anxiety is a significant problem in later life and therefore requires recognition and treatment. Burvill (1987), in his critique of the ECA data, pointed out that because presence of generalized anxiety disorder (GAD) was not consistently assessed, the prevalence of anxiety may well have been underestimated. In addition, it has been maintained that multiple symptoms of anxiety may exist in an older adult, without necessarily meeting specific diagnostic criteria for an anxiety disorder (Gurian & Miner, 1991). Overall, however, it is agreed that 10% to 20% of older adults experience clinical levels of anxiety and would benefit from treatment (Sheikh, 1992).

When mental health needs in late life have been unrecognized and untreated relative to other age groups, older adults have not been targeted as an actual population for mental health services. They are more likely to be treated by general medical practitioners. Low use of mental health services by older people, therefore, often implies that their mental health problems are embedded in other health care systems. Insufficient mental health referrals from general medical providers hold serious implications for older people, influencing effectiveness as well as appropriateness of treatment. When older people enter psychotherapy, the mental health practitioner needs to know that various forms of affective distress may be expressed in more somatic frames in old age. Besides, the fact that older people are at greater risk for medical health problems makes an understanding of diagnostic issues a critical element of case formulation.

Developmental and Aging Issues

The assumption that older adults must cope with specific developmental issues originated with Erikson (1963, 1968), who translated psychosexual stages into ego development and focused attention on developmental tasks of later life. Erikson assumed the existence of unresolved developmental conflicts throughout the life span, the focal themes of the second half of life being generativity versus stagnation (middle age) and integrity versus despair (young old adult). These focal themes are perceived as normative developmental transitions and are elaborated in more recent texts as major developmental tasks of late adulthood (e.g., Calarusso & Nemiroff, 1991). One implication of this perspective is that any meaningful psychotherapeutic approach must take into consideration the psychological tasks of this developmental epoch with which older adults are dealing. To the extent that aging involves the experience of personal (e.g., physical), interpersonal (e.g., loss of spouse), or social (e.g., occupational) loss, the patient must reintegrate his or her sense of self based on changes in the psychological, physical, or social spheres.

The normative aspect of late life development was elaborated by Butler (1963), who argued that reminiscence was a normal activity of later life and that life review therapy would be especially appropriate to older adults (Lewis & Butler, 1974). Several techniques for the psychotherapeutic use of the life review are described. The basic approach involves asking the patient to write or tape aspects of a biography, allowing the therapist to notice areas emphasized as well as excluded. The person's life work, then, may be an organizing factor with regard to identity and self-esteem. Tobin (1991) suggested that the use of the past to recapture and reaffirm the current self works particularly well with older people in comparison with people of other ages. The usefulness of the past apparently is not a function of its length per se but rather of how it can be used to maintain a constancy of the self when confronted with age-associated decrements and losses. It has been maintained that caution should be exercised with patients whose current perspectives are focused on bad images of the past or re-creations of intense traumatic experiences (Sadavoy, 1994).

McAdams (1993) amplified Erikson's concept of generativity as continuous with identity. The life story report may be a significant indicator of well-being by late life, as would be predicted by Butler's (1963) concept of life review. Reminiscence as therapeutic strategy, then, is the means by which the life story is further elaborated. The adequacy of the normative model has been questioned in terms of the relevance of telling one's life story in a therapeutic context. McAdams (1990) suggested that older people may move "beyond story making" (p. 153) and then prefer focusing on their present life. In a study of older women's life histories, Ruth and Öberg (1992) reported that the women had difficulty seeing their lives as continuous and coherent stories. Ruth and Öberg also noted that the women described their lives more in relation to significant others and more often presented a "we" story than an "I" story. Observations in clinical as well as nonclinical contexts suggest that for some, a sense of having lived a continuous life is not at all apparent. Therefore, the therapeutic focus should vary, balancing past history and present needs.

A more recent variant of life story as a central therapeutic strategy with older patients was described by Viney (1993). By unifying personal construct therapy (derived from Kelly, 1955) with narrative treatment approaches, Viney (1993) gave accounts of elders' stories in three dimensions: *self-limiting* stories, such as, "I worry about the future"; *self-empowering* stories, such as "I enjoy my life now"; or *age-related (developmental)* stories, which are more or less related to age-cohort-shared experiences (e.g., retirement). In addition to her focus on how the individual creates more or less disruptive constructs about his or her life, this approach illustrates how age is conceived of as a relative and not a normative therapeutic issue. Some stories may be age related; others may not be.

The psychological developmental process may be understood in terms of experience. As people age, they are exposed, both as age cohorts and as individuals, to a large variety of problems. Through this process, they come to learn which types of coping strategies are generally ineffective and which types can best achieve their goals. They also may develop *vulnerabilities* and *self-constricting* adaptational styles. Balanced against a potential increase in coping repertoire, however, is the fact that older adults are not, by virtue of their age, experts at dealing with problems related to functional or other types of losses. Various types of losses can be accompanied by growing constraints and the need for greater efforts to maintain a sense of control and efficacy. Atchley (1991) elucidated some of the possible consequences of the more serious challenges of health or relational loss: interrupted continuity in way of life, need for more extreme coping methods, reduced capacity to use defenses otherwise used, rusty skills in using feedback from others, and changes in reference groups.

The point to be underscored is that age itself is not stressful but certain conditions associated or combined with age may be. Even these conditions do not uniformly impinge on the lives of people of the same age. Also, many of the challenges that occur in the latter stages of the life course are not abrupt or discrete events. They are more or less scheduled or expected events. One may, therefore, prepare for transitions by the process of *anticipatory* coping. Some losses will come suddenly and be followed by other losses. Still, what makes a loss and what regulates duration and severity must be seen within circumstances preceding and following it, together with the actual coping strategies used. To conceptualize late-life problems in terms of pure topical issues or themes can at best lead to simplistic descriptions and not to any essential degree contribute to augmenting diagnostic and therapeutic skills. How each person adapts in response to changes and losses is a critical therapeutic factor. This factor is more a matter of individual variability than how older people as a group adapt (Papouchis & Passman, 1993). We now turn to a brief presentation of central empirical studies addressing the question of whether psychotherapy works.

Empirical Investigations

Recent reviews on psychotherapy with older adults present a convergent picture of the efficacy of varieties of psychotherapy and psychosocial interventions (Gallagher-Thompson & Thompson, 1995). Attention is increasingly focusing on short-term psychotherapy, and controlled studies have been performed to evaluate efficacy of the various approaches. Studies reviewed include brief forms of cognitive, behavioral, psychodynamic, personal construct, and control mastery therapies (Gallagher-Thompson & Thompson, 1995). Several studies also have compared the effectiveness of different forms of psychotherapy.

A comprehensive series of comparative studies of individual short-term (16–20 sessions) outpatient psychotherapy with depressed older people (experiencing a current episode of major depressive disorder) has been conducted (Gallagher-Thompson, 1992; Thompson & Gallagher, 1984; Thompson, Gallagher, & Breckenbridge, 1987), comparing cognitive, behavioral, and brief psychodynamic approaches. About 70% of those completing treatment in all groups demonstrated substantial improvement across treatment approach, whereas patients placed in a waiting list control group did not demonstrate improvement (Thompson et al., 1987). A 2-year follow-up study showed a comparable extent of maintenance of treatment gains in all three groups (Gallagher-Thompson, Hanley-Peterson, & Thompson, 1990).

A study among older caregivers of impaired relatives, comparing brief psychodynamic therapy with cognitive–behavioral therapy, revealed that efficacy of each approach was related to length of caregiving (Gallagher-Thompson & Steffen, 1994). Psychodynamic therapy worked better with those caregivers who were new to caregiving (less than 44 months), whereas those who had served longer as caregivers improved more with cognitive–behavioral therapy. At a 1-year follow-up, these gains were maintained (Teri, Curtis, Gallagher-Thompson, & Thompson, 1994).

Studies comparing cognitive and behavioral approaches with other forms of psychotherapy have generally reported only minimal differences. Recent findings from meta-analyses of 17 controlled empirical studies indicated that treatment (cognitive, psychodynamic, reminiscence, and eclectic) was reliably more effective than no treatment on both self-rated and clinician-rated measures of depression (Scogin & McElrath, 1994). The fact that only minimal differences among treatment approaches were found may be related to the possibility that patients who benefit more from a specific treatment have been randomly dispersed across treatment modality and, as such, minimize intertreatment differences (Beutler & Clarkin, 1990). Findings of variable response to treatment need further exploration to reveal potential effects of individual difference and variation in client variables.

From a health service perspective, it is generally accepted that pharama-cotherapy is the most manageable, if not necessarily the most effective, approach to treatment of affective disorders in older adults. However, a general implication drawn by Scogin and McElrath (1994) is that psychotherapy compares favorably with results of studies using antidepressant medication (mean *d* = .57; Schneider, 1994) as treatment modality and, as such, challenges endorsement of pharmacotherapy as the optimal treatment of choice for late-life depression. Also, caution is required in the administration of psychotropic medication to older patients, both because of the presence of age-related biological modifications and because of the possibility of somatic comorbidity (Higgitt, 1992). Numerous studies have identified an overrepresentation of older people among those receiving long-term prescriptions of benzodiazepines (e.g., Higgitt, 1992), although patterns of noncompliance among community-dwelling older people are revealed in some studies (e.g., Lepola, Leinonen, & Koponen, 1994). A growing awareness of considerable self-administration of medication has alarmed health authorities, and alternative treatment models are needed.

Implementing a Psychotherapy Program

Theoretical and Conceptual Position

Over the years, thinking about therapy has evolved under the influence of several sources, inside and outside psychodynamic circles. Of particular importance to our present approach are recent developments within relational psychoanalysis (see, e.g., Mitchell, 1988; Wachtel, 1997) and psychoanalytic self psychology (see, e.g., Muslin, 1985). Influence from cognitive–behavioral theories and systems theory has also been significant. Individual members of our clinical staff differ as to how strongly they endorse particular theoretical statements from the various schools. Hence, for the sake of inclusion, in this brief account of our theoretical and conceptual position, we stay at a fairly high level of abstraction.

At the most general level, our approach may be classified as *integrative psychodynamic*, meaning that various therapeutic techniques and interventions may be productively combined within the same, psychodynamically informed, treatment (Wachtel, 1993, 1997). The model builds on the assumption that clinically, psychopathology can be meaningfully described in terms of vicious cycles in the patient's interaction with other people. In his or her attempt to achieve a goal, such as to satisfy need gratification or to establish satisfying relationships with others, the patient typically acts in ways that create an unwitting repetition of past disappointments and traumatic experiences. At the center of this ironic situation is the patient's characterologically based defenses and pathogenic beliefs (acquired from early traumas) about herself or himself and others (Weiss & Sampson, 1986). Together, these defenses and beliefs impede the patient's functioning, adversely affect his or her self-esteem, and make him or her vulnerable to feelings of guilt, shame, anxiety, and emotional pain. Accordingly, a general therapeutic challenge is to help the patient interrupt life-constricting vicious circles. This may imply that the patient learns new ways of integrating experience and more flexible and adaptive ways of relating. Such learning might most profitably start within the relatively safe, respectful, and confiding climate of the consulting room.

While retaining basic psychodynamic concepts such as unconscious motivation, conflict, anxiety, and defense, the integrative model implies *cyclical processes* by which internal states and external events continually re-create the conditions for the recurrence of the other (Wachtel, 1994). Opposing the view of unconscious motives as always independent variables, in a cyclical perspective, such motives might well turn out to be dependent on how the person characteristically relates to other people. In other words, unconscious wishes, fantasies, and motives are as likely to result from a person's interpersonal behavior as to cause it. Causality is being defined in circular rather than linear terms.

To succeed in evoking meaningful therapeutic change, the therapist must actively attend to repetitive cyclical maladaptive patterns in the patient's interpersonal behavior. These patterns will unavoidably unfold also within the therapy context (the transference). By being subject to the patient's unwitting attempts to draw her or him into particular (transferentially determined) roles, the therapist is in a unique position to identify and to emphatically respond to the more subtle aspects of the patient's maladaptive interpersonal style and defensive maneuvers.

In a cyclical perspective, the traditional question of what comes first: insight or behavioral change? is no longer meaningful. Because the cycle has no clearly defined beginning or end, it is—in principle—possible to interrupt at any point. That is, insight may generate change in behavior, and new behavior may as well generate new insight. The two continuously and reciprocally act on each other. Furthermore, appropriately induced changes in the patient's physical or social environment may have a positive influence on both experience and behavior.

Thinking about psychopathology in cyclical rather than linear terms has the additional advantage that change may be brought about by different therapeutic strategies and tactics. For example, with a well-grounded psychodynamically informed case formulation, and a well-established therapeutic alliance, the therapist may choose to combine dynamic explorative and more supportive–didactic techniques (e.g., exposure training and homework assignments) within one treatment. In many cases, such integrated therapeutic approaches have a synergistic effect on the patient's improvement.

With a majority of the therapies in our clinic organized according to brief or short-term formats, the therapeutic interchange is usually focused on troublesome issues in the here and now. The patient is seen as an individual who struggles with adaptive tasks, more or less typical for his or her age group. This should not be understood as a recommendation for one-sidedly pursuing so-called developmentally appropriate goals, such as accommodating to one's forthcoming retirement or possible physical impairment or accepting one's own mortality. In our experience, to emphasize such issues too strongly with physically healthy older patients may be very counterproductive and even border on ageism (Martin & Wilson, 1984).

In principle, to identify critical adaptive tasks and appropriate treatment goals is not different for older patients. This follows from the very fact that there is no single, coherent, easily defined group that makes up older people. Hence, selection of an appropriate therapeutic focus and the setting of meaningful treatment goals always should be tailored to the individual. As with younger patients, the number of possible complaints and troublesome life issues is legion, even though issues related to bodily function, family development, and loss—for obvious reasons—turn up more frequently than in therapies with adolescents and younger adults.

A patient's efforts to master a given challenge or adaptive task may be hampered either by factors in the present life situation or, more typically, by lifelong maladaptive patterns of thought and behavior. In fact, this is what brings him or her into therapy. Although material that emerges from probing into the patient's past (e.g., as part of the life review) may be useful to understanding the origin and development of a particular maladaptive pattern, such information is not necessary for breaking vicious cycles in the patient's present life. Consonant with the opinion of many seasoned therapists (see, e.g., Appelbaum, 1978), we have found that the pursuit of genetic insight as a critical agent of change may be overvalued, often at the negligence of transformative interpersonal and relational (common) factors in the therapeutic situation. As maintained by Alexander more than 50 years ago (Alexander & French, 1946) and amply confirmed by recent empirical findings (Weiss, Sampson, & the Mount Zion Psychotherapy Research Group, 1986), substantial and long-standing change may result from new (corrective emotional) experiences provided by the very interaction between patient and therapist in the here and now.

Recent research also has shown that patients regulate their own treatment to a larger extent than previously recognized (Weiss, 1993). They enter therapy with an intent, or unconscious plan, to disconfirm pathogenic beliefs by testing them in relation to the therapist. The therapist's task is to help the patient carry out her or his plan, and the therapist uses his or her inferences about the patient's plan to guide the interventions. In testing, the patient acts in accordance with his or her beliefs, that is, by reenacting with the therapist critical scenarios with significant others. For instance, if a patient believes that she or he should always live up to ideal standards and that she or he will disappoint, not to say hurt, those who care for her or him if she or he does not, she or he may test this belief by showing little progress in therapy. Similarly, a patient who expects to be punished or criticized for strivings of independence or self-direction may test the therapist by not showing up for a given session. In this process, the patient unconsciously monitors the therapist's attitude toward the pathogenic beliefs that the patient is working to change. To pass a test, the therapist must act opposite to the patient's expectations. If the therapist fails, he or she may contribute to further discouragement, guilt feelings, and self-accusations in the patient by reinforcing the patient's pathogenic beliefs and maladaptive relational pattern.

It probably goes without saying that with an interactional and mastery-oriented approach to therapy, such as the one here described, we emphasize the cooperative working relationship between therapist and patient. By focusing on the patient's present reality, current life situation, and interpersonal relationships, the therapist becomes an active participant in the therapeutic exchange. Her or his style is less formal, and she or he projects more empathy, support, symbolic giving, and self-disclosure than most traditionally oriented psychodynamic therapists would allow. Technically, she or he may shift flexibly between exploratory, supportive, and didactic interventions, even within the same session. Under certain circumstances, for instance with a patient under great stress, the therapist might find it appropriate to offer direct advice. In Sullivan's (1953) terms, the therapist's stance might be described as that of a *participant observer* rather than one who acts as a semidetached listener and spectator to the patient's narratives and behavior. As already discussed, the therapist uses his or her awareness of the patient's characteristic interpersonal pulls and pushes to provide the patient with opportunities for learning. To be able to do this in a therapeutically productive way (i.e., passing the patient's tests), the therapist should continuously monitor his or her own countertransference feelings, particularly as they relate to the patient's perceptual (parataxic) distortions and maladaptive role reenactments. However, to trust his or her feelings as a reliable source of knowledge about the patient, the therapist should be sufficiently aware of problematic patterns in his or her own interpersonal and relational style. Otherwise, he or she will run the risk of mixing up aspects of his or her own unresolved conflicts and emotional dilemmas with those of the patient. Especially when working within a clinical setting like ours, with most therapists much younger than their patients, therapists should be critically aware also of possible countertransference feelings associated with the topic of aging. This may include myths, prejudices, and stereotyped ideas about older people or unrecognized fears in the therapist of her or his own aging.

The Outpatient Clinic

Since 1993, the Outpatient Clinic for Adults and Older People, University of Bergen, has been the first and only specialized outpatient clinic in Norway offering psychotherapy and counseling to older patients. The clinic is one of three outpatient units at the Department of Clinical Psychology, responsible for the graduate clinical training of students with an average of 3.5 years of prior psychology studies. The shift in profile from treating younger adults to including older patients was made known mainly through media (national TV news, radio programs, and newspaper articles). In addition, general practitioners in the Bergen area were informed by a pamphlet also aimed at the patients. An arbitrary cutoff of 60+ years of age was used to define the older clients. Consequently, the proportion of adults of 60 years or more admitted to the clinic has changed from about 9% in 1992 to 30% in 1996. The relative proportion of patients between 50 and 60 years of age was 5% in 1992, whereas the comparable figure in 1996 was about 20%. The clinic does not offer psychotherapeutic services to psychotic patients or to patients with serious cognitive impairment.

When patients are admitted to the clinic, the SCL–90–R (Derogatis, 1983) and the Target Complaint Questionnaire (Battle et al., 1966) are administered. After the fifth session, the Working Alliance Inventory (Tracey & Kokotovic, 1989) is administered in addition to the SCL–90–R, a procedure repeated at termination. Additional standard measures used are the WHO-10 Well-Being Index (Bech, Gudex, & Staehr Johansen, 1996) and the Psychosocial and Environmental Problems and Global Assessment of Functioning (Axis IV and Axis V, respectively, of the *Diagnostic and Statistical Manual of Mental Disorders*, American Psychiatric Association, 1994). Diagnosis is defined in terms of the *ICD–10 Classification of Mental and Behavioural Disorders* (World Health Organization, 1993).

One of our initial concerns related to older patients was a fear of jeopardizing the working alliance by introducing psychometric instruments too early in the course of treatment. However, experience has taught us that our concerns were overstated, and we are now far less inclined to reduce the formal assessment procedures.

Approximately 70% of the patients registered (during 1993–1996) were women. Nearly 30% are between 60 and 67 years of age; another 20% are 67 years of age or older. Approximately 20% are widow(er)s, a finding related to age. Regardless of age, the most common diagnostic groups are anxiety disorders, various forms of depression, somatoform disorders, and minor adjustment disorders. Not surprisingly, older patients report having more medical problems than our younger patients.

There is a predominance of self-referred patients, independent of age. About one tenth of the patients do not enter therapy after admittance, a finding that does not relate to age. Nearly two thirds of all therapies last 15 sessions or less, regardless of age. The older adults tend to have their sessions given at a more flexible schedule. Flexibility nearly always indicates more sparsely distributed sessions for the older as compared with younger patients.

Academic as well as clinical training is presented within the broader context of life-span developmental psychology. This implies that training in geropsychology is given as part of the regular graduate courses in relevant areas (e.g., psychopathology) and as a clinical practicum. The practicum is defined as a skill-focused, experiential training with adults of all ages. Students are expected to present their ongoing cases, which have been weekly videotaped, in supervision groups (four students per group) and at regularly scheduled case conferences.

Case Vignettes

In the first case described below, the patient's ability to work through ambivalent feelings in a family conflict is illustrated. The patient is essentially challenged as to her capacity for dealing with the current consequences of a long-standing conflict.

Coping With the Threat of a Significant Loss

Patient A, a woman in her early 70s, presented for treatment complaining of a severe family conflict originating in long-standing marital discord. At two earlier occasions, she had initiated to leave her husband but was not able to implement her decision. Periodically, she developed somatoform symptoms for which she received medical treatment from her general practitioner. The patient's elder daughter had for many years the role of negotiator whenever disagreement and tensions worsened, resulting in the father being rejective of his daughter and eventually making further contact between father and daughter extremely difficult. Patient A's younger son was the only one feeling relatively comfortable visiting the family house. The daughter openly started accusing her mother of not taking responsibility in the conflict, implying an explicit claim for the mother to leave her husband. Being the only child of well-off parents made Patient A relatively independent of her husband, in spite of her not working outside her home. She entered therapy as a self-referred patient. Although she demonstrated obvious psychological distress, she appeared to be integrated, with a relatively distinct understanding of her problems. Mrs. A was very concerned about her husband's reaction to her involvement in therapy. His apparent approval mainly was due to the fact that he considered his wife to have a personal problem, and he made it clear that he would not be involved in her treatment.

Diagnostic issues. On entering therapy, Mrs. A was diagnosed in accordance with the *ICD–10* criteria of adjustment disorders (F43.2). Her target complaint was a feeling of inability to cope with her current problems and of being in the midst of losing everything she had fought for. She showed autonomic signs of panic anxiety (tachycardia), panic attacks, suicidal ideation, and mood instability. These symptoms had lasted for about 6 weeks. Before our first meeting, she had been through a medical examination, with negative findings on vital parameters. She had been given antidepressant medication, which she referred to as being of minor help. In spite of sleeping about 7 hours per night, she often felt exhausted on awakening. In accordance with SCL–90–R criteria, she exhibited a significant symptom profile (Global Severity Index; score = 69); the Anxiety and Depression scale showed the primary elevated values.

Therapeutic focus. It became evident that marital conflict was less severe in later years, in terms of intensity and frequency of tensions. The couple had in certain respects come to terms with one another, but at the cost of not seeing their daughter and her family. Contact between the patient and her daughter always involved hiding and lying. Verbal aggressive assaults from the husband often occurred in the presence of neighbors and friends, resulting in social withdrawal. In addition to the obvious marital conflict, there was a normative aspect present, explicitly expressed by the patient saying, "A wife can leave a husband, but a mother cannot accept losing her daughter." Another issue initially raised was related to her planning for a divorce at the age of 73. Realizing what this might cause in terms of disapproval and negative sanctions, leaving her husband seemed overwhelming and associated with feelings of shame.

The patient framed the current psychological threat as that of losing her daughter and grandchildren. Coping with this threat made a new claim on the patient of which she had no apparent response. The anxiety that she was experiencing, therefore, was primarily related to the prospect of losing her future.

Therapeutic tasks. An immediate therapeutic task was related to the fact that the patient was highly anxious. To reduce her sense of helplessness about the current situation, previous positive coping experiences were explored. Socializing the patient into therapy and defining attainable goals were easily accomplished because the patient was able to articulate on what she wanted to focus: improving her relationship with her daughter and reducing her anxiety reactions. To keep her focused on the agenda, a brief relaxation exercise was introduced at the beginning of each session.

Although the patient was not diagnosed with concomitant personality disorder, the unfolding of her psychological vulnerability seemed associated with her way of relating to others, apparently making her cope in an avoidant, dependent manner. She had considerable guilt for having given her daughter a parental role and initially described her in a very idealized way. Her idealization of the therapist also became apparent and was accepted in the initial phases of treatment, but after a while these defenses were needed less. Viewing collaborate or transference issues from the perspective of the patient's history of significant relationships, the relationship with the therapist may therefore serve as a bridge encouraging the patient to reestablish old or develop new relationships. Gradually, the patient started questioning her avoidant reactions, wondering whether she really wanted to leave her husband or if she primarily wanted to avoid conflict with her daughter. She was given ample opportunity to discuss ambivalence toward her daughter and to consider whether she was able to leave her husband without developing a dependent relationship with her daughter.

As the therapy relationship evolved, there was a tendency by the patient to ask for direct advice and solutions. She expressed feeling comfortable in our sessions, symptoms became less intense, and she obviously wanted her therapist to give her advice on whether to divorce. Finally, therefore, she was confronted with the issue of defining the risks that she feared if leaving her husband. Her fear of abandonment and of being left alone was expressed with anger, along with a strong desire to educate the therapist to what it felt like to risk one's future. Challenging and confronting her made the therapist resemble her daughter, except that the therapist did not tell her what to do but rather to decide for herself and consider the pros and cons related to her dilemma.

Termination. After this point, there were 8 more sessions spread out over several months, and we gradually terminated therapy after a total of 16 sessions. She showed considerable improvement in mood and reduced guilt and started to look for a new place to live by herself. As part of a maintenance guide, she was given advice to be aware of potential danger signals that might bring her back to therapy. This was not perceived as an invitation to continue therapy, but she expressed feeling comfortable with the knowledge of this possibility.

In the case above, the therapist initially worked to strengthen the adaptive capacities of the patient, offering support and reassurance in the midst of intense anxiety and profound guilt. The long-standing conflict with the husband was recognized, but the current problems with her daughter were emphasized in treatment.

The realignment of relationships with children is also an issue in the case vignette that follows, representing a significant stressor for the patient. Contrary to the patient described above, this patient represents a case of withdrawal and not of an open conflict.

Coping With Loneliness

Patient B, a 77-year-old widow with the diagnosis of recurrent endogenous depression without psychotic features (F33.2; ICD–10) was referred to our clinic by her general practitioner. She had suffered from depression since early adulthood and for years had received antidepressive medication. At referral, she had been a widow for 4 years. Two years after her husband's death, she had been hospitalized for a suicide attempt. The patient had three grown children and grand- and great-grandchildren. When admitted, she was not considered suicidal. The doctor described her as an intelligent woman who was motivated to find out which aspects of her own behavior kept her family at a distance.

Diagnostic issues. The initial SCL–90–R indicated primarily anxiety symptoms but also a mild depression; both were reflected on the Target Complaint Questionnaire. She did however mention loneliness as her primary problem and related her loneliness to the death of her husband and to her own fear of being a nuisance to her family. The patient was assigned to a student therapist.

Therapeutic focus. The patient entered therapy with a distinct inclination to explore past relationships to reveal what aspects of her own present functioning made her feel lonely and depressed. During the first five sessions, the patient to a large extent set the agenda by introducing what she considered significant life events that had contributed to the current symptoms. Among the themes presented were significant family relations, old ones as well as present, and her inclination to always be of assistance to others. From early adulthood, she had always felt guilty whenever she asserted her own needs. Looking back, however, magnified her feelings of guilt, and after the fifth session, she felt considerably worse, with strong feelings of worthlessness. At this point, she considered terminating therapy, but because of the potential suicidal risk, the patient was contacted by the supervisor. She agreed to continue for at least three sessions. When confronted with the immediate worsening of her anxiety and depression, the patient claimed that it had been necessary to work through the feelings and that despite all her faults, for which she was to blame, she would not be regarded as a person that avoided confronting her own failures.

Therapeutic challenge. At this point, the student therapist introduced a reformulation of the patient's relationship with her children and grandchildren. As the patient gradually came to consider her children and grandchildren to be sound, caring, and self-assertive individuals, she was asked if any of her sacrifices as a parent could have contributed to this development. The patient accepted that it was very likely that her parental behavior had supported the development of their own life course. She also considered it likely that her children would be able to handle it if she stated more clearly that she wished for more contact with them. It became apparent that she hardly ever asked them for any favors, let alone invited them for family gatherings, because she expected them to be bothered by her requests and to feel guilty if they had to decline invitations. Instead of accepting help and invitations, she instead turned them down, to demonstrate that she was autonomous and in no need of more frequent contact. She felt certain that they experienced her needs as a nuisance and would not put them in an embarrassing situation by suggesting more frequent contact.

The next three sessions were spread over 6 weeks. During these sessions, the patient's assertiveness and autonomy became more apparent, and she reported that the children were relieved by what they considered a new vitality and openness in their mother.

Termination. Therapy was terminated after 11 sessions. She reported improvement, which was reflected both in the Target Complaint Questionnaire and in the SCL–90–R. She was able to feel and express anger and also reflected on the fact that her own family (parents and husband) were victims of their own upbringing. In addition to renewed positive interest in her children and grandchildren, she started taking more interest in her life apart from her children and began helping people in less favorable situations than hers.

In the case above, the patient entered therapy with an expressed wish to review her life, a wish that was recognized by the young therapist. By facilitating the completion of her unfinished business, current relationships were eventually emphasized.

The probability of dramatic change is high as a result of therapeutic work with older patients. The final case vignette illustrates the trauma of losing a spouse as an unexpected event during an intense therapeutic encounter.

A Case of Nonassertiveness and Physical Symptoms

Ms. C, a 72-year-old woman married to a former police officer 3 years her senior, was referred for psychotherapy by her family doctor. She had consulted him because of enduring pain, mostly located in her forehead, with radiation down her face and neck. She also complained of weakened memory and difficulties in concentrating and sleeping. The latter made her feel chronically fatigued and exhausted, and she was very concerned about her health in general.

Diagnostic issues. Her family doctor had sent Ms. C for a thorough neurological examination, but the examination yielded no physical explanation for her complaints. Thinking of her condition as a neurotic depression with psychogenic pain (dysthymia, F.34.1; persistent somatoform pain disorder, F.45.4, ICD–10), the doctor then prescribed antidepressants and sleeping pills, which Ms. C reported to have only modest symptomatic effect. Despite this, she continued to take her medication regularly.

Ms. C's initial reaction to going into psychotherapeutic treatment could be described as ambivalent. She feared that her being in psychotherapy might make people think of her as "crazy." She also questioned if a psychologist could really do anything to relieve physical pain, and she was very concerned that a psychotherapist might request that she stop taking pills.

The therapist, a female graduate student in clinical training, responded to the patient's concern by saying that there was no reason to withdraw medication as long as she used it according to prescribed dosages. This seemed to make the patient more at ease.

Therapeutic focus. As her initial strategy, rather then focusing on issues of pain and medication, the therapist chose to direct her efforts into establishing a sound therapeutic bond to Ms. C. This was done, for example, by inviting her to describe typical situations and episodes from her ordinary daily life. The patient responded positively to the therapist's invitation and easily recounted episodes that included her husband, children and their spouses, grandchildren, or neighbors.

An underlying theme in most of Ms. C's narratives was a feeling of being dominated by others or of being more or less subtly taken advantage of. For instance, she did all the domestic work, despite the fact that her physically and mentally healthy husband had retired 15 years ago. She also found it difficult to engage her husband—on whom she was very dependent—in joint, pleasurable activities, such as going to a movie or just taking a walk together. Likewise, her children (two sons and a daughter) constantly asked for her assistance, for example, to cook when they had dinner parties or to take care of their dogs and cats every time they traveled.

When relating such episodes, Ms. C nonverbally—and mostly outside of her own awareness—communicated feelings of bitterness, disappointment, and even hostility. To the therapist's question of why she didn't say no more often, she typically replied that it was not her way or that it would just make her feel guilty. She also said that having grown up as an oldest child with eight siblings, she had become accustomed to taking responsibility for the well-being of others since very early in life.

As therapy proceeded, the vicious circles resulting from the patient's lack of self-assertiveness and setting of limits became a main issue in the therapeutic discourse. The therapist, very tactfully, started to challenge her suppression of negative feelings associated with particular social situations or interpersonal episodes by asking questions such as "What were your feelings then?" or "How did you want that particular situation to be?" At first, the patient reacted with marked resistance to such interventions by replies such as "I think I didn't have any particular feelings" or "I have always thought that it is best to concentrate on the positive." However, partly assisted by the therapist's mild but continuing confrontations, she gradually became more aware of her true feelings and, encouraged by the therapist, was able to express them more freely. This seemed to have a strengthening effect on the already good working alliance between the two of them.

In the middle of her 12th therapy session, the patient revealed that for a couple of weeks, she had experimented in trying to get along without medication and that, to her great satisfaction, things had worked out quite well. Her sleep had significantly improved, and she was experiencing less pain.

Therapeutic changes. For the next 2 months, the therapist intensified her challenging of Ms. C's pathogenic beliefs and her maladaptive interpersonal pattern. This prompted Ms. C to begin to question her long-held idea that by saying no, or by expressing negative feelings, she would automatically hurt her loved ones. At this stage in therapy, the patient frequently seemed to test the validity of this idea by acting more assertively toward her therapist during the sessions. Then, with the therapist's support and active encouragement of her new behavior, Ms. C became gradually more assertive also in relation to her family members. Contrary to her expectations and fears, the family, although hesitantly and somewhat bewildered at first, seemed to approve of her new style. Her youngest son had even jokingly commented, "Mom, you obviously must have chosen a smart shrink!" There were also indications that Ms. C's more direct and less complaining interpersonal style made her company more attractive, which in turn had further positive effects on her sense of well-being and on her self-esteem.

When Ms. C had been in therapy for about 6 months, her husband died very suddenly. This made it necessary to concentrate most of the therapeutic work for the next couple of months on the patient's grief reactions and grief work. Taking into consideration her strong and lifelong dependency on her husband, one had to be open to the possibility of a serious therapeutic setback. However, Ms. C went through the grief period without any severe symptomatic relapse, and gradually therapy could proceed on the same track as before the death of her husband.

Termination. Therapy was terminated after 29 sessions, distributed over a 14-month period, with increasingly longer intervals between sessions toward the end of treatment. At termination, Ms. C's condition was clinically judged as substantially improved. She reported that she felt more comfortable in her daily life, and she had adjusted fairly well to her situation as a widow. The latter was exemplified by her description of episodes in which she had felt proud of her own coping and autonomy. Although she was still periodically overconcerned about her physical health, she also jokingly characterized herself as an "incurable hypochondriac," and her original symptoms and complaints had been significantly diminished. Medication was used only occasionally.

In this case, there was a need for the therapist to socialize the patient into treatment by devoting extra time in establishing a sound relationship. In spite of the trauma that occurred during therapy, the patient was gradually able to refocus on the initial challenge from her therapist and to explore alternative coping strategies for more satisfying relationships.

Therapeutic Adaptation

According to our conceptual position, then, current clinical psychology is a sound foundation in developing competencies in clinical practice with older adults. However, integral to clinical geropsychology are specific types of knowledge—among others, knowledge of the diversity of normal as well as pathological aging, along with specific assessment issues. At the introduction to geropsychology, students are taught to use decision trees in narrowing down possibilities for diagnosis (e.g., differentiating subtypes of dementia). In contrast, case formulation in a psychotherapeutic context serving older adults more often involves a focus on *ruling in* problems, enlarging the field of view to encompass a broad range of factors and their interactions. An extensive part of this knowledge, therefore, relates to diagnosis and initial case formulation.

Although any single theoretical orientation for the application of psychotherapy with older adults is likely to be recommended (Teri & Logsdon, 1992), there is a need for each approach to address relevant age-related issues. These issues can be described in terms of *common problems* that bring older people to therapy and specific *relationship factors* in psychotherapy with older adults (Zarit & Knight, 1996). Knight (1992) described psychotherapy with older adults as distinctive in terms of content issues and the reaction of younger therapists who find talking about death, grief, and adjustment to disability fundamentally difficult.

Common Problems

Common problem areas presented with more frequency by our older clients are grief, relationship conflicts, and various psychosomatic complaints. Many of the normal events associated with aging—such as loss of significant others, changes in one's own health, or a decline in a close family member's health—are likely to elicit vulnerability. Grief, therefore, is often a principal focus of therapy, whether the relationship with the deceased was problematic or primarily positive. It is not always a question of working through the loss, but of various legitimate feelings evoked by the loss. Thus, in addition to applying grief-therapeutic principles as we traditionally know them, we also have to take into account the social constrictions that older patients may struggle with in their efforts to deal with a serious loss. As one widow expressed it, "When can I stop mourning and start living?" In our experience, the greatest loss for many of our older clients is that they have to face a shrinking social network and social support base, neither of which is easily replaced. What this may imply in terms of the therapeutic relationship is commented on below.

Problems brought into therapy are often related to conflicts in current, close relationships. In recent literature, the extent of such problems has been documented. A study reported by Miller and Silberman (1996) found that 42% of an older sample reported that to recover from their depressive episodes, they needed to resolve interpersonal conflicts, tensions, and disagreements. Focusing on marital issues, no patient elected to divorce his or her spouse during therapy, and many long-standing conflicted relationships remained without particular changes. In keeping with Miller and Silberman, we find that the most frequent disputes are with children, followed by spouses, and then by the patient's own siblings. Although divorce is not a common solution, we have, as illustrated in one of the case vignettes above, witnessed that clients in their early 70s have decided to divorce. A strong motive for divorce in these cases has been to improve positive interaction with their children and grandchildren.

The presenting problem of many clients relates to psychosomatic pain and distress and is likely to include depression, anxiety, and adjustment disorders. The problem may be presented as an ailment or in terms of various functional constrictions. The psychological problems are to a large extent comorbid with medical illness and may therefore complicate treatment. Older people facing physical limitations may find themselves having to rely on others for tasks they were once able to do on their own. Coping with various kinds of dependency, then, is a recurrent theme. Not surprisingly, however, a focus on psychosomatic distress may open the door to relational loss as well as relational conflicts, as illustrated above.

Relationship Factors

Facilitating patients' access to therapy and establishing an effective therapeutic relationship in each case are crucial to all forms of psychotherapy and to all groups of patients (Newton & Lazarus, 1992). The well-documented underuse of mental health services by older adults reflects central patient and therapist factors often referred to as *barriers* to psychotherapy (e.g., Shmotkin, Eyal, & Lomranz, 1992). At a more practical level, it may also reflect accessibility and reimbursement levels, implying that the provision of treatment may initially involve going beyond traditional referral sources (e.g., recruiting patients through local newspapers).

Once the older patient has entered treatment, particular attention has been given to the need for socializing the patient, implying that the roles of both therapist and patient need to be directly and verbally articulated to the patient, to establish a sustainable working alliance. Within cognitive–behavioral approaches, the term *therapy education* is often used (Gallagher-Thompson & Thompson, 1996), referring to the responsibility of the therapist to inform the older client about psychotherapy. We find this term especially relevant with regard to the older client's expectations about psychotherapy. Some patients may have the belief that psychologists are an extension of their physician. When referred to psychotherapy by their primary care physician, they may enter therapy with a fairly constricted medical definition of their difficulties. In addition, it may come as a surprise that the therapist offers weekly appointments and that help is being provided in a rather unfamiliar way, compared with earlier treatment experience. Identifying and addressing a client's expectations about psychotherapy may, of course, be relevant for younger adults as well. But in terms of maximizing therapeutic effect with older adults, we find a careful discussion of the client's expectations and an explanation of the limits of therapy to be central elements in establishing the relationship.

A less formal and more active relationship with the older patient may imply giving more concrete assistance and advice, involving family members, and coordination of various health and social services. The necessity for greater activity by the therapist may often be related to the older patient's physical deficits and relational losses. From one perspective, the problems confronting older patients may appear more concrete and less amenable to change. It appears, then, that the variation in needs of older patients dictates the eventual greater activity of the therapist.

In terms of actual as well as anticipated losses experienced by older adults, the patient may use the therapist for "emotional refueling" (p. 701, Newton & Lazarus, 1992). This may involve a greater flexibility by the therapist to show an easily recognized caring, such as touching. When students are taught about how psychotherapy hinges on the collaborative therapeutic relation, various types of caring may appear "too close" and trigger their fear of accelerating dependency in the older patient. In the same vein, receiving gifts from older patients without looking for some subtle reason may also appear frightening. It seems critical in therapy training, therefore, for the therapist to learn how to modify the position on therapeutic neutrality when needed.

With regard to the process of therapy, our experience is that the therapist may need to be more flexible in setting the duration and the frequency of sessions. Setting a time limit on therapy may reinforce the patient's confidence in his or her ability to resolve the problem and, as such, to accelerate the therapeutic process. Continued contact on an infrequent basis may, on the other hand, be more appropriate than a fixed termination. This primarily relates to patients who have few present close relationships or who experience further potential or actual losses.

Conclusion

In terms of common problems or issues brought to therapy by older adults, the fact that older adults are at greater risk of significant losses may often be reflected in psychotherapy, either as the issue in focus or as an interacting factor. In addition, older adults may present their psychological distress in various ways, making diagnosis and case formulation critical issues in therapy planning. Coping with loss, however, is related to a continuum of individual vulnerability and robustness, implying that we have to understand what the loss represents for the individual in terms of psychological threat and efforts to cope with it. Preparing younger therapists for therapeutic work with older adults implies teaching them to focus on variation in affective health in older patients as much as on central geropsychological problems. When younger therapists experience this variation, they will, to a larger extent, be able to integrate basic knowledge of clinical psychology and relevant geropsychology. In turn, this has significant implications for building a genuine therapist–patient relationship. What contributes to a patient's benefit from psychotherapy may involve various factors. Our primary challenge is to make our students see that age alone is neither an inclusion nor an exclusion criterion for applying psychotherapy to older patients.

References

Alexander, F., & French, T. M. (1946). *Psychoanalytic therapy*. New York: Ronald Press.
American Psychiatric Association. (1994). *Diagnostic and statistical manual of mental disorders (4th ed.)*. Washington, DC: Author.

Appelbaum, S. A. (1978). Pathways to change in psychoanalytic therapy. *Bulletin of the Menninger Clinic, 42,* 239–251.

Atchley, R. C. (1991). The influence of aging and frailty on perceptions and expressions of the self: Theoretical and methodological issues. In J. E. Birren, J. E. Lubben, J. C. Rowe, & D. E. Deutchman (Eds.), *The concept and measurement of quality in life in the frail elderly* (pp. 207–225). New York: Academic Press.

Battle, C. C., Imber, S. D., Hoehn-Sarie, R., Stone, A. R., Nash, E. R., & Frank, J. D. (1966). Target complaints as criteria of improvement. *American Journal of Psychotherapy, 20,* 184–192.

Bech, P., Gudex, C., & Staehr Johansen, K. (1996). The WHO (ten) Well-Being Index: Validation in diabetes. *Psychotherapy and Psychosomatics, 65,* 183–190.

Beutler, L. E., & Clarkin, J. F. (1990). *Systematic treatment selection: Toward targeted therapeutic interventions.* New York: Brunner/Mazel.

Blazer, D., George, L. K., & Hughes, D. (1991). The epidemiology of anxiety disorders: An age comparison. In C. Salzman & B. D. Lebowitz (Eds.), *Anxiety in the elderly* (pp. 17–30). New York: Springer.

Burvill, P. W. (1987). An appraisal of the NIMH Epidemiologic Catchment Area Program. *Australian and New Zealand Journal of Psychiatry, 21,* 175–184.

Butler, R. N. (1963). The life review: An interpretation of reminiscence in the aged. *Psychiatry, 26,* 65–76.

Calarusso, C. A., & Nemiroff, M. A. (1991). Impact of adult developmental issues on treatment of older adults. In W. A. Myers (Ed.), *New techniques in the psychotherapy of older patients* (pp. 245–265). Washington, DC: American Psychiatric Press.

Derogatis, L. R. (1983). *SCL-90-R: Administration, scoring & procedures manual.* Baltimore: Clinical Psychometric Research.

Erikson, E. (1963). *Childhood and society* (2nd ed.). New York: Norton.

Erikson, E. (1968). *Identity: Youth and crisis.* New York: Norton.

Gallagher-Thompson, D., Hanley-Peterson, P., & Thompson. L. W. (1990). Maintenance of gains versus relapse following brief psychotherapy for depression. *Journal of Consulting and Clinical Psychology, 58,* 371–374.

Gallagher-Thompson, D., & Steffen, A. M. (1994). Comparative effects of cognitive–behavioral and brief psychodynamic psychotherapies for depressed family caregivers. *Journal of Consulting and Clinical Psychology, 62,* 543–549.

Gallagher-Thompson, D. (1992). The older adult. In A. Freeman & F. Dattilio (Eds.), *Comprehensive casebook of cognitive therapy* (pp. 193–200). New York: Plenum.

Gallagher-Thompson, D., & Thompson, L. W. (1995). Psychotherapy with older adults in theory and practice. In B. Bongar, & L. Beutler (Eds.), *Comprehensive textbook of psychotherapy: Theory and practice* (pp. 359–379). New York: Oxford University Press.

Gallagher-Thompson, D., & Thompson, L. W. (1996). Applying cognitive–behavioral therapy to the psychological problems of later life. In S. H. Zarit & B. G. Knight (Eds.), *A guide to psychotherapy and aging: Effective clinical interventions in a life stage context* (pp. 61–82). Washington, DC: American Psychological Association.

Gatz, M., & Finkel, S. I. (1994). Education and training of mental health service providers. In M. Gatz (Ed.), *Emerging issues in mental health and aging* (pp. 282–302). Washington, DC: American Psychological Association.

Gatz, M., & Smyer, M. (1992). The mental health system and older adults in the 1990s. *American Psychologist, 47,* 741–751.

Gurian, B. S., & Miner, J. H. (1991). Clinical presentation of anxiety in the elderly. In C. Salzman & B. D. Lebowitz (Eds.), *Anxiety in the elderly: Treatment and research* (pp. 31–44). New York: Springer.

Higgitt, A. (1992). Dependency on prescribed drugs. *Review in Clinical Gerontology, 2,* 151–155.

Kelly, G. A. (1955). *The psychology of personal constructs.* New York: Norton.

Knight, B. G. (1992). *Older adults in psychotherapy: Case histories.* Newbury Park, CA: Sage.

Koenig, H. G., & Blazer, D. G. (1992). Epidemiology of geriatric affective disorders. *Clinics in Geriatric Medicine, 8,* 235–251.

Lepola, U., Leinonen, E., & Koponen, H. (1994). The treatment of sleep disorders in the elderly. *Nordic Journal of Psychiatry, 48,* 251–255.

Lewis, M. I., & Butler, R. N. (1974). Life review therapy: Putting memories to work in individual and group psychotherapy. *Geriatrics, 29,* 165–172.

Livingston, G., & Hinchliffe, A. C. (1993). The epidemiology of psychiatric disorders in the elderly. *International Review of Psychiatry, 5,* 317–326.

Martin, G. A., & Wilson, P. (1984). Psychological interventions with older adults. In J. R. McNamara (Ed.), *Critical issues, developments, and trends in professional psychology* (Vol. 2, pp. 66–107). New York: Praeger.

McAdams, D. P. (1990). Unity and purpose in human lives: The emergence of identity as a life story. In A. I. Rabin, R. A. Zucker, R. A. Emmons, & S. Frank (Eds.), *Studying persons and lives* (pp. 148–200). New York: Springer.

McAdams, D. P. (1993). *The stories we live by: Personal myths and the making of the self.* New York: Morrow.

Miller, M. D., & Silberman, R. L. (1996). Using interpersonal psychotherapy with depressed elders. In S. H. Zarit & B. G. Knight (Eds.), *A guide to psychotherapy and aging: Effective clinical interventions in a life-stage context* (pp. 83–100). Washington, DC: American Psychological Association.

Mitchell, S. J. (1988). *Relational concepts in psychoanalysis.* Cambridge, MA: Harvard University Press.

Muslin, H. (1985). Beyond the pleasure principle. In J. Reppen (Ed.), *Beyond Freud: A study of modern psychoanalytic theorists.* Hillsdale, NJ: Erlbaum.

Newmann, J. P. (1989). Aging and depression. *Psychology and Aging, 4,* 150–165.

Newton, N. A., & Lazarus, L. W. (1992). Behavioral and psychotherapeutic interventions. In J. E. Birren, R. B. Sloane, & G. C. Cohen (Eds.), *Handbook of mental health and aging* (2nd ed., pp. 699–715). San Diego, CA: Academic Press.

Papouchis, N., & Passman, V. (1993). An integrative approach to the psychotherapy of the elderly. In G. Stricker & J. R. Gold (Eds.), *Comprehensive handbook of psychotherapy integration* (pp. 437–451). New York: Plenum.

Regier, D. A., Boyd, J. H., Burke, J. D., Rae, D. S., Myers, J. K., Kramer, M., Robins, L. N., George, L. K., Karno, M., & Locke, B. Z. (1988). One-month prevalence of mental disorders in the United States. *Archives of General Psychiatry, 45,* 977–986.

Ruth, J. E., & Öberg, P. (1992). Expression of aggression in the life stories of aged women. In K. Björkquist & P. Niemela (Eds.), *Of mice and women: Aspects of female aggression* (pp. 133–146). San Diego, CA: Academic Press.

Sadavoy, J. (1994). Integrated psychotherapy of the elderly. In E. Chiu & D. Ames (Eds.), *Functional psychiatric disorders of the elderly* (pp. 499–517). Cambridge, England: Cambridge University Press.

Schneider, L. S. (1994). Meta-analysis from a clinician's perspective. In L. S. Schneider, C. F. Reynolds, B. D. Lebowitz, & A. J. Friedhoff (Eds.), *Diagnosis and treatment of depression in late life: Results of the NIH Consensus Development Conference* (pp. 361–374). Washington, DC: American Psychiatric Press.

Scogin, F., & McElrath, L. (1994). Efficacy of psychosocial treatments for geriatric depression: A quantitative review. *Journal of Clinical and Consulting Psychology, 62,* 69–74.

Sheikh, J. L. (1992). Anxiety and its disorders in old age. In J. E. Birren, R. B. Sloane, & G. D. Cohen (Eds.), *Handbook of mental health and aging* (2nd ed., pp. 410–432). New York: Springer.

Shmotkin, D., Eyal, N., & Lomranz, J. (1992). Motivations and attitudes of clinical psychologists regarding treatment of the elderly. *Educational Gerontology, 18,* 177–192.

Sullivan, H. S. (1953). *The psychiatric interview.* New York: Norton.

Teri, L., Curtis, J., Gallagher-Thompson, D., & Thompson, L. W. (1994). Cognitive/behavior therapy with depressed older adults. In L. S. Schneider, C. F. Reynolds, B. D. Lebowitz, & A. J. Friedhoff (Eds.), *Diagnosis and treatment of depression in late life: Proceedings of the NIH Consensus Development Conference* (pp. 279–291). Washington, DC: American Psychiatric Press.

Teri, L., & Logsdon, R. G. (1992). The future of psychotherapy with older adults. *Psychotherapy, 29,* 81–86.

Thompson, L. W., & Gallagher, D. (1984). Efficacy of psychotherapy in the treatment of late-life depression. *Advances in Behavior Research and Therapy, 6,* 127–139.

Thompson, L. W., Gallagher, D., & Breckenridge, J. S. (1987). Comparative effectiveness of psychotherapies for depressed elders. *Journal of Consulting and Clinical Psychology, 55,* 385–390.

Tobin, S. S. (1991). *Personhood in advanced old age*. New York: Springer.

Tracey, T. J., & Kokotovic, A. M. (1989). Factor structure of the working alliance inventory. *Psychological Assessment, 1*, 207–210.

Tweed, D. L., Blazer, D. G., & Ciarlo, J. A. (1991). Psychiatric epidemiology in elderly populations. In R. B. Wallace & R. F. Woolson (Eds.), *The epidemiologic study of the elderly* (pp. 213–233). New York: Oxford University Press.

Viney, L. L. (1990). The construing widow: Dislocation and adaptation in bereavement. *Psychotherapy Patient, 3*, 207–222.

Viney, L. L. (1993). *Life stories: Personal construct therapy with the elderly*. New York: Wiley.

Wachtel, P. L. (1993). *Therapeutic communication. Principles and effective practice*. New York: Guilford Press.

Wachtel, P. L. (1994). Cyclical processes in personality and psychopathology. *Journal of Abnormal Psychology, 103*, 51–54.

Wachtel, P. L. (1997). *Psychoanalysis, behavior therapy, and the relational world*. Washington, DC: American Psychological Association.

Weiss, J. (1993). *How psychotherapy works: Process and techniques*. New York: Guilford Press.

Weiss, J., & Sampson, H. (1986). Testing alternative psychoanalytic explanations of the therapeutic process. In J. M. Masling (Ed.), *Empirical studies of psychoanalytic theories* (Vol. 2, pp. 1–26). Hillsdale, NJ: Analytic Press.

Weiss, J., Sampson, H., & the Mount Zion Psychotherapy Research Group. (1986). *The psychoanalytic process: Theory, clinical observations, and empirical research*. New York: Guilford Press.

Williamson, G. M., & Schulz, R. (1992). Physical illness and symptoms of depression among elderly outpatients. *Psychology and Aging, 7*, 343–351.

World Health Organization. (1993). *The ICD-10 classification of mental and behavioural disorders*. Geneva, Switzerland: Author.

Zarit, S. H., & Knight, B. G. (1996). Psychotherapy and aging: Multiple strategies, positive outcomes. In S. H. Zarit and B. G. Knight (Eds.), *A guide to psychotherapy and aging: Effective clinical interventions in a life-stage context* (pp. 1–13). Washington, DC: American Psychological Association.

24

Psychotherapy With Older Adult Families: The Contextual, Cohort-Based Maturity/Specific Challenge Model

Bob G. Knight and T. J. McCallum

As has been noted by Qualls (1996), family therapies were originally developed with a focus on child-raising families, and the approach only recently has been applied to understanding families for whom the "identified patient" is an older adult. Older adults, whether seen individually or in the family context, are often referred by family and may be vulnerable to being the identified patient for a dysfunctional family. Knight (1994) wrote about the family issues inherent in the individual psychological assessment of older adults and the communication of assessment results to the older client and her or his family. In this chapter, we propose to examine family therapy and family systems theory within the contextual, cohort-based maturity/specific challenge model (CCMSC) that Knight (1996) proposed as a guideline for considering the adaptation of therapies to older adults.

According to Qualls (1996), family therapies attempt to intentionally alter the structure or function of the family, to benefit one or more members. Qualls further explained that interventions are defined as family therapy either when the locus of intervention is family interaction or when assessment reveals that the client problems involve the family's structure or functioning. Only intervention targeted at the structure or functioning of the family should be considered family therapy.

Qualls (1996) defined *later life* families as those in which concerns about aging are central to the distress of adult family members. On the basis of this definition, the crux of therapy may focus on concern about the aging process itself, or the manner in which aging may directly or indirectly affect the ability of the family to fulfill the needs of its members.

In what follows, we first apply the CCMSC model to family therapy and consider the implications of knowledge about maturation across the adult life span, cohort effects, the social context of older adults, and the specific challenges of late life for work with older families. After that overview, the implications of a family-centered view for assessment and for intervention with older adults are explored further. Finally, ethical issues involved in choosing between individual and familial perspectives with regard to problems of older adults are discussed.

The CCMSC Model and Family Therapy

In the CCMSC model, older adults are seen as more mature than younger ones in certain important ways but also are recognized to be facing some of the hardest challenges that life presents to adults, including adjusting to chronic illness and disability as well as frequent grieving for others. The special social context of older adults and the fact that they are members of earlier born cohorts raised in different sociocultural circumstances may require adaptations that are not dictated by the developmental processes of aging. In what follows, maturation is discussed first, followed by cohort differences and contextual factors as important potential sources of difference in working with older adults and their families in therapy. Finally, specific challenges that are not unique to later life but are more commonly experienced in old age are introduced.

Maturation and Family Systems

The question of developmental maturation poses some interesting dilemmas when applied to family systems rather than to individuals. As noted in the CCMSC model, individuals pass through several family systems over the course of their life cycles: family of origin, one (or more) families established in adulthood, the dispersed and extending family formed by adult children as they form their adulthood families, and the family structures as one moves into grandparenthood, great-grandparenthood, and so forth. In principle, any one of these families can be observed to age and to face changing developmental tasks as its members age. On the other hand, every family system can be seen as being at several differing stages of development, depending on which member's developmental point of view is adopted. That is, a given family is the family of origin for some members (the minor children), family of adulthood for others (the child-raising parents), and a late-life family for others (grandparents and great-grandparents of the minor children). In this important sense, every family system is at all stages of maturity at once, simply because all families are multigenerational. It follows that the classification of a family as aging already reflects a decision to identify the key problems of the family as those centering on the older members, a nontrivial decision from a clinical standpoint. Real family crises can evolve around older family members; on the other hand, real crises involving marital problems, problems with children, and individual psychological disorders in younger family members can be displaced onto the older adult.

The CCMSC model suggests that the insights of maturational views of adult development and aging can be applied to family work to assist in counteracting any tendency to automatically assume that the older members are frail, impaired, and in need of care. In the absence of diseases (see the section on the Specificity of Challenges in Late Life, to follow), older members can be expected to show growth in the direction of cognitive complexity, development of expertise in areas of experiential competence such as family and relationships; androgyny, at least in the sense of acquiring role competencies and interests stereotypically associated with the opposite gender; and a greater emotional complexity with better comprehension and control of emotional reactions. All of these factors at once shape and are shaped by the family system dynamic as the adults develop into older adults.

Cohort Differences

Another dimension of our understanding of older adults from life span development is the ability to separate the effects of maturation from the effects of cohort membership. Much of social gerontology could be summarized as the discovery that many differences between the old and the young that society (and therefore psychotherapists) has attributed to the aging process are due, in fact, to cohort effects. Cohort differences are explained by membership in a birth-year-defined group that is socialized into certain abilities, beliefs, attitudes, and personality dimensions that will stay stable as it ages and that distinguishes that cohort from those born earlier and later (e.g., in the United States, Baby Boomers are between the GI Generation and Generation X). Thus, cohort differences have ramifications for family systems therapy.

Cohort differences, although not developmental, are real. Working with older adults involves learning something of the folkways of members of earlier born cohorts, just as working with adolescents or young adults demands staying current in their folkways and worldview. During times of rapid social and technological change (e.g., the twentieth century), cohort effects may overwhelm advantages of developmental maturation. Preparation to do therapy with older adults in a family systems setting has to include learning what it was like to grow up before one was born.

As noted some years ago by Bengtson, Cutler, Mangen, and Marshall (1985), families are composed of different cohorts, bound together by familial solidarity. We would propose that one source of conflict within families is the acting out of cohort conflicts. Family members of successive generations are, among other things, members of differing cohorts and so have differing views of the world, and of the family, conditioned in part by cohort membership. This is most simply expressed in the cry of children everywhere to parents that "you can't understand me, you grew up in the _____s." In conflicted families, it may be quite helpful to separate cohort-based conflicts from other parent–child conflicts. That is, understanding that some familial disagreements are not really expressions of a parent denying adult autonomy to the grown child, but cohort-based differences in values and life experience, can be helpful in reducing familial tensions. It is often easier to discover cohort-based assumptions and to come to terms with them by relating to, or by recalling relationships with, nonfamily acquaintances who are cohort mates of the target family member. For example, it may be easier to hear what divorce meant in the 1930s from your parents' cohort mates than from your parents. The realization that one is getting a cohort-based perspective from one's parents rather than personal criticism may be helpful in improving relationships.

Successive cohorts also grow up in different kinds of families. Much of the sociology of changing family structures points to these types of cohort effects. For example, later born families tend to have beanpole rather than pyramidal structures (small and equal numbers of members across generations rather than more members in each successive generation), later born families are more likely to have divorced and remarried members, and later born families in the twentieth century have become more and more multigenerational (four and five or more generations alive at once is becoming common).

Change in family structure across cohorts also implies that older family members are likely to have differing expectations and assumptions about family structure and their role in it than will later born family members. These changing values can be a source of familial conflict and grist for the mill of family therapy. For example, earlier born cohorts tend to emphasize that in their day older family members lived with them and were automatically given respect. Exploring the way in which the value of respecting older family members has altered over successive cohorts can help these family members see this change in societal terms rather than in personal, intrafamilial terms. That is, it is not just that younger family members are not giving them the respect that they are due, but that society has changed. It is also often helpful to explore the particulars of multigenerational households and the ambivalence that often surrounded respect for elders even in the early twentieth century. Often people lived together because they had no choice, and the current older cohort will recall having felt relieved to get away and establish their own home. Respect also often was rooted in an authoritarian family structure against which the children of that generation (the current older family members) rebelled and consciously decided to be less authoritarian with their own children. They are then reaping the consequences, both positive and negative, of those decisions.

As elucidated by Bengtson, Rosenthal, and Burton (1990), Hagestad (1990), and Gatz, Bengtson, and Blum (1991), all of these changes in family structure change the familial experience and tend to emphasize the long-term nature of adult-to-adult familial relationships and the role of parent care as well as child care. Among other things, one may spend more time on elder care than on child care, for example, if a parent gets a dementing illness in her or his 60s and then lives out a full life.

The Social Context of Older Adults

Another complication for understanding older adults in family systems is the need to understand the distinctive social milieu of older adults in the late twentieth century. This context includes specific environments (age-segregated housing and age-segregated social and recreational centers) as well as specific rules for older adults (e.g., in the United States, Medicare regulations, Older Americans' Act regulations, and conservatorship law). An understanding of this social context that is based on both knowledge of what is supposed to be and experience of actual operations is important to the understanding of what older people say about their experiences in these settings.

Although understanding the social ecology of various environments is not terribly difficult, many family members of older adult clients may be steeped in their own lives and may not have taken the time to examine their older adult relatives' perspective. Important knowledge concerning the formal network of health and social services for older adults and the formal distinctions between different levels can be learned in an educationally oriented session or two. Some informal visiting at such places can do a great deal toward providing a more experiential framework for understanding the environments of older people. Also, because each nursing home, senior recreation center, and senior meal site tends to develop its own social ecology, site visits play an important role when decisions concerning daycare or placement must be made.

One goal in family systems therapy with older adults is to have other family members to consider the older person's point of view as it may relate to the family functioning as a whole. Familiarity with the older adult's social environment is helpful to that end. An older adult relative's resistance to family efforts to solve problems may be due to the specific characteristics of a service setting—not all senior recreation centers are fun—or to the family thinking only of age-segregated solutions (for some older adults, age-integrated activities such as college classes may be more appropriate than an age-segregated setting). Families may see these more context-based objections as stubbornness or a refusal to take advice from younger family members. Visiting available programs and thinking about how they appear to oneself and to the older family member can be helpful in taking that member's point of view.

Attention to social context also suggests that the best available social resources for older family members may not be what either the older adult or the younger members would wish for in an ideal world. Discussing this fact openly, and making the best of real available resources, is often a better strategy than trying to convince an older relative that a program is really better than she or he perceives it to be.

The Specificity of Challenges in Late Life

Many older adults and their families seek help in therapy to deal with problems that threaten psychological homeostasis at any point in the life span: chronic illness, disability, and the loss of loved ones to death. These problems are not unique to late life but are more likely in the latter third of life. In general, the CCMSC model would argue that much of what is perceived as being special about working with older adult families is related to these types of problems rather than to the age of the identified patient.

The specific nature of these problems is important to the practice of psychotherapy with older persons and their families. Just as the deficit side of the loss–deficit model ignores evidence of maturation, the perception that generic losses are normative in late life fails to do justice to the specific nature of the losses incurred. Clinical experience suggests that the family faces different problems depending on whether the loss is a family member through death or a functioning family member to dementia or whether the family is called on to assist a relative with loss of vision or loss of ambulation. Recognizing the specificity of loss and reconceptualizing losses as challenges imply that some losses can be overcome through rehabilitation counseling as well as adjusted to through grief counseling.

Chronic illness and disability. Experience in therapy indicates that emotionally distressed older families are often caring for older relatives who are chronically ill or physically disabled, or both, and who, along with their families, are struggling to adjust to these problems. Family dynamics may shift, and roles may change or reverse as families attempt to cope with such difficulties. This aspect of working with older adults involves specialized knowledge and specialized skills compared with other areas of psychotherapeutic practice where physical problems and the physical dimension of the person can be more safely ignored.

Illness, especially disorders of cognition and emotion, is likely to become a taboo topic in the family systems sense (Neidhardt & Allen, 1993). A taboo topic is a problem of which everyone is aware but which is not openly discussed. Considerable energy can be spent concealing the problem from the one person it affects the most, the person who has the disorder and who is most keenly aware of it.

For example, dementia is likely to be treated as a taboo topic. Often, everyone in the family is aware that something is wrong with the affected older relative, but no one speaks of it, and in particular, no one wants to speak of it with the relative. Family members may assume that the older adult will not be aware of any changes and should not be told. This, unfortunately, has the effect of creating a family social environment shrouded in secrecy. As the cognitively impaired older adult is already experiencing difficulty comprehending complex social interactions and may often feel anxious and overwhelmed, these secrets may lead to increased suspiciousness and anxiety.

Because an older relative's disability is a network event, families respond to it as they have learned to respond to other crises in the family. These responses will typically have both emotional and instrumental components. On the emotional side, there are often various combinations and degrees of guilt and blaming. Rationales for blaming oneself often go back decades, raising unresolved childhood or adolescent issues and placing them in the new context. Instrumental tasks emerge when the older adult's capabilities decline and changes in the family system become necessary. For example, if Mom has always "held the family together" or if Dad resolved disputes and helped with taxes, then someone will need to take over these duties and the family will have to adjust to the new configuration. In general, the least adaptive outcomes occur when families try to maintain the status quo: Financial problems may ensue if Dad is expected to continue handling the household bills while he is in the middle stages of a dementing illness, and family social life may suffer if the children wait for invitations from Mom, who is now depressed. The period of adjustment is likely to be uncomfortable, and there may be competition for taking over (or avoiding) the new roles and responsibilities, but a consciously negotiated new homeostasis is likely to be preferable to the alternatives.

Grieving. Another specific challenge to older adults involves working through grief. Although loved ones die throughout our lives, the experience is more common in later life. Older adults seeking help for depression frequently have experienced several deaths of loved ones in the preceding months or years. Grief may be a principal focus of therapy when there are multiple losses within a short period of time, when there is unresolved grief from losses that occurred earlier in life, or when the relationship with the deceased was problematic for some reason.

Clinical grief work consists of three main components: expression of emotion, putting the loss in perspective, and adjusting to life without the deceased. Expression of emotion involves a good deal of persistence. Putting the loss in perspective is often a personal process that has ramifications for adjustment to life without the deceased. Within a family context, adjusting to life without the deceased means the adjustment of the family system to accommodate the loss of the deceased and the roles he or she played in the family (Brown, 1988).

The process of grief work rarely unfolds neatly into these delineated areas but often overlaps in a messy manner in any given therapy. It is person specific in terms of the person lost and often complicated with older adult families by the multiplicity of deaths. Family systems theory also reminds us that everyone in the family is grieving, not just an identified client. One of us (BK) once saw a middle-aged son for a consultation regarding how best to encourage his father to seek counseling for unresolved grief. During the interview, the son repeatedly referred to the father's being unable to get over the death of "his wife." Toward the end of the hour, the therapist inquired if the father's wife was the son's mother. The son nodded and then cried throughout the remainder of that visit.

Caregiving. For older adult families, the emotional adjustments to caregiving may be similar to grief work, in that the impaired relative is unable to fill former familial roles, especially when the impairment is cognitive or when a physical impairment is extreme. Many caregiving families may be dealing with the loss of the roles played by the care receiver while she or he still lives rather than having lost that person to death. The progressive and debilitating course of many dementing diseases forces caregivers to both accept changes and losses in the person they care for and begin to develop new ways of living their lives as caregivers. Working with caregivers has evolved as a special topic within clinical geropsychology (see, e.g., Zarit, 1996).

From a family systems viewpoint, it is somewhat paradoxical that caregiving interventions are generally individually oriented interventions (targeted to the "primary caregiver") in what is a prototypical family systems issue: caring for an impaired family member. Cross-cultural perspectives suggest that this may reflect the highly individualistic values of Western, industrial societies; in other cultures, the whole family is seen as providing care (Aranda & Knight, 1997).

Clinical experience also suggests that not all caregiving cases are truly about caregiving. Caregiving may be a convenient "test problem" to present to the clinician. As caregiving issues resolve, it may develop that there are problems in the marriage or conflicts between the caregiver and his or her children that are more conflictual, historical, and complex than the caregiving issues. In a sentence, many caregiving problems and decisions are not really that difficult, the question then becomes "Why is *this* family having so much trouble with caregiving?" The answer is likely to require familial assessment, family history, and a consideration of the entire family system.

Summary

The CCMSC model portrays older families in a complex light that draws on scientific gerontology. Developmental maturation is an individual concept with questionable relevance to the family system, which in a sense is of all ages at once. However, attention to individual maturation warns against identifying older members of the family as frail or impaired. Cohort differences draw attention to cohort-based conflicts within families and to the changing nature of families across successive cohorts. The specially created social context in which many older adults live invites us to understand older adults in a specific context and to help the family understand the older members' specific social context. Finally, some of the problems faced by older adults and their families are encountered more frequently in later life and have come to be identified with old age. Although the problems may require specific expertise, the family systems perspective suggests that to improve family functioning as a whole, one should not narrowly focus on the age of the identified client, but rather examine the functioning of the entire system. In the next two sections, we discuss the implications of the family systems viewpoint for assessment and then for interventions with older adults and their families.

Assessment as a Family Network Event

The older adult client does not exist in a vacuum. The older person lives in a social environment, often one that includes one or more family members. At this point in time, older families rarely seek help as a family unit but come in for the assessment and treatment of an older family member. Thus, the clinical assessment of an older client can be understood as an event initiated by a family system. The family context provides a perspective that should influence the manner in which the clinician handles the feedback session; the anticipation of a family feedback session can shape the assessment itself.

It is important to assess the family system as well as the client, and certain broad features of the family should be included in that assessment. Ascertaining the client's historical role in the family system can help the clinician to understand the disturbance in the family system that is caused by the client's disorder and thus the family's current reaction to that disturbance in the system. If the client has been impaired for several years, then it may require some careful history taking to retrieve the memory of the client as a fully functioning individual and to determine the importance of the individual for this particular family. If the clinician can interview several family members, then he or she may be able to envision the historical alliances and conflicts within the family network. As with families of any age (and with any presenting problem), histories of abuse, violence, and incest should be carefully reviewed.

A thorough assessment of family context as well as the older adult client's psychological functioning is necessary to make these decisions. Understanding the family context assists the clinician in understanding the problem, in helping the family understand the problem, and in planning interventions. For the client and the family, receiving the conclusions of the assessment begins a long process of attempting to understand and cope with problems identified in the assessment. A family-oriented feedback session can be an important tool in assisting the older adult and his or her family through this process.

A conjoint assessment feedback session can achieve several goals at once. It brings the family together, provides the opportunity to educate everyone at once about the assessment results, and it can provide a common understanding of the interventions that are to follow. There are also significant reasons for having even an older person with dementia present during assessment feedback. It provides a chance to model open communication about dementia, it provides opportunities to demonstrate the cognitive impairment to family members still in denial, it allows the client to contribute to discussions about the situation the family faces, and it allows for a candid response from the older adult to the emotional climate of the room.

Talking with clients who are suffering from dementia about their cognitive impairment does not come naturally to most professionals. Both the resistance to discussing dementia and the reasons for doing so are analogous to discussing death with the terminally ill: It is an emotionally difficult situation, but it is the client's situation, and he or she has the right to understand the illness.

The clinician should also consider the possibility that the older client is not the only impaired person in the family system. Families often seek help because several people are having problems at once. It is also possible that the decision to care for an older relative may help to disguise problems that originated elsewhere in the system. That is, a couple may take in an older relative to distract themselves from their own marital difficulties. The clinician must be able to identify who in the family is the most emotionally distressed, who in the family is the most impaired (cognitively, emotionally, and characterologically), and whether the problems lie within individuals or are located in the interaction patterns between individuals. These decisions are partly assessment questions and partly strategic decisions about the success of different intervention approaches. A very impaired relative (due to dementia, psychosis, character disorder, or substance abuse) may not be willing or able to benefit from treatment, and the focus may then shift to helping those who are upset by the impairment to cope better with it. Individual intervention may be chosen over family intervention on the basis of who is willing and able to come to therapy rather than of the best approach in an ideal setting. The feedback session may well conclude with a recommendation that several family members seek individual therapy or that the members seek family therapy.

Intervention With Families

Older families are long-standing homeostatic systems (Carter & McGoldrick, 1988; Neidhardt & Allen, 1993); their reactions to a crisis involving an older member are determined at least as much by system issues as by the crisis itself.

The older family is a long-standing system of relationships and roles that now faces the necessity of changing in response to the problem defined by the assessment. Taken together, these concepts are quite similar to the notion of *life event webs* introduced by Pruchno, Blow, and Smyer (1984). Families are linked together in ways that continue even when the system no longer shares a household. The problems of older adults are family problems and resonate throughout the life event web of the various family systems of which the older adult is a member. Assimilating interventions and their implications into the family system may take some time.

Bowen (1978) described the transmission of dysfunction and other family patterns across generations, a key theme for the family therapist working with a multigenerational family system. Whether in work with families or in applying family concepts to individual therapy about family issues, it is notable that people have a much clearer understanding of the impact that their parents have had on their lives and the somewhat mythical power of parents in their lives than they do of their impact on their children's lives. Even within the context of what the therapist may see as an obvious reenactment of a family script, any one adult is likely to perceive parents acting on him or her as powerful figures who do considerable harm (intentionally or not) while viewing her or his relationships with adult children as the children overreacting to herself or himself as another human being with good intentions. Realizing that parents are only human and that children perceive parents as more than humanly powerful and seeing repetition in familial relationships can be useful therapeutic goals in therapy with older families.

Broderick (1993) suggested several modifications to this *cybernetic* model of the family as a goal-oriented system, to constitute what he refers to as a *transcybernetic* model. Three of these seem of particular relevance to this discussion of the later life family. First is the notion of *reflexive spirals*: Much nonfunctional family behavior is the failure to act in goal-oriented ways due to the triggering of overlearned familial behavioral scripts that have a force and pattern of their own and are unconnected to the realities of the current situation. For example, long-standing sibling rivalries may take the place of reality-based decision making when questions arise as to where an impaired relative will live or who will have the power of substitute decision making.

Second, Broderick (1993) called attention to the *psychopolitical* model of family systems. In this view, the family is a collection of individuals who make decisions in the way that other groups do: through communication, persuasion, and power relationships. This model calls attention to the diversity of opinion within families and to the power relationships within families. In this view, conflict over the best course of action to take regarding older family members is normal and should be expected. The issue from a therapeutic standpoint is how and why the decision is made rather than what decision is made. It also calls attention to the power differential within the family and poses the question of the role the therapist should play with regard to less powerful members. Older adults in therapy are often in this less powerful position.

When called in by another family member as a consultant, the therapist should beware of siding with that first caller against other family members, quite likely including the older client. The therapist needs to be aware of who he or she is working for and to be clear with other family members about that allegiance—whether it is to a specific family member (first caller, the one paying the bill, or the older adult) or to the family as a unit (implying compromise of individual members' goals to reach a family one). This view of therapy implies that the family therapist is something of a diplomat: able to negotiate differing viewpoints and reach a compromise decision that can be seen as everyone winning rather than everyone losing.

Finally, Broderick (1993) argued for the contextualization of family therapy in a way that parallels the contextual aspect of the CCMSC model; his label for the familial context was the *opportunity matrix*. This points to different families having different resources to address problems (due to socioeconomic status and to the resources of the community in which they live). In this regard, the aging component is to call attention to the resources available in the aging network. Broderick also uses this term to cover the family's use of space and time to regulate emotional connectedness. With regard to the older family, one can note that they are more dispersed spatially than the child-raising system and have less frequent contact as well. The emotional and psychopolitical meaning of which family members are close and which are distant in time and space should be explored, with an eye on the other aspects of distance making as well (e.g., job opportunities that take children away from parents to whom they are emotionally quite bound).

This last point leads to an important practical consideration of working with older family systems: It is more difficult to get all the members together for conjoint sessions. Depending on how the family is conceptualized, "all" may be quite a lot of people (starting with the older adult, think siblings, spouse, children, grandchildren, great-grandchildren, nieces, nephews, cousins, long-term friends, and so forth). Who is present and who is absent will affect both what is known about the problem and what can be done about the problem. Who is absent should always be of concern to the therapist: The absent person is empowered to play a spoiler role with regard to any outcome of family sessions.

Even if the number of people is manageable, geographic distance may limit contacts. Every opportunity should be taken to include family members who are in town for a visit and to communicate long-distance with those who are not accessible in the local community. The therapist needs to model inclusiveness and open communication to the greatest extent possible. The more barriers the family erects to these actions, the more important the actions are likely to be.

Countertransference and the Older Family

Perhaps the most difficult question facing the therapist working with the older family is "Who is the client?" The question can be answered with the whole family in mind or with any one member. The outcome of intervention is likely to be quite different depending on whether the therapist chooses (consciously or otherwise) to favor the interests of the older adult, a middle-aged child, the young adult grandchild, and so on.

If the issue is not carefully examined, there is considerable room for therapists to choose the family member closest to their own age and gender, to their role in their own family, or whichever position enables them to act out their own problems. There clearly is room to speculate that the tendency to focus on the needs of caregivers rather than the older, frail family member in the United States and the typical but incorrect assumption that caregivers are mostly middle-aged daughters (in fact, primary caregivers are mostly spouses; see Gatz et al., 1991, p. 407) reflect the personal concerns of aging service providers rather than the needs of older adults or their spouse caregivers.

The Borg Family in a Family Context

Ingmar Bergman's film *Wild Strawberries* has entered the literature on psychotherapy with older adults through the writing of Butler (1963) and of Erikson (1978). More recently, Knight (1996) used it to demonstrate the effects of using the CCMSC model on a specific case. In this chapter, we return to the story of the film, to reinterpret it within a family systems context.

The first point we would make is that Isak Borg may be the *identified client* of earlier writing but is not the real client. The main conflict within the Borg family system is between his son Evald and Evald's wife, Marianne, over the question of whether to have a child—and more generally over Evald's coldness, which Marianne recognizes as a characteristic of Isak as well. As the film evolves, it is clear that the same formal and distant style of parent–child relationship is characteristic of Isak and his mother also, and so we have an example of the transmission of this pattern across three generations. The problematic marriage may also be viewed as a repetition of Isak's problems with Evald's mother, with similar cause (the distant husband) but differing effects (adultery vs. estrangement).

Cohort changes may be seen in the familial context in the shift from Isak's very large family of origin to the family he established in adult life (his wife and one child, followed presumably by himself and one child, with the help of the long-time housekeeper). His son finds the idea of a childless family of adult life quite acceptable.

Their social context is that of a relatively well-off Swedish family in the 1950s. Their family decisions are not likely to be limited by economic or social limitations. For example, it is not economically critical to Isak that Evald repay the loan that his father has given him.

We should note that the specific-challenge aspect of the CCMSC model does not seem to apply to the Borg family. That is, they are not dealing with problems generally thought of as late-life problems. The possible exception would be the highly speculative notion that Isak may be working through, or avoiding, unresolved grief for father, siblings, and the loss of his wife. If he were available for interview, one might want to explore this possibility; however, the simpler hypothesis is that the Borgs are coping with non-age-graded problems of family living. This fact serves as a useful reminder that many older families are coping with issues and themes that are present throughout life.

The issue of recurring patterns is obvious in Isak's (and Evald's) relations with women and with the formal pattern of their own conversations, including the one near the end of the film in which Isak offers to dismiss the loan and Evald insists that it must be repaid. Although there is some hope in the fact of Isak breaking the pattern, Evald's response reminds us that it is an established pattern and will need time and repetition of new patterns, to change.

The psychopolitical issues in the family illustrate the power of the older generation in decision making (Isak with regard to Evald and Isak's mother as the matriarch). It is also clear that Evald feels that he can unilaterally decide that he and Marianne will remain childless. It would appear that her leaving him for a while and the appeal to Isak's authority as the father are moves on her part to change the psychopolitical balance of power in this regard.

Within the family systems perspective, we would argue that the car trip assumes the role of a surrogate family system that allows for playing with different roles. The ejection of the couple from the car can be seen as a rejection of their style of fighting. Evald and Marianne can then be seen as playing the role of parents vis-à-vis the younger hitchhikers, a role that leads Evald to a more positive view of family and a more engaged style of parenting, as well as to an alliance with Marianne to save their real family system.

Summary

Family systems theory suggests a different level of analysis and several types of questions that differ substantially from those posed in individual interventions. The focus is on relationships among people rather than intraindividual processes. The history of familial relationships is important for understanding multigenerational transmission of values, dysfunction, and relationship scripts and for working on recurring patterns of interaction. The psychopolitical concept brings attention to power relationships among family members and the manner in which decisions are made. The opportunity matrix within which the family is embedded influences their interactions with one another and their choices within the larger society. Countertransference issues are likely to emerge earlier and be even more potent within family contexts than within individual interventions.

A key issue in the application of family systems theory to older families is when to apply it. As we have noted throughout the chapter, real and strategic considerations may limit the opportunities to actually have an entire family meet together for multiple sessions. However, it is often possible to "think family" even when one cannot "do family": the Bowenian notion of family therapy with individual clients (see Bowen, 1978). We would argue that it is virtually always beneficial to think family, even when involved in individual interventions with older adults or with younger adults who are caring for older ones.

Ethical Issues

Family therapy poses a number of ethical issues in a different form than in individually oriented interventions. First, as has been noted earlier, is the question of to which client relationship the therapist owes fidelity (see Fitting, 1984, 1986, for discussion of fidelity as an ethical principle in therapy relationships). Therapists can enter family systems (in some sense, they are always entering family systems, even when doing individual therapy) as an ally of any one member or as an ally of the whole system. The choice of whose therapist one is is itself fraught with value-laden choices. At the very least, the choice should be clearly communicated to all involved family members, and the therapist should wrestle with the implications of the choice. What one knows and what one chooses to do are likely to be very different depending on where the family system is entered. As a class exercise, we ask students to role-play a multi-generational family. Afterward, we discuss (among other things) what one would do if he or she were the older adult's therapist, the middle-aged daughter's therapist, the college-age granddaughter's therapist, or the whole family's therapist. Each role leads to different, and often to opposed, actions and outcomes.

Confidentiality is tricky in the conjoint family therapy context. In our view, almost any arrangement can be agreed to, as long as it is agreed to and clear to all family members. The best strategy is likely to be the agreement that nothing should be disclosed to the therapist that cannot be used in the family session. This allows for open communication and the full use of what is known. In some circumstances, families will not disclose information that may be useful under these terms. The therapist then has to consider whether there is any value in knowing things that cannot be used, as well as whether sensitive information may become usable in time.

The issues of beneficence and autonomy are often in conflict with regard to individual older clients (see Knight, 1996) and are likely to arise in family therapy with older families, both as conflicting values within the family and as ethical conflicts for the therapist. When older family members are frail, everyone struggles with the question of whether it is more important to respect their autonomy or to be beneficent and take care of them. The key problem in beneficence of course is who gets to decide what the "good care" option is. Just as therapists can influence, intentionally and unintentionally, individual clients who are ambivalent about complex decisions, the family therapist may influence the family by subtle cues or more overtly by taking sides in the psycho-political battle within the family over competing notions of beneficence or over the balance between autonomy and beneficence. Within families that are themselves divided over complex issues, it is quite difficult to adhere to the principle of guiding process without guiding outcomes.

With regard to autonomy, the older adult relative within a family is presumed competent by the clinician until the assessment demonstrates incompetence. Many families may already define the older adult client as "incompetent" and exclude him or her from decision making. Although this exclusion from decision making within the family is sometimes based on cognitive impairment, it can also be based on depression, dependency, passivity, or intra-family power struggles. The psychologist must avoid accepting the family's viewpoint and joining the family against the older adult. At some point in the progression of dementia, this principle may require modification. Unfortunately, at this time, the point at which that is appropriate is not clearly definable (see Grisso, 1994, for more detailed discussion of competency and dementia).

Conclusion

The CCMSC model applies scientific gerontology to the understanding of family systems and suggests that in a sense, all families are older families. The specialized aspects of working with older families likely arise from the specific challenges facing older relatives and the family system (i.e., chronic illness, disability, grief, and caregiving), from the need to integrate cross-cohort views and to work with multiple adult generations of the family structure, and from the need for both family and therapist to understand the social context of older adults in age-segregated societies. Applying family systems to assessment and intervention with older adults points to a number of ways in which family theory leads to a very different perspective on working with older adults and their families than do individually oriented theories, including raising the question of whether the older adult is the person who should be the focus of psychological intervention.

References

Aranda, M. P., & Knight, B. G. (1997). The influence of ethnicity and culture on the caregiver stress and coping process: A sociocultural review and analysis. *Gerontologist, 37,* 342–354.

Bengtson, V. L., Cutler, N. E., Mangen, D. J., & Marshall, V. W. (1995). Generations, cohorts, and relations between age groups. In R. H. Binstock & E. Shanas (Eds.), *Handbook of aging and the social sciences* (2nd ed., pp. 304–338). New York: Van Nostrand Reinhold.

Bengtson, V., Rosenthal, C., & Burton, L. (1990). Families and aging: Diversity and heterogeneity. In R. H. Binstock & L. K. George (Eds.), *Handbook of aging and the social sciences* (3rd ed., pp. 263–287). San Diego, CA: Academic Press.

Bowen, M. (1978). *Family therapy in clinical practice.* Northvale, NJ: Aronson.

Broderick, C. B. (1993). *Understanding family process: Basics of family systems theory.* Newbury Park, CA: Sage.

Brown, F. H. (1988). The impact of death and serious illness on the family life cycle. In B. Carter & M. McGoldrick (Eds.), *The changing family life cycle* (pp. 457–482). New York: Gardner Press.

Butler, R. N. (1963). The life review: An interpretation of reminiscence in the aged. *Psychiatry, 119,* 721–728.

Carter, B., & McGoldrick, M. (Eds.). (1988). *The changing family life cycle.* New York: Gardner Press.

Erikson, E. H. (1978). Reflections on Dr. Borg's life cycle. In E. H. Erikson (Ed.), *Adulthood: Essays.* New York: Norton.

Fitting, M. D. (1984). Professional and ethical responsibilities for psychologists working with the elderly. *Counseling Psychologist, 12,* 69–78.

Fitting, M. D. (1986). Ethical dilemmas in counseling elderly adults. *Journal of Counseling and Development, 64,* 325–327.

Gatz, M., Bengtson, V. L., & Blum, M. J. (1991). Caregiving families. In J. E. Birren & K. W. Schaie (Eds.), *Handbook of the psychology of aging* (3rd ed., pp. 405–426). San Diego, CA: Academic Press.

Grisso, T. (1994). Clinical assessments for legal competence of older adults. In M. Storandt & G. R. VandenBos (Eds.), *Neuropsychological assessment of dementia and depression in older adults: A clinician's guide* (pp. 119–140). Washington, DC: American Psychological Association.

Hagestad, G. O. (1990). Social perspectives on the life course. In R. H. Binstock & L. K. George (Eds.), *Handbook of aging and the social sciences* (3rd ed., pp. 151–168). San Diego, CA: Academic Press.

Knight, B. (1994). Providing clinical interpretations to older adults and their families. In M. Storandt & G. R. VandenBos (Eds.), *Neuropsychological assessment of dementia and depression in older adults: A clinician's guide* (pp. 141–154). Washington, DC: American Psychological Association.

Knight, B. (1996). *Psychotherapy with older adults* (2nd ed.). Newbury Park, CA: Sage.

Neidhardt, E., & Allen, J. (1993). *Family therapy with the elderly.* Newbury Park, CA: Sage.

Pruchno, R. A., Blow, F. E., & Smyer, M. A. (1984). Life events and interdependent lives: Implications for research and intervention. *Human Development, 27,* 31–41.

Qualls, S. (1996). Family therapy with aging families. In S. H. Zarit & B. G. Knight (Eds.), *A guide to psychotherapy and aging: Effective interventions in a life-stage context* (pp. 121–138). Washington, DC: American Psychological Association.

Zarit, S. H. (1996). Interventions with family caregivers. In S. H. Zarit & B. G. Knight (Eds.), *A guide to psychotherapy and aging: Effective interventions in a life-stage context* (pp. 139–162). Washington, DC: American Psychological Association.

25

Interventions in Nursing Homes and Other Alternative Living Settings

Steven H. Zarit, Melissa M. Dolan, and Sara A. Leitsch

Residential environments such as nursing homes and other institutional facilities are important and challenging arenas for psychological interventions. Once considered to be warehouses, nursing homes have seen rapid innovations in the design of facilities and programming to meet special needs of older, disabled residents. Geropsychologists can work with other staff, as well as with patients and families, to create an optimal setting that maximizes residents' remaining abilities while minimizing the consequences of chronic disease and disabilities for a patient.

The residents of nursing homes and institutional facilities are increasingly frail. Although the composition of resident populations varies somewhat from country to country, it is generally the case that nursing home residents are characterized by comorbidities, that is, multiple health problems that limit functioning in significant ways (Manton, Cornelius, & Woodbury, 1995). Common medical problems leading to nursing home placement include stroke, hip fracture, heart disease, and diabetes (Ferrucci, Guralnik, Pahor, Corti, & Havlik, 1997). Residents typically need assistance with two or more activities of daily living, such as bathing, dressing, transferring, or using the toilet.

Residents' mental health problems add another layer of complexity to their care. The need for mental health services in institutional settings is considerable. As Smyer and his colleagues (Smyer, Brannon, & Cohn, 1991) have emphasized, nursing homes have become the mental hospitals of contemporary society. Surveys of residents have found that between 50% and 90% suffer from one form of mental disorder (e.g., German, Shapiro, & Kramer, 1986; German, Rovner, Burton, Brant, & Clark, 1992; Rovner, Kafonek, Filipp, Lucas, & Folstein, 1986). Many of these patients have Alzheimer's disease or another dementing illness, and many experience depression, anxiety, and a variety of other acute and chronic problems. Despite this high prevalence, most patients receive little or no mental health treatment (Smyer, Shea, & Streit, 1994).

Psychologists who work in long-term care settings need a variety of knowledge and skills, such as an understanding of dementia, delirium, and depression, and the other common disorders of later life; the ability to conduct an assessment leading to differential diagnosis; familiarity with common diseases and medications so as to understand their psychological implications and to work effectively with medical staff; knowledge of the behavioral management of the types of disruptive behavior typical of some dementia patients; and a systems perspective to understand the relationships among staff, patients, and the patients' families. In this chapter we emphasize the unique characteristics of institutional settings, as well as recent trends in how those settings are organized. We consider models of care, as well as the use of environmental design to achieve therapeutic goals in traditional and nontraditional care settings, and we look at staff issues in long-term care. With that as a foundation, we then turn to the role of the psychologist in these care settings.

Critical Features of Institutional Settings

The fundamental premise of this chapter is that older people with multiple health and mental health problems have an increased sensitivity to environmental demands (Lawton & Nahemow, 1973). According to Baltes (1988), increasing biological vulnerability in old age creates greater environmental potential in both optimizing and hindering behavioral outcomes among aged individuals. Kahana (1982) noted that losses in such domains as health and social roles often reduce the options available to maintain an environment that meets personal preferences. Even with the declines that may accompany aging, older adults have the potential proactively to affect their environment, as well as to be influenced by it (Kahana, 1982). Understanding the role of the setting is critical to development of effective psychological interventions in long-term care settings.

The implementation of care in institutional settings revolves around three related themes, (a) the nursing home as a medical facility, (b) the autonomy–security dialectic, and (c) dependency. An understanding of these issues is an important element in developing therapeutic interventions.

Medical Models of Care

Despite recent innovations in care, the nursing home setting represents an outgrowth of the medical model tradition. The medical model (Parsons, 1951) is based on a method of care and service delivery patterned after an acute care hospital in which health and safety are the primary goals. Therefore, the routines, philosophy of care, and atmosphere derive primarily from those practices within hospital settings. As suggested by Regnier (1994), aspects of the physical environment of nursing homes, such as building codes, safety considerations, room shape, number of residents per room, and distance from each room to the nurses' station, stem directly from hospital design.

The relationship that exists between staff members and residents in nursing homes is also modeled in a medical tradition that defines the staff as the decision makers and the older residents as "sick" patients (Lidz & Arnold, 1990). In such an environment, the older resident is perceived as helpless and dependent (Baltes, 1994). Staff are trained in routinized delivery of physical and health care to residents that restricts opportunities for autonomous, self-directed behavior. Despite obligatory statements to the contrary, what matters most in nursing homes is delivery of health care, not the quality of residents' lives.

The Autonomy–Security Dialectic

A second pivotal issue in how care is organized is the balance that is set between residents' autonomy as adults and their need for security, or what Parmelee and Lawton (1990) have called the *autonomy–security dialectic*. According to Lawton (1989a), these human needs form a dialectic because both are essential for well-being. Unfortunately, this balance is often easily disrupted, as satisfying one need in a given situation often leads to the frustration of the other. Particularly for the older adult, achieving an overall sense of balance between independence and support is often a difficult task.

In a short-term medical setting, patients are treated as dependent and many decisions are made for them (e.g., what foods they eat, when they eat and sleep). These decisions are made for the purpose of expediency so that routines in the hospital can be maintained. Having to conform to a hospital's routine is at best a short-term annoyance. Nursing homes, however, have carried over many of the same routines, emphasizing the dependency of the resident and the need for organizational efficiency over autonomy.

There are, of course, legitimate needs for security. Typically, placement of an older adult from a private residence into residential care occurs to assure physical safety and security, as well as psychological peace of mind for family members who may be concerned about the ability of an older person to function adequately at home. The benefits of security include increased feelings of support through the availability of assistance and contact with others (Carp, 1987; Sheehan, 1986).

On balance, however, nursing homes find it easier to stress security over autonomy. This excessive helping may actually lead to further decline in competencies. An optimal environment is one that fits an individual's capacities or slightly exceeds them so the individual is challenged to function at his or her best (Lawton & Nahemow, 1973). In other words, to be appropriate, an environment should be stimulating, but not overwhelming. An environment that is too supportive may encourage excess disabilities, boredom, or dependent behavior. Alternatively, a context that is far too demanding or complex for a person's competence level may also promote incapacity due to the excessive stress it creates.

Dependency Scripts

Baltes and her colleagues (Baltes & Horgas, 1997; Baltes & Reisenzein, 1986) proposed a specific mechanism whereby institutional settings lead to dependencies and excess disabilities. This mechanism, called *dependency-support scripts*, describes a process of rewarding residents in long-term care settings for dependent, incompetent behavior, while ignoring or even punishing self-sufficiency. Conducting detailed behavioral observations of interactions in nursing homes, Baltes and Wahl (1992) reported that dependent self-care behaviors have the highest probability of securing immediate and reliable support and attention from others. Further, staff members adhere to this script for behavior regardless of the competence level of the older resident. While this interaction pattern may be appropriate for older adults who are unable to perform independent self-care behaviors, adults who are capable are at serious risk for over-compensation by staff.

These studies have also indicated that the vast majority (approximately 80%) of dependent self-care behaviors in residents were the result of compliance with staff instructions, rather than requests for help (Baltes, Kindermann, Reisenzein, & Schmid, 1987). Furthermore, older residents reported being fully aware that they were not performing behaviors that they were competent to perform (Wahl, 1991). Clearly, then, the emphasis on security in institutional settings is manifested in reinforcement of dependencies.

Therapeutic Models of Residential Care

The deficiencies of nursing homes have long been recognized, and have led to proposals for restructuring them to support specific therapeutic goals. As Lidz and Arnold (1990) eloquently stated, "one way to increase the importance of autonomy in a nursing home is to separate its medical care function from its residential function" (p. 67). Toward that end, therapeutic models of care have placed a greater emphasis on autonomy and have focused on the domain-specific deficits and strengths of the impaired resident, rather than assuming global impairment. In general, the goal of such settings is to keep residents independent and autonomous in a comfortable environment. A therapeutic model is designed to stabilize and build on the competencies of residents in order to create a supportive, yet challenging environment that maximizes the potential for prolonged functioning (Regnier, 1994). This philosophy of care is seen as a more humane, cost effective, and therapeutic alternative to the medical model (Cohen & Day, 1994).

Nursing Homes: Special Care Units for Dementia

Special care dementia units represent an attempt to bridge the gap between the medical model tradition and a more therapeutic approach to care. These units are typically designed for dementia patients, although units can target residents prone to falls or with other special physical needs. Specialized care often involves aspects such as reduction of stimulation, professionally trained staff, individualized activities, environmental modifications, and more direct involvement of families of residents, but there is considerable heterogeneity among units and no standard criteria for special care exist (Ohta & Ohta, 1988).

Cohen and Weisman (1991) have outlined several therapeutic goals to be met in dementia facilities. First, these environments should attempt to balance resident needs for safety and security with those of autonomy and privacy. In addition, such settings should promote maintenance of functional abilities and competencies through activities that are tied to familiar tasks and routines, as well as through an environment that is stimulating and challenging. Further, the facility should support a positive social climate and promote interactions among residents. Finally, a dementia-specific facility must be flexible and able to adapt to the changing needs of residents throughout the disease progression. Clearly, the focus of such a model is not solely on promoting health and safety, but instead is on building on residents' strengths while providing support for their deficits. Although complex behaviors may not be actualized, this environment stresses the ability to perform many simple tasks and behaviors critical to daily functioning and well-being.

Defining the characteristics of special care. Designation of what constitutes special care is controversial and there is a great deal of diversity among units that offer specialized dementia care (Maslow, 1994). Common goals of the units include sustaining activities of daily living, increasing quality of life, diminishing behavior problems, and dealing with physical difficulties (Maslow, 1994). The method through which the units achieve these goals varies. Many nursing homes have created special dementia units by putting locks on doors to traditional nursing home wings but do little else in the way of programming or care. While locked doors or special alarm systems that alert staff when patients wander off the unit are the most common feature of special care units (Maslow, 1994), other possible characteristics include a higher staff to resident ratio, special training for staff, a safe outdoor area, a specialized floor plan, color coding, and family support groups. Ideally, special care units will offer a variety of dementia specific activities for the residents, such as cognitive stimulation and exercise programs for smaller groups. In reality, special care units are no more likely to provide special activities for residents than are any other units, but nonetheless cost more on average than other units (Maslow, 1994).

Resident characteristics. The obvious characteristic that most residents of dementia specific special care units (SCUs) have in common is their dementia, however the severity of the dementia varies. Although they are usually more cognitively impaired than residents of other units, SCU patients tend not to be as physically frail (Holmes, Teresi, Weiner, & Monaco, 1990; Maslow, 1994; Mehr & Fries, 1995). Typically, they need assistance from staff with their activities of daily living (Holmes et al., 1990), are often younger than residents of other units, are more likely to participate in activities, and are less likely to be restrained (Maslow, 1994; Rovner, Steele, Shmuely, & Folstein, 1996). Residents of SCUs are more likely to be administered psychotropic medication, but they are less likely to use other types of medication (Maslow, 1994; Rovner et al., 1996). Residents of SCUs are also more likely to fall than residents in other units within nursing homes (Maslow, 1994).

Effectiveness of special care units. Because of the large variability of characteristics among SCUs, any assessment of their effectiveness must take into consideration the specific treatment offered. Several studies have investigated the impact of these units on a variety of outcomes. Cleary, Clamon, Price, and Shullaw (1988) tested the effect of a reduced stimulus unit on residents with dementia. Among the services offered by the unit were more appropriate activities for residents with dementia and unrestrained wandering. Although no significant changes in global severity of dementia were observed, patient weight reversed its downward trend significantly. Furthermore, family satisfaction increased significantly and more interaction was observed on the unit.

Rovner and colleagues (1996) conducted one of the few investigations with random assignment to treatment. Residents just entering a facility were randomly assigned to either a special care unit or to a nonspecialized unit. Characteristics of the treatment unit included a dementia-appropriate activity program, psychotropic drug treatment, and educational rounds. The control unit was in the same institution, and therefore included the same medical treatment, but did not include any specialized programming for the residents. After 6 months, 28.6% of the residents in the special care unit exhibited behavior problems compared with 51.3% of those in the control unit. Restraint and drug use decreased for the treatment group and increased for the control group. There was no significant cognitive deterioration for either the treatment or the control group.

The lack of significant cognitive differences in the outcome underscores a very important feature of dementia care. Goals of treatment should not focus primarily on arresting the deterioration of cognitive abilities. Cognitive decline is part of an ongoing degenerative process associated with Alzheimer's disease or another type of dementia, and efforts to intervene will have only limited impact. Other manifestations of dementia, however, including the patient's behavior, mood, and functional competency, are more responsive to behavioral and environmental intervention and should be the focus of specialized dementia units or other treatment settings. Physical problems, such as the weight loss common among Alzheimer's disease patients, have also been shown to be sensitive to specialized dementia care (Cleary et al., 1988). Appropriate indicators of the effectiveness of the specialized units should include those domains that are sensitive to special care.

Assisted Living Facilities and Group Homes: Alternatives to Nursing Home Care

To meet the recent demand for more flexible residential settings that maximize the independence of disabled older adults, a variety of new types of settings have been developed (Regnier, 1994). These facilities go by many different names, including assisted living, board and care, and group homes. Unlike special care units within nursing homes, these facilities are not located within medical settings and are not regulated as health care settings. They have generally adopted a philosophy of care emphasizing social, therapeutic, and environmental influences on behavior. In other words, they take many of the ideas expressed in special care units and extend them to a nonmedical setting. Typically, these assisted living facilities are more homelike, have less staff (particularly medical staff), and orient their programs around the goal of maximizing independent living.

The therapeutic nature of assisted living makes it a viable alternative environment for residents with dementia. Perhaps the best known of these approaches is group homes for dementia patients in Sweden (Malmberg & Zarit, 1993). Group homes consist of 5 to 7 apartments that are linked together with hallways and common areas and are secured to the outside with a locked door. These facilities have been explicitly developed on a social model to emphasize maintenance of remaining abilities. Programming is built around activities of daily living. To the extent possible, residents assist with cooking, cleaning, or doing their own laundry. The setting also emphasizes autonomy. Residents sign leases to their apartments, and furnish them with their own belongings. They are given keys to the apartments and can go inside and lock the doors. Units are quiet, homelike settings, with little of the institutional quality of nursing homes and perhaps fewer behavioral and management programs. Although residents are able to perform fewer activities than staff had originally anticipated, it has been possible to maintain most residents in group homes until late in their illness or even until death (Malmberg & Zarit, 1993).

Similar noninstitutional care models are beginning to emerge in the United States (Regnier, 1994). What constitutes assisted living can vary greatly from site to site. As with special nursing home units, assisted living or board and care facilities may consist of little more than a locked door, or they may have a well-developed program and well-trained staff. Other homes, however, exhibit just the opposite. The independence of the residents is respected and a variety of services are offered to assist in their daily living.

The Assisted Living Environment and Dementia

The therapeutic model as implemented in assisted living settings may be better suited to meet the needs of cognitively impaired older adults. These individuals may be at greater risk for overcompensation because dementia often creates the need for restrictions in lifestyle and activities fairly early in the disease progression (Cotrell & Schulz, 1993). A more flexible environment that is not governed by strict routines may be better able to support an older resident's needs for attention and supervision. In an intervention to reduce behavioral problems, Beck and Vogelpohl (1995) found that older nursing home residents who were given higher levels of autonomy appeared to be more relaxed and interacted with their environment more. This particular strategy also reduced tension and stress among the staff members caring for the residents. The authors concluded that the less restrictive setting was better able to promote physical and psychological health among these impaired older adults.

Although impairments in memory, reasoning, language, and other cognitive functions are undeniable consequences of dementia, losses are not uniform across areas of functioning. Significant difficulties may be present in one domain, but other abilities may remain relatively intact for a much longer period. For example, cognitively impaired older adults may not be capable of complex decision-making tasks (i.e., managing finances), but they may be quite able to perform more limited independent actions important to daily living such as preparing a snack or taking a walk (Hofland, 1994).

In a similar vein, Fitting (1980) pointed out the fluctuations in decision-making capacity experienced by impaired older adults and the importance of protecting their right to choose as much as possible despite these instabilities. Hofland (1994) suggested that decision-making ability be continually re-assessed to reshape care plans and choices offered to maintain participation of the older adult as the disease progresses. In this way, autonomy may be pre-served, but the person's capacities will not be overwhelmed by environmental demands. Assisted living environments, with their flexible routines and focus on the individual's strengths may be better able to mold to residents' changing competencies.

Due to the emphasis on independence in care routines among assisted liv-ing environments for the cognitively impaired, these settings may be more likely to consider and value past histories of residents. Individuals come to the care environment with long-standing habits and care routines in all domains of functioning. According to Hofland (1995), the environment should be flexible enough to meet the needs and preferences of older residents, rather than be so inflexible as to expect the residents to change their past history to conform to the environment. For example, an individual who would like to have a meal later in the afternoon should not be forbidden because of strict environmental routines that govern all meal times and resident behavior.

Person–Environment Interaction in Long-Term Care Settings

While research suggests that maintaining autonomy in residential settings is beneficial to physical and psychological health, we must remember the wide range of individual differences among older adults in their preferences, desire for, and lifelong patterns of independence. As Hofland (1995) pointed out, choos-ing not to be autonomous is also a valid choice for older adults. In matching persons to their environment, it is important to acknowledge that individuals vary considerably in their needs and preferences, and that this variation is particularly salient among older adults. In an excellent illustration of the importance of individual differences in person–environment fit, O'Connor and Vallerand (1994) argued that nursing home residents with high self-determination personality styles may be better adjusted in homes that provide for freedom and choice. Physical competency may also play an important role in issues of person–environment fit. For example, research by Timko and Moos (1991) indicated that highly functional residents benefited from greater choice and independence in a residential facility much more than did very impaired individuals.

As Kahana and Kahana (1983) warned, we must attend to individual dif-ferences or we may unintentionally increase the incongruence between person and environment, thus creating further stress or discomfort. As we are assess-ing special housing for older adults, we must realize that although a setting may appear beneficial in its effects on residents, these effects may not be evenly distributed and may even be reversed for a minority of residents (Carp & Carp, 1984). Therefore, to evaluate the effectiveness of a particular residential set-ting, it is important to acknowledge the role that person variables play in the dynamic relationship between individual and context.

The assessment of residential settings for older adults must fulfill three standard functions, maintaining competence, providing stimulation, and providing a sense of security and support (Lawton, 1989c). To date, few studies have directly examined all of these issues or systematically compared pertinent information across residential settings. We must consider the effectiveness of programs on problematic behaviors among demented older adults and also the impact such interventions have on quality of life issues (Cotrell & Schulz, 1993). Clearly, environments that do not foster autonomy needs in older residents are detrimental to functional capacity, and research indicates that older adults are aware of the constraints imposed on them by contextual conditions (Wahl, 1991). Residential environments must continue to evolve to meet the needs of older adults as well as maximize their potential.

Staff Issues in Long-Term Care

The social climate of a long-term care environment is largely determined by the staff–resident interactions that take place within it. As previously discussed, staff members are an integral part of the dynamic that defines the goals of a setting as medical or therapeutic. Although it is impossible to thoroughly discuss the role of staff in an institutionalized environment within the bounds of this chapter, staff demands and attitudes are important issues when considering interventions within these settings.

Caring for nursing home residents is a physically and emotionally demanding occupation. A major feature of these settings is the pyramid structure of the staff (Smyer, Brannon, & Cohn, 1991). The few individuals at the top of the staff hierarchy have the most training and expertise but the least contact with patients. In turn, staff responsible for the majority of resident care (e.g., nursing assistants or aides) constitute the bottom level of the nursing home hierarchy and have the least training. In the United States, an average nursing staff for a long-term care facility is composed of 15% registered nurses (RNs), 14% licensed practical nurses (LPNs), and 70% nursing assistants or nurse aides (Institute of Medicine, 1986). It is these nonprofessional nurse aides who perform approximately 80% to 90% of the actual personal care of residents (Waxman, Carner, & Berkenstock, 1984).

Despite their low status position in the nursing home hierarchy, nurse aides are endowed with a great deal of responsibility and are involved with almost every aspect of a given resident's well-being (Aroskar, Urv-Wong, & Kane, 1990). With such responsibilities for the physical and emotional care of residents, however, comes little personal authority or independence. Nurse aides must conform to strict routines and schedules imposed by the administration. An often overwhelming number of routine tasks must be carried out within a short period of time (Wright, 1988). These high occupational demands may cause aides to experience burnout and job stress. Burnout may lead nurse aides to experience physical and emotional exhaustion, as well as reduced feelings of accomplishment and pride in their work (Maslach, 1982). Clearly, burnout may negatively impact the quality of care afforded to residents.

The experience of working within an institutional environment varies with the type of facility. Specific aspects of the environment, instead of the global structure, have been shown to have a systematic effect on staff attitude toward older adult patients. Millard and Smith (1981) found residents pictured without personal belongings surrounding them were perceived as less effective, more dependent, and less socially capable and desirable. Pietrukowizc and Johnson (1991) established that participants who read life histories of residents perceived them as more adaptable, goal setting, and possessed with interactional skills. These findings are particularly relevant to the consideration of assisted living facilities, which lend themselves to personalized rooms and apartments. Staff may, therefore, perceive residents of assisted living facilities as more sociable, desirable, and capable.

The attitude held by staff members can have a profound effect on their behavior toward residents. Brown (1988) showed a positive relationship between nursing assistants' attitude and their behavior toward older adults and the patients' rehabilitation potential (Heller, Bausell, & Ninos, 1984). Furthermore, infantilization and its effect on nurses' behavior has been a primary concern in the literature. Some nursing staff perceive the residents as children and treat them as such. This behavior on the part of staff creates a self-fulfilling prophecy and causes many of the residents to regress into a state of childlike helplessness (Storlie, 1982).

Clearly, several relevant issues regarding staff outcomes in long-term care must be considered. As discussed previously, staff often operate under the assumption that older residents are incompetent, which results in an emphasis on overcompensation for deficits. Such scripts surrounding behavior patterns must be identified in the facility before they can be modified. Specifically, interventions at the staff level have been successful in altering this dependency script and promoting higher levels of independent behavior among residents (Baltes, Neumann, & Zank, 1994). Similarly, perceptions that staff have about residents, their beliefs about the delivery of care, and their level of training in the management of frail or dementia patient residents are crucial issues to consider and may have important implications for intervention attempts.

The Psychologist as a Consultant in Long-Term Care

Effective interventions in long-term care facilities grow out of an understanding of the setting, particularly how autonomy, security, and dependency issues are addressed. Psychologists need to know how to address specific questions about diagnosis and behavioral management, but must keep in mind the larger principles of how care is organized and delivered and how the setting affects behavior.

Psychologists can play an effective role in long-term care settings as consultants. Some consultations will involve diagnostic questions, but more typically psychologists will assist in the development and implementation of interventions for residents' behavioral and affective problems. This is an important role, because other staff are usually too busy to examine the whole of a problem or situation or to put together evidence from multiple sources, such as patients, families, and staff, that are needed for identifying successful interventions. Although psychologists may also conduct psychotherapy with selected individuals, most residents are too disabled to benefit from more than brief treatment.

Consultations focus on individual residents, or, on occasion, their families. The solutions, however, often focus on changing the interaction of residents with staff or between staff and family. Over the long term, psychologists can help staff implement procedures that promote greater autonomy and independence. To play this role effectively, psychologists need to draw upon several sources of information.

The beginning point for the consultant is to understand the setting's organization and the role of staff. As noted previously, long-term care settings have a pyramid structure, with the few individuals at the top of the pyramid typically having the most training and expertise but also the least amount of contact with patients, whereas staff at the bottom of the pyramid have the most responsibility for patient care and the least training. The consultant must try to understand the problem from the perspective of the staff. Their work is often physically and emotionally demanding, especially when caring for difficult residents for which they have little or no training.

Successful intervention must take this hierarchy into account. Consultants must gain the support of the key people in charge of clinical operations, for example, the director of nursing or the head of a specific unit. Although the ultimate goal may be to change the behavior of nurse's aides or assistants, that may not be possible unless the changes are supported by supervisory personnel. Supervisory personnel do not need to be involved on every consultation, but it is helpful to meet with them regularly to assure ongoing support of interventions.

Depending on the setting, physicians may have an important role in the hierarchy. They may be an important referral source or have a key role in proposed interventions, for example, changing the resident's medications. Psychologists need to learn to work effectively with physicians in a number of ways. It is important to be familiar with medical terminology and the effects of common illnesses and medications that affect older people. This knowledge is central to diagnostic questions but also helps the psychologist establish credibility with physicians.

The consultations process begins by obtaining information from the staff person who has made the referral. This first step can clarify the initial consultation and identify the next steps in assessment. Depending on the situation, the consultant will then obtain relative information from other staff as well as the resident and, when appropriate, his or her family. Medical charts or other staff records are an important source of information, and should always be reviewed as part of a consultation. Psychologists also need to know how to communicate effectively in charts, writing clear and brief notes that summarize the main findings and the proposed change in ways that all the staff can understand. Notes that are too long or too technical will be ignored or misunderstood.

Interventions can be made on many levels. Sometimes, the patient's problem can be treated directly, for example, with a change in medication. Often treatment involves changes in how staff approach the patient. These changes need to be clear and simple, so that staff can understand and make the changes.

Short, inservice training sessions on a problem can be a good way of implementing these changes. Changes in daily routines can also be part of the intervention, for example, scheduling more activities as a way of heading off agitation or moving a resident to a different room because of a roommate problem.

It is important to recognize that staff also need emotional support. Their jobs are demanding and they often experience considerable stress. They also become attached to individual residents, and may be upset when that resident declines or dies.

Families also play a key, and often overlooked, role in long-term care facilities. They can be a source of problems, complaining to staff about care or interfering with routines that staff think are best for the resident. Often, problems result because families do not understand how a facility functions, or how to make changes. They may walk up to the first staff person they see to talk about a problem, and not realize that the person may not have anything to do with their relative's care. The consultant's role is often to help families understand the rules of the game, that is, who to go to with concerns and how to phrase those concerns. Families need to learn to mix criticism with praise, so as to get the cooperation of staff. Conversely, staff who are dealing with problem residents need to tell families more than just the bad things that happen. By taking time to work with the family, the consultant can enlist their cooperation as well as help them to feel they can influence the care their relative is receiving.

Some facilities have support groups for families of their residents. In general, groups that are independent of the facility may be more effective, because families can speak freely without fear of reprisals from the staff. They can also learn about the experiences of families who have relatives at other facilities. This information can put their own experience into a broader perspective, as well as provide ideas about how to handle specific problems.

Finally, there are occasions when the psychologist will provide direct treatment to the resident. Short-term psychotherapy may be appropriate for a depressed resident or for someone in the early stages of dementia. Groups are often used in long-term care facilities, but are usually not an optimal treatment. These settings often present many threats to autonomy. Asking people to talk about personal experiences in a group of other residents can be experienced as another threat to their autonomy. Unlike group therapy in the community where participants do not necessarily see each other outside the group, residents of a long-term care facility remain in close proximity to the other group members. Activity or interest groups are a more important strategy. Psychologists can work with staff who lead those groups to understand more about group behavior and to deal with problems that might arise.

Conclusion

Long-term care settings pose a challenge and opportunity for psychologists. Application of knowledge about geropsychology combined with an understanding of the long-term care setting can lead to substantial improvements in residents' functioning and make the facility a better place for staff and families.

Interventions need to be grounded in the knowledge of how settings influence behavior, particularly, issues of autonomy, security, and dependency. New types of long-term care settings offer possibilities for using features of the setting and programming in creative ways to minimize adverse effects and support residents' remaining abilities. Psychological consultation can play a critical role in bringing together information from relevant sources to develop effective interventions.

References

Aroskar, M. A., Urv-Wong, E. K., & Kane, R. A. (1990). Building an effective caregiving staff: Transforming the nursing services. In R. A. Kane & A. L. Caplan (Eds.), *Everyday ethics: Resolving dilemmas in nursing home life* (pp. 271–290). New York: Springer.

Baltes, M. M. (1988). The etiology and maintenance of dependency in the elderly: Three phases of operant research. *Behavior Therapy, 19,* 353–377.

Baltes, M. M. (1994). Aging well and institutional living: A paradox? In R. P. Abeles, H. C. Gift, & M. G. Ory (Eds.), *Aging and quality of life* (pp. 185–201). New York: Springer.

Baltes, M. M., & Horgas, A. L. (1997). Long-term care institutions and the maintenance of competence: A dialectic between compensation and overcompensation. In S. L. Willis, K. W. Schaie, & M. Hayward (Eds.), *Societal mechanisms for maintaining competence in old age* (pp. 142–164). New York: Springer.

Baltes, M. M., & Reisenzein, R. (1986). The social world in long-term care institutions: Psychosocial control toward dependency? In M. M. Baltes & P. B. Baltes (Eds.), *The psychology of control and aging* (pp. 315–343). Hillsdale, NJ: Erlbaum.

Baltes, M. M., & Wahl, H. W. (1992). The dependency-support script in institutions: Generalization to community settings. *Psychology and Aging, 7,* 409–418.

Baltes, M. M., Kindermann, T., Reisenzein, R., & Schmid, U. (1987). Further observational data on the behavioral and social world of institutions for the aged. *Psychology and Aging, 2,* 390–403.

Baltes, M. M., Neumann, E. M., & Zank, S. (1994). Maintenance and rehabilitation of independence in old age: An intervention program for staff. *Psychology and Aging, 9,* 179–188.

Beck, C. K., & Vogelpohl, T. S. (1995). Cognitive impairment and autonomy. In L. M. Gamroth, J. Semradek, & E. M. Tornquist (Eds.), *Enhancing autonomy in long-term care: Concepts and strategies* (pp. 44–57). New York: Springer.

Blake, R. (1986). Normalization and boarding homes: An examination of paradoxes. *Social Work in Health Care, 11,* 75–86.

Brown, M. (1988). Nursing assistants' behavior toward the institutionalized elderly. *Quality Review Bulletin, 14,* 15–17.

Carp, F. (1987). Environment and aging. In D. Stokols & I. Altman (Eds.), *Handbook of environmental psychology* (pp. 329–360). New York: Wiley.

Carp, F., & Carp, A. (1984). A complementary/congruence model of well-being or mental health for community elderly. In I. Altman, M. P. Lawton, & J. Wohlwill (Eds.), *Human behavior and the environment: The elderly and the physical environment* (pp. 279–336). New York: Plenum.

Cleary, T. A., Clamon, C., Price, M., & Shullaw, G. (1988). A reduced stimulation unit: Effects on patients with Alzheimer's Disease and related disorders. *The Gerontologist, 28,* 511–514.

Cotrell, V., & Schulz, R. (1993). The perspective of the patient with Alzheimer's disease: A neglected dimension of dementia research. *The Gerontologist, 33,* 205–211.

Ferrucci, L., Guralnik, J. M., Pahor, M., Corti, M. C., & Havlik, R. J. (1997). Hospital diagnoses, Medicare charges, and nursing home admissions in the year when older persons become severely disabled. *Journal of the American Medical Association, 277,* 728–734.

Fitting, M. D. (1980). Professional and ethical responsibilities for psychologists working with the elderly. *The Counseling Psychologist, 12,* 69–78.

German, P. S., Rovner, B. W., Burton, L. C., Brant, L. J., & Clark, R. (1992). The role of mental morbidity in the nursing home experience. *The Gerontologist, 32,* 152–158.

German, P. S., Shapiro, S., & Kramer, M. (1986). Nursing home study of the eastern Baltimore Epidemiological Catchment Area Study. In M. S. Harper & B. D. Lebowitz (Eds.), Mental illness in nursing homes: Agenda for research (pp. 27–40). Rockville, MD: National Institute of Mental Health.

Heller, B. R., Bausell, R. O., & Ninos, M. (1984). Nurses' perceptions of rehabilitation potential of institutionalized aged. Journal of Gerontological Nursing, 10, 22–26.

Hofland, B. F. (1994). When capacity fades and autonomy is constricted: A client-centered approach to residential care. Generations, 18, 31–35.

Hofland, B. F. (1995). Resident autonomy in long-term care: Paradoxes and challenges. In L. M. Gamroth, J. Semradek, & E. M. Tornquist (Eds.), Enhancing autonomy in long-term care: Concepts and strategies (pp. 15–33). New York: Springer.

Holmes, D., Teresi, J., Weiner, A., & Monaco, C. (1990). Impacts associated with special care units in long-term care facilities. The Gerontologist, 30, 178–183.

Institute of Medicine. (1986). Improving quality of care in nursing homes. Washington, DC: National Academy Press.

Kahana, E. (1982). A congruence model of person–environment interaction. In M. P. Lawton, P. G. Windley, & T. O. Byerts (Eds.), Aging and the environment: Theoretical approaches (pp. 97–121). New York: Springer.

Kahana, E., & Kahana, B. (1983). Environmental continuity, futurity, and adaptation of the aged. In G. D. Rowles & R. J. Ohta (Eds.), Aging and milieu: Environmental perspectives on growing old (pp. 205–230). New York: Academic Press.

Lawton, M. P. (1989a). Behavior-relevant ecological factors. In K. W. Schaie & C. Schooler (Eds.), Social structure and aging: Psychological processes (pp. 57–78). Hillsdale, NJ: Erlbaum.

Lawton, M. P. (1989b). Environmental proactivity in older people. In V. L. Bengston & K. W. Schaie (Eds.), The course of later life: Research and reflections (pp. 15–23). New York: Springer.

Lawton, M. P. (1989c). Three functions of the residential environment. Special issue: Lifestyles and housing of older adults: The Florida experience. Journal of Housing for the Elderly, 5, 35–50.

Lawton, M. P., & Nahemow, L. (1973). Ecology of the aging process. In C. Eisdorfer & M. P. Lawton (Eds.), The psychology of adult development and aging (pp. 619–674). Washington, DC: American Psychological Association.

Lidz, C. W., & Arnold, R. M. (1990). Institutional constraints on autonomy. Generations, 14(Suppl.), 65–68.

Malmberg, B., & Zarit, S. H. (1993). Group homes for people with dementia: A Swedish example. The Gerontologist, 33, 682–686.

Manton, K. G., Cornelius, E. S., & Woodbury, M. A. (1995). Nursing home residents: A multivariate analysis of their medical, behavioral, psychosocial and service use characteristics. Journal of Gerontology, 50, 242–251.

Maslach, C. (1982). Burnout: The cost of caring. Englewood Cliffs, NJ: Prentice-Hall.

Maslow, K. (1994). Current knowledge about special care units: Findings of a study by the U.S. Office of Technology Assessment. Alzheimer's Disease and Associated Disorders, 8, 14–40.

Mehr, D. R., & Fries, B. E. (1995). Resource use on Alzheimer's Special Care Units. The Gerontologist, 35, 179–184.

Millard, P. H., & Smith, C. S. (1981). Personal belongings—A positive effect? The Gerontologist, 21, 85–90.

O'Connor, B. P., & Vallerand, R. J. (1994). The relative effects of actual and experienced autonomy on motivation in nursing home residents. Canadian Journal on Aging, 13, 528–538.

Ohta, R. J., & Ohta, B. M. (1988). Special units for Alzheimer's disease patients: A critical look. The Gerontologist, 28, 803–808.

Parmelee, P. A., & Lawton, M. P. (1990). The design of special environments for the aged. In J. E. Birren & K. W. Schaie (Eds.), Handbook of the psychology of aging (3rd ed., pp. 464–488). San Diego, CA: Academic Press.

Parsons, T. (1951). The social system. Glencoe, IL: Free Press.

Pietrukowizc, M. E., & Johnson, M. M. S. (1991). Using life histories to individualize nursing home staff attitudes toward residents. The Gerontologist, 31, 102–106.

Regnier, V. (1994). Assisted living housing for the elderly: Design innovations from the United States and Europe. New York: Reinhold.

Rovner, B. W., Kafonek, S., Filipp, L., Lucas, M. J., & Folstein, M. F. (1986). Prevalence of mental illness in a community nursing home. *American Journal of Psychiatry, 143,* 1446–1449.

Rovner, B. W., Steele, C. D., Shmuely, Y., & Folstein, M. F. (1996). A randomized trial of dementia care in nursing homes. *Journal of the American Geriatrics Society, 44,* 7–13.

Sheehan, N. W. (1986). Informal support among the elderly in public senior housing. *The Gerontologist, 27,* 176–181.

Smyer, M., Brannon, D., & Cohn, M. (1991). Improving nursing home care through training and job redesign. *The Gerontologist, 32,* 327–333.

Smyer, M. A., Shea, D. G., & Streit, A. (1994). The provision and use of mental health services in nursing homes: Results from the National Medical Expenditure Survey. *American Journal of Public Heatlh, 84,* 284–287.

Storlie. (1982). The reshaping of the old. *Journal of Gerontological Nursing, 8,* 555–559.

Timko, C., & Moos, R. H. (1991). Assessing the quality of residential programs: Methods and applications. *Adult Residential Care Journal, 5,* 113–129.

Wahl, H. W. (1991). Dependence in the elderly from an interactional point of view: Verbal and observational data. *Psychology and Aging, 6,* 238–246.

Waxman, H. M., Carner, E. A., & Berkenstock, G. (1984). Job turnover and job satisfaction among nursing home aides. *The Gerontologist, 24,* 503–509.

Wright, L. K. (1988). A reconceptualization of the "negative staff attitudes and poor care in nursing homes" assumption. *The Gerontologist, 28,* 813–820.

26 ────────────────────────────

Family Caregiving: Stresses, Social Programs, and Clinical Interventions

*Steven H. Zarit, Lennarth Johansson, and
Shannon E. Jarrott*

Family caregiving has emerged during the past 20 years as a major social and clinical problem. The aging of the population has placed an increased burden on society's financial resources, and on families who contribute unprecedented amounts of assistance to disabled older adults for longer periods of time than ever before. Most families willingly provide this help, but often do so at considerable personal sacrifice. Family caregiving has thus become a key issue at several levels—for research, to understand how people adapt to chronic stress and how that stress might be relieved, for clinicians, to develop effective strategies to help families manage the demands placed on them, and at a social policy level, where we need to find ways of meeting the growing needs of an aging population with ever-diminishing resources.

In this paper, we examine the research foundations for understanding family caregiving, some promising social and clinical interventions, and emerging social policy questions about the role of families in elder care. We begin with a discussion of the social and family context for caregiving.

Caregiving and Its Social Context

Most countries are experiencing a historical change in the age structure of their population. Between 1950 and 2050 the proportion of those aged 65 years and older in the population will more than double. The aging of populations in industrial societies presents tremendous and challenging problems in sustaining pensions, health care, and service programs. However, the demographic development that poses the most immediate and dramatic demands is the so called *secondary aging*, that is, an increasing number of the older adults reaching age 80 and beyond. This age group, which is sometimes called the *oldest old*, has the greatest risk of chronic illness and disability. As the most rapidly growing age group in the industrialized world, the oldest old can be expected to place considerable strain on aging services and on the family (Organisation for Economic Cooperation and Development, 1996).

The majority of frail and dependent older adults live on their own, in private households, and often separately from their children. To maintain their independence and to be able to age-in-place (i.e., in their own homes), they may need services and care. Many older individuals gradually become frail and experience poor health and social separation when they are over the age of 80 years. In this situation a whole range of possible needs arises, such as medical and health care needs, personal and domestic care, social support, and sometimes supervision.

Generally, world-wide the bulk of support to older adults—domestic, personal, and social support—is provided by the family (e.g., Lagergren, Lundh, Orkan, & Sanne, 1984; Hokenstad & Johansson, 1990). Much care is given by older wives and husbands to disabled spouses. When an older person does not have a spouse or a spouse cannot provide care, daughters and daughters-in-law are the major providers. However, just as the demographic changes indicate increasing numbers of older adults and increasing needs, other demographic and social changes may be reducing the potential of the younger generations to provide care. Smaller families, higher divorce rates, and increased participation of women in the workforce decrease the resources that are potentially available for helping an aging parent. Among the oldest old, it is increasingly likely to encounter people who have no family supports because they have outlived their children and other relatives (Johnson & Barer, 1997).

Population aging has affected men and women differently. They have different patterns of labor force participation, transitions from work to retirement, and caregiving. Women earn lower wages, live longer, live alone longer, and can have longer periods of frailty and poverty near the end of their lives. For both men and women, there is an increase in time spent living alone and outside a traditional family unit. Historical trends show that the proportion of older adults living in the same household with children has been steadily dropping throughout the world. While the Nordic countries have the lowest rates of shared households, even countries like Japan, which have a strong tradition of filial piety, have shown a proportionately similar decline in recent years (Sundström, 1994).

A central issue is whether the state or the family should be responsible to provide necessary care to older people (Twigg, 1996). In some countries—for example Germany, Austria, and Switzerland—the responsibility to care for a dependent family member is by law a family obligation. This was the case in the Nordic countries until some decades ago. One of the cornerstones of the postwar welfare system built in the Nordic countries is the belief that these family responsibilities should be assumed by the state. In pace with economic growth, the state gradually extended services and care for children, disabled individuals, and older adults. The United States, by contrast, does not formally obligate children to care for parents but also does not have a universal system of long-term care. Most community-based and institutional long-term care services are not covered by Medicare, the health insurance for older people. Instead, people must pay privately for services until their financial resources are depleted. Only then will Medicaid, the health insurance program for low-income individuals, pay for nursing home care and for limited amounts of community services.

A central question, then, concerns whether families should be required to provide a certain amount of help and, if so, how much help should be required. As Daatland (1996) pointed out, care is increasingly, and over longer periods, shared between families and formal services, as dependent older people in a home setting often need help from both parties. Do steps need to be taken to assure that contributions from and burdens on family are distributed in an equitable way, or should it be left to chance as currently happens most notably in the United States?

A Stress Framework for Family Caregiving

It is in the context of growing needs and diminishing social resources that family caregiving should be viewed. Research on caregiving has typically focused on the stresses and burdens placed on the family. A particular emphasis has been on caring for a relative with a dementing illness. This caregiving situation is the most stressful for families because of the patient's behavioral and emotional problems (Birkel, 1987; Grafström, Fratiglioni, Sandman, & Winblad, 1992). We will emphasize this type of care, but recognize that caregiving includes a broader array of family circumstances.

In reviewing the broad field of research on family caregiving, three points stand out as critical: (a) the stressfulness of caregiving, (b) the multidimensionality of stressors and outcomes, and (c) individual differences in adaptation to stressors.

The Stressfulness of Caregiving

Although an obvious point, it is nonetheless worth noting that caregivers experience considerable emotional strain. They report higher levels of depression, anger, and anxiety than do other people their age who do not have caregiving responsibilities (Aneshensel, Pearlin, Mullan, Zarit, & Whitlatch, 1995; Gilhooly, 1994; Schulz, O'Brien, Bookwala, & Fleissner, 1995; Wright, Clipp, & George, 1993). Caregivers' health may also suffer as a result of prolonged care responsibilities, although findings are less consistent on this point than they are for emotional well-being (Schulz et al., 1995).

The Multidimensionality of Stressors and Outcomes

The stresses of caregiving can best be understood from a multidimensional perspective. Rather than a single stress or burden, caregiving is characterized by multiple stressors and problems. Pearlin and his associates (Aneshensel et al., 1995; Pearlin, Mullan, Semple, & Skaff, 1990) provided a useful framework for viewing these stressors. They differentiated among the following: (a) primary stressors, which are those problems that are directly embedded in the older person's illness and disabilities; (b) secondary stressors, which represent the proliferation of stress into other areas of the caregiver's life; and (c) outcomes, that is, the impact of caregiving stressors on the person's physical and emotional well-being. Primary stressors include the amount of assistance that caregivers give to their relatives for performing activities of daily living, as well as managing memory, behavioral, or emotional problems their relatives may have. Examples of secondary stressors include the extent to which caregiving interferes with other family relationships or with one's employment, or places a strain on family finances. Outcomes have typically included depression, anxiety, and anger but also can include positive affect and subjective health.

Caregiving families differ from one another in terms of which stressors are present. The stressors that are present also change over time. The implication for clinical practice is that there is no single type of caregiver stress or burden but, rather, a broad array of potential stressors.

Variability in Adaptation to Stressors

Perhaps the most interesting and important finding in caregiving research is that stressors tell us relatively little about caregivers' outcomes. Caregivers can adapt very differently to similar stressors. Some caregivers are overwhelmed by even minor challenges, whereas others manage reasonably well, no matter what problems they encounter. Still others fluctuate in their functioning over time (e.g., Townsend, Noelker, Deimling, & Bass, 1989). Such dimensions as severity of the care recipient's disease, extent of disability, or level of behavior and cognitive changes account for a surprisingly small portion of the caregiver's well-being (Aneshensel et al., 1995; Zarit, Todd, & Zarit, 1986). Even when caregivers are followed over time, increases or decreases in stress account for relatively small amounts of changes in well-being.

Three factors have been identified that are related to caregivers' adaptation: appraisals of stressors, coping, and social support. Following the work of Lazarus and Folkman (1984), caregivers have rated how much of a hassle or how distressing various problems are (e.g., Haley, Levine, Brown, & Bartolucci, 1987; Kinney & Stephens, 1989; Ouslander, Zarit, Orr, & Miura, 1990; Teri et al., 1992; Zarit et al., 1986). Not surprisingly, caregivers typically appraise behavior problems as most stressful or difficult for them, and assess assisting with activities of daily living as less difficult. Depressive behaviors can also be very stressful (Teri et al., 1992). There is, however, considerable variability in what caregivers find stressful. This is an important distinction in both research and clinical practice. The fact that a particular problem is present does not necessarily mean that families experience it as stressful. The problems that are difficult or challenging for caregivers also change over time (Zarit et al., 1986).

Pearlin and his colleagues (1990; Aneshensel et al., 1995) take a different approach in assessing the subjective element of caregiving stressors. They propose subjective stressors that correspond to the dimensions of primary and secondary stressors in their stress process model. Three primary subjective stressors in their model are role overload (i.e., having more to do than the caregiver can manage), role captivity (i.e., feeling trapped in the caregiving role), and the experience of loss of one's relationship with the care recipient. Two secondary subjective stressors are loss of self-esteem, and loss of self, that is, feeling one's identity is being absorbed by the caregiving role. Caregivers vary in their subjective response to similar stressful events; some caregivers feel overloaded when assisting someone with a lot of behavior problems, but others do not. Similarly, some caregivers find it very difficult to manage a job and caregiving, but others do not, and may even report that going to work gives them a break from their caregiving responsibilities (Aneshensel et al., 1995).

The second factor associated with individual differences in caregiving outcomes is social support. Both emotional support and assistance with caregiving tasks generally are associated with lower feelings of depression or burden (e.g., Aneshensel et al., 1995; Franks & Stephens, 1996; Suitor & Pillemer, 1992). Anehensel and her colleagues suggested that different kinds of support are related to different outcomes. When caregivers receive help with care tasks from family and friends, they experience lower feelings of overload. This type of help, however, is not related to improved well-being. By contrast, emotional support is associated with well-being but has no effect on overload. In contrast to these positive findings, Pruchno and associates (Pruchno, Kleban, Michaels, & Dempsey, 1990) reported that levels of all types of social support were low in a sample of spouses of dementia patients, and support did not buffer caregivers from the negative effects of stressors.

Families can also disagree over the care that patients are receiving, and these conflicts are very upsetting for the primary caregiver. Semple (1992) identified three types of family conflict in caregiving: (a) conflict over the patient's diagnosis, (b) conflict over how the primary caregiver is caring for the patient, and (c) conflict over how much help other family members are giving to the primary caregiver. Although the amount of conflict reported by caregivers is, on average, low, it can have disproportionate effects on well-being. Small amounts of family conflict may cancel out the benefits of more frequent positive interactions (MaloneBeach & Zarit, 1995). Families, then, are not always helpful and support may be embedded in criticism or conflict.

The other main factor affecting caregiving outcomes is coping. Again, the picture is more complex than our theories suggest. It is generally expected that problem-focused coping strategies, which seek to modify stressful events, will lead to better outcomes, but support for this proposition is mixed. Aneshensel and colleagues (1995) found that mastery, which indicates the predilection toward more active coping, was generally related to better well-being for caregivers assisting a relative at home but had the opposite effect when their relative was in a nursing home. Pruchno and Resch (1989) reported that different coping styles have effects on different emotions. Use of emotion focused coping mediated the impact of stress on depression and anxiety, whereas problem focused coping was associated with more positive affect. Likewise, Williamson and Schulz (1993) found that coping strategies varied in their affects depending on the stressor. Wishfulness, which is a type of emotion focused coping, was generally related to higher depression whereas taking direct action was related to more depression when coping with memory problems. By contrast, relaxation was related to lower depression when dealing with memory problems. Use of acceptance was related to lower depression when coping with communication deficits or the decline of one's loved one. These findings suggest that coping strategies vary in their effectiveness depending on the type of stressor caregivers are dealing with.

Appraisals, social support, and coping all affect the relation between stressors and caregiving outcomes such as depression or burden. In other words, disability creates the context in which severe distress may develop, but whether or not a family experiences distress depends on these other factors. Of importance for clinical work is that these factors are potentially modifiable. Caregivers can use social programs that increase the amount of assistance they receive with caregiving tasks and reduce their exposure to some care-related stressors. In turn, clinical interventions can help caregivers develop more effective ways of coping with stressors and identify what family and social resources might be of help.

Social Programs and Their Effectiveness

As more caregivers assume the responsibility of caring for an elderly family member, services have developed to aid the patient and provide respite for the caregiver. Respite includes adult day service centers (sometimes called adult day care), in-home help, and short-term nursing home care (overnight respite). Comparable respite services have developed independently around the world. Service delivery systems reflect a country's cultural and governmental structure, but programs have similar goals and serve similar populations (Jarrott, Zarit, Berg, & Johansson, in press).

Respite services are intended primarily to ease the burden of caregiving, but there are other goals as well. Caregivers hope that the service will benefit their relative, and government officials hope that the programs will sufficiently ease caregiving strain such that family members may continue providing for their relatives at home, thereby reducing the use of more costly institutional care (Cox, 1997). The following discussion provides an overview of respite services and their level of efficacy and considers the development of optimal levels of respite services. We also examine permanent institutional placement and its effects on the family.

Adult Day Service Programs

Adult day service programs (ADS) are intended for individuals with dementia or other disabilities. They provide supervised, structured activity for the client during the day and afford the family caregiver time to rest or tend to other responsibilities (Montgomery, 1995). At the same time, ADS places the patient in a safe environment with individuals of similar abilities and needs.

Typically a client will attend ADS 2 to 3 days each week for about 5 hours each day (Jarrott et al., in press; Weissert et al., 1989). Activities and services vary, but frequently include orientation exercises, physical activity, and reminiscing (Jarrott et al., in press). The program also provides clients with the chance to interact with others (Cicerelli, 1984).

Reports of caregivers' satisfaction with adult day service programs are uniformly high (Gottlieb & Johnson, 1995; Strain, Chapell, & Blandford, 1987; Weissert et al., 1989), but analysis of benefits for the caregiver have had mixed results. Some researchers have reported that day programs have little or no effect on caregiver burden or well-being (Lawton, Brody, & Saperstein, 1989; Montgomery & Borgatta, 1989), but these studies often included caregivers who had very low rates of use of day care or other respite services. Recent research that evaluated caregivers receiving adequate amounts of service has had more promising results (Gottlieb & Johnson, 1995; Zarit, Stephens, Townsend, & Greene, 1996). These studies' findings indicate that day care use results in reductions of care-related stressors (e.g., feelings of overload and strain), improved physical and mental health, better relationships, and increased confidence in caregiving abilities.

A continuing theme in research on day care and other respite services is that those who might benefit from services do not use them or use them infrequently (e.g., Gwyther, 1989; Montgomery, 1995). Caregivers may feel guilty about relinquishing the care of their relative to another individual, assuming it is their responsibility to provide care. Some caregivers report that programs are inaccessible or expensive (MaloneBeach, Zarit, & Spore, 1992). Caregivers who decide against using an ADS program frequently perceive that their relative has different needs than clients at the program (Cohen-Mansfield, Besansky, Watson, & Bernhard, 1994). Factors affecting enrollment, such as cost, inconvenient program hours, or incompatibility between an individual and other clients, also reduce amount of service use. Given the findings of benefits of ADS for caregivers, more effort needs to be made to alter actual and perceived barriers to their use.

In-Home Respite

In-home respite is the most commonly used form of respite for caregivers of elderly patients (Caserta, Lund, Wright, & Redburn, 1987). Respite workers may be companions, homemakers, home-health aides, or nurses. Services can include attending to the patient's housework or physical needs or simply sitting with the patient, either for a short period or overnight. Visits from in-home help may be infrequent, for example once a week for light housecleaning, or extensive, such as a daily visit to sit with the client so the caregiver can leave the house. It may be used for a short period, such as following a discharge from a hospital, or long term for someone with permanent disabilities. Benefits of in-home respite for the caregiver include improved mood (Gwyther, 1989) and decreased time spent in caregiving activities (Berry, Zarit, & Rabatin, 1988). Caregivers are highly satisfied with in-home help and would like more of it (MaloneBeach et al., 1992).

The demand for care has typically been found to exceed the available resources, even though a relatively small proportion of caregivers use in-home respite. In Sweden, where municipalities are charged with providing for the health care needs of all elderly citizens, demands for help have exceeded available services and funding. As a result, municipalities have eliminated some services, such as housecleaning, and have raised eligibility levels, demanding that older adults be more ill or in need before qualifying for services (Malmberg & Sundström, 1996).

Despite their generally positive view of in-home respite, some caregivers report problems with these services. They report that home helpers are poorly trained and unreliable, and that they may not get the same helper each time (MaloneBeach et al., 1992; Montgomery, 1995). Agencies can be inflexible in meeting patients' or caregivers' needs (MaloneBeach et al., 1992).

Overnight Respite

The least common type of respite is short-term institutionalization. Overnight respite may be scheduled regularly for a few nights or less frequently for 1 to 2 weeks (Montgomery, 1995). Short-term institutionalization offers the benefit of an extended period of respite but tends to be less flexible than other respite programs. Institutions usually cannot offer emergency respite because of the cost of keeping a bed free (Scharlach & Frenzel, 1986). It would be expected that dementia patients would have difficulty adjusting to a temporary relocation, but the limited data on this issue suggest no difficulties with these transitions (Burdz, Eaton, & Bond, 1988).

Institutionalization and the Family

Institutionalization of a relative may be viewed as a final release of caregiver responsibility but is accompanied by its own stressors (Aneshensel et al., 1995; Zarit & Whitlatch, 1992). Most caregivers visit their relative regularly and continue to provide assistance after placement (Lingsom, 1997; Zarit & Whitlatch). They often feel the needs of their relative are not being met in the institution (MaloneBeach et al., 1992). Although strains associated with everyday care are reduced, caregiver depression and anxiety does not change (Aneshensel et al., 1995).

Different types of institutions have been developed for specialized needs of the patient and the caregiver. Group homes designed specifically for small groups of older adults with dementia can be found in Sweden. In the United States, assisted living homes designed specifically for dementia patients are being developed to offer a more homelike setting. Creation of a range of special institutional settings such as these may better accommodate the diverse needs of patients and family caregivers who require institutional services at different points in their relative's illness.

Respite as Compliment, Supplement, or Substitute for Family Care

Although respite services have been developed internationally, countries differ in how they frame the question of how much formal help should be available? For example, Sweden aims to provide enough formal assistance that families do not have to provide extra help (Hokenstad & Johansson, 1990). In the United States, the goal is to compliment family help without substituting for that care (Penrod, Harris, & Kane, 1994). Policy makers are concerned that providing high levels of formal assistance will result in the withdrawal of family assistance. Conversely, low levels of formal assistance can leave a caregiver with insufficient help and no other alternative than institutionalization of the older adult. Finding the balance between minimal and optimal levels of formal assistance is a pressing issue in every country as more families require help and as family and national budgets are strained.

The available evidence suggests that formal services supplement but do not replace family help (e.g., Jarrott & Zarit, 1995; Lingsom, 1997). Formal services, however, sometimes appear to facilitate, rather than delay institutional placement (e.g., Miller & McFall, 1991; Montgomery, 1995; Montgomery & Borgatta, 1989; Newman, Struyk, Wright, & Rice, 1990; Scharlach & Frenzel, 1986; Wells & Kendig, 1996). That may be especially the case in the United States where the rate of institutional care is relatively low (about 5% of those people over 65) compared to countries that provide universal access to nursing home care (Doty, 1990).

Clinical Interventions in Caregiving

Building on the findings of caregiver stress and the role of formal services, we turn to a model of clinical interventions (Zarit, Orr, & Zarit, 1985; Zarit & Zarit, in press). Three main components are included: (a) assessment, (b) treatment strategies, and (c) treatment modalities. The goal of the treatment is to lower caregivers' feelings of distress by modifying treatable aspects of the care situation. Approaches that are based on this model have been found to reduce caregivers' feelings of burden and distress and to delay institutional placement (Mittelman et al., 1995; 1996; Whitlatch, Zarit, & von Eye, 1991; Whitlatch, Zarit, Goodwin, & von Eye, 1995).

Clinical intervention begins with a multidimensional assessment of the caregiver and care recipient. Goals of the assessment are to confirm what specific problems and stressors are present in the situation, to identify which stressors are problematic for caregivers and should be targeted for intervention, and to identify what resources caregivers can draw upon. Another consideration is whether medical diagnosis and treatment has been adequate. For disorders such as dementia, it is not uncommon to encounter cases where the diagnostic evaluation was inadequate or, more commonly, where inappropriate or excessive psychotropic medications have been prescribed.

Treatment strategies include information, problem solving, and support. The starting point is providing information so that caregivers can understand their relative's disorder and its implications. Clinicians answer questions that caregivers have about diagnosis and treatment of their relative's illness. Although many of these questions should be addressed by physicians, it is quite common to find that a physician has spent very little time talking about the illness with the family. Even when physicians have previously taken the time to explain these issues, families are sometimes not able to absorb the information, or think of questions later. Caregivers need to have all questions answered before they can look at what they can do to deal with stress.

It is especially helpful to clarify for families why their relatives behave the way they do. In cases of dementia, caregivers often believe that the patient's memory and behavior problems are intentional, or are due to a lack of effort. Problems that often lead to incorrect attributions include when patients ask the same question over again, accuse someone of stealing their things, or insist that a deceased parent is still alive. Caregivers often confront patients about these behaviors, but that usually upsets both patients and caregivers and does not change patients' beliefs. A more productive approach is to help caregivers distinguish between the factual and affective (or feeling) components of these communications. Patients make these statements because they are not processing information accurately. Arguing with them over the facts only makes the situation worse and does not change their mind. Instead of responding to the facts in these statements, caregivers can ask what the patient must be feeling, and respond at that level. Patients who believe someone is stealing their money, for example, are likely to be feeling angry or threatened. Recognizing the affective component, families can reassure patients without getting into the specifics of their accusations.

The second strategy, problem solving, involves teaching caregivers to apply a simple behavioral management technique for behaviors they have identified as troublesome or problematic. Problem solving is a 6-step process (Zarit, Orr, & Zarit, 1985):

1. Assessing when and how often a problem occurs
2. Identifying possible antecedents and consequences of the targeted problem
3. Generating possible solutions for the problem
4. Selecting a solution
5. Implementing the solution
6. Evaluating if the solution has been successful.

Problem solving can be used for many different behaviors, such as agitation, wandering, not sleeping at night, and incontinence.

The third strategy is support. Caregivers often feel alone and isolated and feel that no one can understand what they are going through. Emotional support can decrease these feelings of isolation. The psychologist can be an important source of support, helping caregivers begin to tackle some of the problems they are facing. The psychologist should also help caregivers identify family members and friends who could potentially provide support and assistance as well as help caregivers find the assistance available from service agencies.

These treatment strategies are implemented in three treatment modalities, (a) counseling with the primary caregiver, (b) family meetings, and (c) support groups. Counseling is used to develop a therapeutic relationship with the primary caregiver. It is usually time-limited (e.g., 5 to 15 sessions), but plays a pivotal role. The therapist conveys empathy and acceptance while helping caregivers learn how to manage more effectively the stresses and problems they are facing. These sessions allow caregivers to clarify what their goals are and to examine the alternatives available to them. Another use of these sessions is to plan for a family meeting.

The second treatment modality, the family meeting, has proven to be a powerful tool for helping caregivers. As a source of both support and added conflict and stress, the caregiver's extended family plays a critical role. By involving the family in treatment, the psychologist has the opportunity to address these issues directly. Family meetings recapitulate the three treatment strategies. The psychologist begins by answering the questions that family members have about diagnosis and treatment, so that everyone has a similar understanding of the patient's disorder. It is then possible to use a problem solving approach, this time focused on the caregiver's need for support and assistance. Once families understand the situation, they are usually very creative in developing solutions for the patient's care needs.

A family systems perspective is useful in planning and conducting the family meeting. Working with the primary caregiver, the therapist plans who to invite and where to hold the meeting. It is important to learn such things about the family as who is influential or powerful, who likes or dislikes whom, and what role the caregiver and patient have in the family system. Although the primary caregiver can provide only a limited perspective on these issues, this information provides the therapist with some hypotheses for what to expect during the family meeting.

Family meetings are not family therapy. There is no attempt to change basic ways that families address problems or to modify the structure or hierarchy within a family. That is not what families have requested when they come to a meeting, nor is it necessary for accomplishing the immediate goals of reducing strain on the primary caregiver. Rather, family meetings clear up misunderstandings about dementia and identify resources that can be brought to bear on caregiving issues. Most families of disabled older people have functioned adequately in the past and need only to be oriented to the tasks they are now facing. Except for highly dysfunctional or conflicted families, it is usually possible to make progress on the practical issues of helping the primary caregiver.

The third treatment modality is support groups. Support groups add different dimensions to interventions with caregivers. Groups are a very efficient way of disseminating information among caregivers. Problem solving can also work more effectively as caregivers share their own experiences and suggestions for managing problem behaviors. Talking with people who are going through the same experience can be an excellent source of support.

Groups, of course, have their limitations. Some caregivers are not comfortable talking in groups, and others may initially be too distressed to benefit from a group (Whitlatch et al., 1991). In addition, caregivers do not get as much time in groups to explore their concerns as they do in an individual session. For these reasons, it is often better to use groups for long-term support, rather than as the primary intervention.

Issues for the Future

The important role that families play in caring for frail and dependent older adults has become recognized in most countries. If and how this recognition is transformed into measures to support families is quite a different matter. In fact, in many countries, family caregivers get very little support, or no support at all.

The exchange of care and services may be conceived in terms of a social contract regarding the responsibilities of the family and of the state. The design of this agreement will differ among countries. For example, the Nordic Welfare State is the product of culturally homogeneous societies with relatively minor social cleavages, and widespread support for the concept of "the good state" where individuals should not be burdened with the responsibilities of informal relationships. This concept of joint responsibility has led to shared caregiving for older and frail persons by family and state. Researchers in the Nordic countries argue that this is beneficial for intergenerational relationships as it is easier both to receive and to provide care when one does not have to (Andersson & Sundström, 1996). All parties in the family know that there are alternatives, and they may negotiate for the best mix of both sources of help and care. Because this contract has emerged from a particular social and political context it is possible that the same construction of solidarity between family and state may not be acceptable in other societies.

With regard to the future, there are three central problems that need to be addressed. First, despite the endorsement of the importance of the family in care for older adults, few governments have embraced this goal into their policy of social welfare provision. Second, despite government policy to support informal caregiving, few support programs have been actually implemented at the local level. Thus, it has been more a case of lip-service than of action. Third, even if there exists a policy in favor of supporting carers and service programs that target the needs of older adults and their families, collaboration between formal and informal care is often conditional on the terms decided by the formal services. Consequently, efforts to support informal caregiving must address all of these three problems (Johansson, 1991a, 1991b; Pearlin & Zarit, 1993). One further consideration is that policy efforts should incorporate the perspective of the care recipient, as well as caregiver (Twigg and Atkin, 1994).

In recent years, some countries have developed policies explicitly for supporting family caregivers. In 1994, Norway implemented the Social Service Act, which mandates the local authorities to provide economic and respite support to the caregivers. Another example is the implementation of the Carers (Recognition and Services) Act in the United Kingdom, which gives carers a statutory right of an assessment of the carer's own needs. In Sweden, the parliament revised the Social Service Act in 1997 encouraging the local authorities to support and provide respite for family caregivers. The United States has seen a variety of demonstration projects and local initiatives, but no significant effort on a national level, since the failure of the Clinton health care reform package (McConnell & Riggs, 1994).

Lingsom (1997) reported that families act increasingly as advocates for their older relatives in the formal system. Growth in advocacy groups, both at local and national levels, implies a greater influence on policy making in older adult care. Examples of effective lobbying include the work done by the National Carers Organization in the United Kingdom in lobbying for and promoting the Carers Act and the various Alzheimer's societies that have grown from grass roots caregivers organizations. Daatland (1996) reported on a similar development in Norway, where some municipalities have formalized their collaboration with the families and the elderly in *care contracts*. These contracts define the rights and duties of each party, which provide the families with the confidence they need to continue to care.

It is one thing to argue for extended support to caregivers and quite a different matter to translate this into support programs. In some countries, this shortcoming can be explained by the historic tension between the local governments and the national government. The implementation of the government's policy for the care of older adults is very much a matter of the ambitions and priorities of the local governments. As most local authorities are battling with cost containment, one can understand why carers' support sometimes has been called the "Cinderella services," that is, the kind of services that are always cut back first when spending has to be reduced and costs cut (Andersson, 1996).

In their review of recent experiences of community care in the United Kingdom, Nocon and Qureshi (1996) argued that need for services may be related to qualitatively different features of the caring situation and service system. Observing the U.S. situation, Aneshensel et al. (1995) made a similar point that policy needs to create a user-friendly system of services where service guidelines, including eligibility and cost, are organized in an easy to understand format.

What conclusions can be drawn with regard to future directions in caring for carers? First, the building of a well-functioning support system must be based on a systematic approach—the family perspective. Second, national policy, laws, and regulations can pave the way to a better understanding and promotion of caregiver support. However, in decentralized systems, caring for the carers must be the responsibility of the local authorities. Third, because the concept of the family is changing constantly, the preconditions for intergenerational support must follow suit. Caregivers are an extremely heterogeneous group. Caring for carers must therefore incorporate easily accessible, tailor-made, and personalized support. Finally, there is a growing awareness that support for carers is a prerequisite for mobilizing caregivers in the future, which in turn is of crucial importance for the whole system of older adult welfare. The challenge for the future then, is to strike a balance in pooling family and public resources in a partnership in care.

References

Andersson, L. (1996). Visible and invisible informal care: Swedish elderly care at the crossroads. In V. Minichiello, N. Chappel, H. Kending, & A. Walker (Eds.). *Sociology of aging. International perspectives* (pp. 246–258). Madrid, Spain: International Sociological Association, Research Committee on Aging.

Andersson, L., & Sundström, G. (1996). The social networks of elderly people in Sweden. In H. Litwin (Ed.). *The social networks of older people: A cross-national analysis* (pp. 15–29). Westport, CT: Praeger.

Aneshensel, C. S., Pearlin, L. I., Mullan, J. T., Zarit, S. H., & Whitlatch, C. J. (1995). *Profiles in caregiving: The unexpected career*. San Diego, CA: Academic Press.

Berry, G. L., Zarit, S. H., & Rabatin, V. X. (1988). Caregiver activity on respite and nonrespite days: A comparison of two service approaches. *The Gerontologist, 31*, 830–835.

Burdz, M., Eaton, W. O., & Bond, J. B. (1988). Effect of respite care on dementia and non-dementia patients and their caregivers. *Psychology and Aging 3*(1), 38–42.

Caserta, M. S., Lund, D. A., Wright, S. C., & Redburn, D. E. (1987). Caregivers to dementia patients: The utilization of community services. *The Gerontologist, 27,* 209–214.

Cicerelli, V. G. (1984). A continuing evaluation of older adult day care: Longitudinal evaluation of day care clients and assessment of family caregivers' view (Report to the Gerontological Society of America). Unpublished manuscript.

Cohen-Mansfield, J., Besansky, J., Watson, V., & Bernhard, L. (1994). Underutilization of adult day care: An exploratory study. *Journal of Gerontological Social Work, 22,* 21–39.

Cox, C. (1997). Findings from a statewide program of respite care: A comparison of service users, stoppers, and nonusers. *The Gerontologist, 37,* 511–517.

Daatland, S. O. (1996). Adapting the Scandinavian model of care for the elderly. In *Caring for frail elderly people: Policies in evolution.* (*Social Policy Studies,* No. 19). Paris: OECD.

Doty, P. (1990). Dispelling some myths: A comparison of long-term-care financing in the United States and other nations. *Generations, 14,* 10–14.

Franks, M. M., & Stephens, M. A. P. (1996). Social support in the context of caregiving: Husbands' provision of support to wives involved in parent care. *Journals of Gerontology, 51,* 43–52.

Gilhooly, M. L. M. (1994). The impact of caregiving on caregivers: Factors associated with the psychological well-being of people supporting a dementing relative in the community. *British Journal of Medical Psychology, 57,* 35–44.

Gottlieb, B. H., & Johnson, J. (1995). Impact of day programs on family caregivers of persons with dementia.

Gwyther, L. P. (1989). *Barriers to service utilization among Alzheimer's patients and their families* (Report to the U.S. Congress, Office of Technology Assessment, National Technical Information Service #PB 89–225205). Durham, NC: Duke University Center on Aging.

Haley, W. E., Levine, E. G., Brown, S. L., & Bartolucci, A. A. (1987). Stress appraisal, coping and social support as predictors of adaptational outcome among dementia caregivers. *Psychology and Aging, 2,* 323–330.

Hockenstad, M. C., & Johansson, L. (1990). Caregiving for the elderly in Sweden. In D. E. Biegel & A. Blum (Eds.), *Aging and caregiving: Theory, research and policy* (pp. 254–269). Newbury Park, California: Sage.

Jarrott, S. E., Zarit, S. H., Berg, S., & Johansson, L. (In press). A comparison of adult day care in Sweden and the U.S. *Journal of Cross Cultural Aging.*

Jarrott, S. E., & Zarit, S. H. (1995, November). *Effects of day care on time usage by employed and non-employed caregivers.* Poster presented at the meetings of the Gerontological Society of America, Los Angeles.

Johansson, L. (1991a). Elderly care policy, formal and informal care: The Swedish case. *Health Policy, 19,* 231–242.

Johansson, L. (1991b). Informal care of dependent elderly at home—Some Swedish examples. *Ageing and Society, 11,* 41–58.

Johnson, C. L., & Barer, B. M. (1997). *Life beyond 85 years: The aura of survivorship.* New York: Springer.

Kinney, J. M., & Stephens, M. A. P. (1989). Hassles and uplifts of giving care to a family member with dementia. *Psychology and Aging, 4,* 402–408.

Lagergren, M., Lundh, L., Orkan, M., & Sanne, C. (1984). *Time to care.* New York: Pergamon Press.

Lawton, M. P., Brody, E. M., & Saperstein, A. (1989). A controlled study of respite service for caregivers of Alzheimer's patients. *The Gerontologist, 29,* 8–16.

Lazarus, R. S., & Folkman, S. (1984). *Stress, appraisal, and coping.* New York: Springer.

Lingsom, S. (1997). The substitution issue: Care policies and their consequence for family care. Oslo, Sweden: *NOVA.* (Report Nr. 6).

Malmberg, B., & Sundström, G. (1996). *Age care crisis in Sweden?* Stockholm: Swedish Institute (Report no. 412).

MaloneBeach, E. E., & Zarit, S. H. (1995). Dimensions of social support and social conflict as predictors of caregiver depression. *International Psychogeriatrics, 7,* 25–38.

MaloneBeach, E. E., Zarit, S. H., & Spore, D. L. (1992). Caregivers' perceptions of case management and community-based services: Barriers to service use. *Journal of Applied Gerontology, 11,* 146–159.

McConnell, S., & Riggs, J. A. (1994). A public policy agenda: Supporting family caregiving. In M. H. Cantor (Ed.), *Family caregiving: Agenda for the future* (pp. 25–34). San Francisco: American Society for Aging.

Miller, B., & McFall, S. (1991). The effect of caregiver's burden on change in frail older persons' use of formal helpers. *Journal of Health & Social Behavior, 32,* 165–179.

Mittelman, M. S., Ferris, S. H., Shulman, E., Steinberg, G., Ambinder, A., Mackel, J., & Cohen, J. (1995). A comprehensive support program: Effect on depression in spouse-caregivers of AD patients. *Gerontologist, 35,* 792–802.

Montgomery, R. J. V. (1995). Examining respite care: Promises and limitations. In R. A. Kane & J. D. Penrod (Eds.), *Family caregiving in an aging society* (pp. 29–45). Newbury Park, CA: Sage.

Montgomery, R. J. V., & Borgatta, E. F. (1989). The effects of alternative support strategies on family caregiving. *The Gerontologist, 29,* 457–464.

Newman, S. J., Struyk, R., Wright, P., & Rice, M. (1990). Overwhelming odds: Caregiving and the risk of institutionalization. *Journals of Gerontology, 45,* 173–183.

Nocon, A., & Qureshi, H. (1996). *Outcomes of community care for users and carers.* London: The Open University Press.

Organisation for Economic Cooperation and Development. (1996). *Caring for the frail elderly people. Policies in evolution* (Social Policy Studies, No. 19). Paris: Author.

Ouslander, J. G., Zarit, S. H., Orr, N. K., & Miura, S. A. (1990). Incontinence among elderly community-dwelling dementia patients: Characteristics, management, and impact on caregivers. *Journal of the American Geriatrics Society, 38,* 440–445.

Pearlin, L., Mullan, J., Semple, S., & Skaff, M. (1990). Caregiving and the stress process: An overview of concepts and their measures. *The Gerontologist, 30,* 583–594.

Pearlin, L. I., & Zarit, S. H. (1993). Research into informal caregiving: Current perspectives and future directions. In S. H. Zarit, L. I. Pearlin, & K. W. Schaie (Eds.), *Caregiving systems: Informal and formal helpers* (pp. 155–170). New York: Erlbaum.

Penrod, J. D., Harris, K., & Kane, R. L. (1994). Informal care substitution: What we don't know can hurt us. *Journal of Aging and Social Policy, 6,* 21–31.

Pruchno, R. A., Kleban, M. H., Michaels, E., & Dempsey, N. P. (1990). Mental and physical health of caregiving spouses: Development of a causal model. *Journal of Gerontology, 45,* 192–199.

Pruchno, R. A., & Resch, N. L. (1989). Aberrant behaviors and Alzheimer's disease: Mental health effects on spouse caregivers. *Journals of Gerontology, 44,* 177–182.

Scharlach, A., & Frenzel, C. (1986). An evaluation of institutional-based respite. *The Gerontologist, 26,* 77–82.

Schulz, R., O'Brien, A. T., Bookwala, J., & Fleissner, K. (1995). Psychiatric and physical morbidity effects of Alzheimer's disease caregiving: Prevalence, correlates and causes. *The Gerontologist, 35,* 771–791.

Semple, S. J. (1992). Conflict in Alzheimer's caregiving families: Its dimensions and consequences. *Gerontologist, 32,* 648–655.

Strain, L., Chappell, N., & Blandford, A. (1987). Changes in life satisfaction among participants of adult day care and their informal caregivers. *Journal of Gerontological Social Work, 11,* 115–129.

Sundström, G. (1994). Care by families: An overview of trends. In *Caring for frail elderly people: New directions in care* (Social Policy Studies, No. 14). Paris: OECD.

Teri, L., Truax, P., Logsdon, R., Uomoto, J., Zarit, S. H., & Vitaliano, P. P. (1992). Assessment of behavioral problems in dementia: The revised memory and behavior problems checklist. *Psychology and Aging, 7,* 622–631.

Townsend, A., Noelker, L., Deimling, G., & Bass, D. (1989). Longitudinal impact of interhousehold caregiving on adult children's mental health. *Psychology and Aging, 4,* 393–401.

Twigg, J. (1996). Issues in informal care. In *Caring for frail elderly people: Policies in evolution* (Social Policy Studies, No. 19). Paris: OECD.

Twigg, J., & Atkin, K. (1994). *Carers perceived: Policy and practice in informal care.* London: The Open University Press.

Weissert, W. G., Elston, J. M., Bolda, E. J., Zelman, W. N., Mutran, E., & Mangum, A. B. (1989). *Adult day care: Findings from a national survey.* Baltimore: Johns Hopkins University Press.

Wells, Y. D., & Kendig, H. L. (1996). Changes in carers' capacity and motivation to provide care. *Journal of Family Studies, 2,* 15–28.

Whitlatch, C. J., Zarit, S. H., Goodwin, P. E., & von Eye, A. (1995). Influence of the success of psychoeducational interventions on the course of family care. *Clinical Gerontologist, 16,* 117–130.

Whitlatch, C. J., Zarit, S. H., & von Eye, A. (1991). Efficacy of interventions with caregivers: A reanalysis. *Gerontologist, 31,* 9–14.

Williamson, G. M., & Schulz, R. (1993). Coping with specific stressors in Alzheimer's disease caregiving. *The Gerontologist, 33,* 747–755.

Wright, L. K., Clipp, E. C., & George, L. K. (1993). Health consequences of caregiver stress. *Medicine, Exercise, Nutrition and Health, 2,* 181–195.

Zarit, S. H., Orr, N. K., & Zarit, J. M. (1985). *The hidden victims of Alzheimer's Disease: Families under stress.* New York: New York University Press.

Zarit, S. H., Stephens, M. A. P., Townsend, A., & Greene, R. (1996, August). *Stress reduction for family caregivers: Effects of day care use.* Paper presented at the American Psychological Association Annual Convention, Toronto, Canada.

Zarit, S. H., Todd, P. A., & Zarit, J. M. (1986). Subjective burden of husbands and wives as caregivers: A longitudinal study. *The Gerontologist, 26,* 260–270.

Zarit, S. H., & Whitlatch, C. (1992). Institutional placement: Phases of the transition. *The Gerontologist, 32,* 665–672.

Zarit, S. H., & Zarit, J. M. (In press). *Geriatric psychology.* New York: Guilford Press.

Index

About the Editors

Inger Hilde Nordhus, PhD, is Associate Professor of Clinical Geropsychology at the Department of Clinical Psychology, University of Bergen, Norway. Her research interests focus on problems of mental health and aging, psychological assessment of older adults, and psychosocial interventions in old age. She has a central role in the development of postgraduate specialization in aging psychology in Norway, and serves as editor of the *Journal of the Norwegian Psychological Association.* She has authored several articles and has contributed to various books in geropsychology.

Gary R. VandenBos, PhD, Executive Director for Publications and Communications, American Psychological Association, has worked since the late 1970s in furthering the use of psychological research knowledge on aging to help shape public policy and in disseminating such knowledge. He has coedited several volumes in geropsychology, such as *Psychology and the Older Adult: Challenges for Training in the 1980s* (1982, with J. F. Santos), *The Adult Years: Continuity and Change* (1989, with M. Storandt), and *Neuropsychological Assessment of Dementia and Depression in Older Adults* (1994, with M. Storandt).

Stig Berg, PhD, is Director of the Institute of Gerontology, University College of Health Sciences, Jönköping, Sweden. He has broad interests within the gerontological field particularly in the areas of biology, psychology, and old-age care. His recent research has focused on genetic and environmental sources of variation in the aging process through studies of twins. In addition, he has published several articles and textbooks in gerontology.

Pia Fromholt, MA, is currently Professor of Humanistic Gerontology at The Danish Research Councils and Director of the Center for Geropsychology, Aarhus University and Psychiatric University Hospital, Denmark. She received her master's degree in psychology from the University of Copenhagen and her bachelor's degree in medieval archaelogy from Aarhus University. Her research interests include memory and cognition, aging and adaptation, and coping with mental dysfunction in old age. She has written several articles and contributions to books in gerontology.